The War against Terrorism

The War against Terrorism

Neil C. Livingstone

LexingtonBooks
D.C. Heath and Company
Lexington, Massachusetts
Toronto

*To my wife, Susan; my parents;
my family; and those we love;
that they may never know the
terror of which I write.*

Library of Congress Cataloging in Publication Data

Livingstone, Neil C.
    The war against terrorism.

    Bibliography: p.
    Includes index.
    1. Terrorism. 2. Terrorism—Prevention. I. Title.
HV6431.L58 1982   363.3'2   81–48331
ISBN 0-669-05333-3   AACR2

Copyright © 1982 by D.C. Heath and Company

Published simultaneously in Canada

Printed in the United States of America

International Standard Book Number: 0–669–05333–3

Library of Congress Catalog Card Number: 81–48331

Note Regarding
Source Material

Terrorism is, by its very nature, war in the shadows; therefore, it is a particularly difficult subject to shed light upon.

While much is known about the results of terrorism—the shattered buildings and broken bodies—far less is known about individual terrorists and their patrons, goals, weapons, methods, and organizational structure. The problem is made more complicated by the reluctance of national governments, for obvious reasons, to release information regarding the strategies and techniques they have developed to combat terrorism.

In writing this book, the author has drawn not only on previously published material, interviews, and personal experiences, but also on many intelligence sources, which, by their very nature, cannot be entirely documented. The Palestine Liberation Organization (PLO) does not, for example, publish an annual report detailing its budget and operations; therefore, the author can only rely on intelligence estimates for such information. On other occasions, confidential sources have been utilized that cannot be cited, in order to preserve their anonymity.

Contents

Foreword

Any examination of the vast literature of terrorism—the intentional utilization of psychological and physical force by established regimes and substate groups for the purpose of attaining real or imaginary, broad or limited goals—reveals a proliferation of definitions of this phenomenon. Indeed, the absence of a universal consensus as to who are the terrorists is a major contributing factor to perpetuation of contemporary ideological and political violence. If we cannot agree on the permissibility or impermissibility of using a tactical and strategic force in the struggle for power within and among nations, how can we decide on possible cures?

While the debate over the morality and legality of modern expressions of ideological and political violence will probably continue, it is safe to assume that terrorism as both the weapon of the strong and the weak is now an established mode of conflict. It will continue to persist through the 1980s and 1990s because many of the causes that motivate terrorists will remain unsolved, and new subrevolutionary issues will emerge in the future.

What is particularly disturbing is the fact that the advances of science and technology are slowly turning the entire modern society into a potential victim of terrorism, with no immunity for the noncombatant segment of the world population or for those nations and peoples who have no direct connection to particular conflicts or to specific grievances that motivate acts of violence. Clearly, the globalization of the brutalization of modern violence makes it abundantly clear that we have entered a new Age of Terrorism with all its frightening ramifications.

There are no simple solutions to the problem of terrorism, particularly because future incidents could be more costly in terms of human lives and property. *The War against Terrorism* is a serious effort to address the important question of how the United States and other liberal democracies can cope with the challenges ahead. As a practical counterterrorist manual, this book will probably stimulate a public debate over which recommendations suggested by the author should be adopted by Western societies. This book is required reading for all those concerned with the problem of contemporary terrorism and what can and should be done about it.

Yonah Alexander
Institute for Studies in
International Terrorism,
State University of New York;
CSIS, Georgetown University

1 Introduction

You're no longer a liberal after the first time they [terrorists] try to kill you.—
Guatemalan businessman[1]

Among the Palestine Liberation Organization (PLO) and the Popular Front for
the Liberation of Palestine (PFLP) rank-and-file in southern Lebanon these days,
the most prestigious badge of distinction that can be worn—weather permitting—
is a Soviet-made fur hat. While not of the haute couture variety, Soviet fur hats
are the latest thing in revolutionary chic, for possession of one in many parts of
the world usually indicates that the owner is a graduate of one of the elite
schools and camps operated by the USSR and its allies that train and indoctri-
nate terrorists and other revolutionaries. With each passing month, more and
more fur hats appear in embattled Lebanon and, for that matter, in dozens of
other locations around the world. Ironically, they may soon lose some of their
prestige value as they became too commonplace.

The issue of fur hats is important because it is indicative of the massive
amount of support and assistance that the USSR is providing to terrorist and
revolutionary movements. Despite a common perception to the contrary, this
is a relatively recent development, especially on the scale it is being practiced,
and represents a real departure from the past when most revolutionary terrorist
organizations were independent and essentially operated without measurable
outside assistance.

During the past decade and a half, however, the USSR, operating in tandem
with its Eastern bloc neighbors and various proxy nations, has relentlessly
extended its influence over nearly all of the globe's revolutionary terrorist
movements by means of cooptation, internal intrigue, offers of arms and assistance, and the training and indoctrination of literally thousands of revolutionaries in a vast network of schools and camps scattered around the world that
are operated directly or indirectly by the Soviet State Security Committee
(KGB) and allied intelligence services.

The Soviet strategy is clear. Moscow supports, sustains, and abets international terrorism because it has proved to be a relatively low-cost strategy
for nibbling away at the peripheries of the Western alliance, for undermining
NATO and its member states, and for scoring major gains in the Third World
that could potentially deny the United States and its allies access to critical
sea lanes and raw materials. Moreover, Moscow supports wars of national
liberation and revolutionary terrorist movements as a means of diverting the

1

resources of the industrial democracies from the task of competing with the massive Soviet military buildup.

Genesis of Modern Terrorism

Terrorism is by no means a new form of warfare; it has been witnessed in nearly every conflict of ideas, wills, and national groups in history. The Old Testament contains many references to behavior that, for all intents and purposes, can only be described as terrorism. In the first century A.D., Jewish nationalists known as the Zealots conducted a fierce and unrelenting terror campaign against the Roman occupiers of the eastern Mediterranean. The Zealots enlisted professional killers called *sicarii*, or dagger men, who struck down rich Jewish collaborators in the cities and those who opposed violent resistance against the Roman overlords.

The radical Islamic sect known as the Assassins, which appeared nearly a millennium later, was, as Paul Wilkinson notes, "Perhaps the first organized group systematically employing murder for a cause it believed to be righteous."[2] Inspired by the teachings of Hassan Sibai, the Assassins resisted, for nearly two centuries, efforts to suppress their heretical religious beliefs through a combination of merciless terrorism and fanatical faith in their own certitude and, in so doing, created a murder cult not witnessed before or since. Ritualized murder was elevated to the state of a fine art by the Assassins and transmitted from one generation to the next under the tutelage of the so-called master assassin, referred to as the Old Man of the Mountain. Too small a sect to engage in conventional warfare against their opponents, the Assassins systematically murdered those in positions of leadership and influence among their enemies, achieving political aims through the power of intimidation. Like the Jewish *sicarii*, the Assassins used the dirk or dagger to perform their sacramental murders.

Although terrorist behavior is as old as man himself, the term *terrorism* did not come into popular usage until the 1790s when it was employed to describe Jacobin excesses in revolutionary France. Based on the Latin verbs *terrere*, to tremble or cause to tremble, and *deterrere*, meaning to frighten from, the word *terrorism* has come to mean acts of violence designed to influence political behavior through a process of intimidation.

In the nineteenth century, Spanish insurgents employed incipient terrorism with demonstrable results in their struggle against Napoleonic domination. However, prior to the second half of the nineteenth century, terrorism was fairly rudimentary and took the form chiefly of poisonings, knife attacks, arson, riots, and ambuscades. In its full incarnation, however, terrorism presumes a certain level of technological development, both in terms of targets and the means used to strike at them. In one sense, modern terrorism is the product jointly of the Industrial Revolution, which provided the means and the targets, and the so-called age of revolution, commencing in the late eighteenth century, during which time terrorism found its true focus and expression as a form of revolutionary warfare against the state and the established order.

As Michael Waltzer notes, terrorism, as we know it today, is little more than a century old.[3] The true antecedents of modern terrorism can first be glimpsed in tsarist Russia. By the 1860s, the Russian intelligentsia had grown impatient with the slow pace of systemic reform and sought instead to transform peasant discontent into open revolution. Regarding themselves as avengers of the people, anarchists like Bakunin and his disciple Nechaev became apostles of the renewing force of violence, maintaining that progress was impossible without destruction. Their objective was nothing less than the complete destruction of the state, and anything that contributed to this goal was regarded as moral, and conversely, anything that hindered the realization of their apocalyptic visions was deemed immoral. In this connection, explosives revolutionized terrorist conflict and tactics. With the development of sufficiently powerful, stable, and affordable explosives, terrorists finally had a weapon that would begin to redress the disparity that existed between the firepower of the state and the means available to dissidents to strike back at the state. Organized into secret societies like the People's Will, Russian terrorists launched a campaign of unremitting terror against the state that reached its zenith in 1881 when Tsar Alexander II was brutally assassinated in a plot that included teams of bomb throwers. Prior to the Russian experience, never before had terrorism been used so systematically to bring about the destruction of the state.

Ironically, the Bolshevik Revolution was characterized by relatively few acts of terrorism; it was just not required in view of the internal disintegration of the Romanov state. The Bolsheviks, moreover, while supportive of the concept of mass terror, tended to discount for the most part the efficacy of individual terror and to regard it at best as an ancillary weapon useful only in the early stages of the conflict.

By contrast to the Bolshevik Revolution, systematic terrorism has been a feature of nearly every other conflict in the twentieth century. The Chinese revolutionaries of Sun Yat-sen went so far as to organize a department of terror in the Revolutionary Alliance party that "so completely demoralized the Manchu court that the Imperialists dared not execute self-admitted assassins who were caught red-handed in an attempt to assassinate the prince-regent."[4] It should be recalled that World War I was sparked by a terrorist incident at Sarajevo and that terrorism was used effectively against the Nazis by the peoples of occupied Europe during World War II. It is in the anticolonialist struggles of the postwar period, however, that one finds the first modern terrorist campaigns where terrorist violence was utilized to win international attention and to undermine public confidence in the governments in opposition. Moreover, prior to World War II, the victims of terrorism were nearly always specific individuals singled out for death either in retribution for some action or because of the positions of leadership or authority that they held. Beginning with the revolution in Algeria, the targets of terrorism became less deliberate and more random, as terrorists struck at ordinary people, innocent of any specific crime, in a strategy intended to intimidate the masses by harming the few. Also, if the past quarter century has been characterized by terrorists seeking ever more vulnerable and defenseless targets, then the next quarter century may witness them striking at targets of maximum shock potential—for example, oil refineries, nuclear power plants, architectural landmarks, liquefied natural-gas (LNG) transports, chemical-warfare depots, sporting events, and technological show-pieces like the Concorde supersonic jetliner. To this extent, terrorism promises to be a laboratory for violence in the years ahead.

The Threat

The term *terrorism* is widely misused. It is utilized in its generic sense as a form of shorthand by governments and the media and is applied to a variety of acts and occurrences that approximate terrorism in form but not in substance or, worse yet, that have no real resemblance to terrorism at all. Terrorism, if nothing else, is violence, or threats of violence, but it is not mindless violence, as some observers have charged. Usually, when employed in a political context, it repre-sents a calculated series of actions designed to intimidate and sow fear through-out a target population in an effort to produce a pervasive atmosphere of insecurity, a widespread condition of anxiety. A terrorist campaign that causes a significant threshold of fear among the target population may achieve its aims. In some instances, terrorism is potentially a more effective, especially from a cost-benefit perspective, strategy than conventional or guerrilla warfare. Unlike other forms of warfare, however, the goal of terrorism is not to destroy the opposing side but instead to break its will and force it to capitulate.

Terrorism is very much a product of the weapons available to the terrorist at any given moment. A revolutionary group that does not possess tanks, air-craft, and the other implements of conventional warfare fights with whatever resources it has available. Such a resource may consist of a bottle filled with gasoline and a rag stuffed in the top, a sharpened stake buried in a pit on a well-traveled trail, or a fountain pen packed with puttylike plastic explosive and detonated by an electrical impulse. The day may not be far off when terrorists have at their disposal biological or radiological weapons capable of wiping out tens of thousands, perhaps even millions, of innocent people.

The effectiveness of terrorism as a revolutionary strategy is a matter of record. Terrorism has been used to focus considerable attention on various causes, announcing to the world the existence of certain grievances or reminding it of forgotten agendas and unresolved problems requiring urgent attention. Through the use of violence, terrorist movements have projected their presence and objectives around the globe because, as Robert Taber notes, "Headlines burst bigger than bombs."[5] The embracement of terrorism by certain Palestinian elements transformed the Palestinian issue from chiefly a humanitarian concern into a political problem at the very heart of the Middle East controversy.

Terrorism, moreover, has been employed successfully to embarrass governments and to compel them to grant concessions and pay ransoms used to underwrite new revolutionary activities. It has demonstrated to subject populations the vulnerability of the state and communicated to them that their aspirations can be realized through armed struggle. Terrorism has eroded government authority and diminished the rule of law by so intimidating national governments that they have, on occasion, tolerated terrorists in their midst or declined to punish terrorists in their custody out of fear of reprisals. Other governments have felt compelled to adopt extralegal methods to combat terrorism. Scarce resources have been diverted from more productive uses by national governments forced to defend themselves and their populations from terrorist attacks. Often governments have sought greatly expanded police powers and restrictions on civil liberties in order to combat the problem. In some cases, this has been led to the overthrow of constitutional government, as in Uruguay, and the onset of systematic state repression. The private sector, too, has been forced to spend billions of dollars on elaborate security precautions.

Terrorism has changed the way most of us live. Americans take for granted today the inconvenience of passing through metal detectors and having their carry-on baggage checked before boarding flights. On a broader and more serious scale, terrorism has reduced the quality of life significantly in many nations such as Israel and Northern Ireland. In Belfast, armored vehicles rumble through the streets, foot patrols with their weapons at the ready keep a sharp watch for snipers, and shoppers are searched for weapons and explosives at checkpoints throughout the city. Investigators confirm that the terror is having a deep psychological impact on the people of Northern Ireland, especially the children, noting the rise of suicides, stress-related disorders, and family problems.

In short, terrorists have demonstrated that they can have impact on national and international events far beyond what their often limited numbers and resources would suggest. As the nations of the world become ever more urban, industrialized, and interdependent, and as their infrastructures become increasingly complex, they become more vulnerable to the designs of terrorists. So complex is the modern world and so close the margins for error that even relatively minor terrorist actions can have far-reaching consequences. As illustration, the explosion of a time bomb in an airport flower shop on Gran Canaria, in March 1977 by an obscure terrorist group seeking independence for the Canary Islands from Spain, was responsible for a chain of events that led to the worst civil aviation disaster in history. Because of the bombing, jet traffic was diverted to the airport at Tenerife where, as a result of the confusion and overcrowding this produced, two jumbo jetliners collided, with a loss of 581 passengers. Thus, there can be little question that terrorism presents many extra-ordinary challenges to the modern world in terms of state security, arms control and nuclear proliferation, respect for the rule of law, human rights, international commerce, and the relations between nations.

The Response

The United States and the other industrial democracies are today on the defensive, beset by powerful forces both from within and without that are seeking to undermine their material achievements and to erode their global influence and military posture. In the final analysis, they have only two choices when it comes to dealing with the issue of terrorism. They can either submit to its outrages and provocations, or they can take every step within reason to defend themselves. This book is dedicated to an examination of the latter course of action.

The first half of the book explores the terrorism phenomenon, noting its origins, evolution, and the operational characteristics of terrorist movements. The external lines of support so important to the growth of international terrorism in the contemporary world are documented and described in chapter 2, as well as the methods of financing violence that terrorists have employed. Chapter 3 examines the terrorist personality and socio-economic matrix, and attempts to develop a profile useful in identifying terrorists and predicting their behavior. The too often understated or misunderstood role of the media as the communicators and stimulators of terrorist violence is the focus of chapter 4. In addition, chapters 5, 6, and 7 are devoted to the weapons and targets currently preferred by terrorist groups, together with a discussion of new weapons technologies that may one day be employed by terrorists and the potential targets of opportunity they may be used against.

The second half of the book offers a survey of the many strategies to contain, control, suppress, and ultimately, to defeat terrorism that have been considered by national governments (chapter 8), as well as an examination of the new techniques and countermeasures that can be used by the private sector to deter or respond to terrorist violence (chapter 9). Finally, chapter 10 advances a comprehensive new strategy to confront the problem of terrorism that, if adopted by the United States, could turn the tables and put the terrorists on the defensive.

In writing this book, the author not only has relied upon published sources but also has incorporated his own firsthand knowledge regarding counterterrorism and crisis management that he acquired when he served in government and later as one of the principal officers of an international security firm. Various individuals with experiences on the front lines in the war against terrorism—as employees of the military, various intelligence agencies, and private-sector security companies—also cooperated with the study and provided down-in-the-trenches knowledge about counterterrorist methodologies, often illuminating critical aspects of terrorist operations and capabilities not previously reported elsewhere.

Notes

1. Statement to author, Guatemala City, January 1982.
2. Paul Wilkinson, *Political Terrorism* (New York: John Wiley & Sons, 1974), p. 45.
3. Michael Waltzer, "The New Terrorists," *The New Republic,* 30 August 1975.
4. Henry J. Chisholm, "The Function of Terror and Violence in Revolution" (Master's thesis, Georgetown University, 1948), p. 20.
5. Robert Taber, *The War of the Flea* (New York: Citadel Press, 1970), p. 91.

2

The Organization of Violence: International Support and Financing of Terrorism

The availability of the means to cooperate globally intensifies the sense of obligation to act. — Zbigniew Brzezinski[1]

Political passions and global conflicts no longer stop at national frontiers and, instead, spill over into the international arena with alarming frequency. This has witnessed the internationalization of terrorist violence in recent years, facilitated in large measure by the communications and transportation revolutions that have compressed time and distance as never before. While instantaneous communications and modern jet travel have resulted in greater global cooperation and understanding in some areas, at the same time they have contributed paradoxically to growing international tension and disequilibrium by providing revolutionaries with access to new sources of financing, training, weapons, logistic support, and the ability to forge operational alliances with various affinity groups in countries throughout the world.

Television permits terrorists to communicate their message to the rest of the world, using the universal language of violence. Moreover, it disseminates information about new tactics and methods, provides intelligence about potential targets and government countermeasures, and stimulates random outbreaks of imitative terrorist behavior that is often described as the contagion effect. Technological advances have made it possible to dial directly, at last count, seventy-four countries from the United States, including those as remote as Papua New Guinea, and this, in turn, permits a previously unimaginable degree of coordination between beween terrorist groups. Simply with a dime, one can call anonymously nearly anyone or anyplace in a particular metropolitan area, from an airport terminal to an office building, and allege that a bomb has been placed in that building or facility. This usually results in the evacuation of the building, or a forced emergency landing of a threatened aircraft, which inconveniences hundreds, even thousands, of people, sows the seeds of fear, and often costs taxpayers and the affected companies thousands of dollars. On 22 October 1981, for example, trading was halted on both the Chicago Board of Trade and the Philadelphia Stock Exchange after anonymous callers said that bombs had been placed in those buildings. All it took was a telephone and the price of the call to close the world's largest center for commodities trading.

Perhaps nothing has contributed to the shrinking character of the globe more than modern jet travel that has rendered few terrorist targets more than several hours' flying time from the sanctuaries where terrorists maintain their bases. It is not hard to imagine a terrorist operation originating in the Middle East, striking at a target in Europe, and culminating in a safe haven in Africa or Latin America—all in the space of a twelve-hour period.

The internationalization and diffusion of terrorist violence has produced dozens of transnational nightmares over the past decade that have witnessed scores of nations caught up in conflicts far from their borders that they could neither anticipate nor avoid. Some of the attacks are so far afield from the real source of conflict as to be ludicrous were it not for the casualties and disruption they cause. As illustration, Croatian nationalists took over the West German consulate in Chicago in an attempt to force the German government to release one of their confederates who was about to be extradited to Yugoslavia.

Paris, New York, Washington, D.C., and London have all become magnets for nonindigenous terrorist violence, presumably because all four cities are communications and media centers and transportation hubs and boast large concentrations of diplomatic personnel. Many foreign nationals and diplomats are more accessible targets in Western capitals than in their native lands; because of prevailing freedoms that exist in the West, terrorists are able to orchestrate their attacks with less interference or fear of discovery. During the past decade, for example, conflicts in the Philippines, Chile, South Africa, Yugoslavia, Liberia, Central America, Iran, Northern Ireland, and the Middle East have spawned political violence in Washington, D.C., making it the unofficial terrorist capital of the United States. Similarly, Paris has become a battleground for those from the Middle East as they settle old grudges and policy disputes. In the past three years alone, terrorists have assassinated or attempted to kill current or former officials of Iran, Syria, Israel, Iraq, Turkey, and the PLO in Paris. The Saudi Arabian embassy in the French capital was seized by five Palestinian terrorists in 1975, the Iraqi embassy in 1978, and the Turkish embassy in 1981.

Against this backdrop, one of the most disquieting trends of the modern era is the emergence of transnational terrorist organizations with close linkages to one another, armed and trained by powerful patron nations, whose capacity for violence extends far beyond the geographical regions where their conflicts are rooted. Richard Clutterbuck has cited the classic example of terrorist cooperation that occurred in May 1972, at Lod Airport near Tel Aviv, that saw the "indiscriminate slaughter of Puerto Ricans in Israel on behalf of Arabs by Japanese bearing fake documents acquired in Germany and using Czech weapons acquired in Italy."[2]

The Lod massacre was but one of the many joint operations carried out by the Japanese Red Army (JRA) in collaboration with the PFLP. Another joint JRA-PFLP operation involved an attack on a Shell Oil company facility in Singapore in 1974, netting five hostages, and the simultaneous seizure of the Japanese embassy in Kuwait. The hostages ultimately were exchanged for a ransom and safe conduct to South Yemen in a Japanese Airlines plane.

No longer active in Japan, the JRA is today almost entirely the creature of the PFLP and is dependent on the ultraradical Palestinian group for financing, training, and weapons. It currently embraces the Palestinian cause with the fervor that it once devoted to the goal of revolution in Japan, suggesting that its nihilistic commitment to violence transcends even nationalistic impulses. Fusaka Shigenobu, head of the JRA's Arab section, resides in Beirut where she oversees the remaining terrorist activities of the handful of members that remain.

The JRA is representative of the evolution of multinational terrorist groups that are not wedded to any one cause but that instead serve as hired guns to the highest bidder. Cooperation between terrorist groups has been reinforced by a series of terrorist summits that have brought revolutionaries from diverse struggles together. During the 1970s, terrorist summits were held in Libya, Ireland, and Lebanon. Among the participants at a 1972 summit at the Baddawi refugee camp were Fusaka Shigenobu, Andreas Baader of the Red Army Faction, Abu Iyad and Fuad Shemali of Black September, as well as representatives of Iranian, Latin American, Turkish, and various European terrorist organizations.[3]

Other examples of terrorist cooperation, and there are many, include the murder of the Israeli counsel general in Istanbul, Ephraim Elron, by Turkish terrorists in partial repayment for the training they received in Palestinian camps in Spain and Lebanon. Similarly, the terrorist group led by Ilich Ramirez Savchez, better known as Carlos "the Jackal", that shot its way into OPEC's Vienna headquarters consisted of four Palestinians, one German, and one Latin American. The skyjacking of Air France flight 139 to Entebbe was carried out by two Germans and two Arabs and illustrated the close ties that existed between the PFLP and the Baader-Meinhof gang. Patrick Arguello, a Sandanista (Nicaragua) skyjacker trained in Palestinian camps, was shot to death on 6 September 1970, during the attempted seizure of an El Al Israel 707, and his companion, Palestinian terrorist Leila Khaled, was captured.

Terrorist Patrons

It can be stated flatly and unequivocally that, without the support of powerful patrons and ideologically allied movements, terrorism would be only a minor annoyance instead of a global problem of expanding dimensions. While the complaints that give rise to terrorism are multifaceted and varied, the fact remains that terrorism is, in large measure, the product of a handful of nations that provide the arms, financing, training, safe havens, and other support apparatus to revolutionary and violence-prone nonstate actors. This is a marked departure from previous years, when revolutionary movements were self-sufficient and confined their activities to the country that was the target of their activities. Few received any measurable outside support. Even as late as

1970, Ted Robert Gurr could discover only 19 terrorist groups out of 355 surveyed that "were reliably reported to have gotten material support, training or safe bases from which to operate outside the country in which they were active."[4]

The USSR, by means of its training, indoctrination, and other support activities, has managed slowly, relentlessly to take over—from within—most of the world's major terrorist movements. Since 1969, the Irish Republican Army (IRA) (Provisional wing) has become a doctrinaire Marxist organization that openly proclaims that its goals are, first, to unite Ireland and, second, to produce a socialist revolution in the country. No longer Catholic, its leaders and theoreticians regularly characterize the Republic of Ireland as a facist state. The IRA's leaders travel frequently to the USSR and to other eastern bloc nations, and it receives arms and training from Libya, Cuba, and the PFLP, as well as maintains effective links to the Soviet KGB and Cuban Direccion General de Inteligencia (DGI). The more nationalistic Official wing of the IRA, which has renounced violence, is no longer a serious factor in the Irish political picture.

Twenty years ago, the Basque Homeland and Liberty Movement (ETA) terrorist organization was Catholic, nationalist, and purposefully democratic. Today, it embraces a vision of a separate socialist Basque nation established along the lines of a Marxist-Leninist dictatorship. Similarly, the Tupamaros organization in Uruguay, the M-19 movement in Columbia, and virtually every other urban terrorist/guerrilla organization in Latin America, except the Montoneros of Argentina and various right-wing death squads, have become increasingly Marxist and, conversely, less nationalistic under the careful culti-vation of Moscow and its surrogates, Cuba and the Palestinian resistance.

It is usually impossible to view terrorism outside of the context of East-West relations and competition among the superpowers. The USSR and its Eastern bloc allies are, operating largely through surrogates, the chief sponsors and patrons of global terrorism, and they regard this as an effective and economical strategy for undermining the Western democracies and for making gains in the developing world, without running the risk of outright conflict. The implication is not that a central control room exists in the basement of the Kremlin from which all terrorist movements are coordinated and their acts orchestrated but rather that the Soviets have been quick to recognize the opportunities presented by outbreaks of localized violence and to exploit them for their own purposes. As former deputy director for intelligence of the Central Intelligence Agency (CIA), Ray S. Cline, has observed:

> It's important to realize that when you say the Soviet Union supports terrorism, you do not mean that they direct and command each terrorist activity. That would be impossible and not very useful. What they do is supply the infrastructure of terror: the money, the guns, the training, the background information, the communications, the propa-ganda that will inspire individual terrorist groups.[5]

Predictably, in world forums and policy statements, the USSR opposes terrorism and maintains that states have the right of self-defense when confronted with subversive or terroristic activities by other states. This viewpoint can be traced back to the aftermath of World War I when the new Bolshevik government was fighting for its life, challenged by counterrevolutionary movements that operated from sanctuaries outside of Russia with the aid of the Western democracies. In the protracted military campaign that followed, insurgents struck frequently across the Soviet border in hit-and-run raids.

Despite Soviet condemnation of hijackings and attacks on diplomats, Moscow nevertheless has qualified its opposition to terrorism by affirming that wars of national liberation cannot be considered as terrorism so long as the conflict is confined to the actual country in question. Of course, this support of wars of national liberation does not extend to the Soviet empire in Eastern Europe or to recently subjugated Afghanistan. While the developing world is regarded as an area of open competition between the great powers, and while Moscow rarely shirks from making gains in Europe and other parts of the industrial West, Eastern Europe—the Soviet buffer to the West—has, under the terms of the Brezhnev doctrine, been declared off limits as a zone of competition. Events in Eastern Europe are viewed as matters of internal concern by Soviet policymakers, who wish to preserve the status quo at all costs. Thus, the rise of the Solidarity labor movement in Poland, which is openly challenging the government and the Communist party for political power, represents the kind of threat that may compel the USSR to invade Poland, as it has done in the past in Hungary (1956) and Czechoslovakia (1968). Should the Poles resist an invasion, they probably will resort to terroristic acts against Soviet personnel, facilities, and equipment, just as the Afghans have done. In this event, Soviet reluctance to participate in effective international programs for curtailing and controlling terrorism may come back to haunt Moscow. It is not hard to imagine a scenario with the Soviets on the hot seat instead of the West, striving to enlist sufficient support in the world community to implement effective multilateral remedies for the suppression of terrorism.

Direct Soviet support of terrorism takes many forms. First, the USSR and the nations of Eastern Europe are the largest suppliers of firearms, explosives, and military hardware to terrorist movements, although usually armaments are channeled through conduits like the Cuban state intelligence agency, the DGI, or selected proxy forces like the PLO. The DGI funneled Soviet-made weapons to the Sandanista guerrillas in Nicaragua and is currently serving as quartermaster to insurgents in El Salvador, to ETA terrorists in Spain, and to countless other groups in Africa and Latin America.

Virtually every terrorist arsenal in the world contains largely Soviet and Eastern bloc weapons, and many movements have been provided with Katusha rockets, SAM-7 missiles, RPG7 antitank rockets, and RGD5 hand grenades. The Soviets have even transferred tanks and aircraft to the PLO. In terms of direct funding, the CIA estimates that Moscow spends $200 million a year to support national liberation movements, much of it to groups that actively embrace terrorism as a tactic.[6]

Second, Moscow provides extensive training to terrorists from every corner of the earth. Training programs are reportedly administered by the International Department of the Central Committee of the Soviet Communist Party (CPSU/ IO), which is charged with liaison with all Communist parties not in power. The cornerstone of the training effort is the so-called Harvard of world terrorism, the Lenin Institute in Moscow, that instructs members of Communist parties from outside the borders of the USSR in the finer points of guerrilla warfare, terrorist tactics, manipulation of the media, and subversion. By contrast to the Institute, the Patrice Lumumba University, also located in Moscow, provides academic instruction to non-Communist students from developing countries. Ilich Ramirez Sanchez, known to the world press as Carlos, attended Patrice Lumumba for a short period but was expelled. Students who show proper aptitude are, at the end of their studies, sent to one of the military-style training camps at Baku, Odessa, Tashkent, or Simferopol, where they receive actual terrorist training before returning to their countries of origin. After a careful screening process, for example, the KGB selected ten Mexican students to receive special training and cultivation as the nucleus of an operation, code name Leo, designed one day to overthrow the government of Mexico.[7] These camps are supplemented by additional training centers in East Germany (Pankow), Hungary, and Czechoslovakia (Karlovy Vary near Prague). Thousands of would-be terrorists and guerrillas have passed through these camps before returning home, including at least one in every ten members of the Palestinian resistance.[8]

The USSR, however, is increasingly shifting away from direct ties with terrorist movements, especially those in Europe, in favor of operating through surrogates. The major exception to this rule is the PLO that has for some time maintained an official liaison office in Moscow and is directly supplied, financed, and trained by the Soviets. Although Yasir Arafat traditionally has been accorded the same status as a visiting head-of-state when visiting the Soviet capital, in October 1981, the PLO was extended full diplomatic recognition by the USSR and its office elevated from the status of a mission to a fully accredited embassy. Soviet policymakers believe that open support for European terrorist organizations, none of which enjoy broad popular following, would be counterproductive and likely to damage relations between Moscow and Western Europe. In addition, European terrorism has usually impacted negatively on Communist party prospects at the polls, by reminding the voters of the party's antidemocratic tendencies and propensity for governing by means of violence. This was particularly true in Italy where the Communist party had made significant electoral gains and was on the verge of winning the next national election up to the time of the abduction and murder of Christian Democratic party leader, Aldo Moro, by the Red Brigades. The political fallout over the Moro killing was so great that the Soviets tried, without a great deal of success, to shift the blame to the CIA by launching an extensive propaganda and disinformation campaign that accused the CIA of carrying out the kidnapping and execution as a way of discrediting the Italian Communist party.

Despite the leading role played by the USSR, both directly and indirectly, as quartermaster and armorer of world terrorism, the U.S. State Department has, until recently, been reluctant to place it on a list of nations that support terrorism. Moreover, a draft report, prepared by the CIA during the Carter administration and circulated on Capitol Hill in early 1981, rejects the massive evidence of Soviet support of international terrorism as merely circumstantial. However, with the ascension of the Reagan administration, both of these shortcomings have been corrected.

What does the USSR receive in return for its fraternal support of terrorist movements? Is its support purely based upon considerations of comradeship and ideological commonality? Hardly. The fact is that the USSR regards terrorism as a highly efficient and cost-effective strategy to achieve strategic and geopolitical goals. It is no accident that West Germany, Italy, the United Kingdom, and Turkey, all NATO members, are currently engaged in prolonged military and police campaigns against terrorists, all of which are supported and sustained to some degree by Moscow and its surrogates, and that these struggles are diverting crucial resources away from the external war-making capabilities of those nations. Spain, soon to become a NATO member, is also confronted with Soviet-sponsored separatist movements that embrace terrorism. Similarly, by supporting terrorist/insurgent movements in the Third World—which may one day come to power—the USSR hopes to deny the United States and the West access to raw materials, strategic shipping channels, military bases, allies, and global influence.

By contrast, there have been few terrorist campaigns against Soviet allies in the Third World. There are several possible explanations. The answer may, in part, be attributable to the fact that violent opposition is rendered extremely difficult in tightly controlled political systems where individual activities are closely monitored by an all-encompassing secret police apparatus and where little personal freedom of movement or access to the air waves and mass media exist. Even more important in explaining the absence of terrorism in such systems is the fact that the United States and the industrial democracies do not train, equip, or provide the infrastructure for terrorists opposed to those systems. Anti-Castro Cuban guerrillas are regularly monitored by the United States and interdicted before they can strike at Cuba, although admittedly this has not always been the case. Only recently a group of far-right extremists allegedly affiliated with the Ku Klux Klan and the U.S. Nazi party were arrested before they could launch an invasion designed to overthrow the leftist government on the island nation of Dominica in the West Indies.

The most important Soviet surrogates involved in the support of terrorism are Cuba, East Germany, Libya, Syria, Czechoslovakia, and various elements of the Palestinian resistance. Cuban involvement dates back almost to the very inception of the Castro regime. As early as 1960, Cuba was providing training to Argentine guerrillas, both in Cuba and in Argentina. In April 1974, under Cuba's sponsorship, four Latin revolutionary movements—the Tupamaros of Uruguay, Chile's Movement of the Revolutionary Left (MIR), the National Liberation Army (ELN) of Bolivia, and the People's Revolutionary Army (ERP) of Argentina—came together to form the Junta for Revolutionary Coordination (JRC). A 4,000-acre training facility near Guanabo, Cuba, was established under the control of the Cuban Ministry of the Interior to train and equip JRC terrorists. Other Cuban camps are located at Pinar de Rio in Cabayas province and at Pinar de Agua in Oriente. Carlos the Jackal received extensive training on subjects ranging from forgery and false disguises to sabotage and explosives at Camp Mantanzas near Havana. The three-month-long course at Guanabo even uses U.S. Special Forces manuals to teach urban warfare techniques.[9] The curriculum includes weapons instruction, the use of explosives, collection of tactical intelligence, launching operations, survival techniques, communications, propaganda, and the fabrication of false documents. At the behest of the KGB, Cuba trains members of the IRA, Basque separatists, the Polisario front, the JRA, the Baader-Meinhof gang, the Palestinian resistance, Iranian Mujaheddin, Turks, Kurds, French terrorists, Italian Red Brigades, the Armed Forces of Puerto Rican National Liberation (FALN), and the rank-and-file of countless African and Latin American revolutionary movements. Some PLO recruits are actually trained at the Cuban Military Institute in Havana.

Cuban instructors teach similar courses at virtually every terrorist training facility in the world, from South Yemen to Eastern Europe. Cuban instructors are known to be in Nicaragua, Libya, Lebanon, South Yemen, Syria, Angola, and Ethiopia, to cite but a few examples. The Cuban DGI, headed by KGB personnel, is the chief coordinating arm of the Cuban terrorist connection. Many underground terrorist movements, especially those in Europe and Latin America, have a DGI operative assigned to them for contact and coordination purposes.

Libya

When it comes to supporting international terrorism, Libya is in a league by itself. Shortly after Muammar Qaddafi seized power in 1969, he began lavishing his country's oil wealth on an assortment of terrorist groups, mostly coreligionists, although as Claire Sterling notes, "Almost anybody claiming to be a revolutionary could put the bite on Qaddafi."[10] Challenging both communism and capitalism as inappropriate strategies for the development of the Third

World, Qaddafi sought to chart a separate course, anchored around his peculiar brand of Moslem fundamentalism and Arab nationalism. As Libya's isolation has increased, however, Qaddafi has attempted to shore up his position by moving steadily into the Soviet orbit, while still rejecting Marxism. He has purchased billions of dollars worth of Soviet weaponry. Soviet and Warsaw Pact military advisors stationed permanently in Libya train Libyans in the use of their newly acquired weapons and provide necessary maintenance for the more sophisticated hardware. Soviet and North Korean pilots fly Soviet-made Libyan jets and operate surface-to-air-missile batteries.

Qaddafi has transferred millions of dollars worth of weapons to more than forty terrorist groups around the world. Indeed, reliable estimates indicate that Libya spends some $70 to $100 million a year in direct support of terrorist movements. Among the weapons Qaddafi has provided to terrorist groups are the two SAM-7 missiles with which Palestinian terrorists were preparing to shoot down an El Al Israel airliner at Rome's Leonardo da Vinci Airport in 1973.

In the early 1970s, Qaddafi began setting up training camps in Libya initially designed to provide military training to members of the PFLP and the PLO. Now numbering more than twenty camps in all, the largest at Torca, the camps provide instruction to terrorists of diverse races, nationalities, and political persuasions. It was estimated that in early 1980 more than 7,000 foreign recruits were receiving military training in the various camps.

One of the most unique and shadowy training facilities is located at Ras Hilal, in an old German U-boat installation. There, under the guidance of former U.S. Vietnam veterans and rogue ex-CIA agents, students are given intensive instruction in the finer points of killing, assassination, demolitions, sabotage, and interrogation.

Libyan support for terrorists has also taken the form of providing forged identity documents to known terrorists, permitting terrorists to board Libyan Arab Airways flights carrying arms and explosives, smuggling weapons and explosives to terrorists in Libyan diplomatic pouches, and granting generous cash bonuses to groups and individuals who perform notable acts of terrorism. Carlos the Jackal, who enjoyed a special relationship with Libya during the mid-1970s, was rewarded with $2 million after his successful seizure of OPEC headquarters in Vienna in 1975.[11] As an honored guest of the state, Carlos was given a luxurious coastal villa to use when he was in Libya. Qaddafi also awarded the Black September team that carried out the Munich massacre at the 1972 Olympics an estimated $10 million bonus for a job well done.

On several occasions, Qaddafi has permitted Libya to be used for terrorist summit conferences, such as the 1979 meeting in Benghazi that representatives of more than a dozen terrorist groups attended.

Although Qaddafi's favorite cause is the Palestinian resistance, he has given money, weapons, training, and moral support to the JRA, the Baader-Meinhof gang, the Italian Red Brigades, Nicaraguan Sandanistas, the Moro National Liberation Front in the Philippines, Polisario guerrillas in the former Spanish Sahara, Dhofari rebels in Oman, and perhaps, strangest of all, to the Provisional wing of the IRA. On numerous occasions, he has spoken out on behalf of the IRA, and the British have seized several shipments of arms from Qaddafi that were destined for the IRA. In 1972, he announced that he was going to send money, arms, and volunteers to Northern Ireland to aid the IRA. Reaffirming his commitment in 1978, he observed that, "We regard Northern Ireland as under British colonization. . . . We do not consider the Irish fight to be terrorism."[12] The Irish navy interdicted the S.S. *Claudia* in 1973 and seized five tons of weapons from Libya that were bound for the Provisional IRA (Provos). On board the *Claudia* was Provo leader Joe Cahill. Libya was also rumored to be the source of the U.S.-made M60 machine guns proudly displayed by the IRA at a press conference. U.K. authorities speculate that Soviet-made RPG7 portable rocket launchers used in attacks on U.K. installations in Northern Ireland were obtained by the IRA via Libya. Since the IRA Provos are staunchly Marxist and neither Moslem nor culturally analogous, Qaddafi's infatuation with Irish terrorists is difficult to explain.

Another of the strange causes embraced by Qaddafi is the American Indian Movement (AIM), to which he has lent occasional public support. AIM members reportedly have also received training in Libya and some indirect funding.

Although Qaddafi, in recent years, has had strained relations with Yasir Arafat's Al Fatah, which he has accused of being more concerned about winning political acceptance in Europe than with carrying out terrorist attacks, he continues to maintain strong links with elements of the Palestinian Rejection Front, especially the PFLP. The open break between the mercurial Libyan leader and Yasir Arafat occurred after Qaddafi, who was seeking to punish the late Egyptian president, Anwar Sadat, for his role in the Camp David peace accords, demanded that Al Fatah launch a series of attacks aimed at sabotaging the operations of the Suez Canal, thereby damaging the already desperate Egyptian economy. Arafat refused, and Qaddafi, describing the PLO's diplomatic offensive to win broader world support as "capitulationist," announced a severing of relations with the PLO in January 1980. The move was not unprecedented. In 1973, Qaddafi cut off the PLO's $40-million-a-year subsidy for a period of time in order to put pressure on its leadership to check the leftward and secular drift of the organization.

In recent years, Qaddafi has become increasingly bold and has launched a series of plots and revolutionary schemes designed to expand Libyan influence throughout the developing world. An early supporter of Iran's Mujaheddin, Qaddafi is one of the closest allies of the revolutionary government of Ayatollah Khomeini. He has tried to overthrow the governments of Egypt, Somalia, Tunisia, the Sudan, and Morocco. Libyan troops have intervened directly in conflicts in Chad and Uganda. Libyan volunteers serve in Lebanon with

Palestinian guerrilla units. He has helped Pakistan to finance the development of a so-called Islamic atomic bomb. He has tried repeatedly to have Sudan's President Jaafar Nimeiry killed, and Libyan fingerprints are all over the assassination of Anwar Sadat. Prior to Sadat's murder in October 1981, Libyan hit teams had been infiltrated into Egypt on a number of occasions for the specific purpose of assassinating the Egyptian leader. Israeli intelligence got wind of several plots before their Egyptian counterparts and, in each instance, tipped off Cairo. Libyan agents reportedly also made various mercenaries offers of $1 million cash for Sadat's head; however, there were no takers. Exiled opponents of Qaddafi's regime, nevertheless, have been assassinated in Europe (two in London and two in Rome), and attempts have been made on the lives of Libyan dissidents in the United States, including a Libyan university student wounded in Colorado.

Qaddafi has sought to extend Libyan influence into the Western hemisphere in providing active support of the Sandanista government in Nicaragua. The Libyan government has deposited $100 million in Nicaragua's Central Bank under the control of the so-called prolonged-popular-war faction of the Sandanista front, and talks are currently underway regarding a variety of joint projects. Sandanista junta member, Moises Hassan, who is of Palestinian descent and identified with the prolonged-popular-war faction, is the driving force behind the Sandanista tie with Libya.

The Palestinian Resistance

The PLO remains one of Moscow's principal terrorist surrogates. In return for official recognition by the USSR and lavish economic and military support, the PLO serves as a major disseminator of terrorist training and weapons to other revolutionary organizations.

The PLO is actually an umbrella organization that embraces a variety of separate groups. Al Fatah, the largest component, led by Yasir Arafat, rarely engages in terrorism and instead leaves that to other constituent organizations like Black September, which was created expressly to conduct terrorist operations. More than a thousand PLO members have received training in the USSR since 1974, and this knowledge is passed along to other terrorist organizations in camps operated by the PLO. Moscow, and its client state Syria, are virtually the exclusive suppliers of arms to the PLO. To show his gratitude, Arafat travels frequently to Moscow (his first trip was in 1956) and toes the line with respect to Moscow's foreign policy, predictably condemning China whenever appropriate and applauding Soviet actions like the invasion of Afghanistan.

By contrast to the PLO, however, the ultraradical PFLP truly deserves to be described "as the framework without which international terrorism could not work."[13] Dr. George Habash, the PFLP's leader, maintains that terrorist movements are everywhere confronted by common enemies—namely, capitalism, Zionism, and imperialism. According to Habash, there should be no geographic or political boundaries to revolutionary action; instead, violence should be internationalized, thereby becoming a far more potent force for the West to deal with.

Under Habash's direction, the PFLP is the cornerstone of a world terrorist federation, promoting strong linkages and cooperation between terrorist organizations everywhere, resulting in more than the reciprocity of past years. Today, largely as a result of the PFLP, a worldwide terrorist network exists, permitting the exchange of operational intelligence, arms, training, and manpower. One group often provides logistic support, false documents, and an escape route to other groups engaged in operations on its territory.

Financing Terrorism

Never was the Biblical admonition that money "is the root of all evil" rendered truer than with respect to terrorist violence. Money is the sinew of terrorism; without it the terrorist is reduced to impotence. This is attributable to the fact that weapons, explosives, safe houses, modern jet travel, sophisticated cover operations, and intelligence-gathering activities are expensive, requiring substantial sums of money. Even a relatively small organization like the Italian Red Brigades is forced to raise nearly $10 million a year to cover its expenses.[14] As a result, accountants and bankers are becoming as important to terrorist organizations as bomb throwers and operatives in the field, and some of the larger organizations like Al Fatah and the PFLP have been compelled to develop elaborate infrastructures to raise, manage, and expend the huge sums of money needed to sustain their globe-spanning operations and innumerable personnel.

As Walter Laqueur has observed, "modern transnational terrorism is, more often than not, big business."[15] In this respect, the PLO, perhaps the wealthiest of all terrorist movements, increasingly resembles a multinational corporation in its structure and operations. Its $200–250 million annual budget pays for offices in nearly one hundred countries (including its main headquarters complex in Beirut); the salaries of thousands of employees; a publishing and propaganda arm; a health care and pension system for employees and their dependents; an elaborate intelligence unit that keeps tabs on the Palestinians and the activities of the enemies of Palestine throughout the world; some charitable activities in refugee camps; schools in which the indoctrination of Palestinian youths is conducted; military training facilities; fuel and maintenance for their Soviet tanks and other military vehicles; and arms, ammunition, and the other paraphernalia of war. Also, like all political organizations, a large amount of what is collected must be sunk back into further fund-raising activities designed to ensure a continuing flow of money into its coffers.

In this connection, the PLO derives its funding from a variety of sources. The largest single contribution comes from the USSR and other Eastern bloc nations, in the form of military hardware, training, and propaganda activities. The Soviet contribution is estimated to cost Moscow as much as $100 million a year, some of it funneled through Libya and Syria. The USSR provides the PLO with little in the way of actual funds, however, since it usually suffers from a hard-currency shortage. Therefore, the PLO's operating budget must be raised elsewhere. Various oil-rich Arab governments, including Saudi Arabia, subsidize the PLO, both out of support for Palestinian aspirations and in hopes of buying protection from reprisals and intrigue against their regimes. The Saudis also privately maintain that they hope to gain a certain amount of influence over PLO policies in this manner and thus preserve the moderate and Islamic orientation of the organization. Riyadh has exerted pressure on the PLO on a number of occasions by urging the purge of Marxist, non-Islamic elements. Unlike the wholly Marxist PFLP, Al Fatah and the other mainline organizations that make up the PLO are more nationalistic than ideological, although this situation is changing gradually as more and more of their members are educated and trained in the USSR, Cuba, and other Eastern bloc nations.

The PLO also receives an income from the large investment portfolio it has accumulated over the years, which some observers believe to be valued at more than $100 million. It is reliably reported that the portfolio is administered by the Arab Bank Ltd., a Jordanian institution with branches in many countries.[16] The PLO owns investment property in the West, although its real estate speculation activities have not been entirely successful. According to intelligence sources, it was one of the largest owners of beachfront real estate in Beirut before the onset of the civil war, which not only resulted in the outright destruction of some of their prime investment properties but also sent Lebanese property values plunging. The PLO also operates many legitimate businesses, providing services and products to the Arab world.

Another source of money for the PLO is the imposition of taxes and other levies, which often represent little more than outright extortion, in areas that it controls and by forcing Palestinians living throughout the world, especially those residing in the Middle East, to tithe a portion of their income, usually 5 percent, to the organization. Palestinian so-called bullyboy squads are used to coerce those reluctant to subsidize PLO terror. Prominent Arab businessmen—including reputed billionaire Adnan Khoshoggi—contribute to the PLO on a regular basis in order to protect their property and enterprises and so they may continue to ply the Mediterranean on their yachts without fear of personal harm or attack.

The PFLP operates much in the same manner as the PLO, and its budget is also roughly $200 million a year. Its chief financial benefactors continue to be Libya, Iraq, and Algeria.

Arab student cadres of the PLO and PFLP have been involved in several schemes in the United States to raise money for the cause. Authorities in

Michigan broke up an arson fraud ring operated by Arab students, and in California, an auto insurance swindle, involving more than a hundred PLO sympathizers, was discovered. Members of the California ring purportedly purchased several insurance policies on a single car, and when the car was either allegedly stolen or involved in an accident, they collected damages, sometimes as many as three or four times. Most of the money raised in the two scams is alleged to have found its way into PLO coffers.

No other terrorist groups begin to approach the wealth of the Palestinian resistance organizations. Lacking wealthy oil-rich patron states, other terrorist movements are forced to be more imaginative and resourceful in raising the necessary funds to underwrite their operations. If, as noted earlier, the PLO and PFLP resemble multinational corporations in their operations, then most of the other terrorist groups have more in common with the Mafia or criminal underworld with respect to their fund-raising efforts. Bank robberies, hijackings, kidnappings for ransom, fraud, vice trafficking, the sale of illegal narcotics, the passing of counterfeit money and bogus lottery tickets, the imposition of tolls on highway travelers to guarantee safe conduct, robbery and the fencing of stolen goods, protection rackets, embezzlement, and outright extortion form the backbone of most fund-raising programs. As in the case of the Palestinian resistance, the contributions of the USSR and its Eastern bloc allies, while significant, are usually confined to training, weapons, logistic and mate-rial support, and propaganda activities rather than infusions of direct cash.

Bank robbery remains one of the classic methods of acquiring funds open to terrorists. In his minimanual, Carlos Marighella advocated bank robbery as a means of acquiring supplies and financing for the revolution, although he preferred to view such activities as expropriations. One of the principal tools employed by Russian revolutionaries during the nineteenth century to sustain their campaign against the tsar, bank robberies have been used by numer-ous terrorist groups in recent years to finance their terror, including the Algerian colon organization, *Organisation de l'Armée Secrète* (OAS); the IRA; the Baader-Meinhof gang; the Basque ETA; the Brazilian Action for National Libera-tion (ALN); the Tupamaros; the Weather Underground in the United States; the ERP in Argentina; the Symbionese Liberation Army in the United States; and the Italian Red Brigades. In 1978, the ETA take from various bank and factory-payroll robberies was estimated to be in the neighborhood of $3.5 million. Banking institutions in many countries have responded to the terrorist threat with increased security measures and reduced amounts of cash at teller windows, and this has taken the profit out of many bank robberies. In one incident in Latin America, a terrorist held up a bank and demanded that the teller hand over all his cash. Along with several stacks of real bills, the teller gave the gun-toting terrorist a dye pack—a hollowed-out stack of phony bills with a real bill on the top and bottom and a low-level explosive charge and a powerful dye in the middle. The entire packet was bound, as normal, with a bank wrapper and, from all outward appearances, looked exactly like the real thing. When the explosive is tripped, either electronically or with a time device, the subject is covered with the indelible dye, making it possible to identify him readily as he makes his escape. In this incident, the unfortunate thief jammed the stacks of bills down the front of his pants and hurried out of the bank, disappearing among the crowds along the busy street. Forty-five seconds later, however, the dye pack went off, blowing the man's pants open and covering his groin with flash burns and dye. He was quickly apprehended.

Although the Argentine ERP raised their initial stake by means of a $300,000 bank robbery in Cordoba, they rapidly graduated to kidnapping wealthy Argentines as their chief tactic for raising capital since it paid far better and involved much less risk. Within a relatively short period of time, the ERP had amassed more than $30 million, including a then record $14.2 million ransom paid for the safe return of Exxon executive Victor Samuelson.

The presence of so much cash often produces corruption within the ranks of the terrorists, as happened after a series of IRA bank robberies in Belfast. Nearly one-third of the £17,000 Sterling collected by IRA Provos during one eighteen-month spree of robberies was siphoned off by the organization's leaders for their personal use. In another instance, a Provo bank robber reportedly embezzled £100,000 from the organization and transferred it to an account in the United States.

Banks have not been the only targets of terrorist thieves. Finance companies, warehouses, payroll offices, grocery stores, armored cars, and even small shops also have been robbed by terrorists. IRA gunmen netted $475,000 from one robbery of a postal truck in the Republic of Ireland. Palestinian resistance organizations looted many of the designer shops in Beirut after the beginning of the civil war, and the entire inventory of a prominent designer-name boutique in Washington, D.C., was allegedly purchased at a sizeable discount from Palestinian guerrillas. Occasionally, a robbery has produced unexpected side benefits as in the case of the finance company robbed by Tupamaros guerrillas in Uruguay. In addition to six million pesos, the robbery yielded six ledger books that revealed that the company was engaged in a variety of illegal activities. The Tupamaros turned the ledgers over to authorities for appropriate legal action, thus improving their carefully cultivated Robin Hood image.

Kidnapping for profit has increased dramatically in recent years and is today perhaps the chief source of financing for many terrorist organizations. Although the figures vary depending on the source, more than 4,000 businessmen have been kidnapped and held for ransom since 1974, and tens of millions of dollars in ransoms have been paid to dozens of terrorist groups. One of the reasons that accurate figures pertaining to the incidence of political kidnapping are hard to accumulate is that a portion of what passes for political kidnapping is, in fact, either purely criminal activity or outright fraud. Many of the so-called political kidnappings in Italy, for example, in actuality have been hoaxes designed to circumvent tight currency-export restrictions and taxation. Many kidnappings and ransom payoffs also go unreported every year since some corporate officials hope to keep such news from other employees in their companies.

Perhaps the record ransom to date is the $60 million (plus $1.2 million in food and clothing for the needy) paid to the Montoneros guerrillas in Argentina for the safe return of two Argentine brothers, Juan and Jorge Born.

Kidnapping for profit is a popular fund-raising method because it is such a low-risk/high-return strategy. Unlike robbing a bank or seizing an airliner or building, a well-planned and -executed kidnapping usually entails few risks to the perpetrators. The vast majority of all prime kidnapping targets have inadequate security; if terrorists discover that a particular target is well protected, all they have to do is to move on to another more vulnerable target. In this connection, it should be remembered that Aldo Moro was not the first choice of the Red Brigades; several higher choices were rejected because they were judged to have good security. Moro was the first potential target who was deemed to be truly vulnerable. Similarly, before the fall of the shah in Iran, authorities raided a safe house used by Mujaheddin terrorists and discovered a list of potential kidnap and assassination victims. In every case where surveillance of the potential victim revealed that they had reasonable security, their name had been crossed off the list. One recent study commissioned by a private security firm estimates, moreover, that 90 percent of all business executives who fall into the high-risk category have no security at all and that only a small fraction of the remainder have taken what could be truly described as adequate precautions

Terrorists, of course, have the element of surprise on their side: They can strike at will, whereas the potential victim and his security personnel must be constantly on the alert since even a momentary lapse can be fatal. As a result, 86 percent of all kidnapping attempts are successful. Not only is kidnapping a particularly difficult crime to prevent but also law enforcement authorities have a very poor record of bringing kidnappers to justice. A kidnapper has less than a one-in-five chance of being punished for his crime.

One of the most alarming new money-raising ventures being explored by terrorist groups is trafficking in illegal drugs, thereby combining perhaps the two most significant hard-ball games in the world: drugs and terrorism. The sale of drugs and narcotics is attractive to terrorists from a number of perspectives. Not only does the drug trade produce astronomical profits on a minimal investment, but terrorists, by virtue of their clandestine networks, already have in place what amounts to the necessary transport and distribution infrastructure. Also, their latent capacity for violence serves them in good stead when it comes to protecting their turf and to destroying potential rivals and competitors. Although certain rogue Palestinian elements have been linked to the illicit drug trade, Latin American terrorists are becoming most deeply and systematically involved in the drug business on an organized basis. The Colombian terrorist movement, M-19, not only sells drugs to raise needed operational funds but also provides protection to marijuana and cocaine growers and traffickers. Prior to seizing power, Sandanista rebels allegedly engaged in some drug sales in order to replenish depleted coffers, although this is disputed by other knowledgeable observers. The recent influx of hard drugs into Spain is almost entirely attributable to Basque terrorists who purchase the product in Colombia, whereupon it is shipped to Brussels, then to Paris, and finally to Spain. Turkish terrorists also are becoming engaged in illegal drug trafficking, and recent reports of growing IRA involvement in the marijuana and cocaine trade have surfaced. Four IRA Provos, for example, were apprehended in 1979 with $2.3 million worth of drugs hidden in a load of bananas.[17] Afghan rebels, engaged in an ongoing struggle against the Soviet occupation of their homeland, have, according to some reports reaching the West, been trading opium and hashish for guns and ammunition. Other reports have been received that the Soviets are permitting Western European and Palestinian terrorist organizations access to Afghan drug crops, grown in areas under the control of the puppet government in Kabul, as a means of indirect subsidy. The product is secretly shipped to Europe where it is sold to underwrite terrorist activities.

The involvement of terrorists in drug trafficking is a relatively recent development. While Western governments in the past have been quick to make accusations concerning the involvement of revolutionary movements in the drug trade, little hard evidence has substantiated such claims. Indeed, most terrorist groups have been characterized by a puritanical streak, eschewing drugs not only from a moral perspective but also because they represent a serious security risk to clandestine groups where a high degree of alertness is critical to survival. Moreover, drug usage may draw the attention of the authorities to a particular individual or group for reasons wholly unrelated to their terrorist activities. In both Cuba and Algeria, drug dealers were dealt with severely by the new revolutionary governments; in many cases they were simply rounded up and shot. The U.S. Weather Underground movement identified heroin traffickers as suitable targets of assassination. Nevertheless, some members of the Baader-Meinhof gang, the Weather underground, and presumably other Western terrorist organizations that thrive in the ferment of the university milieu use marijuana, cocaine, and amphetamines on a regular basis.

Terrorists also demonstrate little reluctance to running vice operations if they generate money for the struggle. The IRA is said to be linked directly to various prostitution activities including massage parlors and brothels, and also to extorting protection from other vice operators. The Palestinians also reap profits from vice activities in Lebanon.

Terrorist movements are also buttressed by so-called friendship societies composed of foreign sympathizers, although in some cases they are unwittingly duped into supporting terrorist activities on the pretence that their contributions are going toward charitable purposes. The Jewish Agency's support of the revolt against the British in Palestine remains a classic example of an external organization of multinational composition that engaged in extensive fund-raising efforts ostensibly for humanitarian purposes, a portion of which was used to underwrite terrorist activities or at least to free other monies for the support of terrorism.

The Algerian National Liberation Front (FLN) which openly embraced terrorism in its war for self-determination against France, sent fund-raising teams to the Middle East and Western Europe to collect money from sympathizers. All too often, however, their efforts degenerated into what amounted to naked extortion, where protection from attacks on one's business or person was purchased by making a so-called voluntary contribution to the FLN.

"Irish elements in the United States," writes U.K. parliamentarian John Biggs-Davidson, "have been generous paymasters and armourers to revolutionaries for more than a century."[18] Indeed, the chief beneficiary of U.S. largess over the years has been the IRA, which has received sustained support from U.S.-based aid societies. At one time, "nine-tenths of the Provo's weapons and most of their funds came from the United States."[19] As one foreign policy observer from the Republic of Ireland remarked bitterly, "Americans must enjoy seeing Irishmen kill other Irishmen, otherwise they wouldn't contribute their money to the IRA."[20]

Although once heavily dependent on financial assistance from sympathizers in the United States who tossed their spare change into pots at Irish pubs and Hibernian Society functions in Boston, New York, and other cities where there are large concentrations of Irish-Americans, to sustain and support its activities, the IRA in recent years has developed an elaborate financial infrastructure to raise more systematically the large sums needed to conduct its shadowy war against the British. Today the IRA meets most of its budget—now estimated to exceed $4 million a year—with the income derived from vice operations, the sale of illegal drugs, protection rackets, bank and armored car robberies, kidnappings, and the operation of pubs and other legitimate businesses. Nevertheless, friendship societies in the United States and the Irish Republic still manage to channel thousands of dollars, along with weapons and explosives, to Irish extremists. The largest and most important IRA support group in the United States is the Irish Northern Aid Committee (Noraid) based in the Bronx. In 1980, Noraid raised just under $200,000, less than half the amount its fund-raising activities yielded a few years earlier. U.K. officials, however, report that the hunger strikes at Belfast's Maze Prison resulted in an increase in contributions.

"British officials diplomatically say they are sure that most U.S. supporters of the IRA think that the money contributions are going for charitable purposes," observes George Will. "But the sulphurous propaganda churned out by the IRA's U.S. agents makes it clear that most contributors must know they are subsidizing murder."[21] In this connection, many U.S. politicians of Irish heritage—including House Speaker Thomas P. O'Neill, Senator Edward

Kennedy, Governor Hugh Carey of New York, and Senator Daniel P. Moynihan—
have publicly condemned the IRA's methods and admonished supporters in the
United States not to contribute to it. Nevertheless, their words are still disregarded
by some. In June 1981, three New York men were arrested and charged with
violating federal firearm statutes after they had paid an undercover FBI agent
$16,000 for forty-two automatic rifles, submachine guns, and pistols. Authori-
ties also seized seven automatic rifles, a machine pistol, a flame thrower, and a
pre–World War II 20-millimeter cannon at the home of one of the men, all of the
weapons presumably destined for shipment to the IRA. The men justified their
actions by stating that they were motivated by considerations of social justice in
Northern Ireland. However, gun-running operations in the United States are no
longer as important to the IRA as they once were. Today, the USSR and its Libyan
and Palestinian surrogates provide the IRA with mortars, bazookas, grenades,
RPG7 antitank grenade launchers, assault rifles, explosives, and other weapons.

The surfeit of money accumulated by some terrorist organizations has
often permitted those in leadership positions to enjoy hedonistic life-styles
more befitting jetset capitalists than dedicated, often avowedly Marxist, revolutionaries. It is no aberration that several PLO officials have been assassinated
in recent years while they were on gambling holidays in Cannes or staying
in luxury hotels in Europe. Majed Abu Sharar, Chief of the PLO's public relations section, was killed in October 1981, when a bomb exploded under his
bed in Rome's Flora Hotel on the Via Veneto. Members of the Baader-Meinhof
gang had a penchant for Alfa-Romeo sports cars, fine hotels, gourmet meals,
and vacations on the southern coast of France. The infamous Carlos clearly
savors the good life and is remembered as a playboy during his two years at
Patrice Lumumba University and, later, during the time he spent in Europe.

Conclusion

Recent years have witnessed the constant expansion and diffusion of terrorist
violence. Various factors have contributed to this development, especially
technological innovation, which has facilitated growing linkages between
terrorist movements, and the military and economic support of terrorist movements by powerful patron nations such as the USSR and its proxies.

Technological progress, however, is a reality of the modern world, and
the products of constant innovation—jet travel, instantaneous communications,
and television—are irreversible and increasingly universal, and therefore there
is no practicable means of denying their benefits and advantages to terrorists.
A more serious problem, and one that admits viable solutions and alternatives,
is state sponsorship of terrorist movements.

As noted previously, the USSR is the single most significant patron of
international terrorism and the engine behind the globalization of terrorist

violence. The Soviets clearly view terrorism as a means of surrogate warfare against the West, a low-cost strategy for nibbling away at the periphery of the Western alliance in the eventual hope of denying the United States and its allies critical resources located in the Third World, access to vital sea lanes, and the support of friendly nations around the world. In short, it is part of a grand strategy by Moscow to isolate the United States and the other industrial democracies from the nations of the developing world. By also sponsoring terrorism within the industrialized nations themselves, the Soviets seek to distract them from the gains the USSR is making elsewhere and to siphon away critical resources that could be better used to shore up the faltering national defense capabilities of those nations but that instead must be diverted to combating and controlling internal threats. Terrorism is "clandestine and undeclared"[22] warfare against the West and, therefore, must be recognized as a clear and present danger both to the individual and collective security of the United States and its allies.

Notes

1. Zbigniew Brzezinski, *Between Two Ages*, (New York: Viking Press, 1970), p. 60.
2. Richard Clutterbuck, *Protest and the Urban Guerrilla* (London: Cassell & Co., 1973), p. 258.
3. Edward S. Heyman, "The Diffusion of Transnational Terrorism," in *Responding to the Terrorist Threat*, ed. Richard H. Shutz, Jr., and Stephen Sloan (New York: Pergamon Press, 1980), p. 209.
4. Ted Robert Gurr, "Some Characteristics of Contemporary Political Terrorism," mimeographed, March 1976.
5. Ray S. Cline, quoted by Herbert Krosney, "The PLO's Moscow Connection," *New York*, 24 September 1979, p. 72.
6. Herbert Rommerstein, *Soviet Support of International Terrorism* (Washington, D.C.: Foundation for Democratic Edcuation, 1981), p. 9.
7. Claire Sterling, *The Terror Network* (New York: Holt, Rinehart & Winston, 1981), p. 136.
8. Ibid., p. 292.
9. Samuel T. Francis, *The Soviet Strategy of Terror* (Washington, D.C.: Heritage Foundation, 1981), p. 29.
10. Sterling, *Terror Network*, p. 259.
11. Carlos the Jackal also reported received $5 million from two of his hostages—the petroleum ministers of Iran and Saudi Arabia—in return for their safe release. He is alleged to have subsequently retired, after undergoing extensive plastic surgery to alter his appearance. Other reports have surfaced that he is dead, but most observers suspect that this may simply be part of a carefully calculated disinformation effort to throw authorities off his trail.

12. "IRA and PLO: Alliance for Violence," *Washington Post*, 9 September 1979.

13. Christopher Dobson and Ronald Payne, *The Terrorists* (New York: Facts on File, 1979), p. 169.

14. Sterling, *Terror Network*, p. 302.

15. Walter Laqueur, "The Futility of Terrorism," *Harper's,* (March 1976), p. 104.

16. Dobson and Payne, *The Terrorists*, p. 89.

17. Sterling, *Terror Network*, pp. 151-152.

18. As John Biggs-Davidson has noted, "Outside assistance for Irish revolutionaries is not new: 'England's danger is Ireland's opportunity.' For centuries, separatists allied themselves with the continental empires that were England's enemies. The Jacobinism of the French Revolution affected the United Irishmen of 1789: Bonaparte regretted that he went to Egypt and not to Ireland. The Hohenzollern Empire was content that arms should be supplied impartially to the rival forces of Volunteers who in 1914 drilled in readiness for civil war feared as the result of Home Rule. A greater war supervened. In 1939-40, the IRA conducted a bombing campaign in Britain. They were in contact with Nazi Germany; and the Abwehr penetrated their ranks." See John Biggs-Davidson, "The Strategic Implications for the West of the International Links of the IRA in Ireland," *Foreign Affairs Research Institute* (1976), p. 2.

19. Sterling, *Terror Network*, p. 151.

20. Confidential interview, New York, 1978.

21. George Will, "'Mad Logic' and Ulster Violence," *Washington Post*, 8 February 1976.

22. Paul Wilkinson, *Terrorism and the Liberal State* (New York: New York University Press, 1979), p. 199.

3 Terrorist Profile: The Secret Lives of Terrorists

I am the wound and the knife!
I am the blow and the cheek!
I am the limbs and the wheel—
The victim and the executioner!

—Charles Baudelaire[1]

Who are these people called terrorists, men and women of unquiet heart and brain who wander the lonely slopes of political violence? Are they sane, otherwise normal people thrust into their dark profession out of desperation, confronted with "the anguished and irreversible choice between giving up . . . worthy ends or resorting to unworthy means,"[2] or are they defective personalities who, if they had not become political terrorists, would have found expression for inherent criminal or psychopathic tendencies through some other outlet? What does it mean to be a terrorist, and how are they affected by the pitiless violence they inflict on others? Do terrorists possess an unconscious desire to die, a streak of self-destructiveness that compels them to take ever greater risks? Do all terrorists believe that they are serving justice or some higher calling? What becomes of terrorists when their struggles are over? These are the questions that are explored in this chapter.

Are They Crazy?

Albert Parry alleges that "most political terrorists have not been normal." He goes on to say, "Not all political terrorists are insane or mentally disturbed, but most are."[3] In a published interview, Parry goes even further, maintaining that "most terrorists are crazy, they have to be crazy. In Asia and Africa, they're all crazy."[4] Although it is currently fashionable in some circles to regard most terrorists as defective personalities and mentally unstable, little evidence exists to justify such a conclusion. Mental cases like Donald David DeFreeze, the self-proclaimed field marshall of the Symbionese Liberation Army, are not stereotypical or even common in terrorist movements because, as Conrad V. Hassel points out, few seriously mentally ill persons could command much of a following.[5] This assessment is further reinforced by Dr. Thomas Valk: "Terrorists with mental problems are not likely to be involved in groups, are not going to be acting primarily for political purposes, and by the very nature of their mental affliction, will not be very capable or effective."[6] This is not to suggest that terrorist movements do not serve as magnets for psychopaths and thugs, just as many conventional military organizations do, but rather to affirm that such individuals make up a relatively small percentage of the rank-and-file of most terrorist organizations.

The willingness to kill for a cause or to sacrifice one's life for an ideal hardly can be interpreted as evidence of mental instability or deep-seated psychosis. According to Dr. William D. Davidson, president of the Institute of Psychiatry and Foreign Affairs, such behavior is consistent with the most heroic traditions of the Western world.[7] The Christian martyrs, observes Davidson, are representative of the homage paid to those who gave their lives to perpetuate and advance deeply held convictions—in this instance, religious beliefs. Similarly, the Crusades witnessed tens of thousands of Europeans traveling to the far reaches of what was then the known world to slaughter other human beings for the glory of their faith. "Surely they were not all crazy," posits Davidson.[8] Indeed, men have long gone to war and committed unspeakable acts of violence over disagreements as to "whether flesh be bread, or bread be flesh" and "whether the juice of a certain berry be blood or wine."[9]

"What is normal behavior is essentially relative," observes Davidson; that certain behavior may appear crazy from a particular perspective or vantage point does not necessarily make it crazy.[10] While rejecting the notion that most terrorists suffer from various forms of dementia, many respected authorities concede that terrorists do tend to manifest paranoiac symptoms, characterized by Hassel as "an overwhelming sense of mission."[11] Terrorists are the kind of people who adopt a cause with single-minded devotion and readily regard the failure of the cause to achieve its goals quickly as evidence of the existence of a conspiracy against it. In the distorted logic of the terrorist mind, the existence of a perceived conspiracy is ample justification for the adoption of extreme violence by the individual in order to remove or destroy the obstacles standing in the way of the cause. Rarely does the paranoiac personality stop to consider that opposition to and criticism of the cause may be well founded and that a reassessment of his or her own attachment to the cause would be advisable.

Nearly all terrorists are outwardly normal men and women who display above-average intelligence and ability. Intellectual acumen is critical to the success of terrorist movements inasmuch as the work of calculated destruction takes great resourcefulness, energy, and skill. Nevertheless, a streak of schizophrenia is evident in many terrorists, expressive of an internal struggle between competing impulses that is attested to by the strange dichotomies that are present in some terrorist personalities. The instances of terrorists revealing a gentle, sometimes almost maudlin, sentimental side are not uncommon. In a scene from the theater of the absurd, one of the terrorists who hijacked the German jetliner in 1977 that ultimately landed in Somalia, where it was later rescued by a German assault team, organized a birthday party for a stewardess aboard the plane. Later, the same terrorist watched as the plane's captain was murdered in cold blood. Young Japanese leftist terrorists, responsible for 8 deaths and over 300 injuries during 1974 and 1975, resulting from the terror-bombing of eleven industrial firms during a ten-month period that gripped Tokyo in unprecedented fear, were described variously as nice people, congenial, popular, terrific workers, and punctual. They baked cookies for neighborhood children and were meticulously neat. Many of their neighbors expressed disbelief that their young friends could be merciless killers who slaughtered and maimed with homemade explosives stuffed with weed killer.

Are They Thrill Seekers?

Terrorists also allegedly are drawn to their gloomy profession because they are "counterphobically seeking the excitement of danger, despairing safe routines of regular hard work and slow advancement."[12] According to William F. May, "the brush with death relieves men of that other death—boredom."[13] Indeed, some observers have postulated that the emergence of terrorism in the contemporary Western world is related to efforts by various individuals to escape what others have described as the monotony of human existence. Drugs, permissive sex, alcohol, and religious cults represent some of the contemporary outlets embraced by large numbers of people to avoid the reality of unfulfilled lives in post-industrial mass society. It is quite a leap, however, from alcoholism or religious cults to membership in violent gangs of terrorists pledged to the destruction of the state.

While superficially there is much in the terrorist mystique that might attract individuals who seek an element of sensationalism in otherwise humdrum lives, there is little evidence of men or women becoming terrorists solely for this reason; and it might be added that those who are attempting to satiate some private fantasy that feeds on danger and violence usually do not last very long. Beate Sturm, a young German terrorist who participated in a number of bank robberies, attempted to justify her actions by stating that she was striving to recreate the exciting world of U.S. crime movies.[14] However, she is certainly the exception rather than the rule. While some U.S. and Western European students-cum-terrorists may act out secret fantasies of strength, domination, and danger through acts of terrorism, the great majority of recruits inducted into the ranks of terrorist organizations in Algeria, Kenya, Malaysia, the Philippines, Cyprus, Ireland, and the Middle East (both Zionist and Palestinian organizations) became terrorists as a matter of circumstance, not because of some defective dimension of their personality or to satisfy a secret craving for thrill or danger.

With respect to excitement, the lives of most terrorists, like the lives of spies and other intelligence operatives, have been greatly exaggerated and romanticized. For the average terrorist, his life is one of little excitement and considerable hardship. By contrast to guerrilla warfare, a terrorist may carry out an actual mission or attack only a few times in his whole career. In between missions, terrorists live dull and tedious lives, characterized more by preparation and waiting than action. If the terrorist is a hunter, he is also the hunted. He must be constantly on the alert for signs of danger, always on the move, with few material possessions and meaningful human relationships. Begin comments on this fact in his memoirs:

> Solitude is an unavoidable condition of the underground. Throughout the years of the revolt I had to deny myself almost entirely the pleasure of friendly chats, of meetings with friends, or relatives or acquaintances. The law of the underground forbade "nonessential" meetings.[15]

This condition of loneliness strikes the observer as the most pervasive fact of the terrorist's existence. Nechaev for example, viewed love and friendship as effeminate and a threat to the realization of the revolutionary terrorist's goals.[16] Mere survival dictates that the terrorist must become faceless, indistinguishable from the masses around him, that everything unique about him must be submerged lest he call attention to himself.

In short, being a terrorist is hard work, and it takes an extraordinary amount of single-minded dedication and commitment. According to Nechaev, the revolutionary terrorist "has no interests of his own, no affairs, no feelings, no attachments, no belongings, not even a name."[17] He is dominated by a single, all-consuming purpose—the revolution—and to this end he has broken completely with the outside world, rejecting its laws, mores, and convictions. Everything else is secondary or does not exist to him at all. Members of the Russian terrorist organization known as the People's Will pledged to devote their whole soul and being to the revolution and to forget any bonds of family, love, and friendship. In his minimanual, Carlos Marighella warns that, "Urban guerrilla activity is not like a business deal, or working on the shop floor, or staging a play. It demands the same kind of commitment as rural guerrilla activity, and anyone lacking in the necessary qualities would be better not to attempt it."[18]

A security manual devised for Italy's Red Brigades entitled *Security Rules and Work Methods*, which was discovered in a Rome hideaway, spells out in rigid detail how members of the terrorist underground are supposed to behave. In a page from the method school of acting, terrorists are advised to adopt completely the personality, habits, and mannerisms of the identity they have selected as a cover. According to the manual:

> The role that each comrade chooses must then be consistently demonstrated in his everyday life. If, for example, he has assumed the role of an artisan, he must leave home every day before 8 in the morning and not return before 12:30 P.M., go out again at 2 P.M. and come

back home at 7 P.M. or after. This means that every comrade must organize his own work according to regular hours. . . . The role must be carefully studied so that any irregularities in one's behavior can be explained."[19]

The manual goes on to impress upon members that they should be the very soul of discretion. It preaches against noisy parties and dirty cars and advises them to cultivate the image of hard-working respectability. Comrades "must be decorously dressed and be personally well-kept: Clean shaven and hair cut."[20]

In summary then, there is nothing frivolous or casual about most terrorists; they are profoundly serious people and, by contrast to many flamboyant guerrillas and partisans, terrorists usually go to fanatical lengths to preserve their anonymity. The life of a terrorist, where a high premium is put on the ability to move unobserved through normal society, accords few opportunities for self-aggrandizement. Though terrorism is a worldwide problem of major concern, the public knows virtually nothing about most of its perpetrators who, unlike guerrilla leaders like Che Guevara, have not developed any measure of notoriety or cult following.

As terrorist movements become older and wealthier, a certain amount of corruption tends to set in, and those in positions of command and authority can indulge in acquisitive or hedonistic pursuits if so inclined. According to Robert Moss, the members of the Baader-Meinhof gang "became notorious for their opulent life-style, living in spacious apartments, driving Alfa Romeo sports cars and slipping off to Paris for weekends of 'rest and relaxation' spent in good hotels."[21] However, inasmuch as their life-style departed from orthodox radical underground living habits, it probably served as a cover for their activities and helped them to avoid capture. So flagrant were their hedonistic tendencies that Andreas Baader, Ulrike Meinhof, and other gang members were expelled from a Fedayeen training camp in Jordan in 1970. According to intelligence reports, the gang offended their Arab hosts by their uninhibited sexual escapades, for partaking liberally of liquor during target practice, and for an almost total disregard of even elementary standards of military discipline and professionalism. Thus, despite their notoriety and success, the Baader-Meinhof gang represents an aberration rather than the prototype of a classical terrorist organization. By contrast to the Baader-Meinhof gang, most terrorists are profoundly ascetic individuals, characterized by sacrifice and self-denial. Stern gang (Lohmey Heruth Israel) terrorist, Joshua Cohen, was a total fanatic who, during the initial phase of the Zionist terror in Palestine, lived in the open and subsisted largely on oranges stolen from local groves. Similarly, Yasir Arafat, as Parry notes:

[I]s unmarried, and neither drinks nor smokes. He eats on the run. He is surrounded by security guards, and is himself always armed. Nevertheless, he never sleeps in the same house for more than one night. Sometimes, in fact, he changes his sleeping place twice in one night.[22]

The price terrorists pay, in broken marriages and strained interpersonal relationships, to pursue their calling is heavy. Commander Zero, the Sandanista leader in Nicaragua, complained that the revolution has ruined three marriages. "The first thing we revolutionaires lose is our wives," he said. "The last thing we lose is our lives. Between our women and our lives, we lose our freedom, our happiness, our means of living."[23]

The life of a terrorist is not conducive to marriage; consequently, few terrorists are married, and those who are usually do not remain married for very long. One study of identified and arrested terrorists in Latin America, the Middle East, and Asia estimates that 75 to 80 percent are single.[24] Not only is it difficult for a male terrorist to provide for a wife and family or to meet his obligations as husband and father, but also families are usually easy targets of authorities in their efforts to place pressure on the terrorist. Stories abound of wives and children of suspected terrorists being subjected to lengthy and intense interrogation, imprisonment, and even assassination by counterterrorist death squads.

Background and Recruitment

Whether recruited on a college campus in Western Europe or in a refugee camp in southern Lebanon, terrorists are very much a product of their heritage, acculturation, environment, and life experiences. Family attitudes and home life play an important role in shaping some terrorists. Individuals raised in highly politicized families often have violent beliefs instilled in them at a very young age. It can be surmised that Yasir Arafat's attitudes are very much the product of his father's and older brother's political activism that took the form of membership in a radical Moslem paramilitary organization known as the Holy Struggle, dedicated to the destruction of the state of Israel. Although his father, by contrast, is a multimillionaire, Venezuelan-born arch terrorist Carlos (Ilich Ramirez Sanchez) was raised on his father's radical leftist philosophy and ultimately sent to Moscow for an education. On a broader level, membership in the IRA seems to be very much of a family affair, with membership passed on from generation to generation in a war that has gone on for centuries. The IRA's recruitment efforts are reinforced continuously by songs, stories, and propaganda that bombard young Irish men and women and create an institutionalized hatred of the British.

Occasionally, however, a total anomaly appears in the guise of an individual whose embrace of terrorism is a matter of personal choice and adopted values rather than having anything to do with his or her background or acculturation. IRA Provo leader Sean MacStiofain serves as a good case in point. Born John Stephenson in London, baptized a Protestant, MacStiofain had no discernible Irish heritage. As a young man he abandoned his English name for a Gaelic one, adopted Ireland and its ways with the zeal of a convert, and took up arms against his native country. In another rejection of a personal heritage, the PFLP reported in 1969 that at one of its training camps in Jordan, among a group of ninety volunteers from Western countries, there were six Jews. Although such reports are difficult to verify, Western intelligence sources indicate that the number of leftist revolutionaries of Jewish heritage from the West who have been trained by the PFLP and PLO may exceed fifty.

The reason why most individuals embrace revolutionary violence, however, has less to do with family background and heritage than with negative experiences and education during their formative years. Many terrorists are alienated or adrift from society long before they are drawn into a community of violence, and this is particularly true of Western terrorists. The urge or compulsion to strike out at society may stem from feelings of humiliation, inferiority, and helplessness that have eroded their sense of worth and self-respect. These wounds to one's sense of self-esteem are called narcissistic wounding, and the hostility they are capable of producing in individuals is called narcissistic rage.[25] According to some psychiatrists, the individual who is completely unaccepted and unloved has the choice of either rejecting himself or rejecting the group or society that he believes has judged him wrong.[26] Western terrorist movements, moreover, are full of male and female achievers who fall short of their personal goals and expectations and blame society for their shortcomings. Others are seeking escape from the impersonality, the anomie, of mass society by making violent statements affirming their existence. Whatever factors explain the individual's decision to become a terrorist, psychologists note one common denominator: Almost all terrorists are characterized by a condition known as primary-process thinking whereby one projects his or her own concerns and problems onto the community or society as a whole. This tendency to let one's inner thinking spill over into larger arenas means that terrorists typically seek vast objectives or sweeping change rather than attempt to work out their problems for themselves. This might best be described as the forest-fire syndrome, a classic example of overkill in which one starts a forest fire to warm his hands. In other words, terrorists are the type of people who try to change an entire society to conform to their perspectives rather than to modify their own behavior to adjust better to society.

Are They Elitist?

Nearly all terrorist organizations are quite small, hence there is certainly the element of elitist behavior in the very act of a select group seeking to impose its views on the rest of society. According to figures compiled by Ted Robert Gurr, 86 percent of all terrorist groups had fewer than 50 members, 8 percent had from 50 to 500 members, and only 6 percent had more than 500 members.[27]

Thus, terrorist groups are inherently minority movements composed of those who maintain that they alone possess the special insight necessary to divine what is best for the masses and the courage to take the extreme measures demanded to give substance to their views. As Albert Camus noted, "The whole history of Russian terrorism can be looked upon as a struggle between the intellectuals and absolutism, in the presence of the silent masses."[28]

"All revolts are largely the work of a small band of zealots who furnish the impetus, the leadership, and the enthusiasm for the others, whether few or many," writes J. Bowyer Bell.[29] In this context, terrorist organizations, especially those of a Marxist orientation, often have perceived their role as that of a vanguard, entrusted with the mission of politicizing the masses and demonstrating the vulnerability of the state through violent assaults on its order and institutions. Most vanguard groups consist largely of intellectuals and ideologues who purport to have special insight regarding the plight of the oppressed masses and the means required to deliver it unto the promised land. "Terrorists do not believe in liberty or egality or fraternity," states Walter Laqueur. "Historically, they are elitists, contemptuous of the masses, believing in the historical mission of a tiny minority."[30] Among Marxists, the doctrine of dialectical materialism reinforces this elitism inasmuch as it calls for the creation of a dictatorship that remains in effect until such time as the stage known as communism is realized.

This elitism is also strengthened by the fact that most terrorist leaders, and a large percentage of the rank-and-file in many cases, come from privileged backgrounds and, as such, have enjoyed educational, cultural, and other advantages that set them apart from the masses. In this connection, one of the greatest misconceptions about terrorists is that they are persons with nothing left to lose, to whom nothing else can be done. Nearly all terrorists have other options available to them; few become terrorists out of personal desperation. A significant number of terrorists have had professional training. For example, an unusually large number of physicians have become terrorist leaders, including Dr. George Habash, founder and secretary-general of the PFLP; the late Dr. Wadi Hadad of the PFLP; Argentine-born Cuban revolutionary and martyr Ernesto Che Guevara; and Cuban exile leader Dr. Orlando Bosch. Bosch, previously accused of plotting to kill former Secretary of State Henry Kissinger, was arrested by Venezuelan authorities for the bombing of an Air Cubana plane, with the loss of all aboard. Writer and outspoken proponent of terrorist violence, Franz Fanon, was a psychiatrist. Although they did not have professional backgrounds, Monodeep of the Indian Naxalite terrorist movement, Red Brigades patron Giangiacomo Feltrinelli, and the infamous Carlos came from wealthy families. George Grivas's father was a well-to-do cereal merchant, and according to Grivas, he was raised in "the handsomest house in the village."[31]

While the leadership of terrorist movements is almost always drawn from the middle and upper classes and is usually well educated, the rank-and-file of most terrorist movements is representative of the population from which it came. Hence, it is not surprising that terrorists from the developed nations are almost always better educated than those from the emerging and under-developed countries. Similarly, the size of the terrorist group is also important; the smaller the group the better educated its members tend to be.

Few of the youthful members of European terrorist groups such as Italy's Red Brigades, the German Baader-Meinhof gang, or the JRA faction come from working-class backgrounds; most are children of the middle class. Interestingly, Andreas Baader, one of the founders of the Baader-Meinhof gang, was a high-school dropout and one of the few members of the German terror movement who had not attended university. Similarly, members of the U.S. Weather movement were almost exclusively the product of white, middle- or upper-class homes and had been enrolled as students at the better universities.

The Provisional wing of the IRA is the only genuinely working-class terrorist movement in the developed world. Even the leadership is largely of blue-collar origins, and this fact sets it apart from almost every other terrorist movement in the world. The Quebec Liberation Front (FLQ) and the Peronist terror groups in Argentina are the only other predominantly working-class terrorist organiza-tions to arise in recent years in the West.

Perhaps the Third World terrorist movement that contains the largest number of well-educated members, many of them of middle-class origins, is the Palestinians. Like the Zionists before them, the various Palestinian terror groups are victims of a diaspora, forced not only to survive but also to achieve in a hostile world. Palestinians are found throughout the Middle East in positions of influence and constitute a critical part of the infrastructure of the population and technology-poor but economically rich nations of the Arabian peninsula. Likewise, a significant number of Palestinians are in Europe and North America, often in the professions. When the call to arms went out from the Palestinian resistance, the sons and daughters of the skilled and talented exile community responded enthusiastically and today form the nucleus of the Palestinian terror organizations. Observed one writer:

> And the Black September terrorists are not clod-hopping country boys. . . . The young men who carried out the attack on the Israeli athletes at the Munich Olympics spoke two or three languages each. If they weren't carrying guns, they would not be condemned to live as shoe shine boys or bus conductors. They would be putting their feet up in a lawyer's office or a bank.[32]

Similarly, the ultraradical PFLP is composed largely of "intellectual activists drawn from the largely Christian Palestinian middle class."[33]

Phillip A. Karber has observed that "historically the most dangerous and successful urban terrorism movements have been waged not by a band of disparate intellectuals, but by a highly organized movement incorporating the technical skills and dogged determination found among the blue collar workers and lower echelon middle class."[34] This may be stating the obvious too strongly; however, it should be apparent that terrorist organizations, on the operational level, have little need as a rule for the skills of mathematicians, tailors, priests, college professors, poets, or lawyers. A man or woman who will fill a bottle with gasoline, stuff a rag in the top, light the product, and hurl it at a target is a far more valuable asset to a terrorist organization than someone who can design a nuclear weapon that, in all likelihood, will never be built. Terrorism is, in its most common incarnation, rudimentary warfare and, as such, requires the application of rudimentary skills to rudimentary tasks. The Zionist terror organizations in Palestine had their pick of men with outstanding professional backgrounds but had to actively recruit those with practical skills that could be adapted to the support of their terrorist activities.

Are They Religious Believers?

Contrary to observers like Parry who allege that "most terrorists of our era have been atheists to a man and a woman,"[35] many terrorists were raised in families with strong religious traditions and continue to observe their religious beliefs even after embracing terrorism to achieve their political aims. Indeed, religious extremism remains one of the chief sources of terrorism in the modern world. The struggles in Northern Ireland, Israel, and the Philippines are rooted in the firmament of sharp religious differences and cultural and socioeconomic antagonisms that arise from those religious differences. The skyjackers of a Libyan jetliner commandeered over Italy in December 1981 were members of a radical Moslem Shiite paramilitary group. They demanded that the Libyan government account for the disappearance of a Shiite religious leader on a trip to Libya in 1978.

Few members of Al Fatah or the other Palestinian terrorist organizations are atheists in the literal sense of the word; many are devout Moslems, including PLO chieftain Yasir Arafat, who has made a pilgrimage to Mecca as evidence of his devotion. Admittedly, such a pilgrimage also has a good deal of public relations value in the Arab world. The PFLP is an exception inasmuch as it is characterized by a rather doctrinaire Marxist-atheist orthodoxy, although many of its most prominent members were baptized Christians. The Mujaheddin in Iran and other Moslem religious terror organizations including the ultraradical Moslem Brotherhood, which is active in Egypt and several other Moslem countries, take their inspiration and raison d'être from fundamentalist Moslem tenets and what they regard as secular, often Western, encroachment on their traditional cultures. Although a case can be made that all of the world's great religions countenance the taking of human life under some circumstances, the Moslem concept of Jihad, or Holy War, provides perhaps the best religious justification for acts of terror by Moslem extremist groups.

In summary, it is not unusual to find a practicing terrorist with strong religious convictions; the two characteristics in one individual are by no means inconsistent or mutually exclusive. Recall that the Old Testament, while exhorting believers to observe the sanctity of human life, also celebrates great generals like David, Saul, and Joshua. Many military and wartime political leaders have been men of deep and abiding religious faith, so why should it be any different with terrorists?

Ideology

As a group, terrorists are not highly ideological and are most often linked instead by common experiences and aspirations, or a commonly perceived enemy, rather than by any formal ideology. Indeed, as Walter Laqueur has observed, "one learns more about a terrorist group by looking at its victims than at its manifestos."[36] The only thread of ideology consistently running through the various Palestinian terrorist organizations, for example, is a universal hatred of Israel and a desire to reclaim what is regarded as their homeland. There is little agreement on what form a resurrected homeland would take should a Palestinian state come into being. Some Palestinians are dedicated Marxists, whereas others are fervent Moslems opposed to the establishment of a secular state.

Most public pronouncements and declarations by terrorist groups are alike in their ambiguity and undefined goals and amount to little more than "sloganeering" without expressing any kind of coherent philosophy or doctrine. Terrorist writings are, in many respects, more representative of the existence of a universal revolutionary vocabulary than any kind of substantive ideology and amount to little more than a collection of words with an emotional ring, such as *oppression* and *power to the people*, which are ideal for communicating through the television medium but that display little in-depth knowledge of philosophy, politics, or economics.

The leadership of terrorist groups is always more ideological than the rank-and-file. Increasingly, both the leadership and rank-and-file have received political and military training in the USSR, Cuba, and the Warsaw Pact nations, or in Third World countries under the tutelage of intelligence operatives from Communist bloc nations. Nevertheless, the number of ideologically committed graduates of such training and indoctrination programs still represents a minority of all terrorists. One should not lose sight of the fact, however, that the great majority of all terrorists willingly cooperates with the USSR and regards Moscow as a friend because of the support it extends to them.

If not highly ideological as a group, many terrorists are nonetheless reasonably idealistic, even if their idealism is often perverted. Like most idealists, they also tend to regard the world simplistically, in black and white terms, taking refuge in old theories and easy answers. Many of their ideals are quite laudable;

it is the righteous certitude with which they embrace these ideals, and the violence they embrace to give life to their ideals, that are at issue.

Often the only element of a terrorist program on which a broad consensus exists is the seizure of power. This, of course, has a great deal to do with the fact that terrorism is a destructive force, oriented toward sweeping away the old order, rather than a constructive philosophy focusing on the replacement of the old order with something else. Sorel, quoting Karl Marx, voiced the view that making plans for the shape of things to come after the revolution was a reactionary act.

In many instances, ideology, expressed in manifestos and self-characterizations by terrorist groups, is adopted simply for the credibility it lends to the terrorist organization and as a justification for acts of violence. Moreover, a professed ideology may be utilized to recruit supporters or to enlist external aid, in terms of arms and financing. In this connection, the USSR provides considerable material support to avowedly pro-Soviet Marxist terrorist groups operating around the globe.

Like nineteenth century Russian terrorists, among members of the so-called cult of the bomb who unabashedly professed a nihilistic allegiance to destruction without any corresponding vision of the shape of the system that would replace the one they destroyed, the U.S. Weather underground was notable, if not for its principles, then surely for its forthright articulation of its nihilistic philosophy. "We're against everything that's 'good and decent' in honky America," announced Bernardine Dohrn, its fiery leader. "We will burn and loot and destroy. We are the incubation of your mother's nightmare."[37]

It is not enough to deal with terrorists as rational conscious, goal-seeking beings; there is an unconscious, irrational element often in the psychodynamic makeup of terrorists. Indeed, many terrorists have not so much an ideology as an aesthetic that motivates them, binds them together, and gives them a common identity. In the words of the late radical German student leader "Red" Rudi Dutschke, "We are not bound together by an abstract theory but by an existential disgust."[38]

Terrorism produces feelings of a kind of mystical solidarity with others who consciously have rejected the conventional patterns of life and accepted standards of morality, who have cut all ties with the established social order. For many terrorists, loneliness is already a condition of their lives before they become terrorists; many were loners, misfits, alienated from society, before they found meaning in terrorizing the very society from which they became outcasts. According to William Stevenson, an Israeli intelligence profile of the late Dr. Wadi Hadad of the PFLP suggested that he "derives almost mystical satisfaction from knowing—with others of this organization—that he is cut off from the rest of the world and thus obeys rules and standards of his (and their) own making."[39] This terrorist cult of alienation draws strength from the very fact of its isolation from the rest of the world and provides a release to many of those who embrace its standard from their own inner loneliness and private anguish.

While this aesthetic may stem from reaction to the external world, or the external world's reaction to the terrorists, it is also a function of the terrorist's supraliminal conceit. "The anarchic rebel . . . feels himself not one with God, but God," writes Bertrand Russell. "Truth and duty, which represent our neighbors, exist no longer for the man who has become God; for others truth is what *he* posits, duty what he comands."[40] Like Malraux's fictional terrorist Ch'en, the political reasons that originally motivated his actions become increasingly meaningless. The very act of destruction becomes an end in itself.

Those of artistic or creative backgrounds often are drawn in large numbers to terrorist movements in the West, due perhaps to their propensity to regard the entire world as corrupt and only their art as bordering on truth. They often subscribe to notions of romantic violence and seek, like Malraux's fictional Ch'en, to live their idea, embracing terrorism as a means of giving practical expression to their art. The example of Ghassan Kanafani, a Palestinian writer and artist and member of the PLO who was assassinated, reportedly by the Israelis, in September 1975 when a bomb planted in his car exploded, serves as a good case in point:

> My political position springs from my being a novelist. As far as I am concerned, politics and the novel are indivisible, and I can categorically state that I became politically committed because I was a novelist, not the opposite.[41]

Violence and art have become synonymous in some underground circles, with individuals like Kanafani seeking the passion that comes from killing others.

Age

Terrorism is a youthful profession. The great majority of all terrorists is under 30 years of age. Few statistics are available, but it is known that 63 percent of all Malayan insurgents were under 30 years of age, 81 percent of the members of the Viet Cong were under 29 years of age (the average being 23.8 years),[42] and that the average age of terrorist cadres in other organizations was as follows: 28 in the JRA, 23.2 in the ETA, and 31.2 in the Baader-Meinhof organization and the Berlin-based Movement Two group.[43] In addition, of the 515 Tupamaros terrorists captured between 1966 and 1972, the mean age was 26.[44] Such figures can be deceiving, however, inasmuch as they are reflective in many instances only of the terrorists who were captured or whose names and personal information were released by the terrorist high command or gleaned from background searches by the press and authorities. Since the operational element of any terrorist organization is bound to be younger than its high command and support contingent, such figures tend to be skewed on the young side; nevertheless, they do provide an idea of the age profile of most terrorist organizations. As might be expected, the oldest figures in most terrorist groups are in the high command. In this connection, the key leadership figures in the Baader-Meinhof movement were in their thirties and early forties. Ulrike Meinhof, at 42, was—according to some reports—the eldest member of the organization when she committed suicide in 1976. Carlos Marighella, author of the famous terrorist minimanual, was 58 when he died, one of the oldest known figures to be actively connected with a terrorist movement. The top leadership of the various Palestinian terrorist organizations tends to be the oldest collectively of almost any major terrorist movement, although most are only in their forties, an age at which they would just be entering the senior levels of power in most countries. The IRA also boasts a number of senior leadership figures in their forties and fifties, but they are reportedly being pushed aside by more youthful, aggressive, and ideologically committed challengers.

While few terrorists stay active into their late forties or fifties, either because of the rigorous demands of the profession or simply because the odds catch up with them, there is really no lower age limit for those engaged in terrorist activities. Children have been found in various terrorist movements. A fifteen-year-old boy was arrested in the Netherlands in connection with the bombing of the Israeli embassy. Two thirteen-year-old youths were captured in Brussels after a grenade attack on an El Al Israel office that left four people injured. On a number of occasions, U.S. combat personnel in Vietnam were accused of indiscriminately making war on children, whereas in fact children, some no more than ten years old, were frequently used by the Viet Cong to plant bombs and booby traps designed to maim-and-kill South Vietnamese (ARVN) and U.S. soldiers, as well as South Vietnamese civilians.

Youth is not only ideally suited to the rigors of terrorist activity but also, as one member of the PLO rejection front put it, young people in the sixteen-to-twenty-two-year age range are more receptive to demands for sacrifice than those more senior. General Grivas's firm conviction, moreover, was that only youths in their late teens and early twenties could be shaped into unquestioning assassins who would kill at command.

The nineteenth century U.S. outlaw, Frank James, brother of the legendary badman Jesse James, perhaps put it best when he reflected on his days with the pro-Confederate guerrilla chieftain and terrorist, William Clarke Quantrill:

> If you ever want to pick a company to do desperate work or to lead a forlorn hope, select young men from 17 to 21 years old. They will go anywhere in the world you will lead them. When men grow older they grow more cautious, but at that age they are regular daredevils. Take our company and there has never been a more reckless lot of men.

Only one or two of them were over 25. Most of them were under 21. Scarcely a dozen boast a moustache. Wasn't it Bacon who said when a man has a wife and children he had given hostages to fortune?[45]

Youth's feeling of immortality often results in reckless disregard for personal safety, a necessary attribute of most successful terrorists. In one's youth, ideas also take on the greatest importance, especially political ideas, and considerations of family, property, and position have not yet surfaced as the chief motivating factors in life. Acts of extreme violence are also easier to commit when one is young, before youth's rashness and unfeeling egocentrism are tempered by life's pain and experience. The ability to put oneself in the other person's place, of sharing his fear and commiserating with his pain, is more characteristic of maturity than of youth. For those who have not witnessed suffering and death, murder can have an abstract quality about it; the fact is that many young criminal offenders do not connect the act of shooting someone with the pain and anguish it produces. Moreover, youth is more malleable than age, more capable of adjusting to any circumstance including a climate of brutal violence.

Equal Opportunity Employer

The 11 March 1978 raid by PLO terrorists on Israel that left more than thirty dead and seventy injured was unique, not only in terms of the number of casualties it produced but also in that it was carried out by an eleven-member team, two of whom were women. Commanded by a 25-year-old Palestinian woman named Dalal Mughrabi, who was subsequently killed in the fighting, the raid underscored the new prominence of women as terrorist comrades-in-arms with men. Once relegated to support roles such as collecting intelligence and smuggling arms, women have emerged as full-fledged members of dozens of terrorist movements, eager to assert their equality with men as fighters for the cause.

Modern terrorism is becoming, as recent events illustrate, increasingly sexless. A woman can learn to use a gun as well as a man and is well-suited to the demands imposed by urban warfare. Women, however, are less visible in the rural context, due largely to the fact that terrorist movements based in the hinterland tend to be more tradition bound, with men less likely to yield authority to women or to confer equality upon them. Moreover, the rigors of life in the bush are greater and pose difficulties with respect to stamina and privacy. Some rural terrorists have viewed women as a distracting and disruptive influence.

While women are usually excluded from top leadership positions and still constitute a minority of the membership of most terrorist organizations, they are nonetheless increasing in both influence and numbers, especially in the more sophisticated organizations operating in the developed world. More than half of the known members of the notorious Baader-Meinhof gang in Germany were women, and a cofounder of the organization, Ulrike Meinhof, was a woman. Similarly, the leader of the now largely defunct but formerly prominent Weather Underground movement in the United States was a young woman named Bernardine Dohrn, who in 1981, came out of hiding and surrendered to authorities. Perhaps the most feared female terrorist in the world is Fusako Shigenobu, who helped plan the massacre at Israel's Lod Airport. Currently, the commander of the Arab section of the JRA, Samira as she is known to her Arab colleagues, runs a global network of trained killers and assassins ready to do the bidding of allied movements around the world. Women were also in the majority and played highly visible roles in another former U.S. terrorist group, the Symbionese Liberation Army. In addition to the organizations already named, women have participated in the violent activities of the Croatian separatists, the FLQ, and the IRA, to name but a few examples.

The increasing number of female terrorists parallels the trend in the developed countries that finds an alarming growth in the number of women charged with and convicted of serious crimes. Most observers believe that this is a by-product of women's liberation, in view of the increasing numbers of women who have forsaken traditional roles and sought instead to compete on an equal basis with men for jobs and influence. As a result of the similarities in the acculturation and education of men and women in the more advanced countries, it should come as no surprise that women are becoming more and more politicized, and it follows that a small number will seek violent solutions to political problems just as some men now do.

Despite the greater resistance they encounter, even in more traditional cultures women are "increasingly willing and even eager to release their long pent-up frustration and rage in the service of causes that permit them to assert their equal claim to symbols of liberation and to a fair share of the terroristic action."[46] According to Mona Saudi, a 25-year-old member of the PFLP, she is fighting for recognition of her equal place in society at the same time as she is fighting against Israel. "The presence of any woman in society was a sexual presence," said Saudi. "Now she's becoming a human being equal to men."[47] Because of the large number of women serving in its ranks, the PFLP has endorsed the liberation of women from traditional Arab male chauvinism. The PLO, however, which is less radical and dependent on more conservative Arab regimes for support, has been more cautious in its support of women's liberation, but as a whole, it has responded favorably to resolutions and actions in international forums that benefit women.

Traditional role perceptions by many men have provided women with additional advantages under some circumstances when operating as terrorists. Male security personnel were, on a number of occasions, taken completely off guard by the striking good looks of Palestinian terrorist Leila Khaled, a dark beauty inclined toward mini-skirts and tight-fitting sweaters. Her appearance was so deceptive that security men were lax in the performance of their duties. By contrast to Khaled and motion picture characterizations of female terrorists as beautiful firebrands, nevertheless, most female terrorists tend to be quite plain looking and even take pains to disguise striking and otherwise noticeable features. Carlos reportedly chose his young female companions chiefly for their nondescript appearance and ability to pass unnoticed in a crowd.

The Impact of Killing

It is often said that everyone is capable of at least one murder; nevertheless, the act of taking another human life or willing the death of another human being does not come easily to most people. The vast majority of all criminal murders involves crimes of passion, done without forethought or premeditation, the product of panic, ignorance, or anger and accompanied subsequently by remorse. Only a relatively small number are cold-blooded, calculated terminations of life.

The discovery of whether one is capable of killing, of taking another human life, writes Albert Camus, is the most difficult hurdle to be surmounted before one can become a revolutionary:

> The only really serious moral problem is murder. The rest comes after.
> But to find out whether or not I can kill this person in my presence,
> or agree to his being killed, to find that I know nothing before finding
> out whether or not I can cause death, that is what must be learned.[48]

The first death is the hardest; after that, in the words of Dylan Thomas, "there is no other." Once the threshold is crossed, there can be no return. The commission of some irrevocable act of violence is employed by many terrorist groups not only to test the mettle of its recruits but also as an initiation rite, under the assumption that once the individual has killed, his commitment to the group is absolute; he ceases to exist as an individual and takes on the identity of the terrorist group, becoming a full-fledged member in a community of violence. Even more important, he isolates himself from society, making it exceedingly difficult, if not impossible, for him to return to the life he left behind. The depraved and violent initiation rituals practiced by the Mau Mau ensured that members were outlaws who could never—short of victory—be reintegrated into society.

During wartime, one can usually overcome inhibitions against killing out of a sense of self-preservation; the battlefield is a unique them-or-us situation. However, terrorism is another thing. It is systematic, deliberate cruelty or

destruction visited on one person or a handful of people, and as such it is in
direct contrast to what John Keegan calls the impersonality of modern war.[49]
It is a return to the rhythms of medieval warfare where a close relationship
existed between one's actions and the direct consequences of that action,
however disfiguring, disabling, or fatal. For example, one is not aloft at 30,000
feet in isolated comfort behind the controls of a marvel of destructive technology, pulling levers that release clusters of bombs on unsuspecting populations
below, never hearing the explosions or witnessing the casualties.

At its most rudimentary level, murder all comes down to a matter of scale.
Terrorism gives new meaning to Stalin's oft-quoted remark that, "A single death
is a tragedy, a million deaths is a statistic." Indeed, one death can be comprehended and felt; a million can boggle the mind. It is hard to assess individual
responsiblity for a million deaths, but in the case of most acts of terrorist
violence, no such problem exists; there can be no ambiguity about the cause-
and-effect process. There but for the terrorist someone writhes in agony or no
longer exists, and this power is bound to have a profound effect upon the
terrorist's personal psyche.

Only a psychopath feels no remorse, no regret, over killing another human
being, and as related earlier, available evidence indicates that there are very few
psychopaths in terrorist movements relative to total membership. Some
terrorists appear not to be greatly affected by the violence they inflict on others
and, hence, are commonly mistaken for psychopaths. However, this is often
just a facade. In actuality, the subconscious, which tracks everything and files it
away in the recesses of the mind, is actually storing impressions of the violent
acts perpetrated by the terrorist, but for a variety of reasons their impact is
effectively repressed. Experience with combat veterans indicates that this
information may remain locked away in the brain for years, then suddenly
explode on the consciousness with debilitating consequences in the form of a
mental breakdown or other psychosis.

There is little question that some individuals find it easier to kill than
others; those with the greatest propensity for violence, aside from psychopaths, are usually characterized by the strongest internal defenses against the
negative impacts of killing. Hence, in most terrorist organizations only a relatively small number of individuals repeatedly engage in acts of violence on behalf
of the group.

How a person reacts to death, to killing, is very personalized and not subject
to generalization because, as J. Glenn Gray has written, destruction is, in the
final analysis, a uniquely individual matter.[50] The chief form of self-defense
employed by many terrorists to shield them from the impact of their murders
is to dehumanize their opponents and victims. By regarding them as somehow
less than human, less than feeling, caring people with dreams and aspirations
like themselves, the terrorist is able to destroy them and to banish the guilt,
at least temporarily, that accompanies such actions.

Many terrorists demonstrate a remarkable detachment from their actions and the subsequent effects. Maria McGuire of the Provisional IRA, who ultimately defected, said that initially she did not connect the victims to the explosions she helped to set; there was no cause and effect. Ultimately, however, she was forced to confront the bloody results of her actions:

> Whenever such casualties had occurred before, there had always been the pressure of events to take my mind off them. But now, almost for the first time, I wondered about the crippled and the widowed and the lives that had been changed forever.[51]

Brendan Hughes of the IRA was able to put his actions out of mind so long as he never really saw his victims. "It doesn't bother me as long as I don't see their faces," said Hughes. "I don't want to see the enemy's face."[52] The reality of his violence was brought home to Saadi Yacef, one of the leaders of the terror in Algeria, when he came upon the body of a European friend in the rubble of a bombing he had ordered. Later, when reminded of the deaths that he was responsible for, Yacef wept uncontrollably. For other terrorists, only a single-minded commitment to the final goal and an unwaivering belief in its efficacy, rightness, and attainability has prevented the bloodshed from undermining their resolve.

Among those who survive, few terrorists are not haunted by those who died as a result of their actions. Although vindictiveness and hatred often fade with the passage of years, the memories of violence do not. Almost thirty years after Israel won its independence, Yalin-Mor recalled with sadness the victims of the Stern gang terror. "I am not a bloodthirsty man," he said. "If I would be God at this moment, I would revive all those killed, Jews and British alike."[53] But of course, there is no return from the grave.

Are They Self-Destructive?

Nechaev wrote that "the revolutionary is a doomed man," totally obsessed by the revolution that in the end will consume him.[54] In this connection, it goes without saying that terrorism is a precarious profession with many certifiable risks for the practitioner and that, if one takes enough risks over a protracted period of time, the odds are bound to catch up with him. For all practical purposes, the terrorist is a condemned man who must be prepared to die at any time. Death is more than just an eventuality; it is an ever present possibility. The terrorist has only two choices—victory or defeat—and there is no middle ground. It is like a zero-sum game where one either wins or loses, and this is why Segre and Adler refer to terrorists as "all or nothing men."[55]

This acceptance of death permits a terrorist to carry out what are often suicidal missions, such as the JRA attack on Lod Airport in Israel where the terrorists had virtually no hope of escape or of avoiding death or capture. Only when one is reconciled to forfeiting his own existence for the sake of the cause is he able, like Palestinian terrorists engaged in attacks deep within Israel, to strap on special belts packed with explosives that can be detonated in the event of probable capture. According to May, an individual's very "efficacy as a terrorist depends upon his readiness to kill and his equal readiness to die."[56]

This willingness to die is at the very heart and soul of terrorism and is what makes terrorism such a potent force. It is hard for some people to understand what appears to be a seemingly irrational drive to self-destruction by terrorists. Terrorists, for their part, adopt various rationalizations that have the ring of altruism and selflessness to justify their self-sacrifice. Twenty-year-old Palestinian suicide commando, Abu Bakr, put it this way: "I've friends, desires, dreams, but I put them aside for a new life. I love life. It's to allow my refugees, my people, to find the joys of life that I'm going to die."[57]

Psychiatrists, however, tell us that the real motivation of many terrorists is not altruism or selflessness but egocentrism. They have observed a strong narcissistic dimension in many terrorist personalities that takes the form of a need for recognition. Like the Buddhist monks in Vietnam who burned themselves to death in protest, many terrorists subconsciously believe that through martyrdom they can have an impact far beyond their own existence and in fact achieve a perverse kind of immortality. In the words of another young Palestinian terrorist: "I can die, therefore I am."[58] This is the existential element in terrorism: the notion that we prove our existence through our actions, and that we certify that the actions are ours and no one else's only if they are unpredictable and defy the conventions of both society and nature. It is not hard to see why the existential philosophers are popular among terrorists and their supporters; existentialism provides a tailor-made apologia for terrorism and its culture of violent antisocial behavior.

This perhaps explains why at least four members of the Baader-Meinhof gang, including cofounders Andreas Baader and Ulrike Meinhof, committed suicide in prison. Confined in captivity, they had no one else to strike out against but themselves. Baader and two others took their lives shortly after German commandos rescued a hijacked German jetliner in Mogadishu, Somalia, putting an end to any hopes that they would be ransomed in exchange for the passengers held hostage. Perhaps Baader and his fellow gang members hoped to slip the finite bonds of life and continue, in the existential sense, the process of becoming in death, thereby coming closer to realizing in death what they had failed to achieve in life.

After the Struggle

What becomes of terrorists when their struggles are over, the guns have been stacked, and normalcy has returned? Are they able to make the adjustment to everyday life without trauma, putting their careers as terrorists behind them, or are they haunted men and women who wake up in the middle of the night in a cold sweat, slowly consumed by pasts they cannot forget, that will not go away? Do some exterrorists become perennial misfits compelled by their experiences or by bloodlust to seek other conflicts where they might ply their skills? Or do they just fade away like combatants of many wars?

As a rule, once one goes near the waters of terrorism, it is only a matter of time before he or she drowns. The vast majority of all terrorists can look forward only to lives of hardship, pain, betrayal, imprisonment, disillusionment, and untimely death. Few committed terrorists live productive and fulfilling lives into old age, and those who do are usually associated with successful struggles; but even victors often become victims. Because of the young age at which most terrorists enlist in the struggle and the subsequent preoccupation with killing methodologies, few exterrorists possess salable skills adaptable to peacetime requirements once the struggle is over. They characteristically become last year's men, whom time quickly passes by. There is usually a clear distinction between the men and women who give the revolution substance with their acts of violence and those who dominate the revolutionary state once it comes into being. The terrorist, after his work is complete, often becomes expendable, devoured by the very society his efforts helped to bring into being, at best pushed aside by opportunistic technocrats and ambitious politicians, and at worst purged, exiled, imprisoned, or even executed. Although they formed a critical element in the mythology of the Bolshevik Revolution, few of the early terrorists and revolutionaries survived Stalin's paranoia. Lumped together as malcontents and counterrevolutionaries, the Bolshevik old guard was eliminated systematically as Stalin, fearful of any potential rivals, consolidated his power. Others were purged as scapegoats to justify the government's failure to attain agricultural and industrial goals.

For those who do survive, one thing is certain: The terrorist experience—the act of human beings committing inhuman acts—is not an experience that easily can be pushed aside and forgotten. For most, it is the greatest emotional passage of their lives, never far out of mind for the rest of their days, an episode that influences their every action for as long as they live. Although it bears some similarity to conventional military experience in wartime, terrorism has little of the spectacle of war of which Gray writes.[59] Its memories are rarely heroic. And unlike traditional military men, who often are viewed as having two personalities, one as a warrior, the other as a feeling, caring, sharing, reflective human being—a father, husband, worker—terrorists are singularly one-dimensional people who live, eat, sleep and breathe the struggle. The precariousness of their lives admits few outside diversions or serious human relationships. As a result, many exterrorists are emotionally crippled and throughout their lives, find it difficult to form enduring attachments to other people, places, or jobs.

For those not killed or emotionally scarred, there is often never-ending guilt. The very concept of guilt, in its most basic sense, tends to be culture bound. Psychologists differentiate between so-called guilt cultures and what are known as shame cultures. In this connection, guilt cultures are most characteristic of Western nations with a Judeo-Christian tradition, whereas shame cultures are most often found in the Middle East and Far East. By contrast to guilt cultures where the individual's feelings of guilt are predicated on evaluation of his or her actions from a standpoint of a constant set of stand-ards, in shame cultures what is right and wrong, for example, is more flexible and closely linked to appearances. In other words, if one can perform a certain action and not be caught or exposed, which would result in public shame and humiliation, then the action is deemed to be acceptable. Thus, guilt, in its traditional sense, is far more characteristic of Western cultures and is usually present in the individual irrespective of the underlying reasons that precipitated his or her resort to violence, however justified or worthy those reasons may have been. In more traditional cultures of the Middle East and Far East, feelings of shame are often directly related to whether the terrorist's actions result in success or failure. While the terrorist's conscience may be suppressed during the struggle, afterward, when the idea that initially compelled the terrorist has lost some of its potency, many exterrorists begin to have second thoughts about the efficacy of their actions. This is particularly true if the product of the bloodshed and sacrifice—the revolutionary state—has not lived up to the expecta-tions of its authors. The anguish of having increased injustice while thinking that one is serving justice, to borrow a thought from Camus, is perhaps one of the greatest disappointments in life that anyone can suffer.

A handful of former terrorists has been successful in achieving positions of political power and influence in the aftermath of their struggles; Menachem Begin of Israel and the late Jomo Kenyatta of Kenya are the most notable examples. Similarly, former commander-in-chief of the IRA, Sean MacBride, was awarded the 1974 Nobel Peace Prize and now works for the United Nations (UN). As a group, exterrorists appear to fare no better or worse as leaders than those who come to power through more conventional means. Although he had been a former chief of the dreaded Mau Mau, Kenyatta, before his death, transformed Kenya into an island of moderation, stability, and progress in a sea of poor, strident, harshly ruled black African regimes.

Conclusion

While notable similarities tend to exist among terrorists within a single group or organization, such similarities become far less manifest when one compares the members of wholly different terrorist groupings in different geographical locales engaged in struggles with vastly divergent objectives. All terrorists are not seeking the same goals, any more than their recruitment into a community of violence was compelled by identical circumstances. Clearly, fundamental differences exist between terrorists in the Third World who are embarked upon national liberation struggles and the often pampered, but disaffected, children of the middle class who have coalesced into violent, often nihilistic, terrorist organizations dedicated to the spread of chaos in the postindustrial Western democracies.

The terrorist profile then, as it emerges, is more significant for its omissions than its inclusions. In many respects it is easier to describe what a terrorist is not than what a terrorist is. A few simple generalizations can be advanced, but it must be emphasized that significant exceptions exist in each instance. As a group, terrorists are not typically thrill seekers, not married, not psychopaths, not highly ideological, not from the lower end of the socioeconomic scale, and not exclusively men. As to what traits they evince collectively, it is safe to say that most terrorists are young, elitist in orientation, of above-average intelligence, and believe that they can shape the world to conform to their—or the group's—standards and ideals. All terrorists, by the very definition of their calling, believe that the adoption of extreme violence is a necessary and legitimate strategy to achieve their objectives. and while few shirk from the employment of violence, most are troubled by it, especially in their later years. Finally, the terrorist, as Irving Lewis Horowitz notes, "performs his duties as an avocation."[60] He may live an outwardly normal life that is, in reality, a cover for terrorist activities.

To summarize, it should be apparent that no standard terrorist profile exists and that nothing, with universal application, can be described as a terrorist personality that might assist authorities in identifying terrorists or potential terrorists. In terms of their backgrounds, motivations, and hopes, terrorists are as complex and multifaceted as the members of any other group. Terrorists hail from every continent and are found in both the developed and less-developed world. They embrace every major religion, and their political stirrings run the gamut from far left to far right. No racial or ethnic group seems to have any greater predisposition toward terrorism than any other. Although historically terrorism has been largely a man's preserve, women are surfacing as members of terrorist groups in ever greater numbers. Terrorist movements contain both selfless idealists and the wicked and profane, both reformers and scoundrels, moderates and extremists, those seeking opportunity and those fleeing failure, authoritarian personalities together with those opposed to all constituted authority. The rich as well as the poor are recruited into terrorist organizations, scholars along with the illiterate, those motivated by personal ambition, and those moved by imported ideologies.

Notes

1. Charles Baudelaire, *Les Fleurs du Mal* (New York: New Directions, 1963), p. 318.

2. William A. Hannay, "International Terrorism: The Need for a Fresh Perspective," *The International Lawyer* (April 1974), p. 283.

3. Albert Parry, *Terrorism: From Robespierre to Arafat* (New York: The Vanguard Press, Inc., 1976), p. 23.

4. Interview with Albert Parry, "Terrorism, It's Problems, Solutions," *The Washington Star*, January 12, 1977.

5. Conrad V. Hassel, "Terror: The Crime of the Privileged—An Examination and Prognosis," *Terrorism* 1, no. 1 (November 1977), p. 6.

6. Thomas H. Valk, "Psychological Dimensions of Terrorism," draft of article prepared for the *International Security Review,* (Spring 1982).

7. Interview with Dr. William D. Davidson, president, Institute for Psychiatry and Foreign Affairs, Washington, D.C., February 12, 1980.

8. Ibid.

9. Jonathan Swift, *Gulliver's Travels* (New York: New American Library, 1960), p. 265.

10. Interview with Dr. William D. Davidson, Washington, D.C., February 12, 1980.

11. Hassel, "Terror," pp. 5-6.

12. Frederick J. Hacker, *Crusaders, Criminals, Crazies,* (New York: W.W. Norton and Company, Inc., 1976), p. 75.

13. William F. May, "Terrorism as Strategy and Ecstasy," *Social Research* (Summer 1974), p. 290.

14. Robert Moss, "Counter Terrorism," *The Economist*, Brief Booklet #29, p. 6.

15. Menachem Begin, *The Revolt* (London: W.H. Allen, 1951), p. 291.

16. Sergey Nechaev, "Catechism of the Revolutionist," in *The Terrorism Reader*, ed. Walter Laqueur (New York: New American Library, 1978), p. 68.

17. Ibid.

18. Carlos Marighella, *For the Liberation of Brazil*, trans. John Butt and Rosemary Sheed (London: Penguin Books, no date), p. 65.

19. Red Brigades, "Red Brigades Manual" (Unpublished, Italy, 1970s).

20. Ibid.

21. Moss, "Counter-Terrorism," p. 6.

22. Parry, *Terrorism*, p. 454.

23. " 'Commander Zero': Payoff Political," *Washington Post*, 25 August 1978.

24. Charles A. Russell and Bowman H. Miller, "Profile of a Terrorist," *Terrorism* 1 (November 1977):23.

25. William D. Davidson and Joseph V. Montville, "Foreign Policy According to Freud," *Foreign Policy*, no. 45 (Winter 1981-1982), p. 148.

26. Ibid.

27. Ted Robert Gurr, "Some Characteristics of Contemporary Political Terrorism" (Unpublished manuscript, March 1976, p. 15).

28. Albert Camus, *Notebooks: 1942-1951* (New York: Harcourt Brace Jovanovich, 1965), p. 213.

29. J. Bowyer Bell, *On Revolt* (Cambridge: Harvard University Press, 1976), p. 225.

30. Walter Laqueur, "The Futility of Terrorism," Harper's (March 1976), p. 103.

31. George Grivas, *The Memoirs of General Grivas*, ed. Charles Foley (New York: Frederick A. Praeger, 1965), p. 2.

32. Gavin Young, "Despair Keeps Movement Alive for Palestinians," *Washington Post*, 17 May 1973.

33. Raphael Rothstein and Zeev Schiff, "Why the Fedayeen Kill the Innocent," *Chicago Tribune,* 11 June 1972.

34. Philip A. Karber, "The Psychological Dimensions of Bombing Motivations," *Targets and Tactics* (June 1973), p. 31.

35. Parry, *Terrorism*, p. 531.

36. Walter Laqueur, "The Continuing Failure of Terrorism," *Harper's* (November 1976), p. 70.

37. Bernardine Dohrn, quoted by Parry, *Terrorism*, p. 335.

38. Moss, "Counter-Terrorism," p. 4.

39. William Stevenson, *90 Minutes at Entebbe* (New York: Bantam Books, 1976), p. 46.

40. Bertrand Russell, *History of Western Philosophy* (London: George Allen & Unwin, 1967), p. 657.

41. "Ghassan Kanafani: Alive as Palestine," *Palestine Digest* (September 1975), p. 18.

42. Andrew R. Molnar, with Jerry M. Tinker and John D. LeNoir, "Human Factors Considerations of Undergrounds in Insurgencies" (Research project prepared for the Special Operations Office of the American University, operating under contract with the Department of the Army Washington, D.C., 1965), p. 76.

43. Russell and Miller, "Profile of a Terrorist," p. 18.

44. Ronald H. McDonald, "The Rise of Military Politics in Uruguay," *Inter-American Economic Affairs* 28 (Spring 1975):34.

45. Martin McGrane, "Unscrupulous Opportunist," *Rural Missouri* (July 1979).

46. Hacker, *Crusader, Criminals, Crazies*, p. 37.

47. Rothstein and Schiff, "Why the Fedayeen Kill the Innocent."

48. Camus, *Notebooks*, p. 134.

49. John Keegan, *The Face of Battle* (New York: Vintage Books, 1977), pp. 165-167.

50. J. Glenn Gray, *The Warriors* (New York: Harper & Row, 1967), pp. 97-129, 171-213.

51. Renee Winegarten, "Literary Terrorism," *Commentary* (March 1974).

52. Brendan Hughes, interview in P. Michael O'Sullivan, *Patriot Graves* (Chicago: Follett Publishing Co., 1972), p. 212.

53. Nathan Yalin-Mor, interview, New York City, 16 September 1976.

54. Nechaev, "Catechism," p. 68.

55. D.V. Segre and J.H. Adler, "The Ecology of Terrorism," *Encounter* (February 1973), p. 21.

56. William F. May, "Terrorism as Strategy and Ecstasy," *Social Research* (Summer 1974), p. 281.

57. "The Suicide Squads of Ahmad Jibril," *The Washington Post*, March 2, 1975.

58. Gavin Young, "Despair Keeps Movements Alive for Palestinians," *The Washington Post*, May 17, 1973.

59. Gray, *The Warriors,* pp. 28-29.

60. Irving Louis Horowitz, "Political Terrorism and State Power," *Journal of Political and Military Sociology* (Spring 1973), p. 149.

4

Terrorism: The Media Connection

The television camera is like a weapon lying in the street. Either side can pick it up and use it.
                                                              —Richard Clutterbuck[1]

"Electric circuitry has overthrown the regime of 'time' and 'space' and pours upon us instantly and continuously the concerns of all other men," observe Marshall McLuhan and Quentin Fiore.[2] Perhaps nowhere is McLuhan's global village concept better illustrated than in the matter of international terrorism. Acts of terrorism command wide attention in the media, and terrorist demands routinely are accorded extensive publicity, permitting terrorists to advertise their causes to the world. Under such circumstances, according to David Fromkin, terrorism is transformed into a form of mass communication that amplifies localized acts of violence into worldwide media events.[3] This has resulted in charges by many observers that the mass media, if not the actual accomplice of international terrorism, have surely, at times, become its hostage.

Among the litany of charges and accusations that have been hurled at the mass media, Walter Laqueur has called it "a terrorist's best friend";[4] Frederick J. Hacker alleges that the mass media "serve as propaganda agents of terrorism";[5] and I.M.H. Smart has accused the media of assisting terrorists at every step. Smart goes on to say that the media inform the terrorist of his potential targets and report his acts of violence, "according him some apparent status, giving credibility to his subsequent menaces and communicating his achievements to his own constituency, inside or outside the country in which he acts."[6] The Task Force on Disorders and Terrorism, under the aegis of the National Advisory Committee on Criminal Justice Standards and Goals, goes even further, alleging that, "In many ways, the modern terrorist is the very creation of the media."[7] Such charges have resulted in considerable soul searching and not a little controversy within the ranks of the electronic and print media in countries where the tradition of a free press is strong. Thus, this chapter explores charges that the print and electronic media represent one of the chief contributing factors to the explosive growth and expansion of terrorism in recent years, tracing the origins of the problem and advancing various solutions for dealing with it.

The Power of the Television Medium

Zbigniew Brzezinski has described the modern postindustrial world as a "tech-netronic" society, "shaped culturally, psychologically, socially, and economically by the impact of technology and electronics."[8] Indeed, we live in a highly visual age that has witnessed the emergence of television as perhaps the single most powerful influence in shaping U.S. political and cultural attitudes. Talk to any old hand from one of the three major networks, however, and he will vociferously deny that television was ever envisioned or intended to be anything more than a supplemental source of public information to books, newspapers, magazines, and journals, which have the time and the space for more in-depth coverage and analysis of news. Unfortunately, television has succeeded beyond the wildest dreams of the pioneers in the field. Although the print medium is still a power in U.S. life, especially with respect to influencing the beliefs of the nation's decision makers, it is from the television set that most Americans get most of their information most of the time. Television news coverage, with its compressed glimpses of events, personages, and trends, is a superficial medium that derives much of its popularity perhaps from the fact that it is so compatible with the frenetic life-styles of those who live in the mass postindustrial societies of the West. Moreover, in a world of information input overload, it is readily comprehensible and digestible, and the concise and snappy format of television has created, in the words of Robert MacNeil of National Public Television, "a nation of news junkies who tune in every night to get their fix on the world."[9]

Television is a world stage and everyone wants to be on it, to project themselves or their ideas through its magic, as if that were the only test of one's existence: I am on television, therefore I am. Instead of simply mirroring reality, television creates a new kind of reality and impresses it on the consciousness of the viewing public. For all too many people, what is not transmitted to them via their television sets does not exist. Access to television time is, therefore, in the rawest sense of the word, power, and the struggle for control over the content of television or for time in front of the camera has become intense, a fact that has not escaped the notice of political terrorists.

Revolutionary Propaganda

Almost by their very definition, terrorist organizations are not mass movements and as a rule are small, elitist groups, striving to impress their views on society as a whole without significant popular support. In an effort to enlist a greater following, throughout history, terrorist and other revolutionary vanguard groups have produced pamphlets, leaflets, books, and newspapers in an effort to communicate their frustrations, ideals, and demands to the general public. Rarely did a revolutionary movement in the nineteenth and early twentieth centuries not include a journeyman printer and at least one good pamphlet writer among its ranks. The advent of the electronic media, however, has resulted in a transformation of the communication techniques employed by terrorists. While a revolutionary underground newspaper could be printed by hand at minimal expense in a basement and distributed by a skeleton crew, television and radio stations—today's chief methods of mass communication—require complex and expensive equipment and a skilled staff to operate them. There is no such thing as a clandestine television station; every nation in the world controls, or at least regulates, the television industry and its broadcasts.

While a few pirate radio stations have been operated in-country on a clandestine basis by terrorist organizations, necessitating almost constant movement of the transmitter so that authorities cannot get a fix on it, the only terrorist radio stations functioning on a continuous and uninterrupted basis over a long period of time have been those broadcasting from outside the target country, with the acquiescence and often full support of the host country. Or in the case of Palestinian radio transmissions in Lebanon, the central government is too weak and fragmented to oppose effectively its territory being used for such purposes. In a rather novel method of radio broadcasting, the Tupamaros guerrillas in Uruguay, during their heyday, periodically hijacked radio stations and utilized them to transmit revolutionary messages to listeners and disappeared just before authorities arrived. On one occasion they interrupted a soccer match in the middle of the broadcast and substituted their own programming, and in another, they took control of the F.M. radio station that provided background music to local department stores. Much to the chagrin of many Montevideo shoppers, they replaced the music format with propaganda statements.[10] Another terrorist group from Latin America with a knack for publicity is the M-19 organization in Colombia, which has often been compared with the Tupamaros. In 1974, when still an unknown presence, M-19 placed clever ads in Bogota newspapers such as, "Lack energy? Inactive? Wait for the M-19." Such exploits, however daring and sometimes entertaining, hardly represent a substitute for a broad-reaching continuous means of communicating with the public.

In view of the inability of most terrorist organizations to disseminate their message through conventional mass media outlets, terrorists have sought instead to create news in order to communicate their existence, ideas, and power to the general public, cognizant that established news organizations will report their actions and deeds for them. Terrorists no longer need actually to grind out the propaganda; instead, all they have to do is produce an event and the news media will do the rest. "The media have extended the terrorist's stage," observes Michael Flood. "Television, especially, has increased the visibility of violence and done more for terrorism than perhaps any other single factor."[11]

Publicity: The Mother's Milk of Terrorism

Terrorism properly has been described as propaganda of the deed and armed propaganda in recognition of the fact that the real goal of most terrorist acts is the propaganda derived from it, not the actual toll measured in lost lives and damage inflicted. As Brian Jenkins has observed, "Terrorists want a lot of people watching and a lot of people listening, not a lot of people dead."[12] Terrorist acts, in and of themselves, almost never materially alter the course of the struggle; rather, the objective of terrorism is to convey a pervasive sense of vulnerability, with the fear that accompanies it, to all those who witness the act or to whom it is communicated. The strategy of terrorism, therefore, is to intimidate, to achieve political goals through the threat of violence instead of as a direct result of violence.

Terrorism must have publicity to succeed. "The terrorist act alone is nothing," writes Walter Laqueur, "publicity is all."[13] Thus, to be able to intimidate vast numbers of people with violent acts of limited duration and consequence requires first that the act become a media event—only then will it take on political significance and gravity. Once it is a media event it can be pressed onto the consciousness of the public and used to dramatize the grievances of the terrorist group and to win public support.

This is nowhere better illustrated than in the turbulent Eastern Mediterranean where, for almost thirty-five years, violent terrorist actions have been used as attention-getting devices by groups contesting the narrow strip of land known previously as Palestine and today as Israel.

Mindful that the growing struggle in Palestine would enjoy little popular support among a U.K. public weary from six years of unrelenting conflict, in the period following the end of World War II, the U.K. government sought to keep the conflict under wraps by imposing heavy censorship. It took a brutal act of terrorist violence finally to break through the U.K.-imposed curtain of silence and to propel the issue of Palestine's future to the forefront of international attention. The terrorist incident used to accomplish this tour de force is described by former Stern gang terrorist Nathan Yalin-Mor:

> Whatever we did in Palestine was silenced by British censorship. So we decided to make a breakthrough. We assassinated Lord Moyne in Cairo. He was the symbol of British Empire in the Middle East, so our action was symbolic as well as political. This was the first deed that brought the problem to the forefront.[14]

The U.K. public was profoundly shocked by the cold-blooded assassination of the English statesman, an event too significant to be suppressed by official censorship. The escalating level of violence in the Middle East, embodied by Lord Moyne's assassination, became a matter of open debate in Parliament and in the U.K. press. However, the impact was even greater outside the United Kingdom, where the issue of Zionist claims on Palestine was catapulted to a position high on the agenda of global concerns by the nascent UN organization.

Ironically, as if taking a page from a history of the founding of the state of Israel for inspiration, there can be little doubt that the growth of the Palestinian liberation movement and notions of Palestinian identity are directly attributable—after years of neglect—to the publicity flowing from terrorist violence committed by the PLO and various splinter organizations. A decade and a half ago, the question of Palestinian self-determination was a nonissue, publicly accorded some lip service by the Arab confrontation states but lacking any real impetus or focus. The standard vision conjured up in the minds of most Westerners and not a few Arabs at the word *Palestinian* was that of a bedraggled refugee dwelling in one of the squalid camps in Lebanon, Jordan, or the Gaza Strip. This has all changed today. Through the miracle of television, the image of the Palestinian has been transformed into a dark, gun-toting figure in a ski mask, peering out of a window, a vision that will live in the minds of perhaps as many as 500 million television viewers who watched the protracted drama that unfolded after eight Black September terrorists shot their way into the Israeli dormitory at the 1972 Munich Olympics, killing two athletes outright and seizing and killing later nine others. In the aftermath of Munich, publicity transformed the Palestinian movement into a conscious and visible force to be reckoned with and kept the Palestinian issue at the center of the world stage, by contrast to other less media-wise revolutionary movements such as the Kurds in Iran, the Huks in the Philippines, and a variety of insurgent groups in Africa that have languished far from the glare of the television lights.

As a military threat, however, the Palestinians have shown themselves to be largely ineffectual. This is less a tribute to Israeli diligence in combating terrorism than recognition of basic operational and logistic weaknesses within the Palestinian organizational structure, rivalries between competing Fedayeen groups, and the lack of imagination the Palestinians have demonstrated in prosecuting their campaign against Israel. The growth of Palestinian terrorism has been facilitated greatly by Israeli propagandists intent on winning world sympathy and support by publicizing new and ever more menacing threats to their nation's security. In many respects, the PLO became champions of the Palestinian people as a result of the credibility Israeli accusations lent to the movement, along with much reporting in the world press of what amounted to a mere handful of sensational terrorist attacks like the Munich incident, rather than any decisive victories or a demonstrable show of force on the part of the Palestinians. Thus, a mythology of strength and momentum evolved that the PLO used to transmit a sense of purpose and pride to other Palestinians and to recruit new members and support, and this, in turn, ultimately resulted in recognition of the PLO by the Arab summit at Rabat in 1974, Yasir Arafat's triumphant appearance at the UN, and to what subsequently amounted to de facto UN recognition. Only in recent years has the PLO truly lived up to its billings and become the formidable opponent of Israel that it was purported to be by journalists and Israeli propagandists.

Nothing Succeeds Like Violence

The name of the game in the highly charged and competitive world of commercial television is news value. Thus, there is always a tendency to emphasize

news stories with a sensational element rather than in-depth background exam-
inations of serious issues before a country that may be more elucidating but that
possess far less audience appeal. Indeed, the news is offered up by commentators
and reporters in a manner designed to maximize the sensational aspects of its
content. NBC newsman David Brinkley has remarked, "The one function that
TV news performs very well is that when there is no news we give it to you with
the same emphasis as if there were news."[15]

In this connection, Richard Clutterbuck has observed that "nothing is so
newsworthy as violence," and for this reason, the media is often accused of
dwelling too much on topics like violence and not enough on the more optimistic side of life.[16] This is attributable in large measure to the fact that the
normal ebb and flow of life throughout the world is not in and of itself newsworthy. Violent death, crises, and catastrophes, however, are dramatic aberra-
tions from the norm that lie, in H.L. Nieburg's words, on "the frontier of our
social experience" and that therefore command the attention of the news
media.[17] Terrorism, as an extreme form of violence, is particularly newsworthy
and well suited to the needs of television, which is a highly visual and compact
medium with little time for exposition. Unlike wars and most revolutions,
which are usually protracted and highly complex events that are too broad
in scope to be grasped readily and easily understood, acts of terrorist violence
normally have a beginning and an end, can be encompassed in a few minutes
of air time, possess a large degree of drama, involve participants who are
perceived by the viewing public as unambiguous, and are not so complex as
to be unintelligible to those who tune in only briefly. It has been said, speciously
but with some truth, that terrorism is so ideally suited to television that the
medium would have invented the phenomenon if it had not already existed.

Criticisms of Media Coverage of Terrorism

Former CBS news chief Fred Friendly described the television camera as a
one-ton pencil, in recognition of the fact that the choice of what is presented
on television and how it is presented in many respects is an editorial exercise
and as influential on public opinion as the actual content of the news. In this
connection, the great power concentrated in the hands of the relatively few
people who run the television news organizations, who sit at the anchor desks
and file the stories, carries with it a great measure of public responsibility
to ensure that the media exercise their power prudently and consistently with
the highest journalistic ideals. In societies with a free press, this means the
preservation of the independence and objectivity of the media, both from
being used by the state or by groups seeking to influence or challenge the
state. According to critics, the failure of the press to make adequate judgments pertaining to the motivations behind the news it reports has resulted

in an extraordinary rise of terrorist violence as terrorists seek to disseminate their message through the organs of mass communications. As Eugene H. Methvin testified before the U.S. Congress:

> [T]oo many of our news editors on the wire desks and broadcast desks are just totally unconscious of the extent to which they have become passive patsies for the modern Adolph Hitlers walking around using them for recruiting agents.[18]

Let us now examine some of the specific charges that have been leveled at the news media with regard to its coverage of acts of international terrorism.

Contagion Factor

Chief among the criticisms concerning the treatment of terrorists and terrorism by the mass media is that heavy emphasis on such stories often stimulates others to commit the same crimes. Known as the contagion factor, some evidence suggests that reportage of a bombing, kidnapping, or other terrorist act, especially when it is described in minute detail, often produces a rash of identical acts. The power of the media to trigger contagious behavior can be seen in San Francisco where, during newspaper strikes, the number of suicides, which are always accorded media attention, drops dramatically. Another illustration is the epidemic of skyjackings that occurred in the late 1960s and early 1970s. Even today, hijackings are rarely isolated incidents; most often they occur in clusters, with one incident serving as the catalyst for others, then they enter a period of eclipse until a new incident produces a fresh rash of imitators. This is explained perhaps by the fact that criminals and terrorists are essentially unimaginative individuals, more likely to emulate than to innovate, particularly if the example is successful.

   In addition to those in the news industry, television and motion picture producers also must be sensitive to the problem of violence portrayed on television programs and in commercial films that serve as stimuli to terrorists and criminals to commit similar acts in real life. One of the most regrettable examples of life imitating art, or the power of television to educate viewers in mayhem, occurred in Boston during the early 1970s. After a fictional television depiction of an individual being doused with a flammable liquid and set ablaze, a gang of youths murdered a young woman in an identical manner the following day. The director of the television program, in an interview some years later, described his horror over the imitative violence that the program spawned and admitted that the young woman's death still haunted him and that he could not escape feelings of responsibility over what happened.

   Another example of irresponsible television programming occurred on 21 January 1979, when CBS scheduled the motion picture *Black Sunday* immediately to follow Super Bowl XIII. The film describes a terrorist conspiracy to hijack the Goodyear blimp and to kill the 80,000 spectators at the Super Bowl with a device resembling a Claymore mine mounted to the blimp. The action in the film was set in Miami at the Orange Bowl, coincidentally the same place Super Bowl XIII was scheduled to be played. Miami authorities were highly alarmed and incensed by the graphic depiction of the attack in the film, maintaining that it might plant the idea for a similar assault in the mind of a terrorist or some other disturbed individual, especially in view of the heavy advance publicity given the film by the network. "What's frightening is that Cecil B. is controlling society," one football player is reported as saying, referring to former Hollywood producer Cecil B. DeMille. "And he'll get someone killed in the Super Bowl yet."[19] Although Super Bowl XIII passed without incident, the potential that the sports event would be singled out as the target of violence was greatly increased by the decision to show "Black Sunday" on the same day and by the extensive media hype that preceded it.

Romanticization of Terror

Many observers are also alarmed by what they perceive as the romanticization of terror, maintaining that sympathetic portrayals of terrorists in the media are major sources of support and recruitment for terrorist organizations. "Uniting beauty with terror," writes Renée Winegarten, "many writers, poets, and artists of the *fin de siècle* and after, from Wilde to Kafka, sympathized with or were fascinated by bomb-throwing terrorists."[20] This fascination has continued to the present day, with both news reporters and filmmakers occasionally guilty of attributing false glamour and a sense of derring-do to certain terrorists, thus contributing to the development of what might be called the terrorist mystique. Argentine-born Cuban revolutionary Che Guevara, as a result of adulation showered on him by the leftist press in the West and misguided and superficial treatments of his career in motion pictures like the Hollywood production "Che," became a larger-than-life cult figure, a prophet of revolutionary violence, who inspired young men and women to reject more conventional means of change and instead to adopt violence as a means of transcending impotence and correcting society's ills. As a consequence of the media attention that he received, Guevara has accomplished far more in death than in life. As a footnote, Guevara's revolutionary legacy was evident in the terrorist skyjacking of a German jetliner to Mogadishu, Somalia: The sole surviving terrorist was a young woman wearing a tee-shirt emblazoned with Guevara's picture.

Reporters and filmmakers sympathetic to the revolutionary antiestablishment goals of most terrorists still tend to be the exception rather than the rule; thus, terrorists are becoming increasingly adept at and sensitive to the media requirements necessary to project well on television and in the press. The

Tupamaros terrorists of Uruguay conducted what amounted to a skillful public relations campaign designed to cultivate a romantic Robin Hood image that glossed over their more obvious brutalities. Yasir Arafat, who speaks passable English, has been increasingly receptive to requests by Western journalists in recent years for interviews and is known to have received coaching and advice with respect to his television presence from various media advisors within the PLO ranks. He has toned down his delivery and eliminated most of the bombastic and obviously self-serving statements he used to make. His performances consequently are lower key with fewer extravagant gestures that might be appropriate before large crowds but that do not come across well on television.

Nevertheless, whatever strides Arafat has made in his delivery and content have not been enough to overcome his physical unattractiveness. It is good for Israel that neither Arafat nor any of the other major Palestinian revolutionary leaders possess the charisma and charm necessary to capture the imagination of the Western press and the physical appearance to relate to the television camera; otherwise, the history of the Middle East might well be different today. Former Secretary of State William P. Rogers was commenting on this fact when he suggested recently that Arafat "should change his tailor," on the premise that he would project better if he did.[21]

The Media Manipulated or Held Hostage

Of course, a dynamic tension always exists between the reporter and the interviewee where each seeks to use the interview to his or her advantage. Nevertheless, when the reporter permits himself to be manipulated directly by the news source, it calls into serious question the integrity of the newsperson. The problem becomes even more serious when it involves an entire newspaper or television network.

The willingness of the media to allow themselves to be used by terrorists as a platform for their propaganda is regrettable, but perhaps understandable when one considers the competition that exists within the industry; all too often the only thing that counts is getting the story. How one accomplishes the task is viewed as immaterial. Sensational terrorist incidents obviously generate widespread public interest to which the media must respond. However, in a number of celebrated cases, various organs of the media have permitted themselves to be dominated and used by the terrorists in a manner that exceeds both propriety and common sense. The slavish and truckling coverage the German Television Network devoted to the kidnapping of a prominent German politician by the Baader-Meinhof gang lends credibility to such charges. For three days, reported one German television executive:

[W]e lost control of the medium. We shifted shows to meet their
[the terrorists'] timetable. [They demanded that] our cameras
be in a position to record each of the prisoners as they boarded
a plane, and our news coverage had to include prepared statements
at their direction.[22]

A related but far more difficult problem concerns terrorist demands that
manifestos, declarations, and other propaganda be published in major newspapers or read on television as a condition precedent to the release of hostages
or in order to prevent a violent action like the detonation of a bomb from
occurring. After terrorists took over the European headquarters of OPEC in
Vienna in December 1975, seizing a number of oil ministers and other hostages,
they demanded that the Austrian government agree to broadcast communiqués
calling for a total liberation war against Israel. Closer to home, following a bomb
explosion in New York's Grand Central Station that killed one policeman
and injured three others, four U.S. newspapers and the *International Herald
Tribune*, published in Europe, mindful of a threat by the terrorists who had
concurrently skyjacked a Trans World Airlines (TWA) jetliner to detonate
another bomb, published two documents supporting Croatian independence.
While it can be argued that most terrorist statements have little actual impact,
in many cases because they are unintelligible and full of convoluted prose,
such behavior nonetheless amounts to little more than naked extortion and
blackmail. Editors and publishers, for their part, have usually acceded to such
demands rather than have the blood of some innocent victim of the terrorist's
wrath on their hands. Benjamin C. Bradlee, executive editor of the *Washington
Post*, one of the newspapers forced to print the communiqués of the Croatian
nationalists, later expressed serious reservations about the impact such a practice
could have on a free press: "The first time, the question of lives is more important. But if it gets to be a habit, you've got to think it over again."[23] If the
mass media become too compliant to such demands, the effect will be to invite
threats of violence that can only be averted by publishing or broadcasting
some piece of propaganda.

Achieving Importance

Consistent with Andy Warhol's remark that someday, because of television,
everyone will be able to be famous for fifteen minutes, the desire to be important—to project one's power through the medium of television—is a very real
motivating force on the part of some terrorists. While being a terrorist is often
a nameless kind of fame, it is nonetheless a fact that acts of extreme violence
generate public attention and confer a perverse kind of celebrity status on
the terrorist that some observers have described as a revolutionary ego trip.

Violence becomes the press agent of those who never could have achieved notoriety any other way. Thomas Sowell describes this phenomenon as one of the prime moving factors in the kidnapping and assassination of Italian Premier Aldo Moro:

> For several weeks a group of obscure young men become important. They carried out a deed that made headlines around the world. They had a famous man in their power, to abuse or taunt as they pleased and to kill when they felt like it. They saw the life of the country around them disrupted as police, workers, and others changed their daily routines in response to the event. The Pope, the American president, the United Nations recognized them with appeals and declarations. In normal times, they might never have gotten past the secretaries to see any of these people, much less expect to influence them. With one daring crime, they leap-frogged bureaucracy and protocol, and elbowed their way into the headlines and even into history.[24]

There for a brief moment, the terrorist and his companions are able to bask in their moment in the sun, having produced a momentous event that has propelled them into the forefront of world news, providing them with a fleeting slice of immortality. Of all of the problems that plague the media today, the need to deal with this compulsive hunger for attention, and the exhilarating sense of importance that accompanies media recognition, is critical lest the media become the handmaiden of international terrorism.

Blurring the Line between Reporter and Participant

On a number of occasions, members of the media, in their eagerness for first-hand, fast-breaking coverage of a major news story, have become overly involved, and even direct participants, in the incident. This has been true particularly in hostage situations in which members of the media have become self-appointed conduits of information between the authorities and the hostage takers. In a number of well-publicized incidents, journalists actually have tied up the phone lines leading into the location that is held by the terrorists, thus denying authorities direct communication to the hostage takers and making negotiations even more complex. Media involvement in sensitive negotiations also results in confused and overlapping lines of communication that may raise false hopes or expectations in the minds of the hostage takers. Moreover, many dangers are inherent in permitting an inexperienced newsperson to conduct life-and-death negotiations with desperate men and women, and it is questionable that members of the media can maintain their objectivity under such circumstances and provide the public with unbiased reporting.

During the seizure of the B'nai B'rith international headquarters in Washington, D.C., by Hanafi Muslims, ABC anchorman Max Robinson, then employed by a local television station in the nation's capital, crossed the line of journalistic propriety when the terrorists used him to disseminate their propaganda after Robinson called the besieged building in an effort to obtain an interview with the Hanafi leader. However, Robinson was not the only journalist guilty of misconduct and lack of common sense. A tense situation was created after radio reporter Jim Bohannen incorrectly identified the gunmen as Black Muslims. The terrorists threatened to execute a hostage unless this misperception was cleared up, and reporter Bohannen was forced to apologize on the air to the Hanafis. This example, of course, illustrates the dangers associated with live or too hurried reporting of terrorist incidents. Conversely, other journalists, fearful of inflaming the situation any further, refrained from identifying the hostage takers as *terrorists, kidnappers,* or *murderers,* though any of the terms would have been accurate and descriptive, and thus were guilty of imposing an obvious degree of censorship on the facts. Such restraint would have been more appropriate if it had extended to the actual method of reporting the outrage instead of cosmetic word changes that had the effect of distorting the news.

Breeches of Security

It has been said that government is the only vessel that leaks at the top. Any newsman in the business long enough, with good contacts and confidential sources, is bound to come across information of a highly sensitive nature over the course of his career, and the obvious temptation will be to publish or report it. However, the release of such information may jeopardize lives and even have an impact on national security. Such an instance occurred during the German commando raid to recover the hijacked Lufthansa jetliner in Mogadishu, Somalia, and surprisingly, the guilty party was Israeli television, which should have been far more sensitive to the security requirements of the operation.

An Israeli named Michael Gurdus, who resides in Tel Aviv and is employed by Israeli radio and television to monitor foreign radio transmissions, picked up signals from the plane carrying the German commandos on their mission as it reported back to its base en route to Somalia. No explanation is available as to why the German transmissions were not encoded or transmitted in a more secure fashion. In what was a patently irresponsible decision by news executives, Israeli television reported the impending raid on the 9 P.M. news, several hours before it was scheduled to take place. Although the international wire services picked up the story, they bowed to German requests for a news blackout until the raid had transpired. Similarly, Israeli radio declined to report news of the raid prematurely, maintaining that to do so was unwarranted and unnecessary in view of the circumstances. In retrospect, the Israeli television broadcast could have compromised the entire German operation and resulted not only in Somalia, under pressure from the PLO and hard-line Arab confrontation states, rescinding the permission it had given for the German commando team to land but also in the terrorists panicking, causing them to slaughter the passengers.

Along the same lines, on-the-spot unsanitized, unedited reporting of a news event often can inadvertently provide the terrorists in hostage situations with critical information such as that related to police movements or behind-the-scenes deliberations of public officials trying to resolve the crisis. During the Hanafi incident in Washington, D.C., live television reports from the scene revealed the presence of city employees barricaded on the fifth floor of the District Building, unbeknownst to the terrorists who had seized that building as well as the B'nai B'rith headquarters.[25]

Brutalizing Effect on the Public

Robert G. Bell has noted in his study of skyjackings that a "saturation of media coverage led to public apathy, robbing the terrorist act of its publicity effect."[26] Indeed, some evidence suggests that because of its commonness, the shock value of ordinary acts of terrorism is decreasing. The public has been fed such a steady diet of violence by the media that it is becoming cynical and callous by the fare. This cynicism will inevitably result in an escalation of terror as terrorists strive to reach new heights of brutality and outrage in order to capture public attention. Few potential targets will be spared, and actions previously regarded as unthinkable will become acceptable to terrorists as their desperation to be heard mounts.

Incitement of Campaign of Counterterror

As the ferocity of terrorism increases, attacks close to home, which are reported in graphic detail in the media with grotesque pictures and descriptions, may incite the public to demand vengeance, producing widespread government terror or the creation of counterterror vigilante gangs. This has occurred in Guatemala, El Salvador, Uruguay, Argentina, and Italy in recent years, to cite but a few examples. Moreover, public indignation produced by sensational media reports of terrorist atrocities has provided many governments with the pretext they need to clamp down hard on dissent by outlawing opposition parties, invoking press censorship, and imposing martial law on the country.

False Impression of Strength

The media are guilty of vastly overplaying the threat of terrorism in some parts of the world. The extensive publicity accorded terrorist incidents gives many people in the affected countries the mistaken impression that the wolves are at the door and their countries on the verge of anarchy. This, in turn, often creates a pervasive climate of fear and results in a lack of trust by the citizens of the afflicted country in their governing institutions and the government's ability to protect them. The media, therefore, must take great care always to put the level of terrorist violence into proper perspective, rejecting exaggerated claims of strength and spurious notions of victory planted by terrorist organizations.

Media Circuses

Terrorist actions, especially hostage situations, often have resulted in an army of journalists and television crews converging on the scene to record every grim detail as it unfolds — the fright and emotions, the bloody violence, the barricaded gunmen and ashen-faced hostages, and perhaps even a rare glimpse of a captured ambassador emptying the trash, as occurred in the seizure of the Dominican embassy in Bogota, Colombia. How will the crisis be resolved? No one, of course, knows until it happens, but that is why terrorist incidents make such good theater: the suspense. A portion of the audience that tunes in to watch prolonged coverage of a hostage crisis does so because the possibility of swift and sudden death is always present, rather like the reason some people attend auto races or bullfights.

Often the crush of reporters, cameramen, and equipment lends an out-of-place carnival atmosphere to an otherwise serious and volatile situation and creates congestion and confusion with which authorities must contend in addition to managing the actual crisis. Journalists have, on occasion, shown little sense of decorum or sensitivity to the ordeal that survivors of terrorist incidents have been through. At the conclusion of the Hanafi Muslim seizure of the B'nai B'rith international headquarters in the nation's capital, reporters virtually assaulted the just-released hostages in their frenzy to cover the story. Here was the scene as described by one observer:

> The hostages, many pale and weak from the strain, shrank from the glare of lights while print and broadcast reporters and camera crews swarmed around them for vantage points. There was shoving and elbowing. Hostages who ran were literally chased by cameramen. Some hid their faces behind their coats and sweaters to avoid the camreas.
>
> One hostage's husband punched a photographer in the face while the wife, in tears, shouted, "Animals! Animals!" at the journalists.[27]

Such displays of media excess are unnecessary and profoundly distasteful to all who witness them, not to mention the fact that they bring serious discredit on the whole journalistic profession.

Intensification of Hoaxes and Bluffs

There is always the danger of intensifying hoaxes and false alarms if too much information is released by the media regarding potential targets, destructive technologies, and circumstances surrounding actual incidents, especially kidnapping cases. The level of threats made against the airline and nuclear industries has soared in recent years. Authorities are forced to sort through the threats in an attempt to ascertain which have the ring of validity because if every threat were responded to as if it were legitimate, it would produce chaotic conditions in the affected sectors of the economy, causing untold delays, production shortfalls, and economic loss, measured both in terms of labor hours and revenues. The proliferation of hoaxes has taken the edge off the response by law enforcement agencies to threats of dubious credibility and could potentially result in the authorities underestimating or failing to identify a real threat, with tragic results.

Preoccupation with Reporting the Event, Not the Punishment

Finally, too often only the terrorist act, because of its sensational value, is treated by the media as newsworthy, and too little or no attention is devoted to the subsequent punishment of the perpetrators of terrorist violence. As one Washington, D.C., journalist commented, "The essence of publishing is to take newsprint which you can buy for two cents a pound and turn it into something you can sell for ten cents a pound. What you print, therefore, is what sells the best and that tends to be a combination of sex, schlock and sensationalism." In many instances, the outcome of lengthy legal proceedings against accused terrorists receives only passing notice in the media; hence, the deterrent value of the punishment doled out to convicted terrorists, which potentially could dissuade others from committing the same crime, is negated. A random survey of various newspapers in Europe and the United States confirms that stories focusing on the punishment of terrorists receive less than 5 percent as many column inches of space as stories pertaining to the actual crimes with which the terrorists are charged. Moreover, whereas the terrorist incident is often front-page news, stories detailing the verdicts of prosecutions against terrorists are usually buried in the back of the newspaper—if they are reported at all. The electronic media are even more unresponsive in this regard; as a result of time constraints and a preoccupation with sensational items, follow-up stories focusing on the death or punishment of terrorists are almost never broadcast.

Should Censorship be Imposed?

Terrorism is a unique phenomenon in that it wins few actual engagements with force of arms but nevertheless is almost always victorious in the struggle for publicity. Indeed, the governments of the world are not nearly so effective in using the media to their advantage as their terrorist opponents. As a result, consensus is that media attention devoted to terrorist acts contributes to the growth and spread of terrorism. This has raised the question as to whether some form of news management should be instituted to define and limit the amount and type of news coverage devoted to terrorism. Former Ambassador Andrew Young has gone so far as to call for actual suppression of First Amendment rights during times of crisis. Unfortunately, news management, whatever form it takes—government guidelines, news blackouts, professional standards, or peer review—is contrary to the First Amendment and U.S. practice and traditions. Stephen S. Rosenfeld, however, disagrees with the use of the term *censorship* in this instance: "What is at issue is not political censorship, which is inimical to our traditions and instincts, but crime control," he writes. "Publicity is the sea in which terrorists fish, the handful of desperate isolated figures who commit these acts, swim in. Dry up the sea."[28]

Contrary to Rosenfeld's assertion, censorship by any other name is still censorship. In view of the fact that freedom of the press, to be meaningful, is absolute and indivisible, any abridgment of free inquiry amounts to a total abridgment; to deny this truth is to make democracy as we know it impossible.[29] Aside from the havoc that censorship would wreak to the Bill of Rights, the adoption of some form of government-imposed or -supervised censorship would permit terrorism to succeed beyond the wildest dreams of its perpetrators and would mean the destruction of one of the very institutions whose preservation forms the rationale for resisting terrorism.

Even if it were admitted for a moment that a drastic measure like censorship was justified in response to terrorism, who would be entrusted with the power to decide precisely what should be censored and what should not be censored? The government? A panel of journalists and editors? And if censorship is restricted solely to terrorist activities, who will define what exactly constitutes terrorism? The term has been applied so broadly to such widely different phenomena as to render it virtually meaningless. Because the term so often is used subjectively, the lack of a narrow and precise definition on which broad consensus exists could result in censorship, in the name of combating terrorism, being used as a weapon by those in power against their political enemies. Any criticism judged to be damaging to the government could be suppressed on the pretense that it was contributory to terrorism, as has happened in South Africa, white-ruled Rhodesia (Zimbabwe), and many parts of Latin America. Some say that such abuses could never occur in the United States, but one has only to remember unsuccessful attempts to control or manipulate the news under the Johnson and Nixon administrations in conjunction with Vietnam and Watergate to understand how real the potential for abuse is.

The threat posed by contemporary terrorism to the United States and most of the Western democracies has by no means reached the level of intensity at which such drastic action might be worthy of consideration. As Brian Jenkins has observed, the actual amount of terrorist violence has been greatly exaggerated.[30] In the ten-year period between 1968 and 1978, the National Foreign Assessment Center of the CIA identified 3,043 total incidents of terrorist violence globally that resulted in 2,102 deaths and 5,078 wounded.[31] To put this into perspective, more people die on U.S. highways in a week than are killed or injured annually throughout the world as a product of terrorist violence. Just as we have learned to live with the negative impacts of the automobile, so too will we have to learn to live with endemic terrorist violence, and accordingly, efforts to stampede the liberal democracies of the West into enacting precipitous and repressive laws designed to combat terrorism, whose ultimate effect will be fundamentally to alter the very nature of those societies, must be resisted at all costs. This is not to suggest that the United States and its allies should take a passive stance with respect to terrorism but simply to affirm that censorship or a drastic federally mandated curtailment of the powers and freedom of the mass media is not the answer to terrorist violence. Such an overreaction to the threat represented by international terrorism would be more destructive to the Western democracies than to the terrorists and recalls the old saying of the remedy being worse than the illness.

Need for Industry Self-Restraint

Freedom of the media from government interference is meaningless without corresponding freedom from being manipulated or used as a compliant tool by terrorists and other nonstate actors who are seeking to thrust their message onto a complacent population. However, if the government is ruled out as the conceptualizer and enforcer of industrywide standards for covering and reporting terrorist actions, then the only other realistic alternative is for the media to police themselves.

This should not be too much to ask of the news media. After all, in the United States, most professionals are governed by carefully considered codes of conduct, and attorneys, for example, can be banned from practicing their trade if they violate established ethical canons. The adoption of an equivalent set of standards pertaining to the mass media, with corresponding sanctions for misconduct, is long overdue.

Many of the major news-gathering organizations and television networks have adopted voluntary guidelines governing the reporting of terrorist incidents, especially hostage situations, although virtually none has any teeth. Some news organizations, moreover, have rejected consideration of any such professional standards as an encroachment on their First Amendment rights. Richard C. Wald of ABC News dismisses the utility of voluntary guidelines, stating that "it has been our experience that news events involving terrorists develop in so unpredictable a manner that guidelines are not very helpful and may tend to limit our flexibility."[32] By contrast to ABC's dubious position, most news organizations have found voluntary guidelines useful. A compilation of the main points contained in a survey of such guidelines may be summarized as follows:

> News coverage should be restrained and limited to the facts. Rumors and speculation should not be reported. Every effort should be made to avoid sensationalizing the events, and extreme caution must be taken to avoid using incendiary phraseology.

> Live coverage should be avoided under most circumstances inasmuch as it often provides an unedited platform to the terrorists. This does not preclude on-the-spot reporting so long as it is not broadcast live.

> Avoid the appearance of a media circus. Television coverage should be discreet and as low profile as possible lest it stimulate behavior intended solely for the cameras. Cameras and television equipment should be camouflaged, and high-intensity television lights, which can give away police positions and the layout of the location, should be turned on only after checking with the authorities.

> News personnel should never inject themselves into the story or volunteer their services as intermediaries in hostage situations. Telephone calls to the terrorists only increase their sense of self-importance and tie up telephone lines. News personnel should perform as negotiators only when specifically requested to act in that capacity by authorities.

> If no deadline has been set or even mentioned, news personnel should never inquire about one.

> News organizations should never simulate terrorist acts, inasmuch as they could cause others to emulate the incident. Likewise, reportage involving too much detail—for example, how to manufacture home-made weapons—must be avoided.

> No information should be reported that might aid terrorists in the commission of their crimes, like the disclosure of police positions. Similarly, information that is likely to raise the collective anxieties of the terrorists or contribute to the tension at the scene of the problem— the arrival of a SWAT team, for example—should not be broadcast.

> Statements and obvious propaganda issued by the terrorists should be balanced by contrary information and interviews.

> Avoid the romanticization of terrorists and their struggles; they never should be portrayed sympathetically.

Such guidelines, however, are only part of the answer. As David Anable of the *Christian Science Monitor* has observed, more than self-restraint is needed by the media. Anable cites "the vital importance of perspective in reporting terrorism, of balance, of explanatory background, and of a steady stream of information about potential trouble spots *before* they turn sour and vicious."[33] In this connection, the mass media need to make a far more intensive effort to introduce a greater measure of balance into its reporting of violence and terrorism. This would involve not only coverage of headline-grabbing terrorist outrages but also in-depth follow-up reporting concerning terrorist groups, goals, and methods, with an eye to putting any single incident into its proper context and giving it perspective, noting the long-term consequences of unchecked violence on society and calling attention to the failures and excesses of terrorism, not just to its victories. Moreover, greater emphasis needs to be given to the victims of terrorist violence, despite the fact that such stories lack the dramatic content of the actual incident. As noted earlier, every effort should be made to avoid glamorizing terrorists and their struggles, and with this in mind, coverage should be expanded to include stories regarding the law enforcement officers and officials who must risk their lives to combat the terrorist menace. Only when the problem and its effects can be rendered comprehensible and intelligible to the average man and woman can much of the stress on society produced by terrorism be alleviated.

More cooperation between law enforcement agencies and the mass media should also be encouraged, and efforts by some in the media unnecessarily to denigrate police, FBI, and intelligence organizations in recent years, without proper regard to the critical frontline role they play in combating terrorism, must be brought to an end. Follow-up stories on the prosecution and imprisonment or execution of terrorists should also be stressed in an effort to communicate to the public that crime does not pay and that violence is not a proper method for altering the political system. As the primary entertainment, as well as news, medium in the United States, television should strive to create more solid role models for young Americans and to instill in them a respect for law enforcement and the criminal justice system.

Too little attention is directed at exploring the impact of television violence, moreover, on society, especially on children. Nobody disagrees that too much violence is unhealthy and debilitating and should be de-emphasized in television programming.

By adopting the aforementioned suggestions, the Western mass media can begin to come to grips with the problem of international terrorism. As Yonah Alexander has correctly observed, terrorism is theater;[34] by denying the terrorist the opportunity to project the image that he or she desires, and to use the media as a means of free advertising, then conditions precedent to the defeat of terrorism can be created.

Conclusion

One sure way to defeat terrorism is death by silence. There is little question that if the television cameras were prevented from recording every terrorist incident, there would soon be fewer incidents. Nevertheless, suppression of news and information is not the answer, and such an approach is inconsistent with the goals and traditions of this country. Indeed, such a strategy would likely do more harm to U.S. democracy, for reasons already cited, than to international terrorists. Moreover, it might compel terrorists to escalate the level of their violence in an effort to pierce any curtain of silence that has been imposed, as happened in Palestine in the 1940s. In view of these considerations, what is needed instead is a commitment to better and more responsible management of news relating to terrorism, including the adoption by the news media of a strict professional code, governing the treatment of violence and terrorism by both print and electronic journalists, including stiff sanctions for abuses.

News reporting should not be regarded as a footrace to ascertain who is the swiftest; such an approach serves both the public and the journalistic profession poorly. Rather, emphasis must be placed on the content and manner in which the news is delivered. While we live in a world of instantaneous communication, this does not necessarily mean that we must capitulate to the technology, at the risk of losing control of the medium, and report the news straight from the source as it happens, in its rawest, unedited form. Such an approach confuses news with theater.

In the spirit of Justice Louis Brandeis, who always maintained that sunlight was the best of disinfectants, the mass media should seek to provide more, not less, information to the public regarding the tragic and sobering facts of terrorism. As Alexander Solzhenitsyn wrote in *Gulag Archipelago:* "Publicity and openness, honest and complete, that is the prime condition for the health of any society." Only in the full light of balanced inquiry and reporting can terrorists be seen for what they really are.

Modern terrorism promises to be the ultimate test as to whether the mass media can function effectively, conscientiously, and in the public interest without resort to limitations on its freedom being imposed. The failure of the media to take adequate steps to police themselves surely will result in increasing support for government intervention to regulate the industry.

Notes

1. Richard Clutterbuck, *Living with Terrorism* (London: Faber and Faber, 1975), p. 147.

2. Marshall McLuhan and Quentin Fiore, *The Medium Is the Message* (New York: Bantam Books, 1967), p. 18.

3. David Fromkin, "The Strategy of Terrorism," *Foreign Affairs* (July 1975):692.

4. Walter Laqueur, "The Futility of Terrorism," *Harper's* (March 1976), p. 104.

5. Frederick J. Hacker, *Crusaders, Criminals, Crazies* (New York: W.W. Norton, 1976), p. 161.

6. I.M.H. Smart, "The Power of Terror," *International Journal* (Spring 1975), p. 234.

7. National Advisory Committee on Criminal Justice Standards and Goals, *Disorders and Terrorism* (Washington, D.C.: Law Enforcement Assistance Administration, U.S. Department of Justice, 1976), p. 9.

8. Zbigniew Brzezinski, *Between Two Ages* (New York: Viking Press, 1970), p. 9.

9. *Time*, 25 January 1980, p. 65.

10. Arturo C. Porzecanski, *Uruguay's Tupamaros* (New York: Praeger Publishers, no date), p. 43.

11. Michael Flood, "Nuclear Sabotage," *Washington Post*, 9 January, 1977.

12. Brian Jenkins, "International Terrorism: A Balance Sheet," *Survival* (July/August 1975), p. 158.

13. Walter Laqueur, "The Continuing Failure of Terrorism," *Harper's* (November 1976), p. 70.

14. Interview with Nathan Yalin-Mor, New York City, 16 September 1976.

15. David Brinkley, quoted in Barbara Rowes, *The Book of Quotes* (New York: E.P. Dutton, 1979), p. 215.

16. Richard Clutterbuck, *Protest and the Urban Guerrilla* (London: Cassell & Co., 1973), p. 245.

17. H.L. Nieburg, *Political Violence* (New York: St. Martin's Press, 1969), p. 118.

18. Testimony of Eugene H. Methvin, U.S. Congress, House of Representatives, Committee on Foreign Affairs, Subcommittee on the Near East and South Asia, *International Terrorism*, 93rd Cong., 2d sess., 1974, p. 64.

19. Henry Allen, "CBS' Black Humor Sunday," *Washington Post*, 20 January 1979.

20. Renée Winegarten, "Literary Terrorism," *Commentary* (March 1974), p. 63.

21. *Washington Post*, 21 October 1979.

22. "Terror and Television," *TV Guide*, 31 July 1976.

23. *Washington Post*, 12 September 1976.

24. Thomas Sowell, "The Terrorist as Celebrity," *Washington Star*, 9 August 1978.

25. However, it should be noted that journalists with knowledge that six Americans had been given secret sanctuary in the Canadian embassy in Tehran after the seizure of the U.S. embassy by student militants voluntarily refrained from reporting the story until the Americans had been safely spirited out of the country by Canadian diplomats.

26. Robert G. Bell, "The U.S. Response to Terrorism against International Civil Aviation," *Orbis* (Winter 1976), p. 1343.

27. Tom Shales and Ken Ringle, "Weighing the Media's Coverage at the Close of the Crisis," *Washington Post*, 12 March 1977.

28. Stephen S. Rosenfeld, "How Should the Media Handle Deeds of Terrorism?" *Washington Post*, 21 November 1975.

29. Everyone is familiar with Justice Holmes's admonition that the "most stringent protection of free speech would not protect a man in falsely shouting fire in a theater and causing a panic" (*Schenck* v. *United States*, 299 U.S. 47 [1919]). U.S. legal jurisprudence maintains that the media must accept responsibility for harm or injury that arises from its actions and, therefore, can be punished for abuses of the freedoms granted in the First Amendment. Nevertheless, efforts to restrain the media from publishing prior to the fact—invoking the doctrine of prior restraint—have met with little success.

30. Brian Jenkins, *International Terrorism: A New Mode of Conflict* (Los Angeles: Crescent Publications, 1974), p. 13.

31. National Foreign Assessment Center, CIA, *International Terrorism in 1978* (Washington, D.C., 1979), p. 1.

32. Richard C. Wald, letter, U.S. Congress, House of Representatives, Committee on the Judiciary, Subcommittee on Civil and Constitutional Rights, *Federal Capabilities in Crisis Management and Terrorism*, 95th Cong., 2d sess., 1979, p. 115.

33. David Anable, speech at seminar on Media and Terrorism: The Psychological Impact, Wichita, Kansas, 3-4, March 1978.

34. Yonah Alexander, "Terrorism, the Media, and the Police," in *Terrorism,* eds. Robert Kupperman and Darrell Trent (Stanford, Calif.: Hoover Institution Press, 1979), p. 337.

5 Conflict in the Skies: The Terrorist Threat to U.S. Civil Aviation

D.B. Cooper, Where Are You Now?   —Slogan on T-shirt

No problem better underscores the technological vulnerability of the modern world to terrorism than air piracy. "The airplane at the mercy of the hijacker," observes one writer, "is a dazzling symbol of an incredibly differentiated, accomplished, but nervous, high strung, and fragile civilization."[1] Indeed, our high-speed, aircraft-linked world gives unparalleled power to individuals, even lunatics, bent on producing disruption or winning publicity for a cause, however ludicrous. A good case in point is the deranged woman who, in January 1979, hijacked a scheduled United Airlines jumbo jet from Los Angeles to New York by claiming to possess nitroglycerin and demanding that a popular Hollywood entertainer read a letter on nationwide television that she had authored. Although she subsequently was taken into custody and was found not to have explosives of any kind on her person, she managed to disrupt flight schedules, inconvenience thousands of air travelers, and succeed in "creating media circuses at two of the nation's biggest airports."[2]

Commercial airliners are an inviting target because they embody national prestige and power unlike any other high technology product, and the skyjacking of an airliner is usually front-page news. Commercial aircraft represent a huge capital investment, upwards of $50 million for a new wide-bodied jetliner, and they require great skill and judgment to operate safely and efficiently. Cruising at 550 miles an hour at 30,000 feet above the ground leaves little margin for error; the lives of as many as 400 passengers depend on the cockpit crew's ability to maintain its concentration and to follow normal operating procedures, and any threat to that concentration or to the plane's airworthiness can spell disaster.

Moreover, skyjackers are often dangerously ignorant of the complexities of flying a commercial airliner. In some instances they have not comprehended the need to have adequate flight charts on board when diverting the aircraft to some far corner of the globe. During the skyjacking of a Cyprus Airways flight in 1978, the pilot had to summon all of his powers of persuasion to convince the skyjackers to allow him to identify their aircraft, destination, and flight path. The skyjackers had wanted to keep Tripoli, their intended destination, secret, unmindful of the fact that not only did they risk a collision with another aircraft but also that the Libyans would likely take them for a hostile airplane when they intruded on Libyan air space without identification.

79

A skyjacker on board is extremely distracting, and the explosion of a grenade or a burst from an automatic weapon could incapacitate the aircraft's controls or start a fire. Inasmuch as the average Boeing 747 burns approximately 3,700 gallons of high-octane fuel an hour in cruising configuration, a wide-bodied, long-range jetliner may carry up to 100 tons of fuel or more and is, if improperly operated, a flying bomb.

Emergence of the Problem

The first skyjacking of a commercial airliner occurred in 1930 when a Peruvian Airlines plane was commandeered. Nevertheless, not until 1968 did skyjacking become a significant international problem, affecting relations between nations. By that time, both the geographic focus of skyjacking and the content of the demands made by skyjackers had changed. Ironically, in the years between 1930 and 1968, skyjacking was a relatively rare crime and had most often been employed, by contrast to the situation today, as a means of escape by those fleeing communist oppression. As Clutterbuck notes, from 1945 to 1952, 85 percent of all skyjacking incidents involved refugees fleeing Eastern Europe, and in every instance the skyjacker was given political asylum in the West.[3] "The fact that crew and passengers were killed in the course of some of the incidents was of minor interest to a public more inclined to regard the hijackers as heroic freedom fighters," writes Robert G. Bell.[4] The next siege of skyjackings followed the Cuban revolution, and like most of the previous instances of air piracy, they were committed by individuals escaping the onset of a communist government. Again, U.S. authorities were reluctant to press charges against the skyjackers and instead accorded them political refugee status.

When air piracy emerged as a serious international problem in 1968, it was as a product of two different sets of circumstances in different hemispheres, and whereas in previous years sky piracy had involved the flow of people and planes from East to West, after 1968 the direction was reversed, with most incidents originating in the West and culminating in communist and Third World countries. Initially, most of the skyjackings were what the former acting administrator of the Federal Aviation Administration (FAA), James E. Dow, described as a part of the take-me-to-Cuba phenomenon in which malcontents, thrill seekers, political fugitives, lunatics, and hard-core criminals hijacked domestic flights in the United States and forced them to fly to Cuba.[5] Although the United States had previously confiscated most Cuban planes hijacked to the United States as payment for U.S. assets expropriated by the Castro government, thereby creating an unfortunate precedent that would come back to haunt the United States, the Cubans promptly returned U.S. planes and passengers.

On 23 July 1968, an El Al Israel flight from Paris to Tel Aviv via Rome was hijacked and forced to land in Algeria, ushering in a new, more deadly and ominous era, both with respect to skyjackings and to the conflict in the Middle East. The skyjackers were three young Palestinians, and their act of piracy was clear notice of the expanding boundaries of the conflict in the Middle East. Unlike earlier skyjackings, which were typically the work of disordered minds or carried out for the sake of a ransom or simply as a vehicle for escape from a repressive regime, the Palestinian war against civil aviation was cynical and coldly political, designed to intimidate Western governments, to disrupt Israeli commerce, and to win publicity for its cause. Although their targets were initially Israeli airliners, the Fedayeen quickly enlarged the focus of their actions to include attacks on the aircraft of nearly every major Western nation. Buoyed by initial successes, Dr. Wadi Hadad of the PFLP soon recognized that airline skyjackings and sabotage could be used to put pressure on Western governments that supported Israel and to extract huge ransoms needed to underwrite the activities of his organization.[6] In this connection, it must be remembered that, prior to the drastic increase in oil revenues that occurred following the October 1973 Middle East War and the oil embargo against the West, the various Palestinian terror organizations were not recipients of such generous largess from oil-rich Arab governments as they are today.

Skyjackings reached epidemic proportion in the peak year of 1969, which witnessed eighty-seven attempted skyjackings, sixty-three of which were to Cuba. Nearly half of the attempts were directed against U.S. airliners, and thirty-seven were successful. Although initially the problem was more acute in the United States, Israel took the first major steps to combat air piracy and related crimes.

Following the 1968 skyjacking to Algeria, Israeli authorities overhauled security both at their airports and aboard El Al planes. As a result of these stern security precautions that denied potential terrorists easy boarding of El Al planes, the Fedayeen were forced to change their targets and tactics. In 1968 and 1969, PFLP terrorists attacked flights by the Israeli flag carrier on the ground in Athens and Zurich where security standards were less stringent. El Al offices in Europe were bombed, and employees of the airline were singled out as victims of PFLP terror. Finally, flights operated by other airlines to and from Israel were hijacked, beginning with the commandeering of a TWA flight from Los Angeles to Tel Aviv. Leila Khaled, perhaps the most famous Palestinian sky pirate, and a companion boarded the plane during a stopover in Athens and shortly thereafter diverted the flight to Damascus. The level of violence was escalated again in February 1970 when a bomb, detonated by barometric pressure, exploded aboard a Swissair flight heading for Israel, with a loss of forty-seven lives. A PFLP faction known as the PFLP general command claimed responsibility for the bombing. There could be no doubt by 1970 that the PFLP was waging a merciless war against international aviation, designed to isolate Israel and to damage its already fragile economy.

Although the potential that an El Al airliner will be the target of terrorists is much greater than that of other airlines, the Israeli flag carrier is perhaps one of the securest airlines in the world. El Al planes have been modified structurally and reinforced, or hardened, to reduce the damage that can be done by a bomb in the hold or an attack from without. The cockpit area has been sealed off effectively from the rest of the plane with a reinforced bulkhead and bulletproof door. Pilots have been instructed in terrorist psychology and evasive maneuvers that can be taken to disrupt a skyjacking in progress. Armed sky marshals ride shotgun aboard El Al flights. Passengers and their hand luggage are screened before boarding El Al flights and are forbidden to take cabin luggage to their seats. According to the El Al director general in 1976, Moredecai Ben Ari, El Al security precautions do not rely on a "single line of defense" but on multiple defense mechanisms, any one of which may trap the terrorist or prevent him from carrying out his attack.[7] Ultimately, Israeli authorities put pressure on foreign governments to upgrade airport security at international airports deemed to have lax or negligible security.

In September 1970, the most complex and costliest series of skyjackings in history occurred. When they were over, a TWA jumbo 747 had been blown up in Cairo and three other jet aircraft lay in smoldering ruins on Dawson's field, an old RAF installation, in Jordan. However, perhaps no aviation-related incident produced more international outrage than the infamous Lod massacre of May 1972. Three Japanese terrorists, acting as PFLP surrogates, were able to circumvent Israeli security measures at Lod Airport in Israel. Pulling automatic weapons and grenades from their luggage, they opened fire indiscriminately on passengers in the crowded airport. Twenty-five persons were killed and seventy-six wounded, many of them Puerto Rican pilgrims on a visit to the Holy Land. Later attacks on airports in Rome, Athens, Brussels, and Paris would also claim many casualties, but the Lod incident, together with a series of events in the United States in subsequent months, would produce an international crackdown on air piracy and aviation-related terrorism.

The United States Takes Action

By the end of 1972, 159 U.S.-registered aircraft had been hijacked, slightly more than half having been commandeered to Cuba, and in the minds of most public officials, this argued persuasively for new and dramatic measures to insure the safety of airline passengers and to prevent further disruption of U.S. civil aviation.[8] Two new developments contributed momentum to this trend. This first was a new incarnation of the sky pirate, the famous D.B. Cooper incident, in which a criminal skyjacker extracted a ransom from an airline whose plane he had hijacked and then parachuted into a remote area in the Pacific northwest, realizing that to land at an airport was to invite sure capture. He was never found. The second was the seizure of aircraft by criminals to facilitate their escape. In October 1972, an airliner was hijacked in Houston by a gang of bank robbers from Washington, D.C., who killed a ticket agent in the process. Two weeks later, three fugitives from Detroit hijacked a Southern Airways DC9 and demanded a $10 million ransom, threatening to crash the plane into the Oak Ridge nuclear facility if their demands were not met. Their threat created near panic in Oak Ridge as residents jammed roads leading from the small city. After a hair-raising odyssey that took them from Birmingham to Detroit to Cleveland to Toronto to Knoxville to Chattanooga to Havana (where they were initially refused entry) to Orlando and back to Havana again, the skyjackers finally were arrested, and the plane, crew, and passengers were returned to the United States.

In January 1973, the FAA mandated specific security procedures designed to provide four levels of defense against would-be skyjackers: (1) at the ticket counter, (2) at the boarding gate, (3) on board the aircraft, and (4) at the final destination should the plane be hijacked. The centerpiece of this effort was the introduction, at all major U.S. airports, of magnetic metal detectors, which federal authorities hoped would prevent troublemakers and skyjackers from boarding a plane with concealed weapons or explosives.[9] The metal detectors would render time-consuming manual searches unnecessary. Walk-through metal-detector gateways were installed at boarding gates, and all hand baggage was screened, either manually or with the aid of metallic or electronic hand searchers. The metal-detection gateway works by creating an electromagnetic field within the arch that is disturbed, setting off an alarm, by ferrous or non-ferrous metal carried through by the passenger, with the amount of metal necessary to trigger the machine's alarm dependent on the level of sensitivity at which the machine is set.

Before reaching the boarding gate, the passenger is screened by the ticket agent and other airline personnel who are on the alert for certain telltale characteristics that can identify a potential skyjacker. For example, the ticket agent is usually on the lookout for a young male passenger, traveling alone, who buys a one-way tourist-class ticket to the nearest destination on the scheduled flight, pays with cash, appears to be nervous and avoids eye contact, carries no luggage, and requests—especially if his request is adamant—to be seated in a certain section of the plane. If a passenger fits the profile, security personnel are alerted, and the individual is singled out for a thorough body search and is questioned at length as to his or her travel plans.

If, despite the security precautions, the skyjacker still manages to get aboard the aircraft, tough contingency plans were developed for dealing with the incident, including a firm but flexible posture regarding negotiation and armed federal sky marshals in civilian dress aboard random flights.

A hijacked plane is most vulnerable on the ground, and far more skyjackings that take place on the ground fail than those that occur in the air. As a result, conventional wisdom increasingly supports the notion of strong action by the authorities while the plane is still on the ground, before it is airborne and out of reach. Under some circumstances, authorities can immobilize the aircraft by flattening the tires or by placing barricades on the runway, but such efforts do not always work. In 1972, during the nine-stop skyjacking of a Southern Airways DC9 by three convicts, FBI agents, fearful that the strain on the pilots and passengers was reaching a critical threshold that could result in a catastrophe, made the situation even more precarious by shooting out the tires of the jetliner in Orlando. Undeterred, the skyjackers ordered the crew to take off with flat tires. "They made a nightmare take-off," writes Clutterbuck, "with sparks flying, and the engines became overheated with pieces of rubber being inhaled into the jets."[10]

On the diplomatic front, in an effort to reduce the incentive for skyjackers to commandeer planes to Cuba, several years of informal cooperation with the Castro government on the issue of skyjacking were formalized in a five-year agreement between the United States and Cuba, signed in February 1973, covering both aircraft and ships, whereby each government pledged to return skyjackers for trial or to prosecute them in their own courts and, if found guilty, to punish them severely. Although Castro had welcomed the propaganda value of early skyjackings to Havana and greeted skyjackers as revolutionary comrades-in-arms, such incidents had rapidly become tiresome and disruptive to Cuban aviation, and many of the skyjackers were quickly perceived for what they were: common criminals.

The results of the U.S. initiative were immediate and impressive. In the first year of operation, the system yielded 2,000 guns, 3,500 pounds of explosives, and 23,000 knives and other weapons.[11] The catch in 1974 was 2,400 firearms and innumerable other lethal weapons. Approximately 6,100 persons were denied boarding in the first two years after the new security measures were implemented, and 6,700 were arrested for violations of antihijacking and other statutes. Most significant of all, during the next eighteen months not one successful skyjacking of a flight originating in the United States occurred, whereas during the same period, nearly fifty foreign airliners were commandeered by skyjackers.

During the first seven and one-half years after the installation of the new federal security procedures, skyjacking incidents in the United States were reduced by more than two-thirds.[12] Of the thirty-one successful skyjackings during this period, none was the result of firearms or explosives escaping detection at security checkpoints. In eleven of the incidents, skyjackers avoided security precautions or forced their way aboard the aircraft, and in fifteen of the remaining twenty incidents, the skyjacker's claim of possession of a weapon was discovered to be a hoax.[13] The remaining weapons used to commandeer aircraft included a nail file, a small pocket knife, and a bottle of rum, with which a pro-Castro passenger threatened to burn an Eastern Airlines L-1011 en route from San Juan, Puerto Rico, to Miami. The fact that there were only thirty-one actual skyjackings is remarkable, considering that U.S. airport security stations screen more than 860,000 passengers and 1.3 million pieces of hand luggage daily at 426 airports.

Because of its success, the antihijacking program won broad public support, and most air travelers cheerily put up with any inconvenience that it created. During the early years of operation, however, many unsuspecting first-time flyers were netted by the metal detectors. According to one airport security chief in a rural region of the country: "You wouldn't believe the knives and other weapons some of these people pack and don't think anything of it. Why, a lot of the folks hereabouts regard a knife as a tool, not a weapon. We simply take their knife and hold it until they return."[14] Former Senator Vance Hartke of Indiana, in a noisy scene at an airport, did challenge the right of the FAA to scrutinize a U.S. senator, in view of congressional immunity, but his protests were disregarded, and Hartke found little sympathy for his position.

Since its inception, the airport security program has been updated and refined. In 1977, 2,034 weapons were seized at U.S. airports, the large decrease attributable to the broad awareness of airport security measures. The security check at the boarding gate has given way to the secure corridor at most U.S. airports, which is more efficient, requires fewer personnel to operate, and involves less redundancy of equipment. Today X-ray monitors scan hand baggage as it passes through an inspection compartment on a conveyor belt, displaying the contents on a TV screen that is observed by a trained operator. Metal objects show up on the screen densely whereas other materials are projected merely as shadows. Security personnel also are assisted by portable explosives detectors. When the probe is inserted into a box or piece of luggage or passed over an individual's body, it can detect explosive vapor concentrations while filtering out other competing vapors.

Assessment of Present U.S. Deficiencies

Despite the strides that have been made, however, the system still contains deficiencies and weaknesses. While the current system usually can catch the crazed, impetuous, and unsophisticated skyjacker, it is unlikely to deter a determined terrorist who has approached the problem with careful planning and imagination. Perhaps one of the chief criticisms of current airport security is that the work of actually spotting would-be skyjackers is still essentially manual. In other words, the X-ray monitors, skyjacker profiles, and metal-detection gateways are only as good as the security personnel who use or operate them. The weakness of most airport security jobs such as watching the TV screen on the X-ray monitor or detecting nuances in a passenger's behavior that might identify him or her as a skyjacker is that the jobs are inherently repetitive and boring. In view of the thousands of passengers who pass through security checkpoints every day in most major airports, security personnel often develop an assembly-line syndrome and become casual and sloppy in carrying out their assigned tasks. Handguns and knives in uncharacteristic shapes could escape identification by a bored or, alternatively, over-worked

X-ray monitor operator. A recent congressional hearing noted that a briefcase, containing a pistol sawed longitudinally in half (to avoid violating federal law), carried by a news reporter passed through a number of X-ray screening stations at different airports without detection, despite the fact that the characteristic shape of the pistol had not been altered.[15] While this situation would be improved through the introduction of television screens with higher definition that flashed red or triggered an alarm when any unusual object was detected, as some military monitors do, this would not solve the problem of suitcases and briefcases with deadly firearms built into their frames. Only detectors sensitive to explosive vapor could detect such weapons.

Key to any successful skyjacking attempt is the need to secret some kind of weapon on board to intimidate the crew and to force them to obey the sky-jacker's commands. Under some circumstances, it is possible to carry a small knife or gun through a metal-detection gateway by shielding it from the magnetic field with various wrappings if the sensitivity of the machine is not set at a particularly high level. A would-be skyjacker can test a gateway's sensitivity by walking through the arch with his hand cupped over a heavy metal belt buckle or with a large amount of change gripped tightly in his fist. If the warning buzzer is not tripped, it is a good bet that a heavily shielded gun or knife will pass through undetected. Many other weapons normally will pass scrutiny—for example, nitroglycerine in a perfume bottle in a lady's purse; an aerosol spray can that, when held at arm's length with a lighter under the stream of mist, makes an excellent flame thrower; any sharp object like a pencil that can be plunged through the jugular vein of a stewardess or hostage.

Another, perhaps surer, method for secreting a weapon aboard a jetliner requires an inside man employed by the airline or an imposter posing as an airline employee. The inside man could stow a gun or grenade on the plane, under a seat or in a restroom, during routine cleaning, maintenance, the pre-flight check, or even among the food trays and beverages loaded before each meal. The actual skyjacker would clear security and could go directly to a pre-arranged location to retrieve the weapon once the plane was airborne. The possibility of such a scenario argues, of course, for close screening of airline employees and supervision of workers by someone in authority while they are performing their duties on board the aircraft.

Although all passengers boarding scheduled commercial airline flights in the United States must pass through security checkpoints, private charter passengers are not now routinely scrutinized since they are viewed as being members of affinity groups who therefore would notice the presence of some-one who did not belong to the group. This presumes, of course, that no member of the private charter would be motivated to hijack the aircraft. An armed skyjacker can gain ready access to chartered aircraft like those transporting athletic teams, under many circumstances, and force his or her way on board. Although no private charter has been hijacked, charters provide a rare opportunity to terrorists, improved all the more by the probable notoriety of the affinity group that is taken hostage.

To sabotage a commercial aircraft is relatively easy and requires someone with only a rudimentary knowledge of aircraft mechanics and structural design and access to the target aircraft. In addition to bombs and explosives contained in baggage in the hold, a terrorist dressed as a mechanic or in fact working for the airline could plant explosive devices in the hydraulic system or at other vulnerable points. In many countries, each passenger is required to identify his baggage on the tarmac, and only then is it stowed in the hold. Any unclaimed luggage is not put aboard, and the luggage of any passenger who declines at that point to board is promptly retrieved and subsequently removed. Terrorists have coldly circumvented such precautions, however, by placing bombs in an unsuspecting passenger's luggage. In the case of the TWA flight lost over the Aegean in the early 1970s, the terrorists apparently planted a bomb in one of their own courier's articles of luggage. Unaware of the bomb secreted in his luggage, he boarded the flight in a normal fashion, raising no suspicions. Of course he was lost in the subsequent explosion along with the other passengers, but the sacrifice of one of their number evidently was deemed acceptable to the terrorist high command.

In an effort to upgrade detection of efforts to sabotage aircraft by bombs planted in checked baggage, which is not presently screened, the FAA is underwriting the development of effective systems and procedures for processing checked luggage to ensure that it does not contain explosives. Among the experimental systems designed to identify the presence of explosives that are currently being developed and tested are units based on X-ray absorption, nuclear magnetic resonance, and thermal neutron activation, as well as a system that relies on small animals and is derived from police experience with bomb-sniffing canine units.

For more than a decade, the U.S. Secret Service has inspected the rotor blades of the president's helicopter for telltale signs of tallium, a chemical that weakens metal and causes stress fatigue. Terrorists could sabotage jetliners by applying tallium to control cables, engine mounts, the fan blades in the jet engines, the hydraulic struts in the landing gear, or various portions of the rudder and other control surfaces. The mere threat of tallium being used to sabotage a commercial airliner is probably enough to blackmail an airline company. Although in recent years precision-guided munitions (PGMs) have been used to bring down airliners, in the future terrorists may employ more esoteric methods to sabotage aircraft, such as interfering with marker beacons and other navigational aids or tampering with computers critical to control tower operations. The possibility of this kind of sabotage goes beyond mere speculation. Six air traffic controllers at New York's Kennedy Airport are suspected of having tampered with a computer that caused a Soviet Aeroflot Ilyushin-62 jetliner, on a trip between Washington, D.C., and New York in

January 1980, to travel through airspace reserved for other planes. The plane was carrying Soviet diplomats, including the ambassador to the United States, Anatoli Dobrynin. Letters and numbers indicating the airliner's radar blip had been removed from the main computer at Kennedy; thus, the plane's existence in the crowded eastern flight corridor went unnoticed, which could have produced a midair collision.

Current International Vulnerabilities

While no terrorist problem has been confronted more effectively than air piracy, especially in the United States, fundamental deficiencies abroad remain that pose a serious threat to civil aviation. "Unfortunately, the rest of the world has not been as vigilant," complains former Senator Abraham Ribicoff.[16] For example, at least thirty of the forty-two foreign-carrier skyjackings that occurred outside of the United States in 1977 and 1978 were the product of inadequate passenger-screening procedures at foreign airports. While many nations have implemented comprehensive security checks on passengers and baggage, few systems are so effective as that in the United States, or those adopted by Israel, West Germany, and the United Kingdom. The United Kingdom may well have the tightest airport security in the world as a result of the spillover of violence from the conflict in Northern Ireland. International airports like Rome and Athens, however, are still a disgrace from a security standpoint, and the lack of any viable security measures at many smaller airports in the developing world is simply an invitation to disaster.

The United States is, to date, a signatory to three international conventions—the Tokyo Convention of 1963,[17] the Hague Convention of 1970,[18] and the Montreal Convention of 1971[19]—focusing on air piracy and related questions of international terrorism. In 1974, Congress amended the Federal Aviation Act of 1958 by passing both the Antihijacking Act and the Air Transportation Security Act (Public Law 93-366, 5 August 1974). The antihijacking Act implemented the Hague Convention and gave the president power to suspend air service to any nation that aids and abets any terrorist organization engaged in air piracy and even to suspend air services to nations that maintain normal air services to nations that support air piracy. Air piracy was made punishable by death, though to date no skyjacker has been executed in the United States largely because of the ambiguity surrounding the Supreme Court's ruling on the death penalty. Skyjackers have been put to death, however, in both the USSR and the Philippines. The Antihijacking Act also provides for evaluation of the security measures at foreign airports and permits the revocation by the secretary of transportation (with the approval of the secretary of state) of operating authority to the United States for airlines from countries judged to have inadequate security.

Legislation presently being debated before Congress would further strengthen federal policies and programs aimed at combating terrorism. Several measures are currently pending before Congress to implement the 1971 Montreal Convention and provide for U.S. technical assistance to foreign governments for airport security training, the establishment of a list of states supporting international terrorism and the automatic imposition of economic and trade sanctions against those nations, the identification of dangerous (from a security standpoint) foreign airports with the possibility that the operating authority of air carriers utilizing those airports could be curtailed, and the extension of security measures to all charter flights. However, the most controversial provision of the legislation, and the section that is presently holding up its passage, requires the addition of "taggants"—tiny, plastic-coated flourescent particles that will survive detonation, water, and fire, and can be retrieved by magnet or isolated under a black light—to explosive material to aid law enforcement agencies in tracing the source and purchaser of explosives used in the commission of crimes.[20] While the measure has strong support within the airline industry, representatives of the National Rifle Association (NRA) maintain that the introduction of taggants would be tantamount to federal firearms registration.[21] Moreover, explosives-industry representatives contend that taggants will "not produce the intended results" and that they easily can be removed from any explosive material.[22]

Despite three international conventions addressing aspects of air piracy and the fact that most countries have domestic statutes punishing aerial terrorism, enforcement of such acts still remains an elusive goal, and this is directly attributable to the lack of international cooperation in combating air piracy and aviation-related terrorism. In recent years, determined air pirates who have hijacked international airliners have usually found countries like Libya that, for reasons of compatible policies or attitudes, have been willing to furnish terrorists with sanctuaries and allow them to escape punishment. While Algeria has made it a practice to return ransoms, passengers, and hijacked aircraft, terrorists have, as a rule, been granted asylum. In some instances, skyjackers even have been received as national heroes, and the offenders in this category have not always been leftist governments. Raffaele Minichiello, who hijacked a TWA flight from San Francisco to Rome, was received as a folk hero in Italy and given only a six-month prison term for his crime. Thus, the elimination of safe havens must be considered key to any meaningful suppression of aerial terrorism.

Extradition of skyjackers, however, is complicated by the reluctance of many governments to extradite political offenders, and this is a major hurdle to enforcement of conventions and bilateral treaties aimed at curtailing skyjacking. Although skyjacking is defined as an extraditable offense by the Hague Convention, the Hague conference specifically rejected a Soviet-Polish proposal that would have made extradition mandatory, preferring instead language that would leave national governments a measure of discretion. By making extradition nonmandatory, the gate was opened for arbitrary and capricious enforcement of what was envisioned as the cornerstone of the convention, and hence any state can make a case for refusing extradition or prosecution on the grounds that the skyjacking was a political act.

In July 1978, at the Bonn Economic Summit Conference, the leaders of seven Western nations, including former President Carter, issued a declaration pledging their governments to take multilateral action against nations refusing to extradite or prosecute skyjackers. The seven nations agreed to suspend all air travel to and from such countries, and procedural guidelines to coordinate their actions were developed at a subsequent meeting in London.

In view of the increasing transnational face of international terrorism, and inasmuch as solid intelligence forms the first line of defense against potential skyjackings, a greater willingness to share official intelligence regarding terrorist organizations, their members, and activities is desperately needed. Authorities note that in the intelligence business conclusions are often reached by assembling myriad bits and pieces of what often appear to be unrelated data that when viewed as a whole, can lead to the prediction of certain kinds of imminent behavior such as a skyjacking or airport attack by a terrorist group. A number of would-be skyjackers have been apprehended before the fact as a result of good intelligence. In 1973, for example, a tragedy of major proportions was closely averted at Rome Airport due to timely intelligence conveyed to Italian authorities. On 4 April Italian military police arrested five Arab terrorists, armed with two portable heat-seeking missiles, who were preparing to shoot down an El Al jetliner. Eight months later, however, it was another story. Information regarding a forthcoming terrorist attack at Rome Airport failed to reach Italian police in time. The result was a bloodbath that left thirty-two dead and eighteen wounded when terrorists attacked a Pan American jet with machine gun fire and grenades. Thus, it is clear that some of the major aviation-related tragedies of recent years involving terrorists could have been avoided by closer cooperation between nations that have a stake in maintaining safe and uninterrupted air travel and commerce. In this connection, consideration should be given to an official international clearinghouse for terrorist information that would act both as a repository for terrorist data and as a systematic conduit for up-to-the-minute intelligence regarding the activities of various terrorist organizations and their individual members.

Finally, in the matter of international cooperation, more emphasis must be placed on ensuring that terrorists who are captured are brought to justice and punished for their crimes. Unfortunately, the question of punishment is inexorably linked to the divisions between East and West, the industrial world and the developing nations, and other cleavages that characterize politics among nations and that condition the differing perspectives evinced by various governments on international questions. Reduced to its most basic level, punishment of air pirates depends on whose ox is being gored. As noted earlier, the United

States was extremely reluctant to punish skyjackers in the 1940s and 1950s when most skyjackers were commandeering planes as a means of transport to escape communism. Not until the United States became the victim, instead of the sanctuary, of skyjackers did Washington suddenly become a vociferous proponent of strong antihijacking measures. Even today, despite a harsh attitude toward terrorists on other fronts, the United States and West Germany in a recent test of their commitment to putting an end to air piracy, have demonstrated a lack of courage with regard to punishing skyjackers. For example, in August 1978, two East Germans hijacked a Polish plane to West Berlin. In an effort to avoid jurisdiction in the politically sensitive case, and thereby to duck responsibility for punishing the skyjackers, the West German government appealed to the United States to invoke its postwar rights to oversee air corridors to West Berlin. The United States acceded to the request from its ally and initiated judicial proceedings. The judge and prosecutor were U.S. nationals, and the trial was conducted under the auspices of German law, utilizing U.S. judicial procedures. The German jury found one skyjacker not guilty and convicted the other, not on skyjacking and wounding but on the lesser charge of hostage taking, for which the judge sentenced the skyjacker to time already served—in this case, nine months. The case was a clear example of selective punishment of skyjackers that illustrated that the West was doing exactly what it has consistently condemned other nations for doing. In 1966, the former shah of Iran had been confronted with a similar situation in which a young Soviet pilot defected in a small plane and requested asylum in the United States after landing in Iran. Despite sympathies to the contrary, the Iranian government returned the pilot to the USSR to what could only be anticipated as a dismal fate, consistent with the provisions of an antihijacking agreement existing between Iran and the USSR.

Many governments have been reluctant to punish air pirates severely in the belief that to do so might precipitate further acts of terror by the skyjacker's confederates designed to blackmail the government in question into releasing the skyjacker, as has happened a number of times in the past.[23] As a solution to this problem, some observers have proposed the creation of an international air crimes authority that would have jurisdiction over air piracy and aviation-related crimes.[24] It would have its own prosecution staff, court, judges, and appropriate penal system, and skyjackers would not be returned to the countries against which the crimes were committed but would instead be tried and, if convicted, sentenced and punished by the air crimes authority. Such a solution, however, has little chance of ever succeeding inasmuch as historically nations have been extremely reluctant to subordinate voluntarily their own domestic law to the jurisdiction of an international tribunal.

Thus, international government-level cooperation to combat air piracy and other forms of aviation-related terrorism, while desirable, is unlikely to materialize in any meaningful sense in the near future. According to Moss, "It seems that the most that can be hoped for are sanctions applied by individual governments or by several Western governments."[25]

The only effective multilateral action to date has not occurred at the state level but has taken the form of threatened boycotts by air pilots against nations that harbor skyjackers. Even to outlaw regimes like Libya, which is often outwardly disdainful of international reaction to its policies and pronouncements, the enforced isolation imposed by a pilot boycott not only would be a great blow to national prestige but also would undermine the normal commercial and economic relations of the country.

In the final analysis, however, the ultimate response to air piracy is self-help, in the form of military action by the state or states victimized by the skyjacking. Although the first responsibility for action belongs to the country to which the hijacked airliner has been taken, under circumstances like the Entebbe incident that witnessed deposed dictator Idi Amin's government both aiding and abetting the skyjackers, the nation whose plane has been seized or whose citizens are being held hostage may decide to take direct military action against the terrorists as well as hold the nation collaborating with them accountable. This was the case in the daring 1976 Israeli rescue of more than 100 Israeli nationals and the French crew of the hijacked Air France airbus.

Following Entebbe, various nations have assembled highly trained commando units capable of retrieving hijacked aircraft and passengers from hostile hands—for instance, the crack German border-police unit permitted by the Somalian government to rescue a Lufthansa jetliner that had been forced to Mogadishu. However, it should be cautioned that the incidents at both Entebbe and Mogadishu represented, in many respects, unique situations and involved substantial risks for the Israeli and German governments. Uganda, in particular, was a small, impotent country under erratic leadership. A more sophisticated nation would have detected the approach of the Israeli aircraft and repelled any attempt to rescue the hostages. Remember also that the Israelis bought precious seconds by rolling out a Mercedes automobile that resembled that frequently used to transport Amin, thus throwing the guards at the airport off balance and causing them to hold their fire while the Israelis gained the advantage. Such a simple ruse probably would not have worked in many countries. There is little question that the Israeli government would have fallen if the Entebbe rescue effort had not been successful and had resulted in a debacle. All of this is not to denigrate the Israeli gamble, which in every respect is deserving of praise for its execution and boldness, but simply to affirm that the Entebbe case is not readily applicable to other situations.

The risks associated with a poorly planned and executed military retrieval of a hostage jetliner are illustrated by the attempted rescue by Egyptian commandos of Egyptian hostages taken aboard a Cyprus Airways plane in Nicosia, Cyprus, by two gunmen in 1978, in which the flight crew and hostages were nearly killed despite the lack of resistance by the frightened and inept skyjackers.

The plane had returned to Larnaca, Cyprus, after refueling in Djibouti and being refused permission to land by Libya, Saudi Arabia, Aden, and Lebanon. Although Syrian President Hafez Assad had given his personal assurance to the skyjackers of refuge in Damascus, they were distrustful of the offer and rejected it. Shortly after the hijacked plane arrived at Larnaca, a C-130E transport plane with Egyptian markings landed at the airport without, and this fact is disputed, clearance by Cypriot authorities and disgorged Egyptian commandos who immediately poured automatic weapons fire into the parked jetliner. In the ensuing fray, the two skyjackers never returned a shot, but the commandos continued to blaze away at the cockpit. Only action by Cypriot national guardsmen at the airport, who opened fire on the Egyptians, saved the lives of the hostages and brought the situation under control.

Conclusion

"Hijacking is not a legitimate way of fighting," charges former Stern gang terrorist Nathan Yalin-Mor.[26] Contrary to Yalin-Mor's assertion, however, for most modern terrorists, the question of legitimacy has nothing to do with whether or not a particular form of violence is employed; the bottom line is effectiveness, and skyjacking has been used in the past with considerable effectiveness by various terrorist groups seeking to publicize their causes and to strike out at their enemies. Skyjacking and other forms of aviation-related terrorism will disappear only when they cease to be effective or when the opportunity is no longer available.

In this connection, airport security measures in recent years have made skyjacking not only far more difficult, thus removing opportunity, but also far more precarious from the perpetrator's point of view than many other forms of terrorism. Moreover, the nations of the world are increasingly reluctant to provide skyjackers with asylum as they did in previous years. Finally, and most important, the organized campaign of terror against Israel and its Western allies by the PFLP in the late 1960s and early 1970s failed to disrupt appreciably international commerce, travel, or communications. Despite the loss of life and property that did occur, international aviation was affected only to a minor degree. As a result, the late Dr. Wadi Hadad, former head of the PFLP's foreign operations bureau and the chief proponent of aerial terrorism in the PFLP, was expelled from that organization in a dispute over the continued utility of skyjacking, following the debacle at Mogadishu. Dr. George Habash, leader of the PFLP, is said to have believed that acts of air piracy, once acceptable as a means of winning attention for their cause, no longer served a useful purpose after the multiple skyjackings staged in 1970 and that they were beginning to hurt the Palestinian cause more than help it. Habash was particularly mindful that efforts to win increasing European support for Palestinian self-determination had been set back by the Mogadishu incident. Moreover, as Clutterbuck notes, after the October 1973 Middle East War restored Arab pride lost in previous Arab-Israeli conflicts and provided the Arab confrontation states with new confidence in their conventional military power, they became more reluctant to cooperate with Palestinian terrorists, especially in the matter of aircraft skyjackings. In addition, the 1973 war had demonstrated the potency of the oil weapon and the West's vulnerability to it. Thus, the Arab world, by 1974, had far more effective weapons at its disposal for putting pressure on the West vis-à-vis Israel and for achieving its other policy aims.[27]

While the level of worldwide skyjackings has remained at a high level, it can be predicted that this figure will decline appreciably in the years ahead, especially as more and more nations adopt tough security standards at their airports. Nevertheless, the terrorist threat to civil aviation will persist for some time to come. In the United States, anti-Castro and Serbian-Croatian terrorist groups currently represent the greatest threat to civil aviation. In recent years, two skyjackings and a serious airport bombing have been attributed to Serbian-Croatian terrorists, and during 1979, an anti-Castro group claimed responsibility for a bomb that exploded in the TWA terminal at La Guardia Airport in New York. Authorities are not discounting the possibility that Puerto Rican separatist groups, which have been responsible for the bombing of numerous buildings in New York and other cities, might turn their attention to aviation-related targets in the early 1980s. A May 1981 bomb blast at Kennedy Airport, which killed an airport employee, was attributed to Puerto Rican terrorists. By contrast, the recent rash of skyjackings to Havana by Cubans who fled their native land in the 1979 exodus appears to be a transitory phenomenon.

Internationally, elements of the Palestinian liberation movement can be expected periodically to engage in acts of sabotage, skyjackings, and possibly even missile attacks on civil aviation. Similarly, since IRA terrorists are known to possess ground-to-air munitions, it would not come as a surprise to see a U.K. airliner shot down, perhaps even over the United States, sometime in the future.

While current airport security systems interdict most unsophisticated air pirates, such systems, or any projected systems now on the drawing boards, will deter few dedicated and resourceful terrorists bent on criminal acts directed against aviation targets. Only sound intelligence, together with international cooperation to deny terrorists safe havens, offer the world community any real protection against terrorists and the threat they pose to civil aviation.

Notes

1. William F. May, "Terrorism as Strategy and Ecstasy," *Social Research* (Summer 1974), p. 279.

2. "Jumbo Jet Is Hijacked by Woman," *Washington Post*, 28 January 1979.

3. Richard Clutterbuck, *Living with Terrorism* (London: Faber and Faber, 1975), p. 95.

4. Robert G. Bell, "The U.S. Response to Terrorism against International Civil Aviation," *Orbis* (Winter 1976), pp. 1329–1330.

5. Letter to the editor from James E. Dow, *Washington Post*, 24 September 1975.

6. Colin Smith, *Carlos: Portrait of a Terrorist* (New York: Holt, Rinehart & Winston, 1976), p. 58.

7. "Israel: Airline Business Soars Despite Terrorist Hijackings," *Washington Post*, 15 August 1976.

8. Federal Aviation Administration, Department of Transportation, "Semiannual Report to Congress on the Effectiveness of the Civil Aviation Security Program," 1 January–30 June 1979, Exhibit 7.

9. A variety of other possible security measures had been tested and discarded before federal authorities settled on the systems that were adopted. These included, as part of so-called Project Zeke, a device constructed in the door frame leading to the cockpit that was designed to knock out the skyjacker with an electrical charge long enough for the crew to disarm him. During one test, however, the copilot, not the skyjacker, was knocked out.

10. Clutterbuck, *Living with Terrorism*, p. 109.

11. Ibid., p. 119.

12. FAA, "Semiannual Report to Congress," p. 9.

13. Ibid., p. 2.

14. Interview with airport security official, August 1977.

15. U.S., Congress, House of Representatives, Committee on Public Works and Transportation, Subcommittee on Aviation, *Aircraft Piracy, International Terrorism*, 96th Cong., 1st sess., 1979, p. 64.

16. Senator Abraham Ribicoff, "Diplomacy Is not Enough." *Air Line Pilot* (September 1978).

17. The Tokyo Convention of 1963 (Convention on Offenses and Certain Other Acts Committed on Board Aircraft), which entered into force on 4 December 1969, grants the commander of the aircraft jurisdiction over crimes committed on board and permits him to take necessary action to subdue the skyjacker. The convention also authorizes the pilot to land in any state that is a signatory to the convention and to turn over the skyjacker to authorities, whereupon the state receiving the skyjacker can return him to his state of origin or to the state wherein the aircraft is registered.

18. The Hague Convention of 1970 (Convention for the Suppression of Unlawful Seizure of Aircraft), which entered into force on 14 October 1971, sets up a system that provides for the extradition and prosecution of skyjackers.

19. The Montreal Convention of 1971 (Convention for the Suppression of Unlawful Acts against the Safety of Civil Aviation), which entered into force on 26 January 1973, relates to acts of sabotage, together with acts of violence to persons on board and bomb hoaxes that endanger the safe operation of

aircraft. It also provides for the extradition and punishment of those who would sabotage air navigation facilities.

20. "Taggants" were used as evidence in December 1979, for the first time, to convict a man of explosives violations in a case before a federal court in Baltimore, Maryland. See Bureau of Alcohol, Tobacco and Firearms, Department of the Treasury, newsletter, 4 January 1980, p. 2.

21. Pat O'Brien, "NRA Snags Passage of Anti-Terrorism Bill," *Airline Executive* (December 1978), p. 25.

22. Testimony of Institute of Makers of Explosives before the Committee on Public Works and Transportation, Subcommittee on Aviation, *Aircraft Piracy*, p. 254.

23. For example, at the 1972 Munich Olympics, eleven Israeli athletes were killed by Black September terrorists. Five of the eight terrorists also lost their lives, but the three remaining terrorists were ransomed when fellow terrorists seized a German airliner and demanded their imprisoned confederates in exchange for the airliner and their hostages. The German government capitulated to the terrorist demand. In addition, Leila Khaled, who had been captured during a muffed skyjacking attempt, was also freed as part of an agreement to release hostages seized in a subsequent skyjacking by PFLP gunmen.

24. See Peter Clyne, *An Anatomy of Skyjacking* (London: Abelard-Schuman, 1973).

25. Robert Moss, "Counter Terrorism," *The Economist*, Brief Booklet no. 29 (no date), p. 20.

26. Interview with Nathan Yalin-Mor, New York City, 16 September 1976.

27. Clutterbuck, *Living with Terrorism*, pp. 103–104.

6 Terrorist Weapons: Today and Tomorrow

[T]he greatest benefactor of mankind will be he who makes it possible for a few men to wipe out thousands. —Karl Heinzer[1]

The essence of terrorism is violence. The terrorist communicates with the world through violence—through acts of viciousness, brutality, and wanton mayhem. Thus, the implements the terrorist uses to promulgate his violence are of critical importance with respect to his ability to reach the goals he hopes to achieve. Without weapons, the terrorist is nothing; with them, he is everything.

The power of terrorists is circumscribed chiefly by their access to and choice of weapons and targets. As their arsenals grow, so does the threat that they pose to organized societies everywhere. In years past, the state and its constituent elites had a near monopoly on the implements of violence and the training necessary to utilize them effectively. Weapons and armor were tediously crafted by hand and extremely costly relative to the buying power of the average individual. Moreover, the science of war was the exclusive preserve of the ruling classes. Violence was essentially the prerogative of the state and armed elites, inflicted downward on subject populations or laterally upon other states. The populace at large did not have the wherewithal to strike back effectively at their oppressors; hence, most uprisings were short lived and brutally suppressed. Transfers of power, when they occurred, were usually the result of coups, assassinations, army mutinies, and conquests by other armed elites. Such political violence involving the masses that did occur were rudimentary and took the form of brawls, food riots, and demonstrations.

With the advent of the Industrial Revolution, improved technology and mass production made available for the first time relatively efficient and inexpensive state-of-the-art weapons for mass consumption. It is no accident that the so-called age of revolution, which commenced in the late eighteenth century and witnessed popular uprisings in the United States, France, South America, and central Europe by the midpoint of the following century, occurred concomitantly with the Industrial Revolution. During the nineteenth century, the individual capacity for violence became more widespread and refined, resulting in new nonstate actors coming onto the world stage, asserting their claims to political power and threatening to upset traditional patterns of international behavior as well as the configuration of world power. Today, this trend has reached the point at which a single individual, or group of individuals, has the ability to make war upon the state and to make it effectively.

97

In this connection, Hannah Arendt has written that "the gap between state-owned means of violence and what people can muster for themselves—from beer bottles to Molotov cocktails and guns—has always been so enormous that technical improvements hardly make any difference. . . .In a contest of violence against violence the superiority of the government has always been absolute."[2] By contrast to Arendt's assertion, however, the state no longer enjoys a monopoly on the instruments of violence and, in some cases, not even parity with groups that seek its destruction. Concludes David Fromkin, "Only modern technology makes this possible—the bazooka, the plastic bomb, the submachine gun, and perhaps, over the horizon, the nuclear minibomb."[3] In our modern world, the average individual has access to the technology of violence and the weapons that flow from it; in fact, one person today can hold in his or her hands more raw firepower than that possessed by an entire Napoleonic-era division.

It can be argued that, measured in terms of the absolute numbers of weapons and the combined destructive potential of those weapons, the state still enjoys a vast superiority over insurgent and terrorist groups, but such assertions are basically meaningless. The state will always suffer from the disadvantage that its arsenals are designed primarily to protect it from external threats posed by other nation-states with similarly structured military establishments and arsenals. A state cannot turn a nuclear weapon upon itself without committing suicide, yet terrorists operate under no such restraints. Even tanks and heavy artillery are neutralized when arrayed against a faceless enemy that chooses its targets at random, strikes swiftly, and then melts back into the populace. A heat-seeking missile or chemical weapon cannot be utilized to combat terrorists, but terrorists are quite capable of employing both in the years ahead in an effort to destroy a legitimate government. Thus, modern nation-states find themselves forced to adopt defensive strategies when confronted with attack by terrorist groups, whereas terrorists are in the enviable position of being able to make disproportional use of the new generation of weapons that is now making its appearance in military arsenals.

Terrorists, like their counterparts in conventional armies, are inherently conservative in their choice of weapons and tactics. Thus, despite remarkable advances in weapons technology, most terrorists are still wedded to the gun, the bomb, the knife, and to proven patterns of violence repeated over time with only minor variations.

Nevertheless, there is no standard terrorist arsenal. The range of terrorist weapons is virtually limitless. No object is too complex, or for that matter too mundane, to be discounted as a weapon by imaginative and resourceful dissidents. Ranging from a sharp pencil that could be used to pierce the jugular vein of a stewardess or to blind her, to radiological, chemical, and biological weapons capable of wiping out millions of innocent people, the array of weapons available to modern terrorists is simply incredible. Everyday household items like power drills, oven cleaners, Chlorox, screwdrivers, and cleavers can be used to inflict injury on people.

Among the more novel and bizarre weapons employed by terrorists in recent years were booby-trapped 100-peso notes in Argentina (the notes, which were left lying on sidewalks, were connected to nearby explosive charges); poisonous snakes (mailed to a government official in India and placed in the mailbox of a victim in the United States); disease-bearing ticks mailed to corporate officials in the United States; a crossbow used in the takeover of the B'nai B'rith headquarters in Washington, D.C.; a blowgun with poison darts used to kill a victim in a European hotel lobby; and a golf bag filled with explosives, gasoline, and an incendiary mixture by the IRA. In a variation of the Soviet technique of training dogs outfitted with satchel charges to chase tanks, the Nationalist Chinese plotted to kill Peoples Republic of China (PRC) Premier Chou En-lai by means of a remote-control bomb carried by a dog. And in 1981, Palestinian commandos, taking inspiration from the recreation industry, sought to cross Israel's highly defended borders, in separate attempts, by means of motor-driven hang gliders and a hot air balloon.

Firearms

Because terrorists tend to engage the enemy in small numbers in brief and highly mobile encounters, they favor compact, flexible, lightweight weapons that can lay down concentrated fire. Such weapons are also easier, as a rule, to conceal, which is important to terrorists seeking to travel undetected. Moreover, inasmuch as few terrorists have received military training, including marksmanship instruction and sustained firing-range practice, a high premium is placed on relatively simple weapons that are easy to load, aim, and fire. Exotic weapons are usually rendered impractical because of the difficulty in obtaining ammunition—another important consideration for the terrorist.

Large caliber alone is no guarantee of stopping power. The trend today is toward smaller-caliber weapons with higher muzzle velocity. Studies demonstrate that small-caliber, high-velocity bullets that tumble earlier cause larger wounds and far more tissue damage than conventional ammunition. Wounds even to the extremeties are often incapacitating or even fatal. In Vietnam, it was not unusual for a single bullet fired by an M-16 rifle to tear off a man's arm. Toxic ammunition and various types of exploding ammunition also add to the lethality of a weapon.

Penetration power is also very important. A televised demonstration of a hardened automobile manufactured by a Massachusetts corporation showed the firm's president sitting behind the wheel of one of his company's products while an employee of the firm raked the windows with a Thompson .45-caliber submachine gun. However, the Thompson is hopelessly outdated and few, if any, terrorists use it today, despite Carlos Marighella's endorsement of the .45-caliber machine gun as the ideal weapon of urban guerrillas.[4] Its muzzle velocity is one-third less than many modern submachine guns, and its rate of fire is only

14 percent that of a Czech-made Skorpion Vz61. As a well-known terrorism expert observed, "If it had been a 9-millimeter weapon aimed at the window, you can bet he wouldn't have been sitting there."[5] Nine-millimeter parabellum ammunition is relatively inexpensive and readily available and has extremely good penetration power. Moreover, there is usually little kick or rise to most 9-millimeter weapons, unlike larger-caliber guns.

All shapes and sizes of 9-millimeter weapons are available, including pistols, assault rifles, and submachine guns. Perhaps the most universal terrorist weapon is the submachine gun. The first submachine guns appeared around the turn of the century, but they did not win broad acceptance until World War I when their utility at close-range fighting was demonstrated in European trench warfare. Submachine guns underwent substantial refinement during the interwar period and were adopted by nearly every combatant army during World War II. In the postwar period, submachine guns have become lighter, smaller, and easier to handle. The future of the submachine gun as a military weapon, nevertheless, is open to question as assault rifles become ever lighter and more rapid firing. The USSR, which historically was the greatest advocate of massed submachine gun fire, has phased out such guns as a battlefield weapon. Those who ignore range and accuracy, say detractors of the submachine gun, do so to their own detriment. In this connection, some military observers maintain that the shotgun is superior to the submachine gun for close-range fighting.

The Czech-made Skorpion Vz61 submachine pistol and its cousins, the Vz23 and Vz25 submachine guns, are perhaps the most popular terrorist weapons in the world. The Vz61 was used in the abduction of Aldo Moro and in dozens of other terrorist attacks including the murder of Genoa prosecutor Francesco Colo and the unsuccessful assault on Princess Ashraf in 1977. Carlos the Jackal also carried a Vz61. Weighing only three and one-half pounds (unloaded), it fires .32-caliber (7.65-millimeter) rounds at the rate of 840 per minute and can be equipped with a silencer. The Vz23 and Vz25 are 9-millimeter parabellum blowback-operated weapons that fire at the rate of 600 rounds per minute and that weigh approximately 6.8 pounds (without magazine). The magazine is housed in the pistol grip. All three weapons have a selective fire feature that permits them to be fired in either a single-shot or automatic mode.

Perhaps the most famous, and surely one of the most highly prized, submachine guns is the Uzi, which is produced both in Israel and under license by FN Herstal in Belgium. Designed by Israeli army officer Uziel Gal in the late 1940s, the Uzi was revolutionary in its conception and today is probably the most widely distributed submachine gun in the Western world. In performance it is comparable to the Vz23 and Vz25. It is a 9-millimeter parabellum, selective fire, blowback-operated weapon that fires at the rate of 600 rounds per minute with only limited muzzle climb. It weighs slightly less than one pound more than the Czech submachine guns and has a marginally higher muzzle velocity. The Uzi is an extremely durable and reliable weapon and can be purchased with a corrosion-resistant baked-enamel finish. It can be fitted with a bayonet, a screw-on grenade launcher, and a spotlight that attaches under the barrel. One would suspect, however, that the spotlight would attract hostile fire. The U.S. Secret Service utilizes Uzis in the protection of the president but reduces the length of the barrel by several inches to permit concealment in the attaché case. The Uzi also can be carried under a coat in a specially designed shoulder harness that places the weapon under the weak-side armpit. A civilian version of the Uzi is now available, but it is not fully automatic and the length of the barrel has been extended. Twelve thousand of the weapons reportedly were sold in the United States in 1981.

Many counterterrorist and executive protection units, however, are shifting to the superior Heckler and Koch MP5-series submachine guns. The MP5K is the Cadillac of ultrasmall submachine guns. Of such fine craftsmanship as to prompt one major arms encyclopedia to criticize the "unnecessarily high grade of manu-facture" of the MP5-series weapons, which makes them more expensive than comparable submachine guns, the MP5K weighs 4.4 pounds, is only 12.8 inches long, and fires 9-millimeter parabellum ammunition at a rate of 840 rounds per minute in its automatic mode, with a velocity of 1,230 feet per second.[6] It has so little rise that it can be fired with one hand and is extremely accurate and deadly at close quarters. According to Heckler and Koch sales literature, "The ultrashort design of the MP5K permits it to be employed even where space is extremely limited. Even when carried concealed, the submachine gun is instantly ready to fire."[7] Other MP5-series submachine guns have options such as a burst firing mode, sound suppressors, and special scopes.

Perhaps the smallest, most compact machine pistol in the world is the 3.5-pound, 8.7-inch-long Ingram MAC II. The Ingram is available in three calibers—.45 ACP, 9-millimeter parabellum, and 9-millimeter short—and can be fitted with the most effective flash and sound suppressor in existence, developed by arms dealer and ex-CIA contract agent, Mitchell Livingston WerBell. Called "a giant step forward in the state-of-the-art of killing" the silenced MAC II is an ideal weapon for clandestine operations.[8] Another extraordinarily small and deadly weapon is the 9-millimeter Beretta 93R pistol that fires 3-round bursts with little climb or flash until the 20-round magazine is empty. The 93R pro-vides a viable alternative to a submachine gun and is particularly suited to exe-cutive protection and police activities.

One weapon that deserves special note is the AM180, which fires .22 long rifle ammunition at the cyclic rate of over 25 rounds a second. Its magazine, containing 177 rounds, can be emptied in less than seven seconds with no per-ceptible barrel climb or recoil. It lays down so much concentrated fire that it regularly chews up concrete blocks in demonstrations. Described by its manu-facturer as a weapons system instead of simply a weapon, the AM180 is available with a Laser Lok sight that projects a small bright-orange laser dot wherever the weapon is pointed. The bright-orange dot is the aiming cue for the shooter, and the weapon will strike wherever the dot falls, permitting the shooter to group his shots in an extremely tight pattern. Best results, however, do not occur in strong sunlight since the dot is often washed out and difficult to see. Its manufacturer has developed a prototype four-barrel version of the AM180 that is capable of firing at a rate of more than 6,000 rounds per minute. Needless to say, armed with an AM180, one man is, for all intents and purposes, an army, and in the hands of terrorists, such a weapon represents a real and terrible threat. The AM180 also comes in a self-contained briefcase version. Equipped with a sound suppressor, it fires through a port in the side of the briefcase and is capable of wreaking havoc in a crowded airport or public gathering. A similar briefcase weapon was used in the 1973 assassination attempt on the life of former South Korean President Park Chung Hee, which resulted in the death of his wife.

To its advocates, no weapon is more devastating at close range or in crowd situations than an automatic or pump shotgun loaded with double-O buckshot. Many experienced shooters find a shotgun far more accurate than a submachine gun and easier to aim. Although illegal under federal law, some older-model shotguns hold eleven rounds, and when slightly modified and outfitted with a front grip to minimize rise, they can be fired like a submachine gun. Police and military riot guns are relatively easy to conceal (under a raincoat) and have few peers when it comes to causing pure mayhem. The Ithaca 12-gauge five-shot riot gun with an 18 1/2-inch barrel also comes in a 29 1/2-inch eight-shot civilian model, but either weapon could be used with great effectiveness by terrorists.

Shotgun shells loaded with flechettes (small needlelike darts) are capable of extraordinary wounding power. As a result of its shape, upon impact the flechette bends into a hook and gyrates through the tissue, producing a severe wound. Twelve-gauge shotgun shells have been produced for military application with both twelve and eighteen flechettes per shell.

Although various military observers note that "those who discard the ability to kill at longer ranges do so at their peril," the assault rifle has won little widespread acceptance among terrorists, except as a sniping and assassination weapon.[9] Kalashnikov AK47 assault rifles were used in the assassination of President Anwar Sadat, were employed by some Black September terrorists at Munich, and are still regularly favored by Palestinian infiltrators crossing into Israel. Strictly speaking, however, the AK47 is more suited to battlefield conditions than to close range terrorist strikes. This is also true of the similar Czech-manufactured Vz58V assault rifle carried, in a cut-down version, by JRA terrorists who carried out the Lod massacre. The SVD Dragunov sniper rifle, produced by the USSR, has more than twice the effective range of the AKM and AK47 (900 meters versus 400 meters). Of semiautomatic design and firing a 7.6-millimeter cartridge, it is extremely deadly when mounted with a PS01 telescopic sight. U.S.-made M16 rifles were captured in such numbers by the North Vietnamese when the government of South Vietnam fell that they have been dumping them on world markets, and it is possible to buy one in perfect condition for about $100 in Bangkok. M16s are used by many insurgent groups and, in limited numbers, by a few terrorist groups like the IRA.

Pistols will always be valuable to terrorists as personal defense weapons, but their utility usually ends there. Soviet-made Makarov pistols were carried by every member of the six-person team, led by Carlos the Jackal, that seized the OPEC headquarters in Vienna in 1975.

Firearms are often disguised by terrorists as benign everyday items in order to assist them in deceiving authorities or to pass unnoticed in a crowd. Guns have been secreted in canes, umbrellas, books, attaché cases, cigarette packages and lighters, cigars, fountain pens, toys, and parcels. One of the most innovatively hidden guns was built into the heel of a man's shoe. Cameras were utilized to conceal guns intended for assassination attempts on French President Charles de Gaulle and the shah of Iran. Similarly, minipistols have been built into Polaroid film packs. At many security checkpoints, especially in airports, security personnel click off one picture on each camera to ensure that it is not a disguised weapon. Firearms have also been smuggled through airport X-ray devices in disassembled form, the pieces scattered throughout the passenger's carry-on luggage. Few security personnel recognize the gun parts when they appear on the monitor, and it is a relatively simple matter for an experienced individual to reassemble the weapon once on board the plane in the restroom.

Perhaps one of the most sophisticated killing devices on record is a standard-brand U.S.-made suitcase with a silenced semiautomatic rifle built into the frame. From all appearances, it looks exactly like a normal suitcase; it even holds the customary amount of clothing inside. However, concealed under the grip is a tiny trigger. The shooter simply aims the suitcase and fires; the spent cartridges are not ejected but collected inside the frame. In a crowded airport or public gathering, more than likely no one would detect the weapon as it cut down its intended victims.

The shooter's ability is improved by a number of combat aids. Perhaps the most significant is the ability to see at night almost as well as in daylight as a result of optical devices that strip away the protective cover of darkness. There are two categories of such devices: active and passive. Active devices, based on infrared systems, however, are of decreasing utility since they can be detected by an adversary using night goggles, binoculars, or pocket sights, and thus the shooter is exposed to considerable danger. Undetectable passive systems, based on image intensification and light enhancement, are currently considered superior. The Star-Tron night vision system, for example, which is manufactured by a Smith & Wesson subsidiary, operates on the principle of light intensification. It amplifies available light up to 50,000 times, producing a clean, sharp image on a television screen or through a binocular-type eyepiece. Starlight enhancement scopes are similar but are usually only efficient on clear or moonlit nights.

One technique for disrupting a sniper's aim, especially if he is using an optical sighting device, is to mount high-intensity strobe lights on top of a vehicle or at critical locations around the perimeter of a secured facility; the pulsating light distorts the shooter's vision and causes spots before his eyes.

Bombs and Explosives

Nearly 70 percent of all terrorist attacks involve explosives in some form or another. This is no doubt attributable to two facts. First, bombs and explosives magnify the destruction and slaughter that one person is capable of inflicting. Second, planting a bomb with a delayed timing mechanism is a means of indirect killing and involves less risk to the terrorist than engaging the enemy directly, since he can often be long gone by the time the bomb explodes. Such delayed-action weapons, however, tend to be more indiscriminate than firearms and explosive projectiles. Clutterbuck has, for this reason, described the bomb as "the meanest of weapons."[10]

In many respects, the bomb is the classic terrorist weapon. Ever since the development of gunpowder by the Chinese, imaginative dissidents grasped its potential as a weapon that could be employed against the state. Prior to the nineteenth century, perhaps the most ambitious terrorist plot involving explosives was the 1605 gunpowder plot in England, in which Guy Fawkes and a band of conspirators planted thirty-six barrels of gunpowder under the Houses of Parliament. Fortunately for Parliament, details of the plot were revealed in an anonymous letter to authorities, and Fawkes and his fellow conspirators were arrested and hanged. Not until the nineteenth century, however, did explosives become sufficiently stable and compact so as to be easily portable and readily fashioned into bombs that could be utilized to slaughter and maim.

The wave of revolution that swept over Europe in 1848 witnessed only the limited use of bombs and explosives against the state. As the uprisings were crushed by the superior firepower of the besieged governments, terrorist philosopher Karl Heinzen called for "the invention of new methods of killing," so as to nullify the military advantage enjoyed by the state.[11] In this connection, he urged revolutionaries "to study the mysteries of powder and fulminating silver."[12] Would it not be possible, Heinzen asked, "to devise some sort of missile which one man can throw into a group of a few hundred, killing them all? We need instruments of destruction which are of little use to the great masses of the barbarians when they are fighting a few lone individuals but which give a few lone individuals the terrifying power to threaten the safety of whole masses of barbarians."[13]

Heinzen's dreams were fulfilled with the development of dynamite. Tsarist Russia witnessed the first flowering of the cult of the bomb, as disciples of Bakunin and Nechaev relentlessly attacked the state with bomb after bomb. During the so-called dynamite conspiracy of 1879–1880, numerous attempts were made on the life of Tsar Alexander II, including three attempts to detonate mines under his private train and a powerful dynamite cache exploded in his palace. He died in 1881, a victim of a bomb thrown by a disaffected Polish noble.

Inspired by their Russian compatriots, anarchists throughout Europe discovered bombs and explosives as a means of giving expression to their nihilistic philosophies. Scarcely a week went by that a bomb did not go off somewhere. Only in the United States did the cult of the bomb fail to take hold. The Haymarket Riot in 1886, sparked by a bomb thrown at police, so enraged the public and discredited the U.S. anarchist movement that it was rapidly eclipsed as a factor in U.S. politics.[14] Over the years, as explosives have become ever more powerful, terrorists correspondingly have become increasingly indiscriminate with respect to the targets of their bombs.

There are various types of explosives suitable for bomb making. Principal explosives include TNT, plastic explosive (C_3, C_4, Cyclonite), guncotton, picric acid (TNP), and nitroglycerin explosives (Gelignite, dynamite). Because of its high stability, power, versatility, and the ease with which it can be molded into any shape—from a flat envelope to an umbrella handle—plastic explosives enjoy wide popularity among terrorists. Moss has described plastic explosive—a compound of TNT, Hexogen, and a rubber compound—as "God's gift to the terrorist."[15] Plastic bombs have been disguised as books, parcels, teakettles, letters, transistor radios, baseballs, and candy boxes. Although the Zionist terrorist organization (Irgum Zvi Leumi) was the first to use parcel bombs, slim letter bombs—undetectable to an untrained recipient—were not perfected until the invention of the Polaroid camera that uses flat batteries that provide the electrical charge needed to detonate the explosive. Shaped charges, commonly made from plastic explosives, permit bomb makers to concentrate the destructive force of the explosion in any desired direction or pattern. In this way, they can be secreted in cars, shopping bags, lockers, and suitcases, and the impact of the explosion can be directed in a manner that maximizes casualties and damage.

Bombs may be set off by means of four kinds of fuses: electric, chemical, mechanical, and flame. Mechanical and flame are the most rudimentary. Most often they operate on the principle of a lever or other trigger mechanism held under pressure. When the mechanism is released, it strikes a detonator, thereby triggering the explosion. Many hand grenades are of this design. Pull fuses are similar, except they are "set off by the act of pulling as opposed to the act of releasing."[16] Pressure fuses—a form of mechanical detonation—can be far from crude. While a pressure fuse may be no more complicated than the activation of a detonator by the weight of a train passing along railway tracks, in 1970, a Swissair flight bound for Israel was blown apart, with the loss of all forty-seven aboard, by means of a bomb detonated by barometric pressure. During their struggle against the British, the Zionist terror organization, Hagana, developed an ingenious pressure-detonated bomb that could be placed in a pipeline and travel through all the valves, exploding once it reached the storage tanks.

Chemical fuses usually involve the combination of two or more chemicals that produce a spark necessary to set off an explosion. Most often a vial of acid is crushed or spilled inside a container, whereupon it slowly eats its way through the container wall until it reaches the chemical. In another variation, the acid eats through a wire, releasing a spring and detonating the bomb. Since the amount of time it will take to penetrate the walls of the container can be calculated, the terrorist can delay the blast according to his needs.

Electrical devices, however, are a far simpler and more reliable means of delayed time fuse. Typically, such fuses involve the closing of an electric circuit by means of clock hands touching two terminals simultaneously. Alarm clocks, egg timers, and watches are the most common instruments used by bomb makers in fabricating such devices. Radio signals, which also fall under the heading of electric fuses, are also utilized to set off bombs, including the one that killed Chilean diplomat Orlando Letelier in Washington, D.C., in 1976. The Israelis have perfected an explosive device that is placed in a telephone receiver and detonated by an ultrasonic tone on the other end of the line. Such a device was used to kill a PLO representative in Paris, Mahmoud Hamshari, who was implicated in the planning of the Munich massacre.[17]

For maximum antipersonnel effect, explosives can be combined with scrap metal, flechettes, metal balls, nails, and other objects that are projected outward at high velocity by the force of the blast. One of the earliest and most devastating terrorist uses of an antipersonnel bomb occurred in 1893 when Auguste Vaillant threw two bombs stuffed with iron nails onto the floor of the French Chamber of Deputies, injuring eighty-four members of Parliament. One simple but effective terrorist design involves placing an explosive in a satchel or tennis bag and packing bolts, nuts, nails, and other projectiles around it. When the explosive goes off, the shrapnel creates havoc in a 360-degree circle. Fragmentation grenades operate along the same principle: When the explosive is detonated, the case holding the explosive breaks into tiny fragments that are hurled outward by the force of the blast.

Explosives can be procured in a variety of ways. Often, high-quality military explosives, especially plastic explosives, are provided directly to terrorist groups by patron nations. The USSR and its Eastern bloc allies directly supply the PLO and other terrorist groups with explosives, detonators, and bomb-making instruction. Similarly, Libya dispenses explosives to dozens of allied terrorist movements, allegedly even using its diplomatic pouches to circumvent strict security measures at Western airports. Explosives also can be stolen from military installations or from legitimate mining and construction operations. The problem of theft and poor governmental controls regulating the purchase of explosives has reached scandalous proportions in the United States. According to a 1977 congressional report, "there are so many gaps and so many glaring weaknesses in the federal system of control of explosives that is is virtually meaningless to speak of 'control of explosives'."[18] One writer describes in a mayhem manual how a militant filed a mining claim on a barren piece of desert land and then proceeded to purchase explosives like dynamite legitimately on the pretense that they were needed for his mining operations.[19]

Sophisticated explosives, however, are not always necessary for the manufacture of extremely deadly terrorist bombs. A devastating explosive can be produced by combining common garden-variety ammonium nitrate fertilizer with diesel fuel, oil, gasoline, or kerosene. Ammonium nitrate is roughly equivalent to dynamite having 60 percent nitroglycerine, and is available at most garden supply stores or from farm suppliers. U.S. Treasury agents demonstrated the explosive power of homemade bombs of this type, fabricated from less than $3 worth of common materials, in 1971 tests at Vandenberg Air Force Base in California. In recent years, guerrillas in Latin America have used ammonium nitrate bombs with great effectiveness to shear the wellheads off oil wells.

Fire and Incendiaries

The use of fire as a weapon is as old as recorded human history, and it remains one of the most terrifying of all weapons. The first primitive incendiary weapons were probably devised by the Greeks, who poured pots of burning oil and naphtha on their enemies. Greek fire, invented by a Syrian named Kalinokos of Heliopolis, was first used by the Emperor Constantine Pogonatus in 673 A.D. in the defense of Constantinople (Istanbul) against the Saracens and was perhaps the first real terror weapon in history. Made from sulphur, pitch, petroleum, niter, and quicklime, it resembled napalm in that it clung to everything it hit, burned furiously, and was difficult to extinguish.[20]

The fact that primitive incendiaries were known to the people of antiquity is clear evidence that such weapons lie well within the province of modern terrorists. "For sheer terrorism," gloats one terror manual, "incendiaries can't be beat. They are horrifying to look at and if set off in a crowded room, instant panic is guaranteed. They burn at 4,000 degrees and give out a blinding light."[21] The simplest incendiary weapon is, of course, the so-called Molotov cocktail, made by filling a bottle with gasoline and stuffing a rag wick in the top. The bottle is hurled at the target, and when it shatters, the gasoline is ignited, producing a fiery explosion. Numerous improvised incendiary weapons can be made by utilizing household substances and easily obtainable chemicals. Napalm, perhaps the most universally dreaded incendiary weapon, is composed principally of soap flakes and gasoline. Another fast-burning, easy-to-ignite incendiary is made by mixing three parts potassium chlorate—available at drug stores, swimming pool maintenance companies, and hospitals—with one part of ordinary household sugar. The mixture is ignited by heat, spark, or sulphuric acid.[22] Thermite grenades can be produced by packing thermite in a casing fabricated from ordinary aluminum tubing and then adding an igniter of powdered magnesium and barium and a simple fuse. It can be hurled, time detonated, shot with a sling, or delivered in any number of other ways.

While NATO armies have de-emphasized flamethrowers in recent years, they are still standard equipment for Soviet and Warsaw Pact forces. If supplied to terrorists and used in crowded environments, few weapons could inflict as many horrible injuries or evoke more sheer terror. The Soviet-made LPO-50 portable flamethrower carries more fuel and has more than twice the range of earlier models (200 feet with thickened fuel). The entire assembly—three tanks and a launcher—weighs only fifty pounds and could be concealed relatively easily.

Terrorists could terrorize a city through acts of widespread arson. Similarly, they could have a serious impact on the economies of various nations by torching fields and setting crops on fire. Large-scale forest and brush fires also could be set deliberately.

To date, terrorists have shown, for the most part, little interest in incendiary weapons, preferring instead fragmentation devices. However, Puerto Rican FALN terrorists have usually combined their bombs with a small tank of propane that acts like an air-fueled incendiary.[23] While most military explosives are solids, air-fueled incendiary weapons are now being introduced that are based on the explosive power of certain vapors or aerosol clouds of small particles that explode when combined with air. It has long been known that coal-mine explosions occur as a result of high concentrations of methane gas and air. Similarly, dust can build up in explosive concentrations in grain storage elevators. However, not until recently could systems be developed to disperse and detonate fuel-air mixtures adequately. Today, terrorists could pump propylene oxide, acetylene, or compressed methane into buildings or secure areas and then ignite it.

Missiles and Rockets

The increasing capacity for individual destruction is nowhere better illustrated than in the appearance of portable, shoulder-fired, wire-guided, and heat-seeking missiles in terrorist arsenals. In Rome (1973) and Kenya (1976), authorities apprehended terrorists preparing to shoot down civilian airliners with Soviet-made heat-seeking missiles. During the recent conflict in Rhodesia, prior to the advent of majority rule, two airliners, both four-engine Air Rhodesia Viscounts, were shot down by Patriotic Front guerrillas using ground-to-air missiles. Forty-eight people were killed (ten of them in hostilities on the ground after the crash) in September 1978 in the first incident, and fifty-nine died on 12 February 1979 in the second incident.

In both Rome and Kenya, and more than likely in the downing of the two Rhodesian airliners, the terrorists were armed with shoulder-fired SA-7 surface-to-air missiles that have a range of more than two miles. The SA-7 weighs approximately 23 pounds and costs under a $1,000 to produce. Among the terrorist groups known to possess SA-7s are various Palestinian factions, the IRA, and a number of African revolutionary movements.

Various countermeasures are effective against the SA-7 missile, including certain evasive maneuvers, the ejection of flares from the target aircraft, and afterburner extensions. The most critical periods in any flight are the takeoff and landing. Despite the limited punch of the SA-7 warhead, which contains only a pound and a half of high explosive, any passenger aircraft—including a four-engine Boeing 707—would be extremely vulnerable during these two maneuvers. The U.K. government is so concerned about the possibility of an airliner being targeted by a terrorist equipped with an SA-7 that security and military personnel at London's Heathrow Airport regularly hold exercises aimed at thwarting such an attack.

Baader-Meinhof terrorists in West Germany, who claimed responsibility for the unsuccessful September 1981 attack on the life of General Frederick J. Kroesen, commander of U.S. Army forces in Europe, used a Soviet-made RPG7 grenade launcher in the attack. The weapon has a range of between 1,000 and 1,650 feet. It fires a 3.7-pound fin-stabilized grenade that is capable of penetrating 320 millimeters of armor plate. Given the failure of the projectile to damage General Kroesen's hardened limousine seriously, however, such claims must be reevaluated.

One of the most remarkable new weapons to appear in the past decade is the Armbrust 300, a privately developed antitank weapon produced in West Germany. Unlike the other antitank missiles discussed, the Armbrust is a preloaded one-shot disposable weapon. It produces no flash, no noise, and no smoke and therefore can be fired from concealment. Since it has no back blast, it can be fired from a small room or inside a building, unlike any other comparable munition. It weighs slightly over thirteen pounds loaded and can penetrate twelve inches of armor. As Brian Jenkins has noted, the Armbrust 300 is "an ideal weapon for urban guerrilla warfare, and could be used as a weapon of assassination."[24]

Chemical/Biological Weapons

It would take a gifted group of individuals operating under optimal circumstances, with all of the requisite facilities and materials, to produce a nuclear device from the ground up, and even then it would be extremely difficult to do and would involve considerable personal risk to the participants. By contrast, any reasonably competent graduate-level chemist or biologist has within his power the ability to manufacture—with only limited resources and in the privacy of his own home or garage—chemical and biological weapons of mass destruction that could be used to terrorize a whole city and even an entire nation. The threat is perhaps best expressed by the writer of a contemporary terror manual: "A militant with an eighth grade reading level can fix up a mad scientist's laboratory out of odds and ends and with easily purchased chemicals become more dangerous than a foreign saboteur."[25]

Perhaps the first recorded use of chemical warfare occurred in 424 B.C. at the siege of Delium during the Peloponnesian War when the Greeks used sulphur fumes against their enemies. Although an attempt was made to outlaw the use of chemical weapons in the Geneva Protocol of 1925, both the United States and the USSR have stockpiled tons of chemical and biological agents. Recently, the USSR has been accused by the United States of using toxic chemical agents in Afghanistan. Only small amounts of some lethal substances are needed to destroy whole societies. In 1960, for example, one U.S. general estimated that two planes, each carrying 10,000 pounds of biological agents over the United States, could kill or incapacitate 60 million Americans.[26] Botulinal toxin (botulism), which ranks number one as a natural biological poison, is far more lethal than even plutonium. With a minimum lethal dose of .00003 μg./kg., estimates indicate that one-half ounce, properly dispersed, could kill every man, woman, and child in North America. To put the toxicity of botulinal toxin into perspective, the amount needed to kill one person has been likened to "a flea on a 100 mile long train, the flea's presence being able to derail the whole train."[27]

The United States has virtually no defense against a large-scale chemical or biological attack. Vaccines and antidotes are not stockpiled in anywhere near the quantities needed to provide adequate protection either to the public or to U.S. military units. To illustrate U.S. vulnerability to a sophisticated terrorist attack using chemical or biological agents, during the past twenty years, reportedly both the White House and the Pentagon were found to be vulnerable to a chemical or biological attack after simulated tests were conducted. While the White House water and ventilation systems today are protected by sophisticated filtering units, Richard C. Clark has written that the U.S. Army has developed certain viruses that can survive filtration chemicals.[28] Of course, if the U.S. Army can do it, so, too, can the Soviets, and perhaps even terrorists.

The leading synthetic chemical agents that are stockpiled for military application are phosgene (carbonyl chloride); mustard gas; hydrogen cyanide; GB nerve gas, or sarin (isopropyl methylphosphonofluoridate); and its more lethal cousin, VX nerve gas [S-(2-diisopropylaminoethyl) 0-ethyl methyl phosphonothiolate]. VX and related nerve agents are odorless, colorless, nonvolatile, and extremely dangerous when either inhaled or absorbed through the skin. In tests conducted by the army, one drop of VX absorbed through the skin was enough to kill a dog. In a highly publicized incident in 1968, near the Dugway Proving Ground in Utah, 4,000 sheep were killed when VX gas escaped from the facility. Not only has the U.S. government acknowledged that a small amount of its inventory of VX is presently unaccounted for, but also both the United States and the United Kingdom have declassified the formula for making it and it has been widely published. According to one source, a quart of VX, which is enough to kill several million people, costs approximately \$5 to manufacture.[29] Moreover, no domestic laws prohibit the manufacture of nerve agents and its possession by private citizens.[30]

VX nerve gas is not the only lethal chemical agent missing from military stockpiles. Fifty-three steel bottles containing mustard gas, which were awaiting destruction, were stolen from ammunition bunkers in West Germany, and German authorities expressed concern that Baader-Meinhof terrorists were behind the theft.

To illustrate further the ease with which certain deadly chemicals can be acquired, U.S. authorities now believe that the mysterious so-called yellow rain used by the USSR and its client states in Laos, Kampuchea, and Afghanistan, and possibly even South Yemen some years ago, is a fungus known as T2 toxin. T2 toxin can be purchased readily through the mail in the United States. Ostensibly for research purposes, one company offers T2 and four other toxins for less than \$100.[31]

On a microlevel, deadly chemicals are extremely convenient and economic tools for selective assassinations. The assassination of Bulgarian defector Georgi Markov is a good case in point. Markov, the first of three Bulgarian exiles living in the West to be attacked, was jabbed in the leg while walking along a London street by a man with an umbrella. The man apologized, then jumped in a cab and disappeared. Markov soon fell desperately ill, and within four days he was dead. He told doctors before he died that he had been assassinated, but they could find no evidence to support his allegation, despite the fact that they could not discover the cause of his illness. It was not until French surgeons removed a tiny pellet, approximately the size of a pinhead, from the back of another Bulgarian exile, Vladimir Kostov, that the mystery surrounding Markov's death was solved. The pellet, a remarkable piece of microengineering, was fabricated of an exotic alloy of 90 percent platinum and 10 percent iridium and had two tiny holes drilled into it that authorities speculate contained poison, probably ricin (derived from castor beans) or a superconcentrated dose of a relatively commonplace substance like nicotine. It is believed that the umbrella was in reality a compressed-gas-powered gun that fired the pellet into the victim's flesh. In a variation on the same theme, it would also be possible to inject a deadly bacteria like Septicemia or a chemical poison into a victim by means of a hypodermic needle concealed in the tip of an umbrella.

Materials made public by the Senate Intelligence Committee reveal that CIA technicians had developed an electric gun, called a bio-inoculator, capable of silently firing tiny poison darts that allegedly would dissolve in the victim before an autopsy could be performed. The weapon was accurate up to a distance of fifty feet. The poisons utilized in the darts ranged from cyanide to stonefish toxin.

King Hussein of Jordan narrowly escaped death a few years ago when assassins substituted acid for his nosedrops. Similarly, terrorists could administer Prussic acid (hydrocyanic acid) to an intended victim by means of a child's water pistol. If shot in the face, the victim would be rendered unconscious almost immediately, and death would follow within a few minutes. Nicotine sulfate, a popular insect poison, has the unique property that it can be absorbed through the skin. It could be hurled on a victim from a drinking mug or cup and, if not washed off immediately, could produce fatal results.

Experiments have been conducted at the CIA utilizing dimethylsulphoxide, better known as DMSO, which also can be absorbed directly through the skin. DMSO currently is used in some locales to give relief to arthritis sufferers. However, because of its ability to piggyback various medications into hard-to-reach joints and other afflicted parts of the body, DMSO could be combined with various chemical or biological poisons and administered to an unsuspecting victim. One scenario involves rubbing a DMSO/poison compound on the steering wheel of an auto. The substance would be absorbed through the driver's hands, and a few blocks later he would slump over and die, his death most likely attributed to natural causes. The DMSO/poison compound could also be put in a felt-tip pen. The assassin would only have to brush the tip of the pen against the intended victim's hand to carry out the plot. Such scenarios are purely speculative, however, and much work needs to be done to determine the transmissibility of various substances when combined with DMSO in view of the fact that, in some instances, the skin will permit the DMSO to penetrate but will reject the piggybacked substance.

By contrast to years past when poisons could be detected easily by a skilled pathologist, modern poisons are often, as noted earlier, high concentrations of rather ordinary substances. One drop of pure nicotine, for example, which can be extracted from pipe tobacco or cigarettes, is enough to kill an adult. A very high index of suspicion would be necessary for a medical examiner to consider the possibility that an apparent heart-attack or stroke victim died as the result of being infected with cobra venom, shellfish toxin, pure nicotine, or any of dozens of other chemical or biological poisons. According to Dr. N.J. Holter, "A good advantage to terrorists is that everyone is too lazy to find the real source of death, or not experienced enough."[32] Even then, only a skilled toxicologist would likely discover the real source of death.

On a macrolevel, terrorist scenarios include dumping toxic or incapacitating chemical compounds into city water systems. There have been recorded threats to dump both lysergic acid diethylamide (LSD) and nerve gas into urban reservoirs in this country, and the Los Angeles police, acting in conjunction with FBI agents, arrested a man who was preparing to poison the city's water system with a biological poison. The drug aminazin produces a loss of memory and interferes with muscular control and, hence, could be used to render an entire population helpless and incapable of defending itself. Mind-altering substances like LSD would produce highly negative behavioral changes in the target population and could lead to chaos and societal breakdown. According to Senate testimony in 1977, it was revealed that the CIA had run tests on aerosol spray cans containing LSD that simply could be sprayed on the intended victim.

Sexual habits could be profoundly altered as well. A 1974 study described how the U.K. penal system was preparing to introduce a sexual depressant into its prisons. "The opportunity to generate a new kind of anti-social behavior as a by-product of what is a benignly intended development," observed the study, is the kind of problem to which law enforcement agencies must be increasingly sensitive.[33] Scientists also have isolated what are, in effect, long distance messenger chemicals known as pheromones, which are secreted by humans and animals, that allegedly can be used to manipulate behavior, mood, and sexual attraction. Pheromones secreted by boars to induce sows to mate with them, for example, are routinely used to prepare sows for artificial insemination. The potential for surreptitiously modifying the behavior of a subject population through the use of things such as drugs and pheromones is not the stuff of fantasy; it is already a reality. Not only does it require special attention, but also authorities should monitor closely research being done in this area that might be utilized for antisocial purposes.

Some chemical compounds apparently have been developed for military use that affect equipment and hardware rather than human beings. One such chemical is an antilubricant agent that causes equipment to break down.[34] There are also reports of an emulsifying agent that can be sprayed on roads and highways to make them impassable.

The failure of a significant portion of the harvest in many agriculturally dependent and overpopulated countries could spell disaster for the leadership in power. In 1977, a Palestinian plot to undermine Israel's citrus exports by injecting oranges with dangerous contaminants, and thereby to disrupt its already tenuous balance-of-payments position, was uncovered. A similar effort by Huk terrorists in the Philippines to contaminate Dole pineapples had surfaced a few years earlier, but Philippine authorities had discovered the plot and hushed it up before any damage could be done. Chemical herbicides such as 2,4D and 2,4,5T could also become potent terrorist weapons against agricultural production. Used by the United States in Vietnam as part of an antifoliage and antifood campaign against North Vietnam and the Viet Cong, they are not difficult either to purchase or steal and could be employed to lay waste to vast tracts of land. While fissionable material and many poisons are subject to extremely tight security and controls, only routine precautions are taken to ensure that one of the deadliest of all manmade poisons, TCDD (2,3,7,8-tetrachlorodiben-zoparadioxin), known as Dioxin, which is a by-product of the manufacture of 2,4,5T and Silvex herbicides, does not fall into the wrong hands.

Absolute panic could be guaranteed if terrorists announced that they had sprayed a solution of benzidine over a populous area, either by air or from a tall building. Medical researchers note that benzidine can cause cancer up to twenty years after a single exposure.

The sabotage by terrorists, either covertly or overtly, of chemical plants and railway tank cars carrying dangerous chemicals such as poisonous chlorine gas also represents a potentially dangerous threat. Moreover, oil spills and spills of deadly chemicals into rivers and sewer systems could be accomplished by sabotaging equipment or simply turning on key valves. Although some risk is involved in handling what are often rusted and unstable containers, chemical dumps—many of them abandoned—represent a virtual treasure trove to serious-minded terrorists intent on inflicting mayhem. Such toxic chemicals can be dumped into rivers, reservoirs, or used to contaminate agricultural land. Many are unstable and explosive and can be utilized also to create intense fires and incendiary blasts.

Another sabotage scheme involves the changing of labels on dangerous chemicals stored in sacks or oil drums. The effectiveness of this can be demonstrated by the inadvertant contamination of livestock feed with highly toxic PCB several years ago in the upper Midwest.

Recalling the great plagues that decimated Europe during the Middle Ages, and parts of Africa and Asia even more recently, it is clear that various germs and biological agents conceivably could be utilized by terrorists with even more devastating impact than the detonation of a nuclear bomb. There was originally some speculation that the first outbreak of so-called legionnaire's disease in Philadelphia might be a terrorist action. While this was subsequently discounted, one observer noted, "It demonstrates what terrorists could do."[35]

Among the virulent biological agents that attack humans are those that produce Rocky Mountain spotted fever (rickettsial), yellow fever (viral), Q fever (rickettsial), anthrax (bacterial), typhoid fever (bacterial), glanders (bacterial), melioidosis (bacterial), dengue fever (viral), Rift Valley fever (viral), pneumonic plague (bacterial), and botulinal (toxin). Glanders, melioidosis, botulism, and pneumonic plague are associated with a high rate of fatalities.

Biological warfare could become extremely attractive to terrorists because of the relative ease and lack of expense required to manufacture deadly viruses and microorganisms and because they are highly suitable to covert dispersal. In 1977, a U.K. military laboratory actually advertised the sale of infectious bacteriological organisms in order to defray administrative overhead costs at the laboratory.[36]

The effectiveness of biological weapons has been recognized for many centuries. Plague-infected cadavers that had been catapulted over the walls produced a serious outbreak of the plague and broke the three-year siege of Feodosiya, on the Black Sea, in 1346.[37] The British spread smallpox among the Indian allies of France during the French and Indian Wars by distributing infected blankets to them. More recently, during the 1962 Cuban missile crisis, the United States was ready to bombard Cuba with an infectious biological incapacitating agent but relented only at the last minute.

Large quantities of anthrax bacteria would not be technically difficult to produce. Various treatment-resistant strains have been developed that can be dispersed easily through aerosol methods and that have a life of up to twenty years in the soil of affected areas.

Among the potential scenarios for biological malevolence are political assassinations carried out by using microbiological aerosols. In addition to methods already discussed, terrorists could spawn epidemics or administer virulent biological poisons to a target population by utilizing aerosol canisters or by dusting a city in crop-duster fashion. One estimate suggests that one aircraft could infect an area of almost 1,500 square acres with yellow-fever virus in a single outing.[38] The yellow-fever fatality rate for unvaccinated individuals is 30 to 40 percent, but it can be as high as 85 percent in virgin areas having no immunity to the disease.[39]

Live bacteria can be carried safely and conveniently by terrorists in light bulbs. When the release of the bacteria is desired, all the terrorist has to do is leave the light bulb on a subway track or roadway where it will be broken within a short period of time. The delay, however, permits the terrorist to remove himself safely before that happens. Bacteria can also be dispersed by means of explosions. They can be fed into a building's air conditioning or ventilation system, or simply dumped into an urban water system. Infected or contaminated parcels and letters also can be sent through the mails to unsuspecting victims.

Clark and other writers have raised the specter of genetic research by terrorists or their sympathizers with the intended purpose of creating laboratory monsters—disease-resistant strains of bacteria and viruses that could present special hazards to mankind.[40]

Terrorist Arsenals of the Future

The terrorist has elevated death and destruction to an art. He possesses the power to engage in mass murder, to reduce man's proudest accomplishments to rubble, to give immediacy to all resentments, and to strike out at all authority. Only the power of modern weapons makes this possible. Indeed, the new generation of weapons now beginning to appear in the world's military arsenals is not only revolutionizing the battlefield but also enabling terrorists and other malevolent nonstate actors to achieve what David R. Milbank has called "disproportionately large effects from the employment of minimal resources."[41] In the words of Ralph Lapp, "Technology now endows an act of irrationality with the greatest of consequences for society."[42] And, if this is the cause for alarm, just over the horizon are weapons, on the drawing boards or in various stages of development, of such awesome destructive power as to dwarf the imagination and capable of giving shape and form to our worst nightmares.

In this connection, following the lead of the world's military organizations, technologically competent terrorists in the not too distant future may strike out at society by creating famines and epidemics, altering weather patterns, and even blackmailing humanity with Buck Rogers-type weapons capable of producing "a hideous storm of terror."[43] The new frontier of weaponry flowing into the world's military arsenals will likely include destructive technologies based on lasers, electromagnetic waves, both ordinary and optical light, acoustic (or sound) waves, charged particle beams (CPBs), and high-energy vortex rings. Such technologies promise to transform the whole landscape of low-level warfare as well. Armed with these new technologies, mass murder could become the prerogative of one individual intent on single-handedly making war on society.

Both the USSR and the United States are engaged in research aimed at the development of CPB weapons, wherein subatomic particles are propelled at unbelievable velocities, approaching the speed of light, at military targets. Comparable to a bolt of raw energy, virtually anything in their path would be obliterated. Critical to the success of such a weapon, however, is the need for an enormous prime energy source, which presently is far from being realized. Nevertheless, a new power source known as the compensated pulse alternator has demonstrated an ability to produce extremely high energy pulses.

Work is also progressing on advanced laser weapons, but as with CPB weapons, the energy levels needed for such weapons still have not been attained. According to Anthony Tucker, however, "compared with lasers, high energy particle beams look extremely promising."[44] Approximating the death rays of science fiction, lasers operate on the principle of superconcentrated beams of light particles projected along a threadlike optical wave band. Until recently, the primary military application of lasers related to the targeting of munitions. However, the United States purportedly has experimented with lasers that one day may be able to knock planes and even satellites out of the air. At the present time, neither technology has been perfected and therefore are beyond the capabilities of any terrorist movement, but the day may come when CPB and laser weapons will be a fixture of military arsenals, and it can be anticipated that the development of small, compact, portable, highly efficient weapons based on the same technologies and suitable for the battlefield will follow.

The wounding power of a weapon is correlated in large measure to the velocity of its projectile. The velocity of small-arms projectiles is expected to increase significantly over the next decade or two, bringing with it new problems in treating wounds and firearm-related injuries. Even more terrifying is the prospect of the development of electromagnetic guns, with which a bullet can achieve a previously unimaginable velocity. Experimenters at the Los Alamos Scientific Laboratory have already fired plastic projectiles at velocities of more than 22,000 miles an hour, ten times the muzzle velocity of the world's most advanced rifles. The new weapon is called the railgun, and scientists postulate that, utilizing this technology, it might one day be possible to accelerate matter to velocities approaching the speed of light. The implications of such a development are enormous. According to Anthony Tucker, "The 'power density' of matter travelling at 10 percent the speed of light is a billion times that of the most mind-boggling laser. At that velocity the bolt energy of 1 gram of matter (the mass of a 0.22 airgun slug) would approximate to that of 1,000 kg of TNT."[45]

It is also possible to kill human beings with intense concentrations of light and sound, and in lesser concentrations, they can be used to disorient individuals severely. Optical light, for example, has an intrinsic brilliance at close range greater than the sun. Sound, in doses exceeding 120 decibels, will rupture the eardrums and in laboratory experiments has been focused strongly enough to set fire to objects. The day is not far off when light and sound weapons will be used in combat. A small light and sound weapon, which resembles an ordinary flashlight, is currently available and has been utilized successfully in executive protection activities. With a million-candlepower bulb and a piercing noise, the device temporarily disorients and incapacitates would-be attackers, with no permanent or lasting side effects. Like stun or flash grenades, this device is ideal for blinding or incapacitating adversaries like skyjackers in crowded environments where firearms are not feasible. Another passive electronic weapon, marketed under the name Taser, shoots a pulsating electric current into anyone who comes into contact with its antenna-like probes.

Microwaves may also have battlefield applications. Scientists believe that they can stop the heart and warm up the brain, producing death just as a high fever does. The problem with microwaves is focusing them in intense enough concentrations. If this problem is overcome, nations will be hard pressed to discover countermeasures to protect their populations.

New technologies for manipulating the human consciousness from afar are also being explored by U.S. and Soviet researchers. Although the results are far from conclusive at this time, should such techniques be perfected and employed by either hostile powers or terrorist organizations, public officials—perhaps even whole societies—could become telepathic targets, their behavior altered from hundreds, perhaps even thousands, or miles away without their ever being cognizant of it. Along similar lines, the USSR has been bombarding the United States with low-level radiowaves in recent years, the purpose of which remains a mystery to defense analysts, although some speculation has centered on experiments in behavioral modification.

On a more mundane, but in many respects no less terrifying, level, terrorists could threaten the economic viability of whole nations by creating infestations of agricultural pests like the Mediterranean fruit fly, which in 1981 threatened a substantial part of California's $14-billion-a-year farm industry. In a related development, Fidel Castro charged in 1981 that the United States was making war on the Cuban economy by infecting two of the island's principal crops with sugar rust and tobacco mold and by decimating its hog population with African swine fever. He also accused the United States of releasing mosquitos carrying dengue fever that has afflicted several hundred thousand Cubans on the island. More than likely, however, the dengue fever was brought back to Cuba by troops serving in Angola.

National economies also could be negatively affected by large-scale weather manipulation. Cloud seeding and other rain-making techniques could be used to cause flooding, reduce mobility, damage agricultural production, and disrupt ordinary patterns of life.

Mayhem Manuals

It is not necessary to attend a KGB-run training facility in Odessa or Baku, or a Palestinian camp in Lebanon, in order to learn the finer points of killing, maiming, and inflicting mayhem. Literally thousands of books—the product of a growing publishing industry devoted to mayhem manuals—will teach a would-be terrorist the fundamentals of bomb making, assassination, forgery, sabotage, knife fighting, torture techniques, and sniping. Such manuals are available to anyone, regardless of age, mental health, or criminal record, with the price of purchase. While most buyers are apparently benign armchair warriors, who apparently enjoy reading about how to kill and maim fellow human beings, mayhem manuals are extremely valuable to terrorists and criminals eager to hone their destructive skills and are widely circulated among terrorist groups, both in the United States and abroad.

The five-volume *How to Kill* series stands alone in terms of sheer depravity.[46] Each crisply written volume contains ten lessons—illustrated with lurid drawings and photographs—focusing on subjects such as smothering, poisoning, neck breaking, splitting someone's skull with a hatchet, decapitation, garrotting, stabbing, and shooting. The author, John Minnery, surveys a wide variety of weapons including hit grenades, blow guns, crescents, silent grenades (perfect for "large gatherings such as ballrooms, receptions, or press conferences"), bicycle-pump hypodermics, ice axes, butterfly land mines ("adaptable for air piracy and conference crashing because of its low metallic signature and size"), shoe guns, killer knuckles, and booby-trapped urinals. He describes how to make an antitank weapon in one's home that can be set up opposite an apartment building and fired by remote control. This is accompanied by a detailed examination of the kinds of shrapnel one might use in the grenade fired by the weapon. One of the most gruesome deaths outlined by Minnery, which he calls the "Barrel of Laughs," involves stuffing a live victim into a standard oil drum, buttocks first. "Since he [the victim] cannot extricate himself," Minnery writes, "he will expire from constricture and muscle exhaustion."[47]

How to Kill, volume 1, is loaded with information on how to assassinate VIPs, providing tips on where to stand, the choice of weapons, where to aim for maximum effectiveness, and various shooting techniques. It even advises potential assassins to consider using explosive ammunition such as that fired by John Hinckley, Jr., at President Reagan in March 1981. Minnery concludes by observing that, "The will to kill, the complete lack of sympathy and compassion, and no hesitation in killing the subject is paramount. You must take his life as detachedly as you might swat a fly or crush an ant."[48]

A good deal of the material in Minnery's books seems designed to assist the would-be political assassin. Not only does he discuss bogus campaign buttons that are in fact nails that can be driven into a victim's heart, but also he describes exploding microphones that can be placed in front of political speakers.

If one desires to make a murder look like a suicide, Minnery provides the reader with a handy twelve-point checklist of things to do to fool the authorities. He also details the best weather conditions for killing, calling it "bio-climatology applied to necrotechnics." In this connection, he notes on the one hand that warm, sunny days are the best time for shooting or stabbing a victim since "there is no obstruction to blood or breath circulation." Cold, blustery days, on the other hand, are the "best time for strangulation, choking and some poisonings." By taking into account such factors "when planning a hit," Minnery asserts, the killer can hope to gain an extra edge or advantage.[49]

Minnery's books are by no means unique. Other publications available to students of mayhem are *Mantracking, Special Forces Demolition Techniques, Ambush and Counter Ambush, Deal the First Deadly Blow, Handbook for the Irish Republican Army, Assassination: Theory and Practice, Training the Gunfighter, The Revenge Book, Improvised Weapons of the American Underground, Home Workshop Silencers I, Bloody Iron, Unconventional Warfare Devices and Techniques, Improvised Munitions Systems, Boobytraps, Sniping, Elements of Explosives Production, CIA Explosives for Sabotage,* and *Combat: House to House. Hi-Low Booms* gives the reader formulas for making 230 different explosive mixtures in the home. *Surreptitious Entry* and *Lock Picking Simplified* provide the reader with an introduction to planning and executing so-called black-bag jobs. An old favorite of left-wing underground groups is *The Anarchists' Cookbook,* a bomb-making manual available over the counter at many bookstores. It is also possible to purchase revolutionary tomes like *150 Questions for the Guerrilla,* by General Alberto Bayo, "the man who trained Che and Castro," and Carlos Marighella's *Mini-manual of the Urban Guerrilla,* at many bookstores.

Among the books that deserve special attention is *The Poor Man's James Bond.*[50] Written by a far-right radical, Kurt Saxon, during the Vietnam War, and "affectionately dedicated to Lee Harvey Oswald, James Earl Ray, Sirhan Bishara Sirhan, and Senator Ted Kennedy," it has recently emerged as one of the staples of the survivalist cult. It described in florid detail how to make pipe bombs, fire bombs, napalm, dynamite, zip guns, so-called people's grenades, and poisons and has sections devoted to pursuits such as blowing up a car, beating a metal detector, and evading pursuit.

Saxon also informs his readers how to modify an old Winchester Model 12 shotgun into a so-called Saxon Special that can be fired like a submachine gun. Despite federal regulations prohibiting more than three shells in a shotgun, Saxon waxes euphoric about his eleven-shot creation. "Think of it!" he exudes. "Eleven great billows of Single O Buckshot in about four seconds. Clear the street in as short a time as it takes to swing the gun. Really piles 'em up. And noise? Lord, what noise!"[51]

In a section entitled "Testing Poisons," Saxon notes that, "The best subject is a wino. . . . Put the dose you want to test in a half full fifth bottle of sweet wine. Then tuck it in the next alley where the wino will be sure to find it. . . . If the nest has a dead wino in it the next morning you've figured out the right dose."[52]

According to a transcript of a conversation recorded by federal agents, George Korkala, accused with Frank Terpil of trying illegally to sell 10,000 machine guns to police undercover agents, described, in a page from Saxon's book, how he helped test the effectiveness of 50 kilos of cyanide he sold to Middle Eastern terrorists. The poison was slipped into a patron's soup in a Beirut restaurant. The patron took one spoonful of soup and slumped forward, face in the soup bowl, dead.

A companion piece to *The Poor Man's James Bond* is *Arson by Electronics,* which was prepared by the State of Florida in order to educate law enforcement officials to recognize fires and explosions of a criminal nature. Unfortunately, it is so detailed that Saxon reproduces the study to teach aspiring arsonists how to start fires and get away with it.

Three other books that rank as classics in the bizarre realm of mayhem manuals are *Black Medicine: The Dark Art of Death* and its sequels, *Black Medicine,* volumes 2 and 3.[53] The first volume is an anatomical study of all the vital points of the human body or, in the author's words, the "one-hundred-and-seventy parts of the human body where a minimum of force will produce a maximum impact on the person's ability to fight." It includes photographs of how to cut someone's throat and how to blind them with a spray can of insecticide. Also, a section for pistol-wielding assassins discusses the body's chief zones of vulnerability to bullets. Volume 2 is a discussion of improvised weapons, ranging from chainsaws and oven cleaners to ludicrous suggestions such as throwing a cat in your opponent's face. The third volume in the trilogy, *Black Medicine III,* is subtitled "Low Blows," and the publisher's promotional literature warns that, "*Low Blows* is not for readers with weak stomachs." Nevertheless, the public is urged to "buy now, before you need to use these secrets in the streets."

While such literature not only offends our sensibilities but also, in the wrong hands, both frightens and threatens peaceful and orderly societies, it is not illegal. Although there may be some merit in permitting serious researchers and law enforcement officials to have access to such materials, there is no compelling or persuasive reason that it should be available to everyone. Free speech is indeed a prerequisite for a free society; nevertheless, in a world beset by soaring crime and the scourge of transnational terrorism, there have to be some limits, as Mr. Justice Holmes indicated when he wrote, "The most stringent protection of free speech would not protect a man falsely shouting fire in a theater and causing a panic." If it is illegal to cause a false panic by shouting fire in a crowded theater, then it follows that there should surely be some restraints on printing and distributing books and pamphlets that instruct individuals how to firebomb the theater and murder the audience. Such publications cross the line that separates constitutionally protected free speech from activities that threaten the lives of U.S. citizens and the national security.

Conclusion

The nature of warfare has been revolutionized in recent years by, on the one hand, the increasing power and accuracy of nuclear weapons that have rendered them efficacious only as a mode of mutual deterrence and, on the other hand, by the development of awesome yet relatively accessible and inexpensive weapons that have placed unparalleled power in the hands of a single combat soldier or terrorist. This has produced a strange asymmetry in the defense capabilities of the great powers, where they are capable of destroying the world in the flick of an eye but are all too vulnerable to the designs of a lone terrorist. Indeed, as Hannah Arendt has observed, "The more dubious and uncertain the instrument of violence has become in international relations, the more it has gained in reputation and appeal in domestic affairs, specifically in the matter of revolution."[54]

In this connection, it is not surprising what terrorists have done in recent years. What is surprising is what they have not done in view of the extraordinary range of new weapons and targets available to them. They tend to be profoundly conservative, wary of experimentation, and inclined to employ weapons and tactics that are already proven rather than to innovate. For the foreseeable future, it is unlikely that terrorists will be armed with anything more deadly than plastic bombs, automatic weapons, shoulder-fired missiles, and grenade launchers. This is not to minimize the impact that terrorists will have in coming years but simply to assert that no evidence suggests that a dramatic departure from previous modes of terrorist conflict will occur. As Frederick J. Hacker has noted, the Molotov cocktail, because of its simplicity and the commonness of its ingredients, is a "much more decisive invention than the atomic bomb."[55]

The day may come, however, when terrorists seek to develop a weapon of mass destruction, such as a chemical or biological weapon, that could be used to unleash an epidemic of violence. Unlike nuclear weapons, control of such substances and related technologies is difficult, if not altogether impossible. Time is on the side of the terrorists. They can make countless attempts to build or employ a fright weapon, fail every time, and more than likely emerge no worse for wear. By contrast, the embattled governments of the world need only let down their guard once for a worst-case scenario to occur.

Notes

1. Karl Heinzen, "Murder," in *Die Evolution* (Biel: February/March reprinted in Walter Laqueur, *The Terrorism Reader* (New York: New American Library, 1978), p. 59.

2. Hannah Arendt, *On Violence* (New York: Harcourt, Brace & World, 1977), p. 48.

3. David Fromkin, "The Strategy of Terrorism," *Foreign Affairs* (July 1975), p. 683.

4. Carlos Marighella, "The Minimanual of the Urban Guerrilla," mimeographed, p. 23.

5. Interview with General Joseph J. Cappucci, retired from the U.S. Air Force, July 1978.

6. Major-General John Owen, ed., *Infantry Weapons of the NATO Armies,* 2d ed. (London: Brassey's Publishers Ltd., 1979), p. 26.

7. Heckler and Koch, Defense Technology Division catalog, 1978.

8. Jim Hougan, *Spooks* (New York: William Morrow and Company, 1978), p. 35.

9. Major-General John Owen, ed., *Infantry Weapons of the Warsaw Pact Armies,* 2d ed. (London: Brassey's Publishers Ltd., 1979), p. 49.

10. Richard Clutterbuck, *Living with Terrorism* (London: Cassell and Co., 1973), p. 144.

11. Karl Heinzen, "Murder," in *The Terrorism Reader,* ed. Walter Laqueur (New York: New American Library, 1978), p. 62.

12. Ibid.

13. Ibid.

14. By contrast to European terrorists who often favored bombs as a tool for assassination, U.S. assassins have used firearms in the commission of nearly every assault on major public figures, including the successful assassinations of Presidents Abraham Lincoln, James Garfield, William McKinley, and John F. Kennedy; Senators Huey Long and Robert Kennedy; and the Reverend Martin Luther King, Jr. Similarly, guns were used in the unsuccessful attempts on the lives of Presidents Andrew Jackson, Theodore Roosevelt, Franklin D. Roosevelt, Harry S. Truman, Gerald Ford, and Ronald Reagan, and the assassination attempt that left former Alabama Governor George Wallace paralyzed.

15. Robert Moss, "Counter Terrorism" *The Economist,* Brief Booklet no. 29 (no date), p. 10.

16. Clutterbuck, *Living with Terrorism,* p. 78.

17. For an excellent discussion of fuses, see Christopher Dobson and Ronald Payne, *The Terrorists* (New York: Facts on File, 1979), pp. 122-125.

18. U.S. Congress, Senate, Committee on the Judiciary, *Control of Explosives*, 95th Cong., 1st sess. p. 18.

19. Kurt Saxon, *The Poor Man's James Bond* (Eureka, Calif.: Atlan Formularies, 1972), pp. 13-14.

20. Bernard Brodie and M. Fawn, *From Crossbow to H-Bomb* (Bloomington: Indiana University Press, 1973), pp. 14-15.

21. Saxon, *Poor Man's James Bond,* p. 24.

22. U.S. Army, *Special Forces Demolition Techniques,* reprinted from Army Field Manual FM 31-20, December 1965, (Boulder, Colo.: Paladin Press, no date), p. 33.

23. Brian Jenkins, "The Potential Arsenal of Tomorrow's Terrorists," in *Protection of Assets* ed. The Merritt Company (Los Angeles: The Merritt Company, 1974), pp. 18-21.

24. Ibid., pp. 18/23.

25. Saxon, *Poor Man's James Bond,* p. 2.

26. Richard D. McCarthy, *The Ultimate Folly* (New York: Alfred A. Knopf, 1969), p. 27.

27. Letter from Dr. N.J. Holter of the Holter Research Foundation, 21 January 1977.

28. Richard C. Clark, *Technological Terrorism* (Old Greenwich, Conn.: Devin-Adair Company, 1980), p. 111.

29. Lowell Ponte, "The Dawning Age of Technoterrorism," *Next* (July/August 1980):53.

30. Clark, *Technological Terrorism,* p. 110.

31. *Washington Post,* 23 September 1981.

32. Interview with Dr. N.J. Holter of the Holter Research Foundation, 23 December 1976.

33. Criminal Justice Project, William R. Drake, director, and Thomas E. Kelly, ed., "Community Crime Prevention and Local Official" (Report prepared under Contract no. 73TA990004 by the Law Enforcement Assistance Administration, U.S. Department of Justice, and the National League of Cities-U.S. Conference of Mayors, Winter 1974), p. 23.

34. Stockholm International Peace Research Institute, *Weapons of Mass Destruction and the Environment* (New York: Crane, Russak & Company, 1977), p. 34.

35. Interview with Dr. N.J. Holter of the Holter Research Foundation, 23 December 1976.

36. Clark, *Technological Terrorism,* p. 108.

37. Stockholm International Peace Research Institute, *Weapons of Mass Destruction,* p. 41.

38. Ibid., p. 43.

39. Ibid.

40. Clark, *Technological Terrorism,* p. 140.

41. David L. Milbank, "International and Transnational Terrorism: Diagnosis and Prognosis," Draft Working Paper (Washington, D.C.: Conference on International Terrorism, U.S. Department of State, 25-26 March 1976), p. 18.

42. Ralph Lapp, "The Ultimate Blackmail," *The New York Times Magazine,* 4 February 1973, p. 12.

43. John Webster, *The Duchess of Malfi.*

44. Anthony Tucker, "Beam Weapons," in *International Weapon Developments,* 4th ed. (Oxford: Brassey's Publishers Ltd., 1980), p. 15.

45. Ibid., p. 23.

46. Minnery, John, *How to Kill,* Vols. 1-5, (Boulder, Colorado: Paladin Press, 1973-1980).

47. Minnery, John, *How to Kill,* Vol. 4, (Boulder, Colorado: Paladin Press, 1979), p. 84.

48. Minnery, John, *How to Kill,* Vol. 1, (Boulder, Colorado: Paladin Press, 1973), p. 51.

49. Minnery, John, *How to Kill,* Vol. 3, (Boulder, Colorado: Paladin Press, 1979), p. 35.

50. Saxon, *op. cit.*

51. Ibid., p. 28.

52. Ibid., p. 48.

53. Mashiro, N., *Black Medicine,* Vols. 1-3, (Boulder, Colorado: Paladin Press, 1978-1981).

54. Arendt, *On Violence,* p. 100.

55. Frederick J. Hacker, interview in the *Washington Post,* 9 February 1977.

7 Targets of the Future: New Frontiers of Terror

I can take a troop of Boy Scouts and train them to sabotage the pipeline system and shut down 80 percent of the energy going to the Eastern coast.
—Maynard M. Stephens[1]

Terrorism is war without limits, and as such, virtually anyone or anything is fair game as a terrorist target. Nothing is sacred. In some instances, the more sacred a potential target the better, because that will guarantee the production of even greater public revulsion and horror and, hence, the communication of the terrorist's message to an even larger audience. The attack on the life of Pope John Paul II in May 1981, as he greeted tourists in St. Peter's Square, serves as a good case in point. Few other assassination attempts could have produced the same profound shock and dismay, the political reverberations, and the worldwide outpouring of grief that the attack on the Pope inspired.

The modern terrorist, however, does not go begging for targets. As John Webster wrote in *The Duchess of Malfi,* "death hath ten thousand doors for men to take their exits."[2] In this connection, the range of targets available today to terrorists and other violent nonstate actors is a virtually limitless horizon, restrained only by the terrorist's imagination and the weapons available to him. Terrorist targets have ranged from airliners, military depots, power transmission lines, department stores, movie theaters, embassies, and innocent civilians to Israeli athletes at the 1972 Munich Olympics, an interstate bus hijacked in the Bronx by a Panamanian native serving in the U.S. armed forces, swimming pools in San Jose poisoned with a powerful herbicide, the offices of a rugby club sponsoring the U.S. tour of a South African team, citrus crops injected with mercury, and a Vermeer painting stolen from a museum and held for ransom. During the period of turmoil preceding the collapse of the shah's regime, Iranian terrorists vented their hatred on anything Western, including movie theaters and places that sold liquor, targets that normally would have aroused little anger in most other places.

Some terrorists perfect an ability to strike at one or two types of targets, whereas others will attack anything. One spate of attacks in Rome, noteworthy more for its eclecticism than its effectiveness, witnessed terrorists firebombing at least a dozen targets in less than ninety minutes, including cars, buses, a police

---

Portions of this chapter appeared in Neil C. Livingstone, "Low-Level Violence and Future Targets," *Conflict* 2, no. 4:177–219.

barracks, four branch offices of the Christian Democratic party, and telephone company offices.

This chapter examines the universe of new targets available to the perpetrators of low-level violence. While the targets identified hereafter are most often referred to in the context of terrorist violence, terrorism is but one distinguishable form of low-level violence, and many of the targets also have relevance in the context of guerrilla warfare, insurrections, partisan activities during military occupations, labor strife, and violence perpetrated by organized crime and other deviant nonstate actors. Moreover, in the event that a state of belligerency exists, these same targets must be considered prime objectives of saboteurs and fifth columnists.

According to Robert Taber, the ideal terrain for a successful guerrilla operation is a country "that is more rural than urban, mountainous rather than flat, thickly forested rather than bare, with extensive railway lines, bad roads, and an economy that is preponderantly agricultural rather than industrial."[3] By contrast to the requirements for guerrilla warfare, the ideal staging ground for revolutionary terrorism is just the opposite: Modern terrorism thrives best in an urban, industrial, nontraditional environment. The more complex and interdependent the society and its infrastructure, the more vulnerable it usually is to the designs of "technoaggressors."[4] In this connection, Hannah Arendt has observed that "bigness is afflicted with vulnerability,"[5] and herein lie both the threat and the strength of contemporary terrorism. The complexity of our modern world affords violence-prone nonstate actors with unparalleled and previously unimaginable opportunities for mischief. A very few people who know how the system works can inflict tremendous damage on it. Our overbuilt cities and their slender lifelines—water, power, sewers, communications—are especially vulnerable to terrorists. This vulnerability would have been impossible in past centuries. "One hundred and fifty years ago if someone wanted to put out all of the lights in a village, he had to go from house to house to do it," notes Walter Laqueur. "Now he blows up one generator and all of the lights in the city go out."[6] The great power blackout in New York, or the strike by a handful of bridge tenders that virtually paralyzed the city, though not the result of terrorist action, serve as vivid examples of what terrorists could do. Indeed, any basic or essential service upon which large numbers of people depend constitutes an attractive target for violence in view of the disruption such an action is likely to produce and the resulting and far-reaching publicity it is sure to generate.

However, the threat does not end with the city. Whole societies and their complex economies, food production and distribution systems, communications networks, energy production, and storage and transport systems present the contemporary terrorist with unparalleled opportunities for disruption. According to Brian Jenkins:

> We are reaching the point of industrialization and population growth when the technical interdependencies of modern society—food on fertilizer on energy on fuel on transportation on communications—are so great and the margins of surplus so slim that a minor disruption in any single area can have tremendous cascading effects on nearly everything else.[7]

Ironically, the more complex an interdependent society becomes, the more vulnerable it becomes to rudimentary, even primitive, weapons. According to one CIA official, in the hands of a knowledgeable saboteur who knew where to throw it, one brick could shut down operation of the Panama Canal for up to three weeks. Similarly, as Robert Moss has noted, it required only a single mortar round to inflict $5 billion worth of damage on the U.S. military base at Khe Sanh in 1968.[8]

It is not terrorism, measured by the yardstick of the past, that is truly frightening but instead the future potential of terrorism. Just as civilians and their homes and cities are no longer exempted from the patterns of conventional twentieth century warfare, so too, under most circumstances, are there no exemptions from terrorist violence. Terrorism is battle with no quarter, no holds barred, and from the perspective of most terrorists, anything is fair game, nothing is too sacred to be considered a target, unless it is felt that the ensuing backlash would outweigh any practical benefit that would be achieved by striking successfully at the target in question.

In the not too distant future, terrorists may attack targets such as nuclear power plants, LNG transport vessels and storage facilities, power grids, subway systems, refineries, microwave stations, urban water systems and water impoundments, levees, and dikes. Many of these targets, including those that fall into the category of the so-called catastrophic targets, are protected only by minimal or rudimentary security systems.

Which Nations Are Most Likely to Become Terrorist Targets?

Terrorism is a rare phenomenon in societies under strict authoritarian rule. For example, terrorist violence in the USSR and other Eastern bloc countries has been negligible in the postwar period and confined largely to an occasional airline skyjacking by someone seeking political asylum in the West. The only other reported terrorist incidents in the USSR in recent years include the bombing of a crowded Moscow subway in 1977 that left several people dead and as many as twenty injured and the 1969 disturbance by a man dressed in the uniform of a Soviet army lieutenant who fired a number of shots into a motorcade carrying four Soviet cosmonauts. Most likely, the USSR and its allies have suffered other degradations at the hands of terrorists that go unreported in the West because of the state management of news in those societies; nevertheless, the level of violence is most assuredly still quite low by Western standards.

While some of the issues and complaints that give rise to terrorism certainly exist in the USSR, the preconditions that facilitate its growth and development do not. Indeed, terrorism is incompatible with tightly regimented systems that place harsh restrictions on individual mobility and interaction and in which the influence of internal secret police organizations is pervasive.

By contrast, the societies most vulnerable to terrorism today are those that are the most open, where the highest degree of personal mobility and the most extensive personal freedoms exist along with government safeguards against arbitrary action by the state against critics and opponents. The terrorist finds the most unhindered climate for recruiting members, procuring arms, disseminating propaganda, and conducting operations against the state in such open societies.

"Terrorism occurs only where governments put a high price on life and civil liberties," notes a recent editorial in the *Washington Post,* referring to South Moluccan terrorism in the Netherlands. "You may have noticed that nobody seems to try taking hostages in, shall we say, Eastern Europe. You haven't heard much lately about the Tupamaros of Uruguay; the government there has settled their hash through methods the Dutch would never countenance."[9] Authoritarian governments recognize few legal or moral restraints when combating terrorism. Operating most often under the aegis of internal security statutes or martial law, which provide a thin veil of legitimacy to their actions, state police and military organizations hunt down and round up suspected terrorists and their supporters. Many are imprisoned, tortured, and even executed without regard to considerations of due process.

In the liberal democracies, high premium is put on a government's ability to govern without resort to violence; legal and constitutional safeguards against violations of individual rights usually take precedence over considerations of political necessity. "If the government is provoked into introducing emergency powers, suspending habeas corpus, or invoking martial law," writes Paul Wilkinson, "it confronts the paradox of suspending democracy in order to preserve it."[10] In 1979, Italy suffered from the highest level of terrorist-related violence in the world, not Israel or Northern Ireland or any of the other regions characterized by protracted terrorist conflicts. As a consequence, stern new laws have been enacted in Italy to give the government sweeping powers—at the expense of Italian democracy—that were not even previously demanded by outspoken right-wing politicians. Similarly, in recent years, the governments of both Argentina and Uruguay have adopted draconian measures to combat endemic terrorist violence, abandoning any pretense of democratic government. Argentina, moreover, has been cited by the Inter-American Human Rights Commission for violations of human rights in conjunction with the methods it has employed in its struggle against terrorism.

In view of the fact that the ground rules for combating terrorism in the United States and the liberal democracies of Western Europe are far more restrained than in totalitarian regimes, out of consideration for the maintenance of civil liberties and a commonly held belief in the need for a measured response to internal violence, such countries will remain terrorist targets, if only by small groups of malcontents, for the indefinite future.

Historically, sustained outbreaks of terrorist violence were most often associated with the Third World since terrorism was, in many instances—for example, Algeria, Kenya, Cyprus, Israel, Angola—employed as a strategy for throwing off the yoke of foreign domination and achieving independence. With the decline of European colonialism, however, terrorism also has declined in the Third World, to be supplanted by relentless state terror in many countries.

Today, in the Third World, the societies most vulnerable to internal turmoil and terrorism are those in which economic progress has been noticeable but in which real gains cannot keep pace with rising public expectations. This leads inevitably to social and economic stress and ultimately to disparate elements within the society resorting to violence to get what they perceive as their rightful share of political power and the national wealth. Recent terrorist violence in El Salvador, Colombia, and the Philippines serve as good examples of the vulnerability of transitional developing nations to this kind of discontent.

Just as many terrorists are otherwise normal men and women for whom things have not gone well, whose personal ambitions and fortunes have been frustrated, such as the large number of JRA members who turned to terrorism only after failing to win entry to prestigious universities, it should be noted that in nations where the engine of progress suddenly slows down and general economic stagnation and political malaise set in, leaving many people, often with newly awakened aspirations, frustrated and disillusioned, an extremely high potential for terrorist disruption exists. Until World War II, Uruguay and Argentina were among the stablest and most upwardly mobile nations of Latin America, but when a prolonged period of economic decline occurred, public frustration gave rise to the Tupamaros movement in Uruguay and to dozens of far-left and far-right terrorist groups in Argentina.

In a situation analogous to the absence of terrorist violence in the USSR and the Eastern bloc countries, terrorism rarely occurs in the most wretched countries from an economic point of view, the so-called Fourth World—the poorest of the poor, the twenty-five most impoverished nations. This is in part due to the fact that, almost without exception, every one of these nations is ruled by a harsh authoritarian regime. Even more significant, public apathy and the weight of centuries of inertia in such countries are simply too great to be overcome easily. To understand this lesson, one has only to recall Guevara's mounting despair and disillusionment with the Bolivian peasantry, which he compared to unfeeling stones, when he was attempting to transplant the Cuban revolution onto the South American mainland. Ordinarily, people will take up arms against the established order only when there is some reason to believe that they can improve their condition through their actions.

Choice of a Target

While a person can become a victim of terrorists purely by happenstance—because he or she is simply in the wrong place at the wrong time—this does not imply that the decision to strike at a particular target was similarly an indiscriminate or impulsive decision on the part of the terrorist. Quite the opposite; by contrast to those who regard terrorism as mindless and uncalculated, it is most often meticulous, premeditated violence, and the selection of the target is, therefore, a product of careful consideration. Three factors, however, typically form the basis for the terrorist's decision: (1) the weapons available to the terrorist, (2) the question of opportunity (in other words, the vulnerability of the target), and (3) the goal or effect the terrorist hopes to achieve through his action. The first two considerations are fairly self-evident, but what the terrorist intends to accomplish is more complex and open to some debate. Let us examine the major goals of most terrorist actions.

Symbolic

A great majority of all terrorist acts are symbolic, designed to convey a message, usually one of vulnerability, to a specific target population by creating a climate of fear, dread, even panic. The relatively high efficiency of terrorism, according to Phillip A. Karber, is due to its symbolic nature.[11] Hence, terrorists usually seek to maximize the symbolic value of the targets they select. In this connection, Lord Mountbatten's 1979 assassination by IRA terrorists was a symbolic act designed to project the power and resolve of the IRA to the entire world and, at the same time, to convince the British people of the awful price they will have to pay if the government maintains its present course with respect to the conflict in Northern Ireland. As for Lord Mountbatten, he was 79 years old, retired and ailing, his distinguished career behind him. His brutal murder served no practical purpose in the sense that it did not remove a figure instrumental or even directly connected to the problems in Northern Ireland. Mountbatten was killed because he was a popular and respected member of the royal family, a mover and shaker in the era immediately preceding, during, and just after World War II, whose death at the hands of terrorists would have a profound psychological effect on the British public; and as Silverman and Jackson have observed, the psychological consequences of a terrorist act are often more important than the act itself.[12] Thus, public opinion, not the victim, is, in the case of Mountbatten as it is in most instances, the real target of the terrorists.

The sum of the deaths of many ordinary men and women may, in the long run, however, have an even greater impact on public opinion than the assassination of a figure like Mountbatten due to the fact that the general populace can identify more readily with persons like themselves who become victims of terrorist action. The murder of an Aldo Moro or Lord Mountbatten may produce widespread indignation and public grief, but the average individual rarely feels personally threatened by the death of so removed a figure as a premier or an English lord; however, if another ordinary fellow with a similar job, family, and mortgage is killed in a terrorist bomb blast, the average person will begin to feel vulnerable. If the violence persists, he will soon fear not only for his own life but also for the lives of his family, friends, and loved ones, and fear of this kind is debilitating. Terrorism has the greatest impact when it is brought home to the masses of ordinary citizens. "What is more effective?" asks Nathan Yalin-Mor, "To kill ministers responsible for the policies, who can be replaced; or to fight against uniformed men? To convince their parents that it is a senseless war and that it should be stopped."[13] After their enormous losses in World War II, reasoned Yalin-Mor and his Stern gang confederates, the British were, as a nation, physically and emotionally exhausted, and the public would not stand for a new round of fighting and for renewed calls to sacrifice, with the accompanying loss of life and national treasure, in a conflict over a parched strip of land along the eastern Mediterranean that held little, if any, significance to the average British subject. Surely it was not worth the sacrifice of one's own life or the life of a loved one. For the Jewish terrorists, the flag-draped coffins of British sons and fathers and husbands was a strategy to bring the war home to the United Kingdom; and as history records, the strategy was successful.

Not only people but also virtually any target may have symbolic importance. In this connection, the destruction of targets such as a bridge, a power-generating plant, or a transit system could potentially inconvenience thousands of people, disrupting the ordinary flow of life and undermining the public's confidence in the government's ability to govern. This, in turn, could potentially create widespread discontent that might play into the hands of the terrorists. Nevertheless, this kind of terrorism can backfire as it did in Malaya during the 1950s. The Politburo of the Malayan Communist party was forced to order Marxist terrorists to stop "attacking reservoirs, power stations, and other public services. Rubber trees, tin mines, and factories must not be destroyed because of the workers who lose their employment."[14]

Allegiance to Own Community

Although as Laqueur notes, terrorism is always more popular against foreigners than against a terrorist's own countrymen, the targets of terrorist violence are sometimes members of the terrorist's own community.[15] This willingness to kill members of one's own community, even members of one's own family who oppose the will of the terrorists, was best expressed in the Mau Mau oath:

> If I am called upon to do so, with four others, I will kill a European. If I am called on to do so, I will kill a Kikuyu who is against the Mau Mau, even if it be my mother or my father or brother or sister or wife or child.[16]

Terrorism of this kind is utilized as a means of maintaining security, consolidating the terrorist organization's position relative to other groups asserting rival claims to power, and finally, controlling dissent within the community wherein the terrorist's support is rooted. A significant part of the Zionist terror in Palestine was directed against other Jews, many of whom had grave misgivings about a strategy of violence against the British, particularly during World War II when the United Kingdom was one of the last remaining bulwarks against Nazi Germany that systematically was exterminating millions of Jews across continental Europe. According to Robert B. Asprey, "anyone who opposed creation of a Jewish state became fair game" in the eyes of the Stern gang and its followers.[17] Similarly, during the conflict over Cyprus, EOKA (Ethniki Organosis Kypriakou Agonistov) terrorists killed "more Cypriots—as 'traitors' or 'collaborators'—than it did British security forces or government officials."[18]

Punishment

Terrorism can serve as a means of punishing opponents for particularly harsh or unconscionable behavior. For example, Sir Harold MacMichael, the U.K. high commissioner for Palestine, was blamed by Zionist extremists for the drownings of some 800 Jewish refugees aboard the dilapidated tramp steamer, S.S. *Struma,* in 1942, which broke up in rough seas and went down with all aboard after MacMichael refused to permit the ship to land its passengers in Palestine, despite vigorous appeals from a score of nations to reverse his decision on humanitarian grounds. The incident profoundly shocked the Jewish population in Palestine, which was appalled by the high commissioner's seemingly pitiless posture with respect to the *Struma* and its passengers, and outraged world public opinion.[19] In retaliation, Stern gang terrorists under Rabbi Shamir attempted to ambush MacMichael by spraying his car with machine-gun fire, but the high commissioner escaped with only minor wounds. Realizing that a further attempt on MacMichael's life would be most difficult because of beefed-up security measures that had been put into place following the incident, the terrorists determined instead to strike at Lord Moyne, the U.K. resident minister in Cairo, a more accessible target and the only man, it was believed, who could have overruled MacMichael's decision regarding the *Struma.*

During the early 1960s, the OAS attempted repeatedly to assassinate French President Charles De Gaulle in order to avenge what they regarded as his sellout of French Algeria. However, unlike the plot against Lord Moyne, their efforts failed.

Achievement of Military Objectives

Terrorists may select a target such as a bridge, arsenal, computer, oil storage tanks, or a military convoy because its destruction has objective military importance. By denying the enemy certain critical assets, terrorists can hope to make the conflict a more difficult one to prosecute.

Similarly, systematic removal of key government officials, along with leading government supporters, members of the press, military and police officers, by assassination, kidnapping, and intimidation, often will undermine the efficiency and operations of the enemy and have a debilitating effect on the whole society. In the industrialized West, few men or women are truly indispensable or irreplaceable; however, the less-developed countries often have only a small trained and educated elite, and the loss of even a small number of the people possessing leadership or technical skills can be crippling to the government in power. In South Vietnam, for example, the Viet Cong carried out a quiet war of attrition against village headmen, police and military officials, and other leading citizens, and soon the leadership ranks of the South Vietnamese government in many important districts were depleted. Subsequent replacement of these local officials was hampered by a pervasive sense of intimidation as qualified Vietnamese declined to serve in key positions lest they, too, become victims of Viet Cong terror.

Only rarely can the assassination of a key official or head of state change the course of a particular conflict or alter the future of a nation. In the early 1960s, the pervasive belief within the U.S. intelligence community was that Castro's charismatic leadership was indispensable to the Cuban revolution and the maintenance of Cuba as a Soviet puppet state in the Caribbean. After enlisting disparate elements from organized crime and the Cuban exile underground, the CIA launched Operation Mongoose, which involved repeated efforts to assassinate Castro and his principal lieutenants, Raul Castro and Che Guevara. Without question, Castro's removal would have seriously jeopardized the future of Marxism in Cuba in view of the fact that no leader of sufficient stature, or *personalismo*, could have inherited Castro's mantle and governed in his place.[20]

In the final analysis, however, assassination is a risky business and can "politically boomerang if the target is unwisely chosen or the assassination unwisely timed."[21]

Financial Gain

Finally, a target may be selected for its financial potential, especially in instances of kidnappings, bank robberies, and extortion from multinational corporations. Amounts that once would have been regarded as nothing less than sensational, ransoms of $5-10 million dollars in exchange for kidnapped business executives, are relatively commonplace today. The record $61 million ransom paid, in 1975, for the safe return of two Argentine brothers, Jorge and Juan Born, directors of a major industrial concern in Argentina, probably exceeded, in purchasing power, even the ransom paid for King Richard I in 1194. Not only do record ransoms make news, focusing attention on the terrorist group responsible for the action, but also the money procured through such methods often is the lifeblood of terrorist organizations and is used to finance new terrorist operations and the purchase of arms.

Who Is Innocent?

In Algeria, during the war for independence, nationalist terrorists hurled bombs into crowded French cafés and sprayed French pedestrians along the streets with machine gun fire from speeding autos. The object of the terrorists was to generate a climate of fear where no French colon, man or woman, could feel secure; and in so doing, the Arab terrorists introduced a new dimension to terrorist warfare.

Prior to the war for independence in Algeria, terrorists usually struck only at specific targets such as military targets or leading political figures, exercising great care not to kill or injure innocent civilians. The Zionist struggle for Palestine and General Grivas's campaign against the British in Cyprus were notable for their exceptional lack of bloodlust. According to Menachem Begin, "Orders were given, as in all similar operations which the exigencies of war compelled us to carry out, to avoid hurting anybody."[22] This concern for the safety of civilians was reflected in the actions of the Stern gang terrorists who assassinated Lord Moyne in Cairo in November 1944. The two assassins were captured easily because of their reluctance to kill a pursuing Egyptian constable, whom they regarded as innocent of any crime. Nathan Yalin-More later explained how the Stern gang selected its targets:

> [W]e never aimed at British women and children. We never aimed at uninvolved people. We only attacked uniformed Britishers, people in high office or in the secret police. We never took hostages and we never traded innocent people to win demands.
>
> All targets were chosen on rational political grounds, or on organizational grounds. We wanted to show that our fight was against the British Government, not against the local population. We had to prove that the British were not gods, that they were mortal.[23]

While the Zionist terror organizations were basically true to their word, serious breaches of conduct did periodically occur in which noncombatants were slaughtered. The destruction of the Arab village of Deir Yassin by units of the Irgun and Stern left more than 250 Arabs dead, including women, children, and even babies. The brutal attack on Deir Yassin so shocked Jewish sensibilities that David Ben-Gurion cabled his profuse regrets to King Abdullah of Trans-Jordan.

Although the IRA has not been known recently for its restraint, prior to the beginning of the struggle over the future of Northern Ireland in the late 1960s, a conscious effort was made by IRA regulars to insulate the populace from the effects of their actions against the British; nevertheless, it should be noted that their intentions were often better than their execution. Former IRA official and Nobel laureate Sean MacBride described the operational philosophy of the IRA:

> It used to be a rule, always, that you had to take precautions not to injure innocents or civilians. In any action we took, ambushes or military actions, it was always the rule that we had to protect people from the effects of our battles. Very often, areas were cleared beforehand.[24]

Despite isolated efforts to restrict the focus of terrorist violence to legitimate military targets and personnel, the trend has been, ever since Algeria, toward the indiscriminate use of terrorist violence, resulting in what Jenkins has called the "narrowing of the category of innocent bystanders."[25] Most modern terrorists maintain that there is no such category as innocent bystander and that they have the right, if not the duty, to kill anyone who is a national of the country whose government they are resisting. From their perspective, legitimate targets may also include a citizen or national of any country allied to the target country. A Swissair jetliner, sabotaged by the PFLP, crashed shortly after takeoff in February 1970, killing all forty-seven passengers. Only fifteen of the passengers were traveling with Israeli passports. The only crime committed by the others aboard was that their destination was Tel Aviv.

Terrorists justify the indiscriminate use of violence against noncombatants by maintaining that it is possible for all citizens of a particular nation to be considered guilty parties to their government's policies since, by not actively resisting those policies to the point of taking up arms against their government, they are, in effect, condoning them. This was the defense of the nineteenth century French anarchist Emile Henry, who threw a bomb into the crowded Cafe Terminus. At his trial he declared that there are "no innocent bourgeois," inasmuch as society in general permitted children to starve to death in the French slums.[26] Hence, one clearly can become a terrorist target not only through deliberate action but also through the failure to act.

Even if they did not carry their nation's flag or represent their country in an official capacity, Algerian nationalists claimed that all French men and women were beneficiaries of what they regarded as the exploitation of their nation and, therefore, were accomplices of the French government and its policies. This theme was echoed by Sartre, who berated his countrymen for their apathy and quiescence regarding the Algerian issue, saying that "your passivity serves only to place you in the ranks of the oppressors."[27]

In conclusion, George Bernard Shaw summed it up best: "The golden rule is that there is no golden rule."[28] Anyone and everything is a potential terrorist target, and those who fail to take note of the fact that terrorists have, in the past quarter century, dramatically altered the focus and conduct of warfare may be condemned to pay a heavy penalty. As Dr. George Habash of the PFLP has maintained, there are no innocent victims in the world.[29]

New Vulnerabilities

We have entered the most complicated and difficult period of accelerated change the world has ever witnessed. While it will bring many new technological marvels that will fundamentally alter our lives in a positive way, it will also be a period fraught with extraordinary and unprecedented risks that will challenge man's basic resourcefulness in terms of controlling those risks and reducing them to manageable levels. There is no question that the perpetrators of low-level violence have not even begun to explore the opportunities available to them as technology and fast-paced urban development provide an ever expanding array of new and more inviting targets. As Smart has written: "[I]t is, perhaps, surprising that, with the obvious exception of attacks on aircraft and airports, terrorists have not made more frequent and determined efforts to strike at the sensitive nerve centers of the postindustrial city: at its communications or energy systems, its basic services, or its water supplies."[30] It is only a matter of time before terrorists or insurgents strike at one of the so-called catastrophic targets, and when that happens, mankind will only then begin to grasp the real meaning of terror.

Inasmuch as terrorists often seek targets that will magnify the impact of what are often the limited means available to them to strike the target, nothing succeeds like focusing on a highly volatile target that will explode with devastating effect or release deadly fumes, gases, radioactivity, or chemicals into the atmosphere, increasing the initial result of the attack through secondary impacts. A PGM aimed at a building may turn the structure into a shambles and kill scores of innocent people, but if used to rupture an LNG storage tank, it could precipitate a catastrophe of major proportions. Similarly, a fire or bomb set at the main laboratory of the National Center for Disease Control could conceivably result in the release of deadly organisms, such as those that produce lassa fever or smallpox, into the atmosphere.

In the area of critical new vulnerabilities, energy and computers provide a wide range of new targets of opportunity for the terrorist and deserve special discussion.

Energy

Our modern energy dependence represents the Achilles heel of the West and provides many opportunities for grave economic dislocations and catastrophic casualties. The energy chain is vulnerable at every step of the way—from the primary, or production, stage through the transportation, refining, storage, and distribution modes. At the production level, oil wells can be sabotaged and on-shore oil field fires created.[31] However, the approximately 700 offshore oil platforms (jackup, submersible, or semisubmersible types) represent far easier and more spectacular targets. As many as 30 separate wells are often clustered together, and a PGM could be used to turn a $50-million offshore platform into an inferno. Oil well fires normally can be extinguished by very costly and time-consuming methods, but only a few firms have the skills and equipment to combat such major blazes, and their efforts could be easily overwhelmed if terrorists struck at numerous wells in a variety of locations simultaneously.

With respect to offshore platforms, well pipes could be ruptured by explosives or by ramming them with a small boat, producing serious oil spills. Moreover, it is not beyond the realm of possibility that terrorists might physically seize a drilling platform or drillship and hold it for ransom. In view of the remote location of most drilling platforms and their minimal security, such a scenario would take only a few well-trained and -equipped men.

Computer technology plays an ever expanding role in the operations of the oil and gas industry. Oil production in the Gulf of Mexico could be impaired severely by sabotaging the computer centers that regulate and control production. Similarly, a small group of terrorists able to target effectively the essential computer centers that control the operation of oil and natural gas pipelines in the United States could shut down the indispensable distribution of energy throughout much of this country.

Oil supertankers, especially so-called very large crude carriers (VLCC), LNG sea tankers, and other marine gaseous fuels transports, are, in the words of one writer, "floating bombs."[32] Such vessels could be hijacked by terrorists on the high seas and sailed into a crowded harbor where the terrorists could threaten to blow up the pirated ship if authorities did not comply with their demands. The most serious disaster scenario would be an intentional accident involving a fully loaded LNG tanker in a busy harbor. LNG is highly combustible after vaporization; thus, a disaster of major proportions could be created by rupturing LNG tanks or by venting the substance into the atmosphere, resulting in a large vapor cloud covering perhaps many square miles. Depending on the prevailing winds, weather conditions, and other variables, the vapor cloud might settle over the heart of the port city, be it New York, Boston, Baltimore, or any one of dozens of large port cities in the United States and abroad. Should the vapor cloud be ignited, the ensuing firestorm could kill hundreds of thousands of people and result in billions of dollars of damage.[33] Of course, the potential for such a disaster is not confined solely to LNG transport vessels. Terrorists could produce identical results by targeting LNG receiving or storage facilities on land. In recognition of these dangers, the possibility of potential terrorist activity should be kept in mind by federal, state, and municipal authorities during debates over siting of LNG facilities onshore.

Sabotage of LNG vessels or facilities would not require unusual manpower or extensive training. According to a confidential report prepared for the administrator of the Law Enforcement Assistance Administration (LEAA):

> The threat to the LNG system, particularly in the storage, conversion, and transportation postures, could be executed by a single insider, alone or in collusion with outside adversaries, by employing means to disrupt safe operating procedures, resulting in "accidental" compromise of container integrity or by outright sabotage of safety mechanisms, storage vessels or transportation vehicles.[34]

Not only could LNG vessels be boarded easily at sea, since such ships travel unescorted and carry no defensive weaponry capable of repelling an assault, but also while in port, few special security precautions are taken. Although access is supposed to be restricted, little actual effort is made to prevent anyone from the immediate proximity of an LNG vessel. Dock workers with access to the ship or who are engaged in other activities nearby are neither extensively screened nor the backgrounds of the crew members of most LNG vessels and facilities carefully investigated.

A few years ago, North Slope oil producers, who were flaring off a good deal of natural gas, entertained the idea of constructing a liquefaction plant on Alaska's North Slope. They thought the resulting LNG could be carried to a port facility in southern Alaska in a fleet of specially designed Boeing 747s. Boeing, in fact, had already worked up preliminary designs for the aircraft. The plan was discarded, fortunately, but had it not, the fleet of 747s never would have escaped the attention of terrorists as potential targets of opportunity.

Palestinian terrorists have threatened repeatedly to sink an oil supertanker passing through the Strait of Hormuz, which connects the Persian Gulf and the Gulf of Oman, one of the globe's busiest shipping lanes and the pathway for much of the world's crude oil. Between 70 and 144 tankers a day pass through this strategic channel, providing ample opportunity to terrorists. The possible ramifications of such an action are simply incredible. The sinking of a supertanker, either by a mine or a PGM, would likely panic ship owners. Traffic would slow down and perhaps even be brought to a halt. The reverberations would be felt throughout the industrialized West and likely would be reflected in plunging stock values and a flurry of trading on foreign exchange markets. Spot values for crude oil would most surely soar. Although it would take two to four months for any such action to impact directly on the fuel supplies of the developed nations, governments, anticipating shortages, might mandate new conservation measures.

Refineries, tank farms, and pipelines are also highly vulnerable targets to terrorists and saboteurs. Interruption of the pipelines leading from the huge Saudi Ghawar oil field would impact heavily on the United States and the other oil-importing countries. Similarly, sabotage of any of the chief liquid trunk pipelines in the United States would create critical energy delays to major industrial production facilities, electrical power-generating plants, and important sectors of the transportation industry and could eventually impact on national security.

Despite their strategic importance, pipelines, both onshore and underwater, and the pumping and compressor stations upon which the operation of the system depend, are extremely difficult to protect by virtue of their locations and length and can easily be sabotaged with little more than grenades, shaped explosive charges, and even rudimentary fertilizer-based explosives, which were demonstrated to be effective in perforating most pipelines in tests conducted by the U.S. government. According to one report, "The fashioning of a shaped charge in a bandolier-like package around a pipeline, using fertilizer or plastic explosives, cuts the pipe as though snapped by a giant."[35] If terrorists possessed antitank weapons or PGMs, the breaching or perforation of a pipeline would, in the words of one industry expert, be "a piece of cake." The sabotage of natural gas pipelines has even more alarming implications:

[I]f you would sever a pipeline and allow it to drain out of its gas and then [if] during that fast surge of gas coming out of the pipeline, sparks were churned up by the mass, the whole mass could explode starting a detonation down the pipeline and where it would stop, nobody knows.[36]

Repair of sabotaged pipelines provides additional difficulties. Most pipeline companies keep only a limited inventory of critical parts on hand in the event of a breakdown. According to a U.S. government report, "One pipeline company keeps two of each important piece of critical equipment on hand, but if three items of the same were damaged, as much as 19 months delay could be created in the system."[37]

In the event of sabotage to major trunk pipelines, the shift to alternative modes of transportation—truck, barge, or rail—would not be adequate to meet the needs of the nation. Moreover, such conveyances are themselves lucrative targets for hostile action. There are perhaps 20,000 trucks carrying liquid petroleum gas (LPG) on U.S. highways alone. The recent spate of population evacuations as a result of train derailments, where tank cars containing dangerous or volatile cargoes such as chlorine gas and LPG have ruptured, is clear evidence of the hazards associated with such transportation modes.

According to Maynard M. Stephens, perhaps the leading authority on the vulnerability of the oil and gas industry to sabotage and warfare, "The federal and state governments have taken little or no interest in the possibility that petroleum and gas facilities can be victims of sabotage or the focal point of terrorists."[38] Stephens also blames the lack of adequate security on the oil companies for resisting government interference in their industry.

The sabotage of conventional fossil-fuel-fired power-generating plants could knock out electrical power to whole cities and large sections of many states, creating chaos and disrupting industrial production and normal commerce. By cutting the conveyor belt that feeds coal into an electrical generating plant, the plant could be put out of service for days, even weeks, depending on the extent of the damage. Normal health care would be affected adversely, and in some of the colder regions of the United States, the populace could be deprived of heat during the winter months, resulting in cold-related deaths.

Although a good deal of public discussion has been devoted to nuclear power plants as potential terrorist targets, it is difficult to conceive of such a threat in view of the many other targets of opportunity available to terrorists that would have an equal or greater public impact with fewer accompanying risks to the terrorist.

Computers

The face of modern society has been transformed dramatically in the postwar period by the development and refinement of the computer and the resulting information explosion. The computer is the greatest repository and processor of information in the history of the world, and its influence is immeasurable. Everything from the synchronization of traffic lights to the storage of bank account data to customer billings to weather forecasting depends today on computers. The increasing reliance on computers for the normal operation of society has resulted in the creation of "critical nodes whose destruction would be comparable to brain death and thus has greatly increased the potential for major disruption and economic loss stemming from the sabotage of computer facilities or interference with computer operations.[39] The incapacitation of key computer centers, as earlier noted, not only could bring oil production in the Gulf of Mexico to a standstill but also could halt the flow of oil through pipelines, ground civil aviation, prevent electrical production and load sharing in the electric power grid, and disrupt communications.

The theft of computer data is a matter of intense concern to authorities. In our increasingly moneyless society, computers handle more and more of our daily financial transactions. Computer experts agree that this presents a great opportunity to terrorists to steal money through phoney transactions, fraud, or simply by skimming small amounts from a vast number of accounts. "In the tradition of spectacular heists," notes one publication, "there's an element of art to the more clever computer-assisted thefts, with none of the heavyhandedness involved in marching into a bank toting a gun."[40] An entire terrorist movement could be financed from the receipts of computer theft. Vital data could be stolen from computer information banks and ransomed back to the rightful owner. Moreover, certain kinds of private data, such as those contained in tax, police, and medical records, could be stolen and used to blackmail individuals.

The destruction or alteration of computer data is a growing and increasingly serious problem with grave national security implications. By feeding inaccurate data into key computers, a terrorist could sabotage aircraft, trains, pipelines, and other transportation modes. Credit ratings, bank balances, and education and criminal records can be altered by someone with access to the computers where such information is stored.

The alteration of data usually can be detected by computer experts; however, the unauthorized penetration of a computer to steal information often leaves no trace, and this is what makes it such an insidious crime. A criminal or terrorist need not even be present at the location of the computer to commit his crime. A central computer data bank in the United States, for example, can be penetrated by a terrorist in the Middle East who simply has access to a telephone line or a computer terminal and the necessary codes.

One of the chief problems confronting the issue of computer security is the need to prevent abuses by the very people authorized to operate the computer. In many instances, the individuals who commit computer-related crimes are the only ones capable of detecting the crime. For this reason, intensive employee-screening programs must be implemented by companies and concerns that utilize computers containing sensitive data.

Low-Level Violence and Future Targets

The U.S. government is the largest single user of computers in the world; as of January 1978, it was operating 11,328 computers.[11] These computers are used for innumerable tasks including air traffic control, the storage of social security data, and disbursement of federal payrolls, and the plotting of intercontinental ballistic missile trajectories. In this connection, a recent General Accounting Office (GAO) report to Congress was highly critical of present federal safeguards applying to computers, maintaining that existing programs are "fragmented and usually did not extend to protect all sensitive data."[42] Although their audit did not cover controls over national-security-related data in key defense agencies, GAO investigators did not find a single comprehensive computer data security program in any of the ten civil agencies of the U.S. government they reviewed and consequently recommended the creation of a centrally directed program to protect personal and other sensitive data in federal computer systems.

Some doubt has also been expressed about the efficacy of national-security-related computer security programs. Navy scientists, using a telephone, were able to crack a supposedly secure Univac 1108 computer system from the outside during the mid-1970s, when the 1108 was the chief computer used by the national defense establishment as well as by the White House.

The Escalation of Terror

"Man is a pliable animal," wrote Dostoevski, "a being who gets accustomed to everything."[43] Violence, in its many expressions, has always been a pervasive feature of human existence, and as a consequence, the modern world has learned to live with, and even tolerate, a certain level of violence. However, in the process, society is becoming increasingly brutalized by the steady diet of violence depicted on television programming and by network news programs that routinely serve up, as part of the suppertime fare, graphic footage of the world's conflicts, major disasters, famines, and terrorist atrocities, replete with dismembered bodies awash in pools of blood—all in living color. Indeed, the routinization of violence and its trivialization in films and on television have produced an increasingly callous and insouciant global population that is becoming ever more difficult to shock or even to surprise. Unless the target is particularly notable or the incident is accompanied by an unusually high loss of life, most terrorist actions have been pushed off the front page; they just are not news anymore. The only exception to the rule occurs in situations like that existing in El Salvador, where the cumulative impact of daily violence, resulting in the deaths of hundreds of ordinary citizens, ultimately exceeds the climate of terror produced by any single murder or assassination, no matter how prominent the victim.

Terrorists consequently appreciate that they will have to strive constantly to achieve new heights of horror in order to capture the public's attention. One day in the near future some terrorist group will likely make a historic departure from past and even presently anticipated levels of violence by striking out at a target of unprecedented real or symbolic importance that they hope will thrust them and their cause onto the center of the world's stage as never before.

Geophysical and Environmental Targets

The environment can serve as both an ally and a target of resourceful terrorists. Hostile manipulation of the environment can be utilized to kill, to wreck economies, and to undermine national governments. It is a relatively easy feat to trigger avalanches and landslides capable of blocking roads and railway tracks and destroying buildings. It may even be possible one day to create tidal waves that could smash seacoasts by means of underwater explosions.

The destruction of dams, levees, and dikes could produce large-scale flooding, accompanied by extensive loss of life and property. Flooding might also be utilized to destroy a region's agriculture and thereby produce famine. It should be noted that flooding can also result from cloud-seeding and other rain-making activities. Even minor increases in precipitation could have far-reaching effects on climate, food production, and the whole ecosystem of a region.

Forest fires are relatively simple to start and potentially could destroy vast amounts of timber and perhaps even whole villages, leaving workers unemployed and causing collateral economic damage throughout a society. Brush fires in the canyons and hills around some of California's cities such as Los Angeles and Santa Barbara annually result in tens of millions of dollars in property damage and even loss of life.

Agriculture and Livestock

The soft underbelly area of most nations is food production. A majority of the nations of the world are net food importers, and any further reduction in their agricultural and livestock productivity could spell disaster not only for the citizens of those nations but also for the governments in power. Often scarce hard-currency reserves must be used to purchase food imports to make up for shortfalls. In other cases, the importing nation simply cannot afford to import additional foodstuffs so that food lines, rationing, and even malnutrition and starvation are the result. This, in turn, often stimulates protests, civil unrest, and even revolution.

Crops can be attacked by deliberately set rural wildfires, by the release of fertile insect pests and by surreptitiously spraying the fields with insecticides. Various biological agents can be utilized to spread crop diseases, such as in rice (Oryza sativa, Gramineae); wheat (Triticum vulgare, Gramineae); corn (zea mays, Gramineae); potato (Solanum tuberosum, Solanaceae); coffee (Coffea arabica, Rubiaceae); sugarcane (Saccharum efficinarum, Gramineae); rubber (Hevea brasiliensis, Euphorbiaceae), and cotton (Gossypium hirsutum, Malvaceae) fields.[44]

Weather manipulation, particularly rain making, can have a tremendous impact on an area, bringing with it flooding, interruption of planting and harvesting schedules, erosion damage, and increased incidence of crop and livestock diseases.

Any number of human antipersonnel agents or animal viruses could be used to deplete livestock herds. Perhaps one of the most bizarre scenarios to interrupt the food chain involves spraying chemical agents that attack the common honey bee, which is responsible for nearly 90 percent of all crop pollenation.

Sporting and Entertainment Events

Any event, especially a sporting event, that attracts wide public attention and vast crowds potentially represents a prime terrorist target. Press and television are usually on hand at such events, ready to be used by terrorists to record their strike and to convey their message to the world. The dense congregation of people into a small area also ensures, if the object of the terrorist plot is pure mayhem, the loss of a great number of lives. The Palestinian terrorists who struck at Israeli athletes at the 1972 Munich Olympics were cognizant of the unparalleled media attention that such an action would generate. The eventful hour-by-hour drama and the shootout at the Munich airport were followed by an estimated global television audience of more than 500 million people.

The U.S.-made motion picture "Black Sunday" deals with a fictional terrorist attack on a premier U.S. sports event: the Super Bowl. Indeed, security at most major sports and entertainment events is predicated primarily on crowd control considerations rather than the threat of sabotage or a terrorist attack.

Beyond the Super Bowl, other events upon which a terrorist group might focus include World Cup soccer matches; the World Series; a performance at the famous Paris Opera or at the Kennedy Center in Washington, D.C.; a Grand Prix auto race; a major rock music concert; the annual meeting of the World Bank; the Academy Awards presentation; the Miss Universe beauty pageant; major religious observances like an appearance by the Pope; and any large parade.

Technological Showpieces

Few developments capture public imagination like those in the field of science and technology; consequently, new technologies and scientific achievements are extremely newsworthy because of the vast international interest they generate. Many technological marvels are identified inextricably with a particular country and represent a unique opportunity for terrorists to strike at the very core of a nation's prestige and self-esteem. A successful attack on a highly prized technological achievement can be utilized to convey to the world the vulnerability of that nation, and if the ensuing disaster is terrible, really terrible, it may ultimately doom what otherwise might have been a viable technology. The fiery disaster involving the German zeppelin *Hindenburg* at Lakehurst, New Jersey, in 1937 was a major propaganda blow to Nazi Germany and its vaunted claims of German technological superiority. Although initially discounted as the cause of the fatal crash, some contemporary writers maintain that sabotage by anti-Hitler German dissidents ignited the thousands of cubic feet of hydrogen in the zeppelin. What had been a promising new technology was doomed; the rigid airship never recovered from the adverse publicity that had been transmitted around the world in graphic detail on newsreels and in newsphotos of the dying ship as it plunged to earth.

During the inaugural flight of the U.S. space shuttle, *Columbia,* and in the period immediately preceding its lift-off, security was intensified to unprecedented levels at Cape Canaveral, Florida, to guard against possible terrorist attack. Because its fuel is so volatile and its guidance system so delicate, noted one observer, "One well-placed shot from a high-powered rifle could bring her down."[45]

The hijacking or sabotage of the Anglo-French Concorde supersonic jetliner would surely produce similar reverberations and might even result in the discontinuation of Concorde service, which has never operated at a profit in the best of times. No potential IRA action would be as devastating to British morale and prestige as a terrorist-induced crash of a British Airways Concorde. In recognition of the Concorde's attractiveness as a target, an extraordinary security program to protect the Concorde and its passengers has been implemented by U.K. authorities. All checked luggage is X-rayed and fitted with tight bands to ensure that it cannot be reopened prior to arriving at its destination. Only minimal hand luggage is permitted on board. Passengers are screened intensively and searched thoroughly before boarding. While such security precautions have prevented any Concorde-related incidents to date, there is no assurance that the future will not hold a different story, especially if a truly resourceful terrorist group targets the Concorde for destruction.

In 1973, Libya's unpredictable leader, Colonel Qadaffi, threatened to sink the Cunard luxury liner *Queen Elizabeth II* as it steamed up the Mediterranean on an anniversary cruise to take part in Israel's twenty-fifth observance of its independence. While Qadaffi's threat did not materialize, the ship, and other passenger liners, while not exactly technological wonders, possess many of the same national prestige characteristics that make the Concorde such an inviting target.[46]

Perhaps one of the most sensational terrorist exploits that is not beyond the realm of imagination is the hijacking or sabotage of a research or telecommunications satellite. Through the transmission of incorrect operational signals to the satellite, a knowledgeable terrorist could either destroy or even hold a $25 million satellite hostage to his demands. This could be accomplished in a variety of ways including the seizure of a ground station, the penetration of key computers that feed information to the satellite, or by sending erroneous signals from a pirate transmitter. Similarly, the launch vehicle carrying the satellite into orbit is an easy target for a heat-seeking portable munition, and the loss of a satellite and launcher as a result of terrorist action would be a major embarassment to the United States.

Irreplaceable Works of Art and National Monuments

The terrorist bombing of the Palace of Versailles in the late 1970s and the damage inflicted on a number of Renaissance buildings in Italy during recent terrorist-related strife underscore the vulnerability of world-renowned monuments and great works of art to terrorist designs. Often the world's greatest monuments have only limited security and, because of their advanced age and traditional building techniques, are more susceptible to damage than newer buildings. Many terrorists, in fact, have a predisposition for striking at buildings. According to Ted Robert Gurr:

Places are more often chosen as targets than public persons, though when a government building is bombed the act can be assumed to convey a message to someone. The preference for property targets was particularly pronounced in the European countries; in Afro-Asian countries terrorists were less solicitous about human life.[47]

The Grand Mosque in Mecca (which was seized and temporarily held by Moslem extremists in late 1979), the U.S. Capitol (which suffered damage from a bomb planted in a lavatory during the domestic violence that accompanied the Vietnam War), St. Peter's Cathedral in Rome, the Cathedral of Notre Dame in Paris, India's Taj Mahal, the Alhambra in Spain, the Louvre, and the Houses of Parliament in London are representative of the kinds of targets sure to dominate world headlines if they were to be come victims of terrorist violence. Likewise, the theft, defacement, or destruction of great art masterpieces is a relatively easy method of winning worldwide attention or extracting huge ransoms. Recent history contains many notable examples of demented artists and other disturbed persons slashing works of fine art or throwing acid or some other caustic chemical at their surface. One has only to recall the man who attacked Michelangelo's great sculpture, the Pieta, with a hammer to realize what a dedicated group of terrorists with explosives and sophisticated chemicals could do. The threat by a major terrorist group to destroy a thousand significant works of art around the globe if its demands were not met remains a nightmare scenario for all patrons and lovers of great art.

Key Focuses of Activity

Any focus of concentrated activity, or so-called brain center—an airport control tower, the various headquarters of the national media, the New York Stock Exchange, vital computer centers regulating oil or power production, or the control rooms regulating the operations of the main-stem locks and dams along the Missouri River—constitutes a key node of vulnerability. For example, despite relatively tight security precautions at the New York headquarters of ABC, CBS, and NBC, a well-armed and trained terrorist squad conceivably could hijack one of the major networks by seizing the building and taking its employees hostage. The terrorists then could broadcast alternative programming and revolutionary messages of its own design to the entire nation, threatening to kill the hostages if they did not get adequate cooperation from the technical staff of the network or if their transmissions were interfered with by authorities. A standoff that might take days, weeks, even months to resolve could develop, with the terrorists broadcasting the entire period.

Communications

A 1981 study found that the high concentration of communications facilities and services under American Telephone and Telegraph Company's (AT&T)

control rendered the overall communications network of the United States extremely vulnerable to terrorist attack. The study, produced by SRI International, said that the loss of only twenty long-distance relay facilities would effectively put the entire U.S. long-distance phone system out of order. The nationwide telephone communications system is not only critical in terms of coordinating government responses to major emergencies and disasters but also is utilized by the Defense Department in the context of the overall U.S. strategic system. Not only could the relay facilities be put out of commission by well-placed explosive charges or hand-held munitions, but also knowledgeable terrorist infiltrators working within AT&T conceivably could sabotage the facilities from the inside.

Another major vulnerability characterizing the U.S. strategic communications system is the Sunnyvale, California, ground station that not only links all U.S. communications satellites to the Defense Department but also controls many of this country's intelligence surveillance satellites and missile warning satellites. The critical facility is located within bazooka range of a nearby freeway, and it is possible to approach within a few hundred feet of the three large dish antennas. Despite the fact that it is one of the single most vital installations in the entire defense establishment, it is not guarded as a class-A, or top-priority, facility.

Similarly, the present naval communications system, which relies on a series of transmitting stations, is also unacceptably vulnerable to interruption. A single hand grenade or even bullet from a .22-caliber rifle could, under some circumstances, be enough to knock out some of the ground stations.

National Economies

According to Kupperman and Trent, governments must recognize "the range of targets, even economic ones, that are well within the reach of the more imaginative [terrorists]."[48] From a standpoint of results, it is far better to make war on a nation's economy than its people, especially the fragile economies of nations dependent on a single crop or product. Economies are often more vulnerable than people. People are able to endure hardship and omnipresent death and still maintain some sense of normalcy in their lives. However, when people are hungry, when their aspirations are dashed by economic downturn, they become truly vulnerable; disillusionment sets in and they lose their will to resist.

In this connection, the use in an agriculturally dependent nation of defoliants by terrorists to destroy crops promises not only to create widespread economic hardship, adding to whatever discontent already exists, but also to deny the central government resources it had anticipated and had earmarked for the purchase of weapons and ammunition to combat the terrorists. A novel and insidious attempt to weaken further Israel's already tenuous economy occurred in 1978 when Palestinian terrorists injected poison into Israeli oranges, one of that country's chief export cash crops. Investigators later concluded that it was likely that the oranges were spiked at a European port where they had been shipped for repackaging and distribution. Following the hospitalization of five Dutch children who ate contaminated oranges and press reports indicating that four West Germans had also suffered stomach ailments and skin eruptions attributable to the poisoned fruit, a panic swept throughout Europe, and sales of fresh oranges, from all sources, fell off dramatically. If any lesson is to be learned from this case, it is that the power of suggestion alone may be enough to damage sales of an export crop severely if there is reason to believe that it has been poisoned or if terrorists publicly announce that they are going to contaminate it.

The large-scale counterfeiting of currency represents another method terrorists could use to attack a nation's economy. During World War II, Nazi Germany devised a secret program to flood the United States with bogus currency as a means of wreaking havoc on the wartime economy of its principal adversary, but the plot became a victim of the war's termination and reportedly the tons of nearly perfect paper on which the currency was to be printed were dumped into a German lake. If the product is of a sufficiently high quality and distributed on a broad enough scale, counterfeiting by terrorists could be used to erode faith in a nation's legal tender and, at the same time, to introduce an inflationary wild card into the country's national economy.

Public Services

Any public service utilized by large numbers of people can be turned into a lethal weapon by terrorists. The postal systems of various countries have been made the unwitting accomplices of terrorists who have sent letter bombs through the public mails. In 1975, a group calling itself the New World Liberation Front (NWLF) threatened to attack water supply systems in the state of Oregon. For example, mind-altering drugs and deadly poisons could be piped into every home and business in a major metropolitan region if terrorists were able to gain access to the area's water system. In California, police and FBI agents recently arrested a man who was preparing to introduce a biological poison into the Los Angeles water system. In San Jose, California, police, tipped off by an anonymous informant, discovered traces of Silvex, a powerful herbicide, and the chemical 2,4D, which contains dioxin, a suspected cancer-causing agent, in the swimming pools of three apartment complexes.

Banks and Commerce

Banks and domestic corporations are characterized by countless vulnerabilities and are typically ill-prepared to deal effectively with terrorist threats, either of a criminal or political nature. As a consequence, they are increasingly common targets of opportunity to terrorists, especially as a means of raising money to support and sustain their operations. Bank robbery, of course, is one of the most direct methods of acquiring funds and was described by Brazilian revolutionary Carlos Marighella as the just way of financing revolution.

Various schemes have been devised to extort money from local business firms as well. One of the most diabolical involved the contamination with cyanide of shelf products in several California Safeway stores. Unless the perpetrators were given fifty loose diamonds of one carat or larger, they threatened to poison food in every Safeway store in the area. Although the extortionists were captured by police and brought to justice, a well-organized terrorist gang could ruin an entire food chain simply by alleging that they had poisoned random items of food. Or, if their goal was simply to spread terror, they could actually carry out their threat, producing widespread chaos as terrified consumers stopped buying many products and returned suspect foodstuffs to stores rather than to run the risk of poisoning themselves and their families.

In addition to extortion plots, terrorists could perpetrate a variety of frauds and scams against insurance companies by means of false insurance claims. Terrorists have collaborated with holders of kidnap insurance policies to stage phoney kidnappings, in most cases splitting the insurance payoffs with the cooperating victim.

International Business

Multinational companies and their employees are increasingly coming under attack by terrorists, "both for ideological reasons and because they offer the best promise of big money."[49] Threats, assaults, kidnappings, and assassinations of business executives have reached epidemic proportions despite the fact that figures showing the level of incidents are greatly understated.[50] Terrorist writers like Marighella have called upon Latin American revolutionaries to single out North American firms and properties as "such frequent targets of sabotage that the volume of actions directed against them surpasses the total of all other actions against vital enemy points."[51] Some 567 Americans were reported kidnapped abroad in the nine-year span between 1970 and 1978, and over half of the victims were businessmen. Thirty-five were killed by their abductors. A senior business executive from a major U.S. multinational estimated in 1979 that at least three kidnappings or attacks a day on multinational businessmen went unreported in Bogota, Colombia. In one case an executive returned home to find his wife with her throat slashed and a note telling him and others like him to get out of the country. Many of the attacks, if they occur in South America or Africa, are not reported to authorities because company officials believe that the local police and military establishments are ineffectual when it comes to combating terrorism. Moreover, they fear a contagion effect that might spark even more violence if widespread attention were devoted to a successful attack on a particular company. Finally, most firms are reluctant to alarm other employees by emphasizing an attack on the company or one of its workers. Several U.S. companies have been forced to pay what amounts to hazardous-duty pay— large bonuses and incentives—to key personnel in order to induce them to stay in violence-prone areas like Argentina.

Since the early 1970s, Fiat, Italy's largest industrial concern, has been a constant target of leftist terrorists. Between 1972 and 1978, for example, one Fiat executive was murdered, three were kidnapped, and twelve were wounded by terrorists. Since 1978, the violence has intensified. Those wounded in such attacks are often shot in the kneecaps, a particularly painful and crippling method of instilling terror in people. Fiat installations have been the targets of bombings and sabotage, the homes of Fiat executives have been firebombed, and in at least three instances, cars belonging to the company's medical consultants have been set ablaze. The choice of Fiat as a target appears to be predicated not only on the company's high visibility, which gives visibility in turn to those who attack it, but also, even more important, Red Brigades' strategists appear to believe that striking at Fiat is a symbolic thrust at the very heart of the beast: Italian capitalism.

In the future, violence against corporations and corporate executives can be anticipated to intensify to the extent that many major companies will be forced to abandon lucrative markets, depriving developing nations of needed foreign investment and skilled jobs. Violence against individuals connected with major companies will become ever more insidious, with terrorists aiming at mutilation and crippling injuries in many cases rather than death. Wives, children, and other dependents are likely to be singled out more often as targets; while an executive may make a conscious decision to risk his own life, he is normally far more reluctant to put his family in jeopardy. Terrorists may strike at the headquarters of major firms by seizing the premises and holding all inside as hostages until ransom demands are met. They may even decree that all persons who purchase a particular product manufactured by the target corporation are, by their act, declaring themselves to be enemies of the revolution and, therefore, likely targets of terrorist violence.

Distinguished Persons

Over the years, heads-of-state have lived by an unwritten code, characterized by forebearance, with respect to the assassination of rival heads of state, even during wartime. To seek the death of another head-of-state would most surely invite retaliation; therefore enlightened self-interest dictated that the rule was rarely violated. Terrorists, however, are not bound by any such restraints. From their perspective, they are already marked for death so they see no reason to back away from striking out at the chief-of-state of the government they are seeking to topple. The more nihilistic terrorist groups tend to have a greater proclivity toward assassination of government officials and heads-of-state than doctrinaire Marxists. As Peter Calvert notes, terrorists affiliated with well-articulated groups with strong ideological identification tend to subscribe to notions of historical determinism and rarely resort to assassination as a tactic, holding instead that "the processes of history are too broad and powerful to be deflected by the removal of one man."[52]

In spite of Charles Dickens's assertion that "threatened men live long," highly visible persons connected with volatile issues should be fearful for their lives. Executive protection remains a difficult task, for as the historian Livy noted almost two millenniums ago, "There is always more spirit in attack than in defense." The advantage will always belong to the assassin, who can choose his weapon and target at will, then select the time and place for his attack. Those entrusted with the protection of the potential target, however, must be constantly prepared, ever vigilant, and on their toes. They need only let down their guard once for tragedy to strike.

The kidnapping and murder of Italian Premier Aldo Moro and the assassination of the United Kingdom's Lord Mountbatten may only be precursors of an all-out terrorist offensive against world leaders in the years ahead. Prime targets include the Pope, heads-of-state of the Western democracies, leading corporate officials, entertainment personalities, and well-known public figures. Special note should be taken of the fact that nearly all of the members of the U.S. Congress, including powerful committee chairmen, have virtually no security other than that afforded ordinary citizens. On any given day, any member of the U.S. Congress could be kidnapped or attacked by terrorists. To illustrate the point, one need only recall that the chairman of the Senate Armed Services Committee, John Stennis, nearly succumbed to gunshot wounds inflicted by two petty thieves who confronted the Mississippi democrat in front of his home in northwest Washington a few years ago. Similarly, most state governors are protected by little more than one or two state troopers, and in the less-populous states, the governor often travels without any security precautions at all.

Conclusion

When all is said and done, it is clear that terrorists and other "technoaggressors" derive much of their basic strength from modern technology. The rapid progress of technology has provided them with not only a whole arsenal of new weapons but also a seemingly endless horizon of diverse and highly vulnerable new targets. Only the future can tell whether or not the perpetrators of violence will take full advantage of the many new targets of opportunity available to them. One thing is certain, however: The power of destruction now lying within their grasp represents one of the most serious and intractable problems confronting the world in the years ahead.

Notes

1. Maynard M. Stephens, (director of Special Programs, Petroleum and National Gas, School of Engineering, Tulane University), letter to the author, January 8, 1982, p. 2.

2. John Webster, *Duchess of Malfi,* Act IV, sc. 2, 1623.

3. Robert Taber, *The War of the Flea* (New York: Citadel Press, 1970), p. 136.

4. I am indebted to Sigmund de Janos and Stephen Lieff for the term *technoaggression,* meaning "small, hostile actions, directed against technological and industrial infrastructures, perpetrated by specially trained military techno-commandos or by technoterrorists representing recognized or ad hoc political organizations." See de Janos and Lieff, "Technoaggression—An Alternative Mode of Warfare," *Conflict* 1979):257–272.

5. Hannah Arendt, *On Violence* (New York: Harcourt, Brace & World, 1977), p. 84.

6. Walter Laqueur, quoted by David M. Alpern, "More Outrages," *Newsweek,* 26 December 1977.

7. Brian Jenkins, "International Terrorism: A Balance Sheet," *Survival* (July/August 1977), p. 164.

8. Robert Moss, "International Terrorism and Western Societies," *International Journal* (Summer 1973), p. 418.

9. Editorial, "Terror in a Dutch School," *Washington Post,* 27 May 1977.

10. Paul Wilkinson, *Political Terrorism* (New York: John Wiley & Sons, 1974), p. 109.

11. Phillip A. Karber, "Urban Terrorism: Baseline Data and a Conceptual Framework," *Social Science* (January 1973), p. 253.

12. Jerry M. Silverman and Peter M. Jackson, "Terror in Insurgency Warfare," *Military Review* (October 1970), p. 63.

13. Interview with Nathan Yalin-Mor, New York City, 16 September 1976.

14. Wilkinson, *Political Terrorism,* p. 96.

15. Walter Laqueur, "The Futility of Terrorism," *Harper's* (March 1976), p. 104.

16. Andrew R. Molnar, with Jerry M. Tinker and John D. LeNoir, "Human Factors Considerations of Undergrounds in Insurgencies," Research project prepared for the Special Operations Office of the American University, operating under contract with the Department of the Army (Washington, D.C., 1965), p. 173.

17. Robert B. Asprey, *War in the Shadows: The Guerrilla in History,* vol. 2 (Garden City, N.Y.: Doubleday & Company, 1975), p. 848.

18. Molnar, Tinker, and LeNoir, "Human Factors Considerations," p. 172.

19. Some observers maintain that Jewish extremists who arranged the voyage knew that the ship was unseaworthy but willingly sacrificed its crew and

passengers in the hope of creating an incident of worldwide impact that would focus on the plight of stateless Jews seeking admission to Palestine.

20. For a detailed description of Operation Mongoose, see Thomas Powers, *The Man Who Kept the Secrets: Richard Helms and the CIA* (New York: Alfred A. Knopf, 1979).

21. Jerry M. Tinker, *Strategies of Revolutionary Warfare* (New Delhi: S. Chand and Co., 1969), p. 204.

22. Menachem Begin, *The Revolt* (London: W.H. Allen, 1951), p. 81.

23. Interview with Nathan Yalin-Mor.

24. Sean McBride, "Terrorism," *Skeptic* (January/February 1976), p. 11.

25. Brian M. Jenkins, "High Technology Terrorism and Surrogate War: The Impact of New Technology on Low Level Violence," in *The Other Arms Race: New Technologies and Non-Nuclear Conflict*, Geoffrey Kemp, Uri Ra'anan, and Robert L. Pfaltzgraff, Jr., eds. (Lexington, Mass.: D.C. Heath and Company), p. 94.

26. Renée Winegarten, "Literary Terrorism," *Commentary* (March 1974), p. 60.

27. Jean-Paul Sartre, "Introduction," in Frantz Fanon, *The Wretched of the Earth* (New York: Grove Press, 1968), p. 25.

28. George Bernard Shaw, "Maxims for Revolutionists," *Man and Superman* (Baltimore: Penguin Books, 1965), p. 257.

29. Dr. George Habash, quoted in Bowman H. Miller and Charles A. Russell, "The Evolution of Revolutionary Warfare: From Mao to Marighella and Meinhof," in *Terrorism: Threat, Reality, Response,* eds. Robert H. Kupperman and Darrell M. Trent (Stanford, Calif.: Hoover Institution Press, 1979), p. 130.

30. I.M.H. Smart, "The Power of Terror," *International Journal* (Spring 1975), p. 233.

31. For more on wellhead shearing, see N.C. Livingstone, "Weapons for the Few," *Conflict* (1975):314.

32. J. Bowyer Bell, *A Time of Terror* (New York: Basic Books, 1978), p. 106.

33. The explosiveness of LNG is a matter of some debate. According to a study that appeared in *Scientific American:* "The detonation of vapor in open air has not been confirmed even when a high explosive charge served as initiator. Charles D. Lind of the Naval Weapons Center at China Lake, Calif., has been unable to obtain detonations even with charges up to two kilograms." See Elisabeth Drake and Robert C. Reid, "The Importation of Liquefied Natural Gas," *Scientific American* (April 1977), p. 28.

34. LEAA, "Liquefied Natural Gas Security and Safety," unpublished working paper prepared for Richard W. Velde, Administrator, LEAA (1977).

35. Maynard M. Stephens, *Vulnerability of Total Petroleum Systems,* Report prepared for the Defense Civil Preparedness Agency, DAHC 20-70-C-0316 (Washington, D.C.: U.S. Government Printing Office, May 1973), p. 142.

36. Maynard M. Stephens, testimony, U.S. Congress, Senate, Committee on the Judiciary, Subcommittee to Investigate the Administration of the Internal Security Act and other Internal Security Laws, *The Trans-Alaska Pipeline: Problems Posed by the Threat of Sabotage and their Impact on Internal Security,* 1976, p. 12.

37. Stephens, *Vulnerability of Total Petroleum System,* p. 142.

38. Maynard M. Stephens, "The Oil and Natural Gas Industries: A Potential Target of Terrorists," in *Terrorism: Threat, Reality, Response,* eds. Robert H. Kupperman and Darrell M. Trent (Stanford, Calif.: Hoover Institution Press, 1979), p. 222.

39. Kupperman and Trent, *Terrorism,* p. 73.

40. Lydia Dotto, "The New Computer Criminals," *Atlas World Press Review* (August 1979), p. 26.

41. General Accounting Office, *Automated Systems Security—Federal Agencies Should Strengthen Safeguards over Personal and other Sensitive Data* (Washington, D.C., 23 January 1979), p. 8.

42. Ibid., p. 12.

43. Fedor Dostoevski, *The House of the Dead,* pt. 1, ch. 2.

44. Stockholm International Peace Research Institute, *Weapons of Mass Destruction and the Environment* (New York: Crane, Russak and Company, 1977), p. 34.

45. "Countdown Is Continuing for Space Shuttle, *Washington Post,* 8 April 1981.

46. It is reported that Qadaffi did dispatch an Egyptian submarine to sink the *Queen Elizabeth II,* under provisions of a joint military command structure in place as part of a Libyan-Egyptian consolidation plan that was later scrapped. President Anwar Sadat of Egypt, however, upon receiving word of the Libyan dictator's orders to the submarine, instantly recalled the vessel, avoiding a disaster that could have led to a major conflict.

47. Ted Robert Gurr, "Some Characteristics of Contemporary Political Terrorism," mimeographed, March 1976).

48. Kupperman and Trent, *Terrorism,* p. 8.

49. Richard Clutterbuck, *Protest and the Urban Guerrilla* (London: Cassell & Company, 1973), pp. 28–29.

50. In Italy, for example, many reported kidnappings are phoney and, in actuality, are charades designed to circumvent currency export restrictions.

51. Carlos Marighella, "Minimanual of the Urban Guerrilla," mimeographed, p. 35.

52. Peter Calvert, "The Diminishing Returns of Political Violence," *New Middle East* (May 1973), p. 26.

8 States in Opposition: The War against Terrorism

[T]o annihilate modern terrorists with their superior methods of battle, the counterblows must be a hundredfold smarter and stronger than the terrorists' own ways and weapons.
—Albert Parry[1]

Until recently, only authoritarian governments, unrestrained by public opinion or safeguards on civil liberties and guided solely by consideration of self-preservation, have enjoyed any demonstrable success in combating terrorism. The liberal democracies of the West, by contrast, have been forced to tolerate a certain level of internal violence rather than to adopt draconian measures that would undermine their essential democratic character. Indeed, the paradox of modern democracy is that, from the perspective of those wishing to do it violence, its very strengths are also its weaknesses—namely, the belief in innate rights, respect for the sanctity of human life, and rule by will of the majority. Thus, terrorism poses unique and difficult challenges for the nonauthoritarian governments of the world, what Robert Moss calls the "complex problem of applying force in a democratic society,"[2] as they attempt to chart a course between the rival, and equally undesirable, antipodes of overreacting and underreacting to terrorism.

Terrorism is war without limits, and unless the state can respond accordingly, measure for measure, it will be at a considerable disadvantage when confronted with an enemy that is not restrained by the same rules that it is. The Vietnam conflict demonstrated the frustrations associated with waging war by the rules and with restraint against an enemy with little regard for either rules or restraints. This is not to suggest that the only antidote to terrorism is repression and violence but, instead, to recognize the additional burden that modern terrorism places on defense planners and policymakers in the Western democracies who are compelled to combat it without succumbing to the temptation to adopt the same methods and tactics employed by the terrorists. Their role is also rendered difficult by the fact that terrorism is a dynamic strategy,

Portions of this chapter appeared in N.C. Livingstone, "States in Opposition: The War against Terrorism," *Conflict* 3 (no. 2-3):83-141.

predicated on relentless offense, whereas counterterrorism traditionally has been a static, or defensive, strategy and, consequently, often fails for this very reason. Thus, those entrusted with the defense of the state must, in view of the restraints under which they operate, seek ever newer and more imaginative stratagems to control terrorism. Moreover, it must be recognized that terrorism is endemic to the modern world and will not soon disappear. It cannot, in any absolute sense, be defeated or eradicated. Like the multiple-headed hydra of Greek mythology that sprouted two new heads whenever one was lopped off, in recent years, whenever terrorism was brought under control in one struggle, more often than not it appeared anew in another context, in another form, someplace else. And in most of the instances where terrorism disappeared, it was self-terminating, not suppressed by military action by the state in opposition; the revolutionaries who embraced terrorism were either victorious or they de-emphasized terrorist violence as their struggles matured into more advanced stages of revolutionary warfare. Finally, while it is possible to minimize the risks associated with terrorism and to reduce its impact, there is no foolproof defense against it, at least in those regions of the world that place a high premium on democratic institutions and individual freedoms. However, as the United States observed before the Ad Hoc Committee on International Terrorism of the UN, "To acknowledge that there are no easy solutions does not mean that we should not proceed urgently to seek solutions."[3]

Given this introduction, let us now examine the various strategies that have been advanced in recent years to delimit and control terrorist outbreaks in non-authoritarian countries. The particular strategy adopted by any government confronted with a terrorist challenge, of course, depends on the nature of the threat, and it is impossible to say, without a detailed examination of the special threat together with a careful analysis of the resources available for employment against it, which strategy or combination of strategies is likely to result in a maximum advantage for states in opposition.

Legal Remedies

In recent years, efforts to win international cooperation for the control of international terrorism and the punishment of terrorists have met with little success. Central to this movement have been various attempts to develop a body of international law, through the promulgation of various conventions and treaties, that would define certain acts of terrorism as international crimes and make the punishment of their perpetrators universally binding on all nations.[4] Supporters of international legal action against terrorism note that piracy on the high seas was not eradicated until it was made a universal crime, permitting any nation to punish pirates despite their nationality or where their crimes were committed.

The first attempt to designate certain individuals—other than pirates—as the enemy of governments occurred in 1856 after an assassination attempt on the life of Napoleon III of France. The assassination of a head-of-state or member of his family was subsequently excluded by Belgium from the list of political offenses for which a nation might offer political asylum or refuse to extradite the offender. Referred to as the "attentat clause," it was incorporated into many extradition treaties.

Another attack on a head-of-state ultimately precipitated the most extensive effort prior to the postwar period to develop a unified international response against terrorism. In 1934, King Alexander I of Yugoslavia was assassinated, along with Louis Barthou, the president of the Council of the French Republic, in Marseilles, France, by Macedonian revolutionaries. The resulting international outrage compelled the League of Nations to draft a convention on international terrorism in 1937.[5] The convention, which was signed by twenty-three states but ratified by only one, India, was motivated greatly by self-interest on the part of diplomats and heads-of-state who were fearful for their lives and desirous of developing strong sanctions as a deterrent to further assassinations. Nevertheless, the League's efforts to arrive at a workable convention for repressing certain acts of terrorism was undermined by petty bickering among the participants and stormy confrontations over wording and definitions. By the time the convention was submitted to the signatories for ratification, it had been overtaken by the onrush of the events leading up to World War II.

Not until the 1960s were efforts revived, this time by the league's successor organization, the UN, to address the problem of international terrorism within the context of international law. However, as Leo Gross has observed, "The work of the United Nations on terrorism in its various manifestations has been in response to events and consequently piecemeal."[6] Three conventions have been drafted to date to meet the terrorist challenge to international civil aviation and another in response to the growing number of terrorist attacks on diplomats (Convention on the Prevention and Punishment of Crimes against Internationally Protected Persons). The draft Convention for the Prevention and Punishment of Certain Acts of International Terrorism, submitted to the General Assembly in September 1972 by the United States, was an attempt to devise a means of preventing the export of violence beyond the actual areas of conflict. While most Western governments, which tend to be the chief targets of terrorism, supported the draft convention as a means of securing a multilateral framework for preventing and punishing acts of terrorism, it was opposed by the Communist bloc states in alliance with most of the countries of the Third World, who demonstrated a greater interest in legitimizing wars of national liberation than in combating terrorism. In addition, many Third World states maintained a strong commitment to the institution of asylum for political criminals; however, no universally acceptable definition of exactly what constitutes a political offender could be agreed upon by the various governments. The Third World/Communist bloc approach concentrated on the eradication of the causes of terrorism, and this, more often than not, provided a convenient pretext for attacking the West and demanding redistribution of the world's wealth. Because of the impasse that developed regarding the rival perspectives concerning terrorism, the draft convention was tabled and is unlikely to be resurrected any time soon.

In view of this and other similar experiences, Walter Laqueur dismisses any idea of multilateral treaty making as an effective method of combating terrorism, contending that "they [conventions] may be of interest to lawyers and insurance companies, but they have not the slightest practical importance."[7] Indeed, efforts designed to reach agreements providing for comprehensive multilateral action against terrorism clearly are doomed to failure, at least for the foreseeable future, because such efforts presume that all states have a mutual stake in global stability and the present world order, not to mention historical, geographical, and economic commonalities that simply do not exist. In the unlikely event that lawmakers are ultimately successful in reaching consensus on a comprehensive convention to combat terrorism, it undoubtedly will be framed in such general terms as to be rendered meaningless. Moreover, enforcement of any treaty will still depend on how each signatory views its national interest on any given issue, and in this connection, nation-states historically have refused to sublimate their domestic law to international law except in situations in which their national goals were advanced by so doing.

At best, all that can be hoped for at this time is some kind of international cooperation on a limited scale. The 1973 agreement between Cuba and the United States, providing for the return of aircraft and skyjackers to their country of origin, which was successful in reducing the number of disruptive, largely criminal, skyjackings plaguing civil aviation in both countries, remains the salient example of a workable bilateral arrangement between two inherently hostile nations. Although Cuba has permitted the accord to lapse, Havana has indicated repeatedly that it would respect the spirit of the agreement.[8] Similarly, regional pacts addressing certain categories of terrorism have been entered into by both the Council of Europe and the Organization of American States, largely because the relative homogeneity of those organizations makes agreement on such questions easier to reach. In July 1978, the United States joined with six other nations—Japan, the Federal Republic of Germany, Canada, Italy, the United Kingdom, and France—in expressing its willingness to suspend all air travel to countries that harbor air pirates by failing either to extradite or prosecute them.

A variety of other legal remedies have been advanced by scholars and diplomats to contain terrorism and to punish its perpetrators, and among the more novel suggestions are an international court or tribunal to try those accused of crimes that are disruptive to international commerce, communications, transportation, and diplomatic exchanges; an international prison to incarcerate terrorists, thereby reducing the likelihood that their confederates will attempt to intimidate national governments in order to win the release of fellow terrorists; and a convention establishing an international antiterrorist police force. It goes without saying that all such proposed legal remedies are predicated on general agreements among governments and that, no matter how well intentioned, they stand little or no chance of being considered seriously, much less adopted, by the world community.

Social Reform

According to former Stern gang member Nathan Yalin-Mor, "The only way to fight terrorism is to solve the real problems. If you do, the antisocial elements will not be able to exist very long."[9] Terrorism neither occurs in a vacuum nor is it generally the product of outside agitation or imported ideologies, though such factors may contribute significantly to its growth and development. At the root of most terrorist outbreaks are real grievances such as the unequal distribution of wealth, the inability to participate in the political process, and systematic government oppression. If no channels exist for the peaceful resolution of societal grievances, violent change often becomes inevitable. However, if the dissidents resort to violence before exhausting all peaceful remedies, it is unlikely they will enjoy significant popular support, as in the examples of the Baader-Meinhof movement in West Germany, the Italian Red Brigades, and the JRA. While terrorist violence by small, nihilistic groups with little public support, who are often more akin to outlaws than to political terrorists, can only be dealt with by means of police or military action, in setting out to control the threat posed by terrorists and other violence-prone political extremists with broad-based support and deep-seated grievances, it must be recognized that inasmuch as terrorism is principally a political problem so too are the most lasting solutions largely political in nature. Indeed, the application of force against terrorists, without any corresponding effort to understand their grievances or to implement specific reforms to rectify what may be legitimate problems, may produce some immediate results but usually does not constitute a viable strategy and may, in fact, only postpone the ultimate threat.[10] "There is considerable historic evidence," write W.T. Mallison, Jr., and S.V. Mallison, "that no governmental attempt to suppress terrorism has been successful in the absence of a political program designed to eradicate the causes."[11] It should be noted, however, that force may be necessary in order to purchase the time needed to implement reforms and to give them time to take hold.

Needless to say, not all political problems can be solved readily, either for the lack of necessary resources or because efforts to satisfy one group's grievances may do harm to another group. This is particularly true of the Palestinian

question and the conflict in Northern Ireland. Both struggles are characterized by rival claims to a single geographic entity, and to displace one group
to redress the damage done to the other is plainly not an efficacious or
equitable option, especially inasmuch as the more powerful party in each case
is presently in control of the disputed territory. While it may be possible to
satisfy the demands of most Palestinians for a homeland by creating a Palestinian
state on the West Bank of the Jordan River and, similarly, to vitiate Catholic
demands for a greater share of the wealth and power in Ulster through aggressive
political and economic reform, a residual level of terrorism can be expected to
persist for some time thereafter, generated by diehards and disordered minds,
that consequently will have to be controlled by means of police and military
action.

High Standard of Government

If successful counterterrorism is, on the one hand, contingent on the progress
that can be made in finding solutions to the issues that give rise to internal
violence, it is also highly dependent on how successful the state is in adminis-
tering its territory and protecting its citizens. Many observers maintain, in this
connection, that the United States was not outfought in Vietnam but rather
outadministered. A well-ordered state responsive to the public's needs, regarded
as legitimate by most of its citizens, and relatively free of corruption offers
few openings or opportunities to revolutionary terrorists.

The ultimate test of any government is how it responds in times of crisis.
If the government is adept at meeting a formidable challenge, it is likely to
enjoy broad public support, but if it should stumble and appear to be incapable
of handling the crisis, even its most ardent proponents will soon desert it.
Once the public loses confidence in their government's ability to govern, it is
usually only a matter of time before that government falls. In order to project
an image of strong, confident leadership, governments confronted with widespread terrorist violence should strive to preserve an atmosphere of normalcy,
of business as usual, so as to prevent an impression that the terrorists have
the power to intimidate it.

A government under assault must never appear to be weak or vacillating.
In this connection, a policy of concessions and appeasement does not deter
terrorism any more than the lenient treatment of terrorists. Moreover, it is a
fact that one successful case of blackmail usually leads to another, and the
perception that the government is knuckling under to terrorists is profoundly
corrosive and undermines the will of others to resist.[12]

This is not to suggest a hard-line policy with respect to terrorism so much
as a policy of firmness in the face of terrorist threats, of a graduated response
to violence instead of precipitous action that is likely to send shock waves

throughout the society and to produce widespread anxiety and misgivings on the part of the populace. If necessary, democratic governments must not shirk from using force to suppress terrorist outbreaks. While democracy and counter-terrorism make, as Moss suggests, uncomfortable bedfellows, this does not mean that democratic societies cannot employ force against their enemies without undermining their constitutional foundations and eroding the fundamental precepts upon which they are based.[13] Nowhere is it written that democratic societies must be impotent or that they serve as doormats on which the lawless and the unprincipled wipe their feet. In the event that it is necessary to adopt emergency measures like a curtailment of civil liberties for the duration of a terrorist-induced crisis, every effort must be made to prevent abuses of those emergency powers because that would tend to alienate the general population. The government's counterterrorist program, moreover, should be designed to produce as little disruption of the daily lives and routines of ordinary citizens as possible.

Strong Intelligence Capability

Timely and reliable intelligence forms the first line of defense against terrorism. Since terrorists may choose the time and place of their attacks from an almost infinite number of possibilities, authorities are at considerable disadvantage in thwarting terrorist violence since they cannot be everywhere at once in equal strength. A well-developed intelligence capability not only may provide authorities with advance information about a forthcoming terrorist operation, permitting them to take steps to avert the incident or at least to minimize the damage, but also aids them in tracking down suspected terrorists and bringing them to justice.

Activities that can be undertaken by intelligence organizations include the surveillance of suspected terrorists and terrorist groups; the infiltration of terrorist movements; the development of informer networks; the design and implementation of contingency systems to respond to terrorist threats; the collection, storage, and analysis of information; and direct counterterrorist warfare. The computer known as the Octopus at the Langley, Virginia, head-quarters of the CIA forms the backbone of the U.S. effort against international terrorism; data from every terrorist movement in the world is fed into the Octopus, along with information detailing the movements and activities of known or suspected terrorists. By assembling and digesting myriad bits and pieces of information, experts ultimately seek to predict terrorist behavior.

In recent years, however, the U.S. intelligence capability has been impaired by extensive public scrutiny by the Congress and media in the aftermath of disclosures regarding the CIA's peripheral role in the Watergate affair and other abuses by it and other intelligence agencies that occurred chiefly in the 1950s and 1960s. These disclosures, together with overzealous efforts by the Congress to reassert its prerogatives and oversight over the activities of the CIA, have had the effect of undermining the morale of the U.S. intelligence community and of greatly reducing its effectiveness. Many of the ablest members of the CIA have sought early retirement or simply left the agency for other employment.

The fear of disclosure has rendered covert action all but impossible and subjects deep cover operations to an unreasonable risk of potential exposure. "With broad consultation on Capitol Hill," observed the former director of the CIA, James Schlesinger, "one Congressman can blackball a covert operation simply by leaking it to the press."[14] Covert operations were defined in an early National Security Council directive known as NSC 10/2 (June 1948) as activities related to "propaganda, economic warfare; preventive direct action, including sabotage, anti-sabotage, demolition and evacuation measures; subversion against hostile states, including assistance to underground resistance groups, and support of indigenous anti-Communist elements in threatened countries of the free world."[15] This last phrase—"support of indigenous anti-Communist elements in threatened countries of the free world"—gave critics of the CIA the most trouble, inasmuch as it had become a justification for shoring up virtually any regime in the world, no matter how wretched, so long as it met the one critical test of being anti-Communist. However, in attempting to limit abuses of this type, congressional critics virtually decimated the entire covert capability of the CIA, including the ability to strike back at foreign terrorists and their supporters.

In this connection, covert action must be viewed as a tool that falls someplace between diplomacy and war in the range of options available to the nation's policymakers. In the absence of an effective covert capability, a nation is left with the wholly unsatisfactory choices of doing nothing in those situations where diplomacy has failed and in resorting to the other extreme of using conventional military force. This nation must rebuild and reinvigorate its capability to carry on a quiet war against international terrorism much the same way the Israeli Mossad does.

Perhaps no intelligence service in the world has had more experience in combating terrorism than Israel's Mossad. Although it is less than one-twentieth the size of the CIA, the Mossad, with approximately 900 full-time employees, has conducted dozens of spectacular operations against Palestinian terrorists and their allies and supporters, including the daring 1976 rescue of 103 hostages at Entebbe, Uganda. Less well known is the fact that the Mossad has engaged in a far-reaching war against the PLO and other Palestinian terrorist organizations, ranging over Europe, North and South America, Africa, and other regions of the globe. In the years since the 1972 massacre of Israeli athletes at the Munich Olympics, for example, the Mossad systematically has hunted down and killed the Palestinian architects and perpetrators of the plot.

The first Palestinians associated with the Munich incident to die were Mahmoud Hamshari, the PLO's Paris representative, who was killed by an electronically detonated telephone bomb, and Al Fatah's Rome representative Wael Zwaiter, who was gunned down on a Rome street. In early 1979, Mossad operatives finally assassinated Ali Hassan Salameh, better known as Abu Hassan, the purported mastermind of the Munich attack, by planting a bomb in his car in Beirut. A close friend of Yasir Arafat's, Abu Hassan was commander of Al Fatah's special operations unit, which was responsible for many of the terrorist strikes against Israel, as well as head of the PLO's internal security forces. Married to a former Miss Universe, he was one of the most colorful, resourceful and charismatic of the Palestinian leaders, and his death left a significant void in Al Fatah's leadership ranks. Incidents like these give the Mossad a fierce and unforgiving reputation and are what make it the most feared intelligence service in the world by terrorists. Nevertheless, the Mossad has not always been on target, as in the celebrated case of a Moroccan waiter, mistakenly thought to be Abu Hassan, who was murdered by Mossad agents in Lillehammer, Norway, in 1973. Five Israelis were sentenced to prison terms by Norwegian courts for their roles in connection with the killing.

Harsh Punishment

Terrorists are the least likely criminals to be caught and punished. This is attributable not only to the difficulty in apprehending terrorists but also to the fact that, even when captured, terrorists are often turned loose or deported by governments fearful that any effort to punish them will serve as an invitation to further acts of violence and blackmail designed to win their release.[16] A recent study prepared by the Office to Combat Terrorism at the U.S. Department of State revealed that 146 people classified as international terrorists had been arrested prior to 1976 and that, of that number, 140 were released without punishment. Another 47 were permitted to escape arrest or detainment "because their own governments chose not to arrest them for offenses committed against another country."[17]

Punishment is important from a societal viewpoint insofar as it reassures the society beset by terrorist violence that retribution is being exacted on those who violate the laws of the land and that their government is acting to protect its citizens from the terrorist menace. To this extent, the swiftness and sureness of the punishment are more important than its severity.

The only real deterrent to terrorism is the knowledge by terrorists that their adversary is vigilant and alert and prepared to take every reasonable counterforce action possible to protect the lives of its citizens, territory, and resources. To this goal, national governments are finding it increasingly expedient to avoid taking prisoners whenever possible—for example, killing terrorists on the spot, thereby removing the stimulus for future terrorist actions. Terrorists who are summarily executed or simply shot down as they attempt to surrender later can be dismissed as casualties of the encounter who died in the fighting that occurred. According to some reports, both the Israelis and the West Germans have given specific orders to their antiterrorist commando units not to take prisoners when the conditions are propitious, which is to say when no journalists or other witnesses are nearby; others suggest that there is no formal command to this effect but that an understanding exists among the officers and men of such units to the effect that prisoners are not desirable.

A strong movement is underway in the West to restore the death penalty, which has been abolished by many countries, in the case of terrorists. In justification, Ernest W. Lefever has observed, "There is one thing you can say for capital punishment; a criminal subjected to it will never repeat a capital or any other crime."[18] Following the murder of a member of Spain's civil guard by Basque separatists, for example, the Spanish government, in 1975, enacted a new law decreeing death for anyone guilty of killing a member of the police, armed forces, or security units during a terrorist, but not a purely criminal, action. The distinction as to what constitutes a terrorist action, as opposed to a criminal action, is left up to the judge. Likewise, in 1979, Israeli Prime Minister Menachem Begin called for the imposition of the death penalty for extremely cruel acts of terrorism, which like Spain's law, is a rather ambiguous standard and calls for a subjective judgment on the part of the judge or court as to what really is a particularly cruel act of terrorism. Nevertheless, the advocacy of a death penalty is especially significant since the only individual ever executed by Israel was Nazi war criminal Adolf Eichmann. Public opinion polls, moreover, in both the United States and the United Kingdom indicate that an overwhelming majority of the citizens of both countries favor the death penalty for terrorists.

At the same time, however some evidence indicates that severe punishment does not always serve as a deterrent to terrorists; many terrorists are fully aware of the fate or punishment that lies in store for them if they commit a particular act of violence and have the misfortune of being caught, yet they go ahead and commit the crime anyway. Obviously, the threat of punishment will not deter zealots of this kind; in such cases, the only advantage provided by capital punishment, according to Representative Lester Wolff, is that the terrorist will die in silence instead of being able to make a political statement in the act of surrendering his or her existence.[19] In conclusion, perhaps the chief argument in behalf of the execution of terrorists, even if the death penalty does not serve as a deterrent, is that it will save governments a good deal of trouble and expense and may even contribute positively to the national psyche.

Boycotting Nations that Support Terrorism

One of the most effective methods—short of using force—to combat terrorism is to isolate countries, both economically or in terms of international travel and communications, that harbor terrorists or support terrorist activities. By threatening to make the offending countries international pariahs, it is hoped that behavior destructive to international comity and stability can be deterred. In 1977, for example, following the skyjacking of a West German jetliner to Somalia, during which the pilot was murdered, the International Federation of Airline Pilots threatened to stage a forty-eight-hour worldwide strike unless the UN acted on the matter of air piracy and collateral terrorist threats to international aviation. The threatened boycott produced a UN resolution condemning airline skyjackings and calling upon all nations to prevent the seizure of hostages as a means of extorting the release of political prisoners. Even nations such as Libya, Algeria, and South Yemen, which had in the past harbored air pirates and provided other support to international terrorist organizations, voted for the resolution in the General Assembly. Their behavior is explained by the fact that few nations can afford to be cut off from access to or communication with the rest of the world, especially those that must import most of their technology and foodstuffs. The U.S. attempt to enlist its Western allies in a program of economic sanctions against Iran in order to win the release of fifty-three U.S. hostages held in captivity by Iranian militants is another example of a boycott being used to apply pressure on a nation that has violated established norms of international behavior.

To be successful, however, boycotts must impose an unacceptable hardship on offending nations and must have widespread support, lest noncomplying countries serve as a channel to circumvent the boycott. This is why congressional proposals to cut off foreign aid and trade with nations accused of tolerating terrorism must be viewed as unsound and counterproductive. In the event of unilateral action by the United States, the black-listed nations have only to turn to the USSR or any of a variety of other nations to fill the void. Moreover, some of the nations most often accused of aiding and abetting international terrorism are major petroleum exporters that have the ability and wherewithal to purchase needed technology and commodities elsewhere.

Isolation of Terrorists from the Population

In view of Mao's dictum that the "people are like water and the army is like fish," the logic of depriving terrorists or insurgents of the life-sustaining medium in which they flourish—namely, the host population—is indisputable and should form the backbone in any long-range counterterrorist strategy. A hostile populace is one of the chief restraints that can be placed on terrorist activities. "It is important," writes I.M.H. Smart, "that terrorists themselves are not entirely immune to the normative constraints of the societies within which they operate. To the extent that they depend upon the connivance, or at least complacency, of some part of the local population, they must be cautious about acting in ways which might offend or alienate them from all support."[20] To this end, propaganda should be utilized to wean the population away from the terrorists because, as Richard Clutterbuck has observed, "The most effective control . . . lies in the minds of the public."[21] In most conflicts, the goals professed by the terrorists will be appealing politically and phrased in such a manner that strikes a responsive chord in a large segment of the population, whether or not the terrorists intend ever to implement the goals. Thus, the government will have greater success in convincing the populace to repudiate the methods of the terrorists rather than their goals. This can be done through graphic depictions of the victims of terrorism and by giving wide dissemination to terrorist attacks on values and institutions that the society at large holds dear. The government should aim, whenever possible, to convey an unflattering picture of the personal lives and habits of the terrorists, portraying them as cruel, atheistic (in countries where there is a strong religious tradition), sexually deviant, or hypocritical people who do not practice the values they espouse. Terrorists will only enjoy significant popular support if the man on the street can identify with them and their cause, and anything that diminishes this commonality will serve to weaken the link between the terrorists and the public. A word of caution, however, must be introduced. National governments must take care not to fabricate adverse propaganda about terrorists, since if it can be proven that any of the government charges are patently false, all subsequent information regarding the terrorists, no matter how correct, will run the risk of being greeted with skepticism by the public.

The government, moreover, must communicate effectively to the public the reasons it deserves their support. In other words, it must make a strong case for itself and not simply offer the public a negative campaign directed against its opposition. The government should formulate an alternative to the terrorists, especially in less-developed countries where poverty and the unequal distribution of wealth and power are often the key factors motivating an individual to join the insurgents. In the Philippines, for example, Ramon Magsaysay, first as defense minister and later as president, won over peasant confidence for the government by taking aggressive steps to address the economic and social ills that weighed heavily upon them. Extensive land reform measures, coupled with a government promise of free land and other opportunities, induced many Huk (from *Hukbalahap*, or People's Army) guerrillas to defect to the government. He also put an end to what Taber describes as "military terrorism" and set much of the army to doing what amounted to socially useful work, "setting up medical stations, building schoolhouses, repairing roads and bridges, helping the peasants get their rice to market."[22] As a result of the Philippine government's aggressive effort to stabilize the economy and provide a more equal distribution of wealth, the Huk insurgency was rapidly eclipsed as a serious threat to the nation, although sporadic Huk resistance continues to this day. The government can also provide monetary rewards to defectors, as the British did in Malaya, and large rewards to the public for information leading to the arrest and capture of terrorists.

The actual physical separation of the people from the terrorists can be accomplished in a variety of ways. The construction by the British of a fifty-mile-long fosse, or ditch, patrolled and booby trapped, in Kenya during the Mau Mau insurrection drastically reduced terrorist infiltration into the country's more populous regions and effectively contained many of the insurgents in the Mount Kenya forest.[23] Similarly, the relocation and resettlement of populations into protected or so-called strategic villages, first employed by Lord Kitchener during the Boer War, provides protection to the civilian population from intimidation and coercion and, at the same time, makes more difficult the recruitment of new members and the collection of food and intelligence by the insurgents. Such a strategy, however, is really only applicable to conflicts in the less-developed world when dealing with a largely rural population, although both Israel and South Africa are taking steps to isolate increasingly their Arab and black populations respectively in an effort to exert more control over them and to prevent their support of terrorists.

One of the most controversial methods used in recent years to isolate terrorists from the population at large is internment. In Belfast, Northern Ireland, U.K. authorities have incarcerated thousands of suspected IRA members and sympathizers on the grounds that they are a danger to the community. An interim custody order permits suspects to be imprisoned for up to twenty-eight days without any form of due process; before the end of the twenty-eight-day period, however, security forces must convince a panel of commissioners that the individual should remain in custody. If the commissioners concur, the individual is held in confinement for an indefinite period, subject to periodic review. While nearly 70 percent of all detainees are released within forty-eight hours, the remainder are interned for weeks, months, even years.[24] No action by the British has provoked more bitterness among Ulster's Catholic minority than the internment program, and it is debatable whether its benefits are worth the alienation it produces and the outrage felt by civil libertarians both in the United Kingdom and elsewhere.

Restrictions on Mobility

Freedom of movement is one of the principal requirements of any terrorist group, and the lack of mobility in the USSR and the Eastern bloc nations accounts in large measure for the relative absence of terrorism in those countries. Strict passport and identity control, including the issuance of national identity cards, serves as a deterrent to terrorism and causes terrorists to adjust their behavior significantly. Similarly, lodging cards like those used in France, which are collected daily by authorities, assist police agencies in tracing the movements of anyone who stays in public accommodations.

Citizens innocent of crimes should have little to fear from such methods;

they will be only slightly inconvenienced. However, the United States takes pride in its unrestricted internal movement and to date has resisted all suggestion of national identity cards, internal passports, or limitations on internal travel. This fact, combined with what some have charged are lax passport and border controls, has resulted in the United States becoming an increasingly popular safe haven for terrorists.

Concentrating on the terrorist's mobility, access to important targets can be reduced by means of cordons and strict security checkpoints like those employed by the British in Northern Ireland that screen people for weapons and explosives and check their identity cards. Curfews are used to keep movement to a minimum at night when terrorists are most likely to stage attacks. It is a relatively simple technical matter to secure key industrial and military targets by ringing the perimeters of such areas with barbed wire and other obstacles, intrusion detectors, and high-intensity lights. Physical security measures should be augmented by regular patrols and entry and exit controlled with special authority permits.

In the event of a terrorist attack, thought must again turn to reducing the terrorist's ability to move and hence to escape. In this connection, both the Israelis and the British (in Northern Ireland) have found that cordoning off the immediate area of the attack and then sweeping it with troops and dogs, conducting careful house-to-house searches, often flushes out the terrorists. Such a response, however, places a premium on speed and the ability of the government to mobilize and position its forces.

Restriction of Access to Weapons and Explosives

Whenever possible, terrorists must be denied access to modern weapons and explosives. Gun-control laws, however, are a poor means of accomplishing this goal and have had little demonstrable impact in preventing terrorists from acquiring the necessary tools of their trade since the kind of sophisticated automatic weapons and modern explosives they favor are not ordinarily available on an over-the-counter basis and usually must be purchased on the black market or in arms bazaars of Asia and the Middle East, stolen from military arsenals, or obtained from the so-called terrorist international or from patron nations committed to the support of various terrorist movements. Once in the possession of terrorists, such weapons and explosives can be smuggled into the country where they will be employed without much difficulty. The fact that the United Kingdom has one of the toughest gun-control laws in the world has not prevented the IRA and other terrorist groups from using guns and bombs on U.K. soil.

Good intelligence and a high degree of vigilance constitute the best strategy for tracing the sources and interdicting the arms, explosives, and supplies destined for terrorist use. Even if it were possible to dry up the supply of weapons and explosives going to terrorist groups, the range of homemade and alternative weapons available to terrorists, many of them constructed from relatively ordinary substances, is absolutely staggering, and any imaginative terrorist need not fear being left unarmed.

Police Force Well-Schooled in Counterterrorist Methods

A nation's police and internal security forces will always be on the cutting edge of the war against terrorism because they will likely respond first to terrorist incidents and often will have the chief responsibility for hunting down and apprehending terrorists. Yet most police organizations, in the United States and abroad, are woefully unprepared to deal with serious terrorist challenges. SWAT (Special Weapons and Tactics) teams are not without utility in suppressing terrorism, but by no means do they constitute an optimal force option. A review of the SWAT training programs employed by a number of prominent police departments in the United States reveals an emphasis on riot control, anti-sniper and reaction force techniques, as well as considerable time honing marksmanship and hand-to-hand-combat skills. The formidable character of the terrorist threat, by contrast, requires that police be schooled in the whole range of counterterrorist techniques and be equipped with modern, highly specialized hardware that has been developed specifically to combat terrorism. Not only will this permit them to act more efficiently and effectively to terrorist challenges, with a corresponding increase in their chances for survival against a well-armed and resourceful enemy, but also it will help to ensure that they do not overreact to the threat or behave in a manner that would impact negatively on public opinion, perhaps even to the extent of winning sympathy and converts for the terrorists. The ultimate test of any successful police operation against terrorists must be the employment of no more force than necessary to bring the challenge under control.

The use of excessive force is a sign of frustration and an admission of the insecurity that accompanies a lack of a clearly defined strategy or proper range of options for combating the enemy. The possibility of embarrassment or defeat at the hands of terrorists often loosens police inhibitions, and while the employment of extreme measures relating to search, surveillance, detention, and interrogation, including systematic brutality and torture, may produce positive results in the war against terrorism, they do so at a terribly high cost. The use of torture, in particular, as Moss notes, "is usually a sign that the security forces are acting on the basis of ignorance" and, once adopted, is often all but impossible to control.[25] Thus, the best safeguard against heavy-handed police methods and the onset of political repression in response to disruptive acts of terrorism is the development of new and highly specialized and refined capabilities for dealing with terrorism. Police should not be called upon to do that for which they are ill-trained and -prepared; to do so is to court disaster.

In the final analysis, the incorrect or inadequate response to a terrorist challenge may only aggravate an already difficult situation, especially hostage situations, turning an otherwise resolvable incident into a tragedy like the Munich Olympics when police were utilized in a desperate attempt to free the Israeli hostages. The end result was one policeman, five terrorists, and all of the hostages killed.

Government-Sanctioned Vigilante Actions

The decline of public confidence that accompanies a government's failure to suppress or contain a terrorist threat often prompts fearful and disgruntled citizens to band together in death squads and other vigilante groupings that adopt the terrorist's own tactics in order to strike back at them. Most prevalent in Latin America in recent years, death squads have fueled the vicious cycle of terror that has gripped nations like El Salvador, Nicaragua, Guatemala, Uruguay, Argentina, and Brazil, witnessing each act of violence answered with an equal or bloodier act of violence. Similarly, Protestant death squads in Ulster often have responded to IRA terror with terror of their own. The June 1980 maiming of two Arab mayors on the West Bank in separate ignition-triggered car explosions, moreover, is thought to be the work of Jewish extremists and may presage the rise of right-wing death squads in Israel.

Often officially sanctioned, many death squads contain a large number of regular police and military officers. Operating usually at night, death squads seek to terrorize the opposition by means of violence and brutality directed against those considered suspected terrorists, their families and supporters. In many cases, the victims simply disappear, while in other instances, the victim's body, which often has been mutilated, is left in a prominent place as a warning and reminder to others. In 1979, it was not unusual for more than a dozen bodies to be discovered each morning in El Salvador, buried in shallow graves, hanging from lamp posts, or dumped along rural roads—victims of right-wing death squads.

Death squads contributed significantly to the defeat of terrorism in the nations of Uruguay and Guatemala, according to Richard Gott, because terrorists had grown accustomed to their opponents playing by rules that they themselves did not observe. The Tupamaros, for example, were totally unprepared to respond to terror when it was turned against them.[26] On the other hand, the murder of a prominent Nicaraguan newspaper editor, which was presumably the work of a pro-government death squad, was the catalyst that touched off open revolt in Nicaragua in 1978 and ultimately resulted in the fall of dictator Anastasio Somoza.

Reprisals

On 14 March 1978, following a bloody terrorist strike in Israel that left 38 Israelis dead and 78 injured, Israel launched a major invasion of southern Lebanon to wipe out guerrilla strongholds and to establish a buffer zone along its northern border. Although it was the largest retaliatory attack in the history of the protracted conflict, it was by no means the first time that the Israelis had retaliated in swift, brutal fashion following a Palestinian terrorist provocation. On 20 February 1973, for example, Israel struck at Palestinian training bases in northern Lebanon in retaliation for the massacre of Israeli athletes at the 1972 Munich Olympics and the bloody attack at Lod Airport by JRA members recruited by the PFLP. The following year, after 28 Israelis, most of them children, died in the storming of a school that had been taken over by Arab guerrillas, Israel commenced a nine-month-long series of retaliatory air strikes against Palestinian military positions, villages, and refugee camps. At least five major Israeli incursions into Lebanon occurred in 1975 in response to Palestinian provocations, including a combined air, land, and sea operation against terrorist bases in Lebanon in the aftermath of the explosion of a bomb-rigged refrigerator that took the lives of 14 people in Jerusalem. In November 1977, 192 people were killed and wounded in southern Lebanon as a result of Israeli air strikes in retaliation for Palestinian rocket attacks that killed 3 Israelis. In a literal application of the Old Testament prescription of an "eye for eye, tooth for tooth, hand for hand, foot for foot, burning for burning, wound for wound, stripe for stripe," in the period between the conclusion of the 1973 Middle East War and early 1978, more than 2,000 Arabs—many of them women and children— perished in Israeli retaliatory raids against Palestinian villages and refugee camps in Lebanon. During the same period, 143 Israelis lost their lives to terrorists.

Although Israel undertook no retaliatory operations in the two years following the big 1978 occupation of southern Lebanon in order not to strain relations with the United States further or to create another impediment to the peace process, the cycle of violence and counterviolence continues unabated. Israel's response in kind to terrorist attacks on its citizens or territory has not always taken the form of air raids and military operations against Palestinian positions and villages in Lebanon. When an agricultural attaché at the Israeli embassy in London was killed in 1972 in the explosion of a letter bomb, the Israelis retaliated the following month with letter bombs of their own addressed to Palestinian officials in Egypt, Algeria, Lebanon, and Libya. Palestinians known to have planned or aided in the execution of terrorist attacks against Israelis have been systematically hunted down and eliminated, as in the 1979 car-bomb explosion that killed Munich mastermind Abu Hassan in Beirut and the subsequent assassination of the PLO's military operations chief, Zuhair Moshen, at Cannes. In 1980, after the murder of six Jewish religious students in the West Bank city of Hebron, Israeli troops bulldozed Arab homes in the vicinity of the attack, forcibly relocated Arab families, and expelled six prominent Arab mayors from the West Bank. Razing Arab homes in the occupied territories, following the arrest—but not necessarily the conviction—of any member of the household, has been a long-standing Israeli practice.[27]

Of course, Israel is not the only nation to employ a policy of systematic retaliation in response to terrorist provocations; reprisals of one kind or another have been witnessed in every protracted struggle during the twentieth century. The theory of retaliation and reprisal is based on the notion of collective responsibility, whereby all of the members of a particular community or group are held accountable for the actions of a few, in the belief that the majority either provides support and sustenance to a violent minority or at the very least is deserving of whatever fate the aggrieved party visits upon it since it has proved itself to be incapable of or unwilling to take effective steps to restrain those members of the community from inflicting injury on others. According to John D. LeNoir and Jerry M. Tinker, examples of collective-responsibility reprisals date back to antiquity, appearing as early as 221 B.C. in China.[28]

The right of reprisal, defined as "coercive measures directed by a state against another state in response to (or 'in retaliation for') illegal acts of the latter for the purpose of obtaining, either directly or indirectly, reparation or satisfaction of the illegal act,"[29] is recognized under international law, although the resort to reprisals as a form of self-help to redress a prior illegal act must be seen as an admission of the weakness of international law, especially with respect to its enforcement. Nevertheless, following the conditions first set out in the Naulilaa Arbitration Award in 1928, reprisals, in order to be legitimate, must have been (1) precipitated by an illegal act on the part of the offending state, (2) preceded by an unsatisfied demand for peaceful redress of the injury, and (3) in proportion to the initial action.[30]

Gerhard von Glahn has observed that Israeli military reprisals have "followed almost automatically the commission of the illegal act."[31] In this connection, Israel's reprisals have been criticized both for violating the rule of proportionality and the requirement that a request for redress be initiated before there is any resort to force. The Israelis respond, however, that any effort to seek peaceful redress would be futile and a waste of time. This was basically the same position the United States took in 1916 when a punitive U.S. expeditionary force of 15,000 men, under the command of General John J. Pershing, was sent into Mexico in pursuit of the Mexican revolutionary Pancho Villa, who had raided settlements in Texas and New Mexico repeatedly during the spring, killing a number of U.S. citizens in the process. In a subsequent public address, President Woodrow Wilson justified the strong U.S. action as a matter of necessity since the Mexican government was incapable of preventing attacks on the United States from its territory: "It was a plain case of the violation of our sovereignty which could not wait to be vindicated by damages for which there was no other remedy."[32]

The question, however, remains: Can reprisals be considered an effective method of combating terrorism? Historically, in Algeria, South Vietnam, the Philippines, Palestine, Cyprus, and Greece, to cite but a few postwar examples, harsh governmental retaliation against significant portions of the civilian population, in response to acts of sabotage and violence, drove far more people into the ranks of the antigovernment forces than they discouraged. It is a fact that if all are made to suffer for the actions of a few, whatever apparent benefit there might be in supporting the national government, or simply standing apart from the struggle, is erased. If one is going to be punished regardless of his or her actions, then where is the profit in collaborating, in being a dutiful servant of the government? Indiscriminate reprisals usually antagonize a whole population in an effort to combat a small minority. In Palestine, for example, only a small portion of the Jewish population initially supported the violent actions of the Zionist terror groups. However, U.K security forces adopted a harsh and heavy-handed program of searches, arrests, and detention that fostered widespread animosity against the British and produced new supporters for the outlawed Zionist underground. According to Bell, "All the tools to repress violent opposition [in Palestine] were used in such a way as to encourage further and more violent opposition: Every attempt to punish the terrorists produced more terror."[33] This also appears to be the case with respect to Israel's retaliatory strikes in southern Lebanon. The Lebanese civilians caught up in the struggle tend to attribute their misery and suffering to the Israelis rather than to the Palestinians, whose presence and activities on Lebanese soil are the stimulus for the Israeli reprisals. One Lebanese civilian told a reporter, "Now that the Israelis are bombing our village, too, we see what the Palestinians have suffered all these years."[34]

Also, the local population that is the target of such reprisals is often powerless to prevent the illegal acts from occurring. In some sections of occupied France during World War II, the Nazis posted the names of prominent local citizens and village leaders in the public squares and declared that, if any more acts of sabotage by the partisans occurred, they would automatically execute the people whose names were on the list. The people of the affected villages, naturally, refrained from any further acts of violence and sabotage; however, the leadership of the underground reacted by importing saboteurs from the outside. Similarly, neither the Lebanese government nor the inhabitants of the affected areas in the southern region of that country have the military power to control effectively the activities of the Palestinians. Thus, repeated reprisals against a population incapable of defending itself or of taking decisive action to remove the source of the controversy amounts to a cruel strategy that, from a practical standpoint, only feeds the hatreds already permeating the region.

All of this is not to suggest that Israel, or any other nation for that matter, does not have the right to "sever the arm of iniquity," as Israeli Prime Minister Menachem Begin has described Palestinian terrorists, but rather to affirm that reprisals, whatever form they take, and any other military actions, must be directed solely at those responsible for the actual violence that precipitated the reprisal. Retaliatory actions are only justifiable, morally and militarily, if it is possible to strike back, in the aftermath of some provocation, at the guilty parties without causing casualties or destroying the homes and livelihoods of those innocent of any crime. Indeed, there is, for the most part, little world reaction to a severe retribution being meted out to terrorists who have committed bloody atrocities. However, if reprisals are relatively indiscriminate and result in high casualties among noncombatants, then the injured party carrying out the reprisal is guilty of the same terrorist behavior as its enemies. While high in symbolic value, the usefulness of most reprisals from a military point of view is quite negligible. Reprisals constitute a punitive tactic that provides, at best, simply a modicum of satifaction to the aggrieved party that an equal or greater measure of blood has been spilled in retaliation for the injuries it suffered. Finally, reprisals like the relatively indiscriminate Israeli raids and air strikes in southern Lebanon are a very high-cost tactic, often resulting in strained relations with disapproving allies and general world condemnation.

Elimination of Safe Havens

The denial of safe havens to terrorists would be a thrust at the heart of the beast and perhaps the single most effective action that could be taken to combat terrorism. The elimination of safe havens, however, under most circumstances must be ruled out as a less-than-viable option inasmuch as any military action against terrorist bases in one country by another country would likely result in an open state of war between those two countries. While there "is no convincing moral argument against such an attack," it would hardly be prudent for Israel to strike militarily at terrorists in nations such as South Yemen, Libya, or Iraq, unless it was prepared for the consequences and perhaps even the intervention of the USSR in support of its client states.[35] The violation of the territory of a weak and fragmented nation like Lebanon or an outcast and misruled country like Uganda, when in hot pursuit of terrorists or attempting to strike at their sanctuaries, may be feasible politically and militarily, but under most circumstances, covert action against the governments that harbor terrorists and provide them with safe havens is a safer and more expedient strategy.

Executive Action

The necessity of maintaining a world order compatible with a society's national interests means that sometimes, under extreme circumstances, systematic murder must be sanctioned and legitimized as an instrument of national policy. This is obviously a painful dilemma for many liberal democracies that are con-

fronted with the equally undesirable choices of behaving like terrorists or sub-
mitting to them. However, it is far preferable to eliminate practicing terrorists
through covert methods than to witness a wholesale curtailment of individual
freedoms and the adoption of emergency legislation that punishes an entire
nation in order to thwart the violent intentions of a few by reducing civil liberties and personal freedoms and subjecting everyone to the arbitrary will of the
state.

Just as it is not a crime to kill the enemy during wartime, so too should it
not be regarded as a crime or a morally reprehensible act when a nation, acting
in concert with its obligation to protect its own citizens from harm, seeks out
and destroys terrorists outside its borders who have committed, or are planning
to commit, atrocities on its territory or against its citizens. The Israeli Mossad,
as noted earlier, has for some time waged a war in the shadows against international terrorism, sending out hit teams to terminate the architects and execu-
tioners of particularly vicious attacks against Israel and its citizens, to let them—
and others like them—know that they will not be permitted to strike with
impunity at Israel simply because they have taken refuge on the soil of another
country. From a moral standpoint, such a policy is far more justifiable than the
indiscriminate retaliatory bombing of refugee camps and villages since only
the guilty are punished. It should be noted, however, that assassinations on
foreign soil run the risk of endangering relations between the nation carrying
out the termination and the nation whose sovereignty has been violated. As a
rule, the targets of such terminations should not be nationals of the country on
whose soil the hit is made so as to diminish the concern of that government over
the incident and to relieve it of the need to retaliate against the offending nation
out of a sense of obligation to its own citizens.

Obviously, state-sanctioned terminations must be controlled and supervised
tightly to ensure that little opportunity exists for abuse. Such methods should
be considered only when the potential target cannot be brought to justice in a
more conventional manner.

Not only terrorists but also the national leaders of the countries that give
them support and sustenance have been targeted for assassination by nations
that are victims of terrorism. It has been reported that Libyan dictator Qaddafi
is the focus of more hit contracts than any other head-of-state. At least a dozen
known attempts have been made on his life, including a 1978 incident in which
the rotor blades of his helicopter were loosened, causing the chopper to crash
with the loss of all aboard. Qaddafi had been scheduled to use the helicopter but
changed his mind at the last minute, thus avoiding an early demise. Saudi Arabia
has, on various occasions, explored the possibility of assassinating Qaddafi in
retaliation for his meddling in Saudi Arabian internal affairs and his support of
elements opposed to the monarchy. Similarly, President Ferdinand E. Marcos
of the Philippines put out a contract on Qaddafi in retaliation for the Libyan
dictator's financial and military support of Moslem Moro secessionists in
southern Mindanao.

Commando Operations

Western governments have employed a variety of nonforce strategies in their
efforts to resist terrorism, including diplomacy, negotiation, concessions, and
cooptation. Occasionally such methods have worked, but more often than not
they have failed or only provided a temporary prophylaxis to an endemic
problem. It is widely recognized that, under most circumstances, making concessions to terrorists only invites further acts of terrorism. This fact, combined
with the failure of the UN to take concerted action to develop effective remedies
to the problem of international terrorism, has resulted in a growing tendency on
the part of national governments to resort to unilateral military action against
terrorism in the belief that, if it is not possible to make terrorists answerable to
the law, then they must be answerable to the gun. Proponents of the military
option justify the decision to employ force by noting that Article 51 of the UN
charter affirms the inherent right of states to self-defense in the face of armed
attack. Acts of terrorism may be considered as constituting an armed attack
since every nation reserves the right to determine when circumstances require
recourse to military action in its self-defense.

    Until recently, the primary responsibility for combating terrorism in most
Western countries fell on the shoulders of the police and internal security forces
or, in extreme circumstances, on army units trained to fight conventional wars
but woefully unprepared for the demands imposed by antiterrorist warfare.
Moreover, conventional troops and military methods are often useless against
terrorists. Not only are contemporary weapons and tactics far too destructive
to be employed in heavily populated urban regions, but also the deployment
of large numbers of soldiers against terrorists simply increases the number of
targets at which they can strike. A nation may possess a strong navy, air force,
and army and at the same time be powerless in the face of a serious terrorist
challenge for lack of proper tools. In the words of General George Grivas, the
Cypriot terrorist leader:

> [O]ne does not use a tank to catch field mice—a cat will do the job
> better. The [British] Field-Marshal's only hope of finding us was to
> play cat and mouse: to use tiny, expertly trained groups, who could
> work with cunning and patience and strike rapidly when we least
> expected.[36]

"Terrorism is a knife that cuts both ways," as Major Henry J. Chisholm
has noted; and in this connection, experience indicates that the best results
against terrorism involve turning the terrorists' own weapons—stealth and
cunning—against them.[37] Counterterrorism demands highly trained and motivated commandos, operating in small groups; skilled in electronics, communications, demolitions, marksmanship, deception, silent killing; and familiar with
terrorist tactics and behavior. Only by turning the tables on terrorists and

making the hunters also the hunted can governments hope to seize the initiative and begin effectively to manage terrorist crises.

In Kenya and Malaysia, the British utilized small expertly trained commando squads to ferret out terrorists and to destroy them. Often such squads included exterrorists who had defected to the U.K. side, in keeping with Laqueur's observation that, "It is the former terrorist, the renegade, who has traditionally been the terrorist's most dangerous opponent."[38] Some of the units, so-called pseudogangs, passed themselves off as insurgents by adopting the behavior, secret signs, oaths, and dress of their opponents. Not only were such teams adept at collecting valuable intelligence, but also they were often able to get the drop on genuine enemy insurgent units and either to capture or eliminate them. Moreover, the existence of pseudogangs promoted distrust among enemy units and eroded cooperation inasmuch as insurgent commanders could never be absolutely certain of the identity of other units that they encountered. Similarly, the French high command in Algeria recognized the advantage of sending out small killer detachments, *commandos de chasse*, to seek out and destroy insurgents.

From such counterinsurgency tactics, the creation of elite specialized commando units capable of reacting decisively to any terrorist threat, from rescuing a hijacked airliner to liberating hostages in a besieged building, was a natural evolution.

General Intelligence and Reconnaissance Unit 269 (Israel)

The first significant use of a specially trained antiterrorist commando unit was on 4 July 1976, when the Israelis carried out a daring rescue mission known as Operation Thunderbolt, designed to free 103 hostages being held, with the cooperation and complicity of the Ugandan government, by pro-Palestinian terrorists at Entebbe Airport, located about twenty-one miles from Kampala. At precisely one minute past midnight, shortly before the deadline set by the terrorists was scheduled to expire, four C-130 Hercules transport planes touched down in the darkness at the almost deserted African airport and disgorged nearly a hundred crack Israeli commandos, together with half-tracks and jeeps armed with 106-millimeter recoilless guns. Confusion was thrown into the ranks of the sleepy Ugandan soldiers guarding the airport, and precious seconds were purchased when a sleek Mercedes limousine, which closely resembled that used by Ugandan dictator, Field Marshal Idi Amin, sped down the ramp from one of the C-130s and accelerated toward the old terminal building where the hostages were being held. As the Ugandan security guards snapped to attention and saluted, they were cut down by Israeli commandos in the limousine.

The raid lasted ninety minutes and was, for all intents and purposes, a complete success. Israeli military planners had expected as many as thirty dead and fifty wounded, but the final toll was far less. Only one soldier, Lieutenant

Colonel Yehonatan Netanyahu, the commander of the mission, died in the raid, and four were wounded.[39] Several civilians also lost their lives and five suffered wounds, but on the whole, the casualties were far lighter than even the most optimistic projections made by the planners of the rescue attempt. Seven of the ten terrorists were killed, together with perhaps as many as forty-five Ugandan soldiers. Soviet-built MIG fighters parked near the new terminal were destroyed, and both control towers at the airport sustained extensive damage. Also left in shambles in the wake of the bold Israeli raid was the prestige of Uganda's former despot, Idi Amin, who at the time was serving as the chairman of the Organization of African Unity.

The courageous Israeli surgical strike was greeted with praise and admiration throughout the Western world, though predictably it was condemned by many Arab and Third World nations as an act of aggression. Israeli Prime Minister Rabin announced to a crowded and exultant Parliament that the operation was "Israel's contribution to the worldwide battle against terrorism."

Lost in the rejoicing over the mission's triumphant outcome, however, was any thought to the devastating consequences that would likely have ensued had the operation failed and resulted in the deaths of the hostages and most of the commandos. In Prime Minister Rabin's blunt assessment, a catastrophe would have represented a great victory for Israel's enemies. Moreover, there is little doubt that Rabin's government would have fallen and that Israel, which at the time was beset by severe economic difficulties and pervaded by a deepening sense of gloom and self-doubt over its growing isolation and the shift of power and wealth to the Arab world that accompanied the explosive increase in crude oil prices, would have been plunged into perhaps the most serious crisis of its short history. As one Israeli official succinctly put it, "If Israel should ever fail to protect her own, she would cease to have meaning."[40]

While the Israelis had served notice that they could and would strike back at terrorists, swiftly and without mercy, far from the borders of the Jewish state, the success of the raid was attributable to a unique and fortuitous set of circumstances and not a little good luck. Uganda, a wretched and backward country under dictatorial rule, possessed neither the capability to detect the Israeli intrusion of Ugandan air space nor well-disciplined and alert troops at the airport. The relatively simple deception of using a Mercedes resembling Amin's to confuse the Ugandan soldiers would not have worked in a more sophisticated environment. Entebbe Airport was located over twenty miles from Kampala, in a realtively isolated area, not in a densely populated urban setting that would have immeasurably complicated the mission. Moreover, Entebbe Airport was only lightly utilized, and no air traffic was scheduled until 2:30 A.M. when a British Airways flight was due to land for short stopover on a run from London to Mauritius. The adjacent country of Kenya cooperated with the Israelis, permitting them to refuel at Nairobi. In sum, the Entebbe raid worked in large measure because it was totally novel. A counterterrorist commando strike on the same scale had never been attempted before, and it was totally unexpected by either the terrorists or the Ugandan military. A word also needs to be mentioned about the role of luck in any military operation. No matter how much planning and preparation goes into a mission of this type, its success or failure, in the final analysis, will depend to some degree on luck, or at least the lack of bad luck. The Israelis gambled at Entebbe and won; they could have lost just as easily, as when Israeli paratroopers, on another occasion, attempted to recapture a school taken over by terrorists in Israel. The school ultimately was liberated, but twenty-two children and six adults perished in the incident.

GSG-9 (West Germany)

The Entebbe raid provided additional impetus, though not the inspiration, for the creation by West Germany of an elite antiterrorist commando unit along the lines of the Israeli General Intelligence and Reconnaissance Unit 269. The bungled effort by the West German police to rescue the Israeli athletes taken hostage by Palestinian terrorists at the 1972 Munich Olympics underscored the deficiencies associated with deploying inadequately trained and equipped police or military units in response to a serious terrorist challenge. At Munich, the West German strategy was initially to induce the terrorists to board a decoy airliner at Fürstenfeldbruck Airport under the pretext that the government had capitulated to their demands and was prepared to transport them to a safe haven in the Middle East. Once aboard, policemen disguised as crew members were supposed to overpower the terrorists. The policemen, however, found the risks associated with the mission unacceptable and refused to go through with it. In desperation, the German authorities decided to position snipers on nearby buildings who were outfitted with rifles with night vision sighting devices in an attempt to pick off the terrorists as they boarded the getaway aircraft. The snipers managed, however, to hit only two (some accounts say three) of the eight terrorists when they opened fire, and in the ensuing melee, nine Israeli hostages lost their lives.

By contrast to that night in 1972 at Munich, when a German Lufthansa jetliner was hijacked to Mogadishu, Somalia, in October 1977, the German government was able to call on a special antiterrorist unit known as *Grenzschutzgruppe-9*, or Border Protection Group Nine, (GSG-9) attached to the German border police. Although the unit, composed of 180 men, had never seen action in the field before, its members had received twenty-two weeks of intensive training, some of it drawing upon Israeli training methods and organizational input, and had sharpened its skills protecting German government officials. Its commander, Lieutenant Colonel Ulrich Wegener, had received special training both in the United States and from the Israelis.

GSG-9 does not report through the conventional military or police command structures, but instead its lines of authority emanate directly from the nation's prime minister and a special cabinet-level crisis management team established to advise him. The unit's chief mission is to strike back at terrorists whenever and wherever the government or its citizens are imperiled, and to this end, GSG-9 can rely upon the most advanced antiterrorist equipment in the world, including special communications and tracking equipment, lightweight body armor reflecting the highest level of the state-of-the-art, specially prepared Mercedes Benz 280SE and Porsche pursuit automobiles, custom-built French helicopters, and advanced weaponry such as the MP5K submachine gun and the Mauser 66 sniper rifle. Every man is trained in skills such as evasive driving, karate, rappeling, scuba diving, knife fighting, and demolitions. Great emphasis is put on marksmanship since it was anticipated that the unit would engage often in hostage retrieval situations where sharpshooters would have to be able to eliminate terrorists without injuring their captives, and German officials wanted no repeat of the abortive Munich rescue attempt. Training films of the unit have shown GSG-9 commandos firing at a speeding auto from a helicopter with submachine guns, hitting both of the dummy terrorists in the front seat without touching the captives in the back seat. Skills like these make the group a formidable opponent against any band of terrorists.

Shortly after Lufthansa flight 181 had been diverted, West German Interior Minister Werner Maihofer activated the unit. With twenty-eight hand-picked commandos, along with thirty medical personnel and communications specialists and a variety of gear, Wegener set off in pursuit of the hijacked airliner in a Boeing 727.[41] The commando unit caught up with flight 181 at Larnaca, Cyprus, but the Cypriot government refused to permit them to attempt a rescue. The hijacked Lufthansa airliner then began an odyssey that took it to Bahrain, Dubai, South Yemen, and a ultimately to Mogadishu, Somalia. In Aden, the terrorists murdered the pilot, dumped his body out onto the tarmac in Mogadishu, and declared that if the government of West Germany did not agree within forty minutes to release eleven of their comrades from prison (plus two Palestinians serving sentences in Turkey) and provide them with a $15 million ransom, they would destroy the aircraft and their ninety remaining hostages. Under pressure from Western governments including the United States, Somali strongman Muhammed Siad Barre finally agreed to permit the German commando team, standing by at that moment in Crete, to attempt a rescue mission. The West Germans bought time to move the commandos into place and lulled the skyjackers off guard by announcing that they had acceded to their demands and were prepared to transport the eleven jailed terrorists to Mogadishu. The terrorists pushed back their deadline by seven hours, the amount of time they calculated it would require for the German plane carrying the eleven freed hostages to reach Mogadishu.

Shortly after 2 A.M., Mogadishu time, the plane with the commandos on board touched down at the airport, unobserved by the terrorists. Almost immediately, Wegener's men went into action. Dressed in dark clothing and shoes so soft that they could crawl along an airplaine fuselage without noise, their faces blackened against glare, armed with MP5K submachine guns and G3SG/1 sniper rifles with infrared sighting devices, they closed in silently on the hostage 727. Utilizing spike microphones to ascertain the exact location of each of the terrorists, the commandos took up positions around and underneath the airliner and on the wings. Ladders quietly were braced against the fuselage by the fore and aft doors on the right side of the plane. In order to concentrate the skyjackers in one location, their leader, known as Captain Mahmoud (real name, Zuhair Akache), was informed by radio from the tower that there were complications, and enraged, he predictably called the other terrorists to the cockpit to decide how to react to the news.

At that moment, the commandos blew off the starboard doors of the plane and the windows out of the emergency exits over the wings. Using stun grenades to blind the terrorists, and wearing protective goggles to shield their own eyes, they poured into the plane and made short work of the terrorists. Three skyjackers were mowed down by submachine gun fire, and one was badly wounded. None of the passengers or crew members was seriously hurt.

Magic Fire, as the operation had been code named, was a complete success from every perspective; the execution and timing of the rescue attempt were faultless, and the fact that no hostages were killed was something just short of miraculous. Wegener and the flight crew were awarded Germany's Cross of Merit for their performance, and the government was praised roundly for its firm and effective handling of the crisis. Perhaps most important, the successful resolution of the skyjacking relieved public pressure on the government and enabled it to reject the most onerous and antidemocratic of the proposed new antiterrorist measures before the German Parliament, designed to combat the rising tide of internal violence. Former radical student leader Daniel Cohn-Bendit, in an interview with a Paris newspaper reported by *The Washington Post*, said the raid was the "moral and political end" of Germany's Red Army faction.[42] What of the eleven terrorists whose freedom the skyjackers had demanded in exchange for the captured jetliner and its passengers and crew? Shortly after word reached them of the defeat of their comrades-in-arms at Mogadishu, three of the eleven jailed terrorists, including the notorious Andreas Baader, committed suicide in their prison cells.

Despite a spate of leftist-inspired riots and bombings, together with the murder of kidnapped German industrialist Hans Martin Schleyer, in retaliation for the raid and the deaths of the three jailed terrorists, Cohn-Bendit's remarks were prophetic: Within eighteen months of the Mogadishu incident, the German Red Army faction was eclipsed as a serious threat to German political stability. Armed with new confidence following the raid, the German government relentlessly hunted down the remaining members of the gang and took effective measures to cut off the support of sympathizers. Moreover, the successors to the first-generation leaders—Andreas Baader, Gunrun Ensslin, and Ulrike Meinhof—proved to be far less adroit or charismatic, and the organization has been driven underground and most of its members are, imprisoned, exiled, on the run, or dead.

Saiqa (Egypt)

If Entebbe and Mogadishu had been unqualified victories over terrorism as part of an expanding get-tough policy by national governments, then the ill-fated Egyptian attempt to rescue a jetliner at Larnaca Airport in Cyprus that had been commandeered by two Arab terrorists surely must be considered a victory for the terrorists. In March 1978, two pro-Palestinian Arab assassins gunned down Egyptian editor Yousef Sibai, a close friend of Egyptian President Anwar Sadat, in the lobby of a Nicosia hotel where he was attending a meeting of the Afro-Asia People's Solidarity Organization. Sibai, the organization's secretary-general, had supported President Sadat's peace initiative toward Israel. Nevertheless, he was a long-time champion of Palestinian rights.

The two terrorists were obvious amateurs who had, most likely, been recruited and instructed by a mysterious third man who left Nicosia prior to the attack. They lacked any clear conception of why Sibai had to be killed and offered later only that he was a spy for Israel—a patently absurd charge. As evidence of their lack of experience, they appeared to have little notion of the vital areas of the body from an assassin's point of view; their shooting was so sloppy that it took Sibai more than a half hour to die despite the fact that he had been shot repeatedly at close range. Further evidence that the two gunmen were not professionals can be deduced from the fact that they spoke only a limited amount of English and, therefore, appeared to have had little exposure to either travel or to Al Fatah's training camps. Moreover, when they demanded Arab intermediaries during the crisis, they were totally oblivious as to which Arab nations maintained embassies on Cyprus—an unlikely oversight if they had been trained hit men.

After shooting Sibai, they barricaded themselves and more than thirty hostages in the hotel's coffee shop. At the end of a four-hour standoff, an understanding was reached between the terrorists and the Cypriot authorities. They released all but fifteen of their hostages and were bused to Larnaca Airport where a Cyprus Airways DC-8 was waiting to transport them to sanctuary in a radical Arab state. The DC-8 took off at 8:30 P.M. with the two gunmen, twelve hostages, and a crew of four, but after a twenty-one-hour journey, during which they were refused permission to land by Libya, Algeria, South Yemen, and Iraq, and refueled following an unauthorized landing in Djibouti, they returned to Larnaca.

Yasir Arafat, meanwhile, had dispatched a twelve-man PLO unit—three senior officials and their bodyguards—to Larnaca to assist the Cypriot government in view of the fact that two PLO representatives were among the hostages still held by the gunmen. They arrived, however, after the plane had departed on its odyssey and, according to most reports, had left Larnaca before the DC-8 returned from Djibouti.[43]

The Egyptian government also informed the government of Cyprus that it was sending a delegation described "as ministers to take part in the negotiations" to Larnaca, but when the Cypriot minister of communications approached the Egyptian C-130E Hercules that had landed at the airfield in order to extend official greetings to the Egyptian delegation, he found instead that the transport plane contained fifty-four members of an elite Egyptian antiterrorist commando unit known as the Saiqa, or "lightning," unit. Upon learning of the deception, President of Cyprus Kyprianou angrily refused to permit the Egyptians to attempt a rescue effort and said that any Egyptian military action would be regarded as a violation of Cyprus's sovereignty. As the C-130E waited at the far end of the runway, negotiations continued with the terrorists for the release of the hostages. When it became apparent that a deal had been reached, whereby the gunmen would be given Cypriot passports, air tickets to Athens, and money to buy tickets onward to a socialist country, the Egyptian commander on the scene, General Nabil Shukry, decided to act unilaterally.

In defiance of the Cypriot government, the ramp of the C-130E was lowered, and a jeep burst from within the aircraft and roared toward the hostage airliner, the commandos sprinting along behind it. Inexplicably, when they were still 300 yards from the DC-8, the commandos opened fire with automatic weapons. The action by the Egyptians was so unexpected that the jeep was able to break through the cordon that had been thrown around the DC-8 by Cypriot national guardsmen and actually to reach the hostage jetliner. At this point, Cypriot national guardsmen began shooting at the Egyptians, and moments later, a blast ripped the jeep apart, killing all its passengers. According to some accounts, the Egyptians had lobbed a grenade at the jetliner that had missed its mark and bounced back into the jeep, whereupon it exploded.

When the confused fifty-minute firefight was over, fifteen Egyptian commandos lay dead on the tarmac, their $6 million C-130E had been destroyed by a Cypriot rocket, and the remaining thirty-nine commandos were in custody. Although the DC-8 had been completely riddled with bullets, incredibly no one aboard had been killed or seriously wounded. According to the co-pilot of the DC-8, Captain Bill Cox, it was fortunate that the Egyptians had been unable to get aboard the captured plane: "If the Egyptians had got on the plane I would be dead," Cox said later. "It was wild, indiscriminate firing. How can they pick out two gunmen from 17 people lying on the floor?"[44] When the fighting was over, the two terrorists surrendered meekly to Cypriot authorities without having fired so much as a shot at the airport.

A postmortem of the incident revealed a tragic set of misjudgments on the part of the Egyptians. Not only did they fail to give the government of Cyprus advance warning of their plan to rescue the hostages, believing that to do so would have jeopardized the mission's security, but also they appeared to have no practical strategy for dealing with the situation in the event that the Cypriots refused to cooperate. Despite the adamant opposition of the government of Cyprus to their mission, they implemented their original plan as though nothing were wrong, believing somehow that, if the mission were successfully executed, the Cypriots would passively accept the flagrant violation of their sovereignty. Moreover, the members of the *Saiqa* unit appeared poorly trained, and it is hard to see how their strategy, even under the best of circumstances, would have resulted in the freeing of the hostages without a significant loss of life.[45] As but one example of the inadequate preparation that characterized the mission, most of the Egyptian commandos, in contrast to the members of the German GSG9 at Mogadishu who wore dark clothing, were outfitted in light-colored desert camouflage fatigues that, at night, made them easy targets for the Cypriots, as well as for the terrorists if they had been observant. A few of the commandos were even dressed in sport clothing and shoes with platform heels as though they had expected to perform undercover roles.

Although there was ample opportunity to approach the DC-8 quietly, preserving the element of surprise and taking it by stealth, the decision to open fire almost 300 yards away from the target, before crossing a broad expanse of open tarmac, must be viewed as the height of folly and lacking any sense of the finesse on which operations of this type are so dependent. The terrorists, believing that an agreement had been reached with Cypriot authorities to end the standoff, were completely off guard and probably could have been overpowered by a handful of commandos without firing a shot. One of the terrorists, who called himself Mohammed, had gone to the bathroom aboard the DC-8 to wash his face, comb his hair, and put on a tie in preparation for surrendering to Cypriot authorities. The doorway to the aircraft was open, and the other gunman was clearly visible at the moment the Egyptians initiated hostilities, an easy target for a sniper.

For its part, the government of Cyprus must also come under criticism for its role in the disastrous affair. The incident at Larnaca is a classic example of a situation that authorities permitted to get out of hand by not taking the necessary steps at an earlier stage to control the crisis before it developed a life and momentum of its own. The Cypriots clearly were negotiating with the terrorists without regard to keeping the Egyptians, who had an obvious interest in the outcome of the affair, properly apprised of their strategy. Cypriot officials later said that, despite their agreement to permit the gunmen to depart for a socialist country (via Athens), they had no intention of letting them get away. Nevertheless, Sadat's skepticism as to whether the Cypriots would have reneged on the agreement and punished the terrorists was well founded and based on the fact that not only did Cyprus have a reputation for harboring terrorist fugitives and permitting them to use the island as a base of operations but also that Cyprus was, at that time, the only country in the world that maintained formal diplomatic relations with the PLO. The permissive climate with respect to terrorism that existed on Cyprus no doubt was an important ingredient in the Egyptian decision to take matters into their own hands.

On 4 April 1978, after having been found guilty of murder at the end of an eleven-day trial, the two terrorists, Zayed Hussein Ali and Samir Mohammed Khadar, were sentenced by a judge to be hanged. The PLO, which had condemned the killing of Sibai as an act of terrorism against the Palestinian people, expressed satisfaction with the verdict, adding a final note of irony to what had been from the outset a puzzling and often convoluted incident.

Dutch Royal Marines (Netherlands)

In recent years, the Netherlands has been plagued by sporadic episodes of terrorist violence fomented by South Moluccans seeking independence for their homeland. The South Moluccan minority in the Netherlands numbers nearly 40,000 people, most of whom came to Europe when the chain of 150 islands known as the Moluccas (formerly the Spice Islands) was absorbed by the one-time Dutch colony of Indonesia in 1949, following the collapse of the South Moluccan nationalist movement. The South Moluccans allege that the Dutch had promised them self-determination, and thus, they have turned to terrorism as a means of winning recognition for their cause and in an effort to put pressure on the Dutch government to support their national goals.

In 1970, South Moluccan gunmen killed a policeman during the seizure of the Indonesian embassy at the Hague that coincided with a visit to the Netherlands by Indonesian President Suharto. Four years later, they took over the building housing the World Court at the Hague, and in April 1975, Dutch police broke up a South Moluccan plot to kidnap Queen Juliana. In December 1975, terrorists hijacked a train in the northern part of the country and the Indonesian consulate in Amsterdam, taking a total of sixty-six hostages in the two incidents. After a fifteen-day siege at both locations, they surrendered, but not before murdering the engineer and two passengers on the train. Although the terrorists involved in the two actions were tried and sentenced to long prison terms, the Dutch population was becoming extremely agitated over the repeated South Moluccan attempts to disrupt their small country and began pressuring the Dutch government to take ever harsher measures to deal with the problem.

Had the terrorists not surrendered when they did, the Dutch authorities had been prepared to launch an assault on the train, using marine commandos who had been practicing such a maneuver almost since the siege had begun.

A similar counterterrorist squad had seen action in October 1974, when it had stormed the Scheveningen jail during a prison uprising led by an Arab terrorist. Thus, when South Moluccan terrorists overpowered another train and occupied a nearby school on 23 May 1977, taking 161 hostages, the Dutch government initially sought to talk out the terrorists, preserving the force option as a last resort. The technique worked to the extent that the terrorists released 105 school children and a sick teacher at the school site, but as the siege wore on, psychiatrists involved in the negotiation process became increasingly worried about deteriorating conditions aboard the train, which they believed could potentially impact severely on the hostages, and the growing instability and eroding discipline displayed by the terrorists. Dr. Dik Mulder, the lead psychiatrist, concluded after twenty days that little further progress could be made in negotiating an end to the standoff, and he recommended that force be employed.[46] The Dutch interior minister and other government officials concurred with the psychiatrist's assessment and ordered the marines, who once again had been practicing assault techniques on a similar train some distance away, into action.

Utilizing listening devices planted underneath the railway carriages and special radars designed to detect heat differentials in various metal surfaces, thereby making it possible to locate the terrorists by fixing on the weapons they always carried, the marines were able to follow the precise movements of the terrorists and therefore to know the exact location of each of them at the moment of the assault. Equipped with night vision devices, the marines moved in noiselessly on the train during the night. As dawn broke, six F104 Starfighter jets swept low over the train, making a tremendous racket, and dropped smoke bombs, thereby creating a diversion. At that moment, the marines rushed the train, and in the brief action that followed, six terrorists and two hostages were killed. As at Entebbe, the hostages died in the crossfire when they panicked and stood up instead of lying down as they had been ordered to do by the marines. When news of the successful assault on the train was conveyed to the terrorists holding the school, they quickly surrendered and the two-pronged incident was brought to a close.

The 100-member marine unit saw further action in March 1978, after South Moluccan extremists took over a provincial government building in Assen, killing 1 man and wounding 5 others in the seizure. The terrorists threatened to kill 71 hostages if the Dutch government did not release 21 of their imprisoned comrades, provide them with a $13 million ransom, and make available a plane to take them out of the country. The terrorists informed the government that they would start executing hostages within a half hour of the expiration of the deadline if their demands were not met. The Dutch government rejected any consideration of compromise with the terrorists and ordered the marines into position around the besieged building. After a shot was heard from within the building and the terrorists subsequently announced that they had executed a hostage, a claim that later turned out to be false (the hostage was only wounded), the order was given to the marines to rush the building. Attacking from two different directions, the marines were able rapidly to overpower the three terrorists holding the four-story building and end the twenty-eight-hour siege. Six hostages were wounded in the action, but authorities indicated that they had expected more casualties.

The consistently strong posture demonstrated by the Dutch government with respect to terrorism and the successive well-executed raids mounted by the Dutch counterterrorist marine unit combined to eradicate virtually the entire South Moluccan independence movement. With most of its members dead, imprisoned, or driven underground, and with little community support because of the bitter hostility their actions had engendered among the Dutch, the movement has been largely inactive in the past two years.

Project Blue Light/Delta (United States)

In May 1977, the White House, in answer to the successful commando-style operations against terrorists by the West Germans and Israelis, and responding to pressure from both Congress and the press, announced the formation of a similar counterterrorist commando force. The force consists of nine special 252-man units, one drawn from each of nine U.S. Army Special Forces battalions. Seven of these units are located in the United States and two abroad (in West Germany and Panama). The core of the force, designated originally as Project Blue Light, is stationed at Fort Bragg, North Carolina. Each unit is supported by elements of the navy SEALs, army Rangers, and the marine reconnaissance and amphibious units.[47]

While Black Beret Ranger units, formed in 1974, had engaged in mock training exercises to free U.S. diplomats and airliners and to retake nuclear installations and oil refineries that had been captured by terrorists, none of the Pentagon's elite commando units—the Black Berets, the navy's SEALs, the air force's Pathfinders, the special forces's Green Berets, or the marines—could be considered a true counterterrorist strike force. None was trained and equipped exclusively to combat terrorists, and U.S. defense planners, mindful of the limitations characterizing each of the existing elite commando units and of the risks associated with "deploying the wrong military instruments out of desperation" against terrorists, saw the need to create a unique force that could respond on short notice with special capabilities in the event of a serious terrorist crisis.[48]

Prior to the inception of Project Blue Light, the Black Berets enjoyed the reputation as the most likely unit to be activated for an antiterrorist operation. However, many observers doubted their effectiveness since, on the whole, their training program emphasized traditional military skills and techniques more suitable to combat conditions than to counterterrorist operations. Moreover, they lacked much of the sophisticated hardware possessed by the British, the Germans, and the Israelis. A U.K. SAS officer, after observing the Black Berets, summed up their inadequate preparation by remarking, "They spend a good deal of time in the swamps eating snake."[49]

By summer 1979, Project Blue Light had given way to a specially constituted new unit, code named Delta. Selected on the basis of physical conditioning, intelligence, attitude, and service record from a pool of more than 42,000 enlisted men and officers, mostly from elite service units, who were invited to try out for the assignment, Delta members represented the cream of the U.S. military establishment. All members were personally selected by Colonel Charles A. Beckwith, the unit's commander and a former special forces officer with a distinguished Vietnam record, who most recently had commanded the Third Ranger Battalion at Elgin Air Force Base in Florida. Beckwith was regarded by many as the preeminent counterterrorist expert within the U.S. military when he was named by President Carter as the commander of Delta. He had received training from both the SAS (U.K.), of which he was an honorary member, and from the Israelis, and he drew upon both experiences in establishing his own organization.

Although now retired from active duty, Beckwith had a reputation as being a superlative training officer and combat leader who instilled a fierce sense of loyalty in his subordinates. Known as Chargin' Charlie to those around him, he had also developed a reputation as a professional wildman, ready to take any risk, attempt any mission, however dangerous, that might be asked of him.

Delta represented a considerable rethinking by U.S. defense planners of the very concept of special commando-style military units in trying to meet the unique demands of urban warfare, advances in modern weaponry, and the threat posed by contemporary terrorism, and consequently, the unit that emerged was different from its predecessors in nearly every respect, including its appearance. Unlike the Black Berets, with their brush-cut hair, Delta commandos, so as to blend in better with local populations during covert missions, wore their hair long, in a variety of styles and cuts, and some members sported beards and moustaches. Patterning the Blue Light training program after the rigorous curriculums of the Germans, British, and Israelis, U.S. commandos were instructed in the techniques of silent killing, rappeling, demolitions, parachute jumping, hand-to-hand combat, knife fighting, marksmanship, scuba diving, communications, lock picking, and first aid. Some members of the unit were also given language training.

Although judgments are difficult because of the extraordinary security surrounding Delta, some knowledgeable observers, while finding that the unit's physical conditioning and commando skills were absolutely first rate, expressed the view that it is still less inventive than its best overseas counterparts and that too much emphasis is placed on physical skills at the expense of time devoted to operational planning and the development of new techniques for dealing with contingencies that may arise as a result of terrorist actions. West Germany's GSG9, for example, working from aircraft manufacturer's blueprints, has spent considerable time devising detailed strategies for retaking nearly every kind of jetliner in use by the world's commercial airlines (including Soviet models).

The first real test of Delta's capabilities came in April 1980, when former President Jimmy Carter authorized a secret rescue mission to free fifty-three U.S. hostages being held in Iran after the seizure of the U.S. embassy by militant students, following the failure of more than five months of diplomatic efforts to win their release. Although not a counterterrorist operation in the strict sense of the word, Delta was selected over other elite counterterrorist military units to carry out the mission because it was determined that it had undergone the most extensive training with regard to hostage situations. Although final authority to proceed with perparation for the surgical strike deep into Iran was not given until mid-April, the mission had been conceived in late November 1979, less than a month after the crisis began. According to a postmortem report prepared by the Joint Chiefs of Staff for the secretary of defense that was later transmitted to the House Armed Services Committee:

> The key to such a bold undertaking was surprise. It was absolutely essential to develop the plans, select the forces, conduct the training, deploy the people and equipment, and execute the mission in an environment of airtight operational security. Secrecy was paramount. The planners recognized that a lean but adequate force that struck swiftly and unexpectedly stood a good chance of rescuing the hostages. A larger, more elaborate force, on the other hand, with its correspondingly larger supporting infrastructure, posed an increased danger of a fatal leak which could have risked the lives not only of the rescue force, but of the hostages whom they were planning to free.[50]

The rescue attempt was similar to the Entebbe, Mogadishu, and Larnaca incidents already described inasmuch as it involved an incursion deep into another nation's territory in order to effect the rescue of hostages. However, unlike previous rescue attempts, the hostage takers in this case were nationals of the country whose territorial integrity would have to be violated and were receiving considerable support from its revolutionary government. Iran, moreover, presented tremendous logistical difficulties for the rescue force since it is a large nation with sophisticated radar and detection equipment—a modern military establishment that, though its effectiveness had been impaired greatly by the revolutionary turmoil, was nonetheless still a potent fighting force to be reckoned with—and because of Iran's proximity to the USSR. Should the Iranian radar not pick up the raiders, it could be assumed that the Soviets would detect them and that Moscow would inform Tehran accordingly. It would be necessary to ferry the rescue force nearly seven hundred nautical miles to Tehran, pause to refuel enroute deep in hostile territory, and then strike at a location (the U.S. embassy) in the heart of a busy metropolitan area. Unlike the three previous incidents cited, which all took place at international airports, there was no suitable runway facility near the target location, necessitating the use of helicopters instead of fixed-wing aircraft, a major disadvantage because helicopters are less reliable and slower than fixed-wing aircraft. Where there were ten terrorists at Entebbe, four at Mogadishu, and two at Larnaca, the Delta force could anticipate finding perhaps as many as fifty terrorists at the captured U.S. embassy, though the figure was likely to be less. Finally, rising temperatures and unpredictable weather conditions in April, including unforeseen sandstorms, could hamper the mission. Despite the difficulties that the mission presented, a plan was developed that, in the president's words, "had an excellent chance of success."[51]

In preparation for the mission, a full-size mockup of the U.S. embassy compound was constructed in the southwestern United States, and four full-scale rehearsals of the raid, with all of its elements, were conducted, in addition to twenty partial rehearsals involving one or more parts of the raid.[52] Meanwhile, other preparations of a logistical and intelligence nature were being made. Six helicopters, RH-53 Sea Stallions (normally used for laying mines), were put aboard the U.S. aircraft carrier *Nimitz* in November, and two more subsequently were included to add a greater measure of redundancy to the mission. The helicopters and crews established a pattern of regular flight exercises in order to deceive Soviet and Iranian observers of their real mission and, at the same time, to keep the equipment in a high state of readiness. A select weather group also was established in November to keep military planners advised as to weather conditions the raiding party could expect to encounter at any given time.

On 24 April 1980, all was in readiness for the rescue attempt, and the order was given to go. Six C130 Hercules air transports took off from an undisclosed location in Egypt, carrying a ninety-member commando contingent, fuel, jeeps, motorcycles, weapons, and sophisticated communications and radar-jamming equipment. To maintain absolute secrecy and to avoid Saudi Arabian air space, the little armada followed a flight path that took them down the Red Sea to the Gulf of Aden, where they were refueled in mid-air, and then on to Masirah Island off the coast of Oman. After a short rest stop, the C130s crossed the Gulf of Oman and entered Iranian air space.

The eight helicopters, meanwhile, had left the deck of the *Nimitz,* operating in the Gulf of Oman near the Iranian coast, shortly after 7:30 A.M. and, flying at little more than 100 feet off the ground, were proceeding to a location about 200 miles southeast of Tehran known as Desert One, where they were scheduled to rendezvous with the C130s and refuel. Once that was accomplished, they were then to continue on to a second location near Garmsar, 208 miles away. Only about 50 miles from Tehran, this was to be the actual staging area for the raid. Here the commandos were to be unloaded and driven to a garage about 700 yards distant where they were to remain hidden until the following night. The helicopters would then be flown to a site about fifteen minutes distant and covered with camouflage netting.

At midnight on 26 April, under the cover of darkness, twenty-six of the commandos were to steal into Tehran in trucks that had been prepositioned near the garage by friendly operatives in Iran. Most were to go directly to the U.S. embassy compound, but a smaller contingent was to be dispatched to retrieve the three Americans being held at the foreign ministry. Although details are not available concerning the strategy and methods that were to have been used to overpower the guards at the embassy compound, it has been speculated that the strike force had precise information concerning the number and exact positioning of the sentries. Equipped with silenced weapons and what one Pentagon official described as a bag of tricks, the embassy was to be secured.

The hostages were then to be driven to Amjadieh Stadium, across from the compound, where they would be met by four of the helicopters and airlifted to an auxiliary airfield near Qom, about fifty miles southwest of Tehran. There the C130s would be waiting for them. Two of the helicopters were to be kept in reserve during the entire operation, only to be used in the event of mechanical problems or, if necessary, to run interference for the other helicopters. A C130 gunship, code-named Hammer, was to be deployed overhead to spray the streets around the embassy and the foreign ministry with heavy-caliber machine gun fire in order to prevent reinforcements from arriving to aid the militants. Once the C130s were airborne, they were to be escorted out of Iranian air space by U.S. fighter planes from the carrier fleet that was waiting in the waters off the Iranian coast.

That was the plan. However, the mission did not work according to plan. Enroute to Desert One, one of the helicopters made an emergency landing with a hydraulic problem that was affecting the rotor blades. The decision was made to abandon the aircraft, and its crew and equipment were picked up by another chopper that had followed it down. Shortly afterward, the remaining seven helicopters encountered a severe dust and sandstorm, and another chopper was forced to return to the aircraft carrier *Nimitz* because its gyrocompass and one of its two altitude indicators had failed. Although six helicopters, the minimum number required to carry out the mission, arrived at Desert One, a third helicopter was discovered to also have a hydraulic problem and would be unable to take off again. In addition, two other choppers reportedly were experiencing technical problems.

In view of the fact that there were only five operational helicopters, Colonel Beckwith, in consultation with the joint task force commander who was in direct contact with the president, decided to scrub the mission. However, during refueling of the helicopters for the withdrawal to the *Nimitz,* one of the choppers collided with one of the C130s, resulting in eight men killed and five injured. Due to the intense fire that ensued, which was certain to compromise

the secrecy of the raid, and the exploding ammunition that was threatening the
other aircraft, Colonel Beckwith gave the order to abandon the helicopters and
to evacuate the location in a rapid but orderly fashion in the remaining C130s.
So ended the first major deployment of the U.S. elite counterterrorist commando unit.

In retrospect, a number of conclusions may be drawn regarding the failed
mission. First, the rescue attempt was aborted as a result of helicopter mal-
functions, and thus the blame, if blame must be attached, rests with those
responsible for the planning rather than the execution of the raid. Every military
operation must be prepared for the unexpected, and if, as Secretary of Defense
Harold Brown indicated, "we recognized that operationally this [the flight to
Desert One] was the most difficult part of the mission," then the military
planners of the mission must be faulted for not building greater redundancies
into the plan in the form of additional helicopters.[53] In this connection, there is
little reason to believe that two more helicopters, or even six more, plus another
C130 to lift the additional fuel required, would have jeopardized the mission by
making it easier to detect. However, it must also be noted in defense of the military planners that they had probably arrived at the unsuccessful plan with the
knowledge that it represented the maximum force option acceptable to President Carter, who was perhaps as near to being a pacifist as any man to serve as
president of the United States.

Moreover, like the old saw about a camel being a horse designed by a committee, the rescue plan that ultimately was adopted was the work of too many
hands, and few of them the right ones; it bore the imprint of policymakers
rather than policy implementors. As a practical matter, it lacked coherence,
cohesiveness, and provided for no clear operational chain of command. The
slapdash command structure, in turn, led to confusion on the ground at Desert
One and to some egregious planning oversights like the failure adequately to
anticipate burn injuries by the airborne medical unit.

The rescue mission also failed to establish proper channels of communications among the various constituent elements involved. The failure of the air
force to transmit critical weather data to the marine helicopter pilots serves
as a good case in point. If too little communication was the problem prior to
the mission, then too much communication hampered its success once the
rescue attempt had been launched. In this connection, Western military
observers are usually highly critical of the Soviet army for its overly centralized
command structure that allows field commanders only limited latitude for
making decisions and that therefore saps initiative and creativeness. Most decisions are made by the high command rather than by field officers who possess
firsthand knowledge of the actual situation. Despite the obvious shortcomings
of the Soviet system, President Carter and his advisors opted to run the rescue
operation the same way, substituting their own judgment for that of the onsite
commander.

Second, the plan approved by the White House had too many predetermined bail-out mechanisms, and not enough backup systems to overcome unexpected problems, confirming a lack of commitment to the original plan on the part of its authors and those who had to approve it. Every mission of this type must accept as a given that it will encounter unforeseen problems, and it must have secondary and tertiary plans to overcome any contingencies that might arise. Moreover, it would appear that the White House tried to make the operation so free of risk that it was doomed from the outset inasmuch as any setback virtually guaranteed that the mission would not proceed. By contrast to the overcaution displayed by the president and his military advisors, "the successful commander has often been the kind of man who deliberately burns his bridges behind him to prevent thought of anything but victory."[54] This is not to argue on behalf of precipitous military adventures but merely to affirm that all commando operations of the type attempted by the United States in Iran carry with them grave risks as well as the potential for great rewards and that any president who dispatches men deep into enemy territory on a desperate mission of mercy must realize that, in the final analysis, he is taking what amounts to a roll of the dice. Perhaps the motto of the SAS (U.K.) expresses it best: "Who dares wins." In this connection, former Undersecretary of the Navy R. James Woolsey has observed that "all military operations are a matter of calculated risk. Daring and surprising ones put heavy demands on equipment and people, but their very audacity can give them cover and protection."[55]

Third, the raid's timing is clearly open to criticism. Not only was much valuable time wasted on many predictably futile diplomatic attempts to resolve the crisis, but also the fact that weather conditions were less optimal for the raid in April than earlier in the year is a matter of record. According to some reports, the United States had forces on the ground in Iran on three previous occasions that were capable of mounting an attempt to rescue the hostages, and each time they were withdrawn in favor of peaceful options. Informed sources, however, confirm that the Air Force Weather Service should have been aware of the 200-mile-long dust storm the mission encountered.

Finally, all other matters aside, the members of the Delta unit conducted themselves with exemplary skill and courage throughout the aborted mission, including some acts of individual heroism after the fiery crash at Desert One, suggesting that they will be more than a match for most terrorists in the future.

This was illustrated by the recent successful deployment of a U.S. antiterrorist team in Thailand. The unit provided equipment and technical advice to an Indonesian commando unit that stormed a hostage Indonesian jetliner in Bangkok, Thailand, on 31 March 1981. The airliner, a DC-10 with approximately fifty passengers aboard, was seized by members of an Islamic fundamentalist group called the *Komando Jihad,* or Holy War Command. Three of the four hijackers were killed in the assault, and a fourth died later at the hospital.

SAS (United Kingdom)

The United Kingdom must be regarded as a superpower when it comes to fighting terrorism. Reportedly the world's finest antiterrorist commando unit, the 900-man strong Twenty-second Regiment of the SAS is an almost legendary organization that was formed during World War II to operate behind enemy lines in North Africa and that later played a significant role in many of the colonial upheavals of the postwar period. Since the introduction of SAS units in Northern Ireland in 1976, U.K. losses to the IRA have been reduced appreciably.

The SAS are the journeymen experts of counterterrorism, seemingly surfacing whenever there is a major terrorist crisis as advisors to the afflicted party or to other commando-style units going into action for the first time. Two SAS men accompanied the West German GSG9 team to Mogadishu and supplied both tactical advice and equipment to them, including the stun grenades. Another SAS team is known to have been dispatched to Rome following the kidnapping of former Italian Prime Minister Aldo Moro. Colonel Charles A. Beckwith, commander of the U.S. Delta unit, and members of nearly every other elite counterterrorist commando unit in the West have received training from the SAS.

The SAS, in May 1980, had an opportunity to demonstrate to the world its considerable skills when five Iranian Arab terrorists, seeking self-determination for the Iranian province of Khuzestan, took over Iran's elegant London embassy, seizing twenty-six hostages, and demanded the release of ninety-one fellow Arabs imprisoned by the Khomeini government, together with safe conduct out of the country. Before a forest of television cameras and journalists, some twenty SAS commandos, dressed in black, armed with pistols and submachine guns, their faces covered with hoods (as is their custom when going into combat), stormed the embassy from the roof and from adjacent townhouses. The decision to take decisive action occurred only after the gunmen inside the embassy had begun to execute hostages.

Tear gas, satchel charges, and stun grenades reportedly were used in the assault. While some of the commandos secured the building, others formed a line and virtually hurled the hostages from one man to the next until the building was evacuated. Three terrorists died in the assault, another died later from wounds he received, and a fifth man, who was also wounded, remains in custody in the United Kingdom. As for the hostages, one was killed and two others were wounded when one of the gunmen opened fire on them as the commado attack began. U.K. authorities currently are looking for a sixth terrorist, Sami Mohammed Ali, known as the Fox, who they believe masterminded the takeover.

In a world where little has been going the United Kingdom's way in recent years, the successful operation against the terrorists holding the Iranian embassy was a great boost to public morale, especially coming as it did on the heels of the aborted U.S. rescue mission in Iran. Home Secretary William Whitelaw was positively euphoric during a press conference after the assault, and Prime Minister Thatcher described it as "a brilliant operation, carried out with courage and confidence," adding that it made everyone "proud to be British."[56]

Other Counterterrorist Units

In addition to those elite antiterrorist commando units singled out for special mention, more than a dozen other nations boast similar units, including France (the *Gigene*), Belgium, Switzerland, Denmark, Italy (Squad R), Indonesia, Austria, Norway, and the British Crown Colony of Hong Kong. Five French antiterrorist experts are reported to have flown to Saudi Arabia in November 1979 to assist the Saudis to drive several hundred well-armed religious rebels out of the Grand Mosque in Mecca. The French advisors allegedly took charge of 3,000 Saudi paratroopers on the scene who were demoralized and discouraged after suffering heavy casualties in repeated unsuccessful attempts to dislodge the rebels holding the Moslem world's holiest shrine and devised a comprehensive plan designed to turn the tide. In addition, they had concussion grenades and debilitating gas shipped from France that could be used to rout the rebels from the miles of tunnels and catacombs underneath the mosque. After a week of careful preparation, the Saudi paratroopers, under the direction of the French specialists, recaptured the mosque amidst bitter fighting, some of it hand to hand. Those rebels not killed in the action subsequently were executed by the Saudi government.

Summary

One of the most effective methods of dealing with terrorism today, especially hostage situations, clearly is a swift and harsh counterattack, executed by highly skilled and intensely trained commando units with the latest modern technology at their disposal. Nevertheless, it must also be recognized that incumbent in such a response are numerous well-documented risks such as those encountered by the Egyptians at Larnaca Airport and by the United States during its unsuccessful attempt to free the U.S. hostages in Iran. Commando-style operations are not, in and of themselves, the final answer to terrorism; they are at best an excellent riposte. While a commando response may provide immediate and temporary relief, it does not strike at the real heart of the problem—the causes that produced the terrorist outbreak in the first place—and hence cannot be regarded as a long-term solution.

New Counterterrorist Technology

In the past, the rapid growth of technology tended to favor the terrorist in the promulgation of his antisocial violence against the state, but in recent years this trend has begun to show a marked reversal. On the one hand, technology has provided terrorists with a plethora of new weapons and targets, but on the other hand, it has increased the state's capability to strike back with authority at terrorists. A critical element in recent successes chalked up by antiterrorist commando units is their increasing reliance on a vast array of newly developed technological hardware, much of it designed specifically for the use against terrorists, that repeatedly has provided the critical margin of victory in engagements with terrorists.

Modern sensors like those described earlier are able accurately to track terrorist movements in a hijacked train or plane, enabling commandos to get a precise fix on their location—a crucial advantage in any siege situation. U.K.-developed stun, or concussion, grenades are another valuable antiterrorist tool, especially in hostage incidents where commandos must exercise extreme caution so as not to kill or injure the people whom they are trying to save. The concussion grenade has a deafening roar and flash that temporarily stuns and blinds terrorists and hostages, allowing commandos to get the drop on the hostiles, but it has no lasting after-effects. Moreover, since the grenade is enclosed in a special covering, it does not spray shrapnal like a normal grenade. The commandos are shielded from the blast effects by heavy goggles and noise suppressors. Among the other passive weapons being developed and tested by antiterrorist squads for use in congested areas where it may be difficult to separate the terrorists from the hostages are low-velocity weapons with bullets that stun but do not kill the target and polyurethane foam that can be sprayed at terrorists from portable backpacks, immobilizing the subjects in a cocoon of foam. Because of the porous consistency of the foam, it completely insulates the subject without smothering him. A skyjack-proof airliner is still a very long way from realization, but one of the possible antiskyjacking systems that has been given extensive consideration is an incapacitating gas on board the aircraft that could be administered through the ventilation system or by means of a special sprinkler system.

A quantitative leap has been made in the field of bomb detection, either on board a plane or in any other closed environment, through the development of the so-called sniffer. In actuality a gaseous chemical detector, the sniffer can detect gunpowder or any other substance it is programmed to detect, even if its consistency is only a few parts per trillion parts of air. The presence of any explosive material triggers an alarm, alerting security personnel. To simplify the identification of explosives, eliminating the need to program the sniffer to detect an unmanageable range of explosive vapors, the federal government wants to require explosives manufacturers to include taggants in their products that can be detected easily by the sniffer, even if they are extensively shielded. Thus, it would be possible for authorities to open the baggage hold of an aircraft and ascertain in a matter of seconds whether any explosives were secreted aboard the plane. Along these same lines, a portable desk-top computerized letter-bomb detector has been devised that is 99.94 percent accurate and that will soon be on the market.

In addition to adding detector taggants to explosives, the federal government is actively seeking to require manufacturers to incorporate identification taggants in all explosives manufactured for commercial use in this country. By recovering taggants after a bombing, authorities could trace the origin of the explosives, and this would assist immeasurably law enforcement personnel and investigators in bringing criminal bombers to justice.

Few skills are more important to an antiterrorist strike force than expert marksmanship and sniping ability. The unfortunate events at Munich in 1972 illustrated the risks that accompany any attempt to pick off terrorists from afar with inadequate gear and training. Contemporary sniping rifles and sighting devices have undergone extensive refinement over the past two decades. Infrared, heat-sensitive, and starlight-enhancement sniper scopes strip the terrorist of the protective covering of darkness. The lightweight and deadly accurate Mauser 66, outfitted with a hair trigger and powerful scope, in the hands of an expert sniper can rip apart a terrorist's skull from a distance of more than 300 yards, making the sniper the terrorist's most feared adversary.

Most counterterrorist commandos wear modern ultralight body armor that can stop a .357 magnum slug at close range, although the impact may break a few ribs and at the very least will leave a severe bruise. Over-the-ear helmets made from advanced plastic compounds are impervious to bullets and shell fragments and are so well cushioned that the wearer can sustain a hit over the head with the butt of an assault rifle with little discomfort.

No counterterrorist unit can survive without timely and accurate information and intelligence about its adversaries. In this connection, modern computer technology provides such units with virtually limitless amounts of information regarding terrorist organizations, their members and characteristics, and also the blueprints and layouts of airliners, office buildings, and even whole cities.

Advanced security systems can reduce the vulnerability of high-probability targets, rendering most locations virtually impenetrable to infiltration or attack, using components such as physical barriers (perimeter fencing, walls, and so forth), electro-optical assessment devices (closed circuit television and night vision systems), locking devices (key/dial/electric/cipher), lighting (sodium/ mercury vapor), and various sensor systems (microwave/seismic/laser field/ seismic-magnetic). Oscilloscopes like the one located in the old executive office building adjacent to the White House can scan radio frequencies for unauthorized transmitters like walkie-talkies that are being operated in a restricted area. Personnel-identification systems based on voiceprints and hand (or other parts of the body) geometry are already replacing less-reliable punch codes, plastic picture identification cards, and fingerprint systems as a means of ensuring rigid control of access points, thereby further reducing the prospect of hostile elements penetrating the controlled area by means of deceiving or defeating the system.

In the final analysis, however, while technology can be an immensely valuable ally to legitimate governments in their war against terrorism, care must be taken so as not to fall into the trap John Ellis calls "technological fetishism," or what he defines as an overdependence on technological hardware, like the United States had during the Vietnam War.[57] Overreliance on technology often produces mental sloppiness, complacency, and—what may be the greatest threat to counterterrorist strike forces—overconfidence. The Israelis, for example, displayed destructive overconfidence a few years ago in the wake of the development of a new razor-sharp wire that they boasted was a breakthrough in perimeter protection and would virtually wipe out traditional infiltration along its borders. Much to Israeli chagrin, however, an inventive U.S. military officer visiting Israel demonstrated that the simple act of throwing a heavy blanket over the wire afforded an infiltrator enough protection to climb over a barrier strung with the miracle wire. The solution was, in effect, so simple that no one had thought of it.

Finally, under some circumstances, high-technology armaments and equipment may even be counterproductive. The U.S.-manufactured M-16, for example, may well be the finest combat rifle in the world, but only when it is working properly. As U.S. troops in Vietnam discovered, the slightest accumulation of grit in the firing mechanism of the M-16 caused the weapon to jam; thus, many elite troops engaged in search and destroy operations opted for using captured Soviet-built Kalashnikov AK-47 assault rifles, a much simpler weapon that "can be smothered in mud and sand and still work perfectly."[58]

Indeed, a sharpened stake buried in a pit along a heavily traveled footpath may be as effective and surely as fearsome a weapon as a land mine. Thus, in the final analysis, technological superiority in a war against relatively primitive adversaries may be no guarantee of victory. Indeed, it must always be remembered that sometimes people on bicycles are best fought by other people on bicycles.

Conclusion

No all-encompassing panacea exists for ending terrorism. A sustained effort must be made to eradicate the causes of terrorism, especially when it is rooted in desperation, injustice, and deprivation, but when that is not possible or in instances where terrorism is more directly the product of disordered minds and anarchistic visions, the only alternative is, in most circumstances, to respond with counterforce. In this connection, revolutionaries have long admonished that revolutions are not dinner parties (Mao Tse-tung), that they do not take place in velvet boxes (Carl Oglesby, former SDS president), and that they cannot be made with silk gloves (Joseph Stalin); all of which is to say that revolutions are brutal, bloody affairs accompanied by pain, suffering, intimidation, privation, and a good deal of horror. Inasmuch, however, as revolutions are not made in velvet boxes, neither can they be suppressed in velvet boxes— a fact increasingly acknowledged by nations around the world that are resisting terrorism as well as those forces that are waging terrorism.

Notes

1. Albert Parry, *Terrorism: From Robespierre to Arafat* (New York: The Vanguard Press, Inc., 1976), p. 128.

2. Robert Moss, "Counter Terrorism," *The Economist*, Brief Booklet no. 29, p. 2.

3. Statement by the United States of America, "Observations of States Submitted in Accordance with General Assembly Resolution (XXVII)," Ad Hoc Committee on International Terrorism, United Nations Document A/AC.160/1, 16 May 1973, p. 4.

4. Precedent for such collective action can be found in international practice governing topics such as diplomatic intercourse and the freedom of the seas. Diplomatic immunity, for example, was an accepted part of international practice dating back to the Greek city-states of antiquity, although the right of diplomatic intercourse was not formally recognized until the nineteenth century, following the Congress of Vienna. Over the years, diplomatic privileges and immunities were codified, but not until 1973 did the UN complete work on the Convention for the Prevention and Punishment of Crimes Against Internationally Protected Persons.

5. League of Nations, "Proceedings of the International Conference on the Repression of Terrorism," Document C.94.M.47.1938.V (Geneva, 1 June 1938).

6. Leo Gross, "International Terrorism and International Criminal Jurisdiction," *American Journal of International Law* (July 1973), p. 509.

7. Walter Laqueur, "The Continuing Failure of Terrorism," *Harper's* (November 1976), p. 74.

8. During the mass exodus of Cubans that began in April 1980, Havana charged that the United States was not living up to the spirit of the agreement inasmuch as a number of Cuban boats were hijacked to Florida and that those responsible were not prosecuted but instead were greeted as heroes. Cuba, by contrast, noted that it had prosecuted every American but one who had hijacked a plane to Cuba during the previous year.

9. Interview with Nathan Yalin-Mor, New York City, 16 September 1976.

10. See Francis M. Watson, *Political Terrorism: The Threat and the Response* (New York: Robert B. Luce Co., 1976), p. 218.

11. W.T. Mallison, Jr., and S.V. Mallison, "The Concept of Public Purpose Terror in International Law: Doctrines and Sanctions to Reduce the Destruction of Human and Material Values," *Howard Law Journal* 18 (1973):14.

12. Laqueur, "Continuing Failure of Terrorism," p. 74.

13. Moss, "Counter Terrorism," p. 23.

14. Interview with James Schlesinger, Washington, D.C., 1975.

15. Thomas Powers, *The Man Who Kept the Secrets: Richard Helms and the CIA* (New York: Alfred A. Knopf, 1979), p. 31. See also Ray S. Cline, *Secrets, Spies and Scholars* (New York: Acropolis Books, 1976), pp. 97-104.

16. Nations fearful of retaliation in the event they prosecute terrorists charged with crimes on their soil should consider, as a possible alternative action, the example of Sweden that, after six terrorists took over the West German embassy in Stockholm and murdered two diplomats in 1975, expelled the four surviving terrorists to West Germany where they were certain to be dealt with severely. Similarly, Kenya—fearing reprisals—handed over to Israel two German terrorists it apprehended as they were preparing to attack an El Al Israel Boeing 707 with a shoulder-fired Strella rocket at the Nairobi Airport in 1976. Although the attempted crime did not take place on Israeli territory, Israel passed a law in 1971 providing that it could prosecute persons accused of crimes against Israeli citizens outside of Israel.

17. Philip Jacobson, "Terrorists at Large," *Washington Post*, 6 November 1977.

18. U.S., Congress, House of Representatives, Committee on Foreign Affairs, Subcommittee on the Near East and South Asia, Testimony of Ernest W. Lefever, *International Terrorism*, 93rd Cong., 2d sess., 1974, p. 65.

19. Ibid., Testimony of Representative Lester Wolff, p. 66.

20. I.M.H. Smart, "The Power of Terror," *International Journal* 30 (Spring 1975), p. 231.

21. Richard Clutterbuck, *Protest and the Urban Guerrilla* (London: Cassell & Company, 1973), p. 259.

22. Robert Taber, *The War of the Flea* (New York: Citadel Press, 1970), p. 121.

23. See Robert B. Asprey, *War in the Shadows,* vol. 2 (Garden City, N.Y.: Doubleday & Company, 1975), p. 974.

24. Vincent Hanna, "Internment: What Are the Facts?" *The Listener* (19 and 26 December 1974), p. 790.

25. Moss, "Counter Terrorism," p. 14.

26. Richard Gott, "Whatever Happened to the Tupamaros?" *The Guardian,* 25 May 1974.

27. U.S., Congress, House of Representatives, Committee on Foreign Affairs, Subcommittee on International Organizations and Movements,

Problems of Protecting Civilians under International Law in the Middle East Conflict, 93rd Cong., 2d sess., 1974, p. 34.

28. John D. LeNoir and Jerry M. Tinker, "Countermeasures Techniques," in *Strategies of Revolutionary Warfare,* ed. Jerry M. Tinker (New Delhi: S. Chand and Co., 1969), p. 300.

29. Wolfgang Friedmann, Oliver J. Lissitzyn, and Richard C. Pugh, *International Law* (St. Paul, Minn.: West Publishing Co., 1969), p. 880.

30. Naulilaa Incident Arbitration, Portugal-Germany, arbitral decision of 31 July 1928, concerning the responsibility of Germany for damage caused in the Portuguese colonies of South Africa, (2 *UN Reports of International Arbitral Awards* [1949], pp. 1011ff.)

31. Gerhard von Glahn, *Law among Nations,* 2d ed. (London: MacMillan Company, 1970), p. 500.

32. President Woodrow Wilson, Speech at Long Branch, 2 September 1916; and *U.S. Foreign Relations,* vol. 2 (Washington, D.C.: U.S. Government Printing Office, 1919), pp. 557-561.

33. J. Bowyer Bell, *On Revolt* (Cambridge: Harvard University Press, 1976), p. 57.

34. Judith Coburn, "Israel's Ugly Little War," reprinted in the *Congressional Record,* 6 March 1975, p. E939.

35. George F. Will, editorial, "Successful Terror," *Washington Post,* 12 August 1979.

36. General George Grivas, quoted in Taber, *War of the Flea,* p. 118.

37. Major Henry J. Chisholm, "The Function of Terror and Violence in Revolution" (Master's thesis, Georgetown University, 20 December 1948), p. 51.

38. Walter Laqueur, "The Futility of Terrorism," *Harper's* (March 1976), p. 105.

39. The Jonathan Institute in Israel, which is dedicated to the study of terrorism, takes its name from the late Lieutenant Colonel Yehonatan Netanyahu.

40. William Stevenson, *90 Minutes at Entebbe* (New York: Bantam Books, 1976), p. 148.

41. Two U.K. SAS officers were on board as well.

42. "Terrorists' Supporters in Europe Hit West German Targets," *Washington Post,* 23 October 1977.

43. "The Strange Affair at Larnaca Airport," *The Economist,* 5 February 1978.

44. "Egyptian Blunder at Larnaca," *Daily Telegraph,* 22 February 1978.

45. Ironically, less than two years earlier, in August 1976, the Egyptians successfully had foiled a skyjacking of a flight from Cairo to Luxor by three Arab gunmen who had demanded to be flown to Libya. Purporting to be low on fuel, the pilot landed at Luxor where authorities were able to talk the skyjackers

into releasing the load of Japanese and French tourists aboard the Boeing 737. Then, posing as airline employees, Egyptian paratroopers took over the plane and captured the terrorists.

46. Dr. Mulder had been utilizing psychological techniques to manipulate the behavior of the South Moluccan terrorists during the siege. According to Dobson and Payne: "He [Dr. Mulder] begins to assert his own will by cutting off all other communications, then controlling what the terrorists shall eat and at what time. He claims that he can eventually tell them when to sleep by bidding them goodnight. In this way it is possible for the psychiatrist-controller to know what the terrorists are doing throughout the day." See Christopher Dobson and Ronald Payne, *The Terrorists* (New York: Facts on File, 1979), p. 154.

47. Richard H. Schultz, Jr., "The State of the Operational Art: A Critical Review of Anti-Terrorist Programs," in *Responding to the Terrorist Threat*, eds. Schultz and Stephen Sloan (New York: Pergamon Press, 1980), p. 33.

48. Brian M. Jenkins, "Upgrading the Fight against Terrorism," *Washington Post*, 27 March 1977.

49. "America's Vulnerability to Terrorism," *Washington Post*, 4 December 1977.

50. Joint Chiefs of Staff, Memorandum for the Secretary of Defense, Subject: Report on Rescue Mission, JCSM-122-80, (6 May 1980), p. 1.

51. President Jimmy Carter, Text of a letter to the speaker of the U.S. House of Representatives and the president pro tempore of the Senate, 26 April 1980, p. 2.

52. Joint Chiefs of Staff, Memorandum.

53. Briefing by the secretary of defense, Harold Brown; and White House, "Internal Transcript," (Washington, D.C., 25 April 1980), p. 4.

54. Maxwell D. Taylor, "Analogies (II): Was Desert 1 Another Bay of Pigs?," *Washington Post*, 12 May 1980.

55. R. James Woolsey, "Sometimes Long Shots Pay Off," *Washington Post*, 28 April 1980.

56. Prime Minister Margaret Thatcher, quoted in *Time*, 19 May 1980.

57. John Ellis, *Guerrilla Warfare* (New York: St. Martin's Press, 1976), p. 59.

58. Dobson and Payne, *Terrorists*, p. 102.

9 Fighting Terrorism: The Private Sector

Only those means of security are good, are certain, are lasting, that depend on yourself and your own vigor. —Machiavelli[1]

Government action against terrorism will always be extremely important, but government action alone is not enough to contain the spreading disequilibrium caused by terrorist violence. National defense against terrorism must be reinforced by strong private sector security programs and countermeasures designed to deny terrorists targets of opportunity.

Moreover, while the state will always respond to acts of terrorism against its citizens and their property inasmuch as each terrorist crime must be regarded as an attack on the social order—and, hence, on all members of society—in addition to the specific victim or victims, the state nonetheless does not have the duty to secure physically all of the assets within its boundaries or to provide comprehensive personal security for every member of society. Indeed, the private sector, both individuals and corporations, must look to themselves as the ultimate guarantors of their own security.

A successful terrorist action is most often the product of a number of factors coming together at the same time, any one of which, by itself, is not enough to overwhelm the system in place to protect the potential target. The mission of any security system is to thwart the union between the target, the opportunity, the means, and the terrorist. The advantage will necessarily always belong to the terrorist, who can choose his weapon and target at will, and then select the time and place for the attack. However, with careful security planning and constant vigilance, terrorist threats can be managed successfully and controlled.

Elements of Good Security

There is still a nearly universal lack of understanding as to what constitutes good security. As illustration, a leading U.S. security expert was consulted in 1979 about providing protection to a European executive whose life had

---

Portions of this chapter appeared in Neil C. Livingstone, "Fighting Terrorism: The Private Sector," *Conflict*, 3 (1981).

recently been threatened by terrorists. The security man was asked to train the executive's chauffeur. "What good is that?" he replied incredulously. "Will the chauffeur always be with him? When he is playing tennis? Taking a bath? Lying with his mistress? One well-trained chauffeur does not constitute a security system." The contract was refused because the security man knew that in order to be effective, any security system must be comprehensive and not simply a series of fragmented components. Simply put, a little security, like a little knowledge, may be more dangerous to the threatened individual than no security at all because it breeds a false sense of well-being and may encourage him to take unnecessary chances. Moreover, many members of the private sector who are concerned about their security tend to create a defense before they analyze the threat, and hence, they often implement unnecessary and useless security programs that bear little relationship to what they really need.

The first step in developing an effective security program or system is a comprehensive analysis of the threat. Once that has been completed, a system can be designed to reduce the vulnerabilities that have been identified. In this connection, no system can ever be rendered entirely free of risk; perfect security does not exist. In view of the fact that security is cumulative to the extent that the more security precautions that are implemented, the more the potential target's vulnerability will be reduced, the degree to which the risk is controlled depends on how serious the threat is and how many resources can be allocated to manage it. In the final analysis, any security system, however, is only as good as its weakest link. After the security system has been implemented, it must be audited periodically to determine how well it is performing, and if improvements or state-of-the-art updating are required, to proceed accordingly.

The following sections focus on the elements of good security and involve a comprehensive examination of counterterrorist programs and techniques that may be employed by the private sector to improve its overall defense against potential terrorist threats.

Vehicle Security

Dawn was breaking in Lagos as the sleek brown Mercedes, belonging to Brigadier General Murtalla Mohammed, the new head-of-state, moved slowly through the half-light, along the feeder road leading from the fashionable Ikoyi section of the city toward the high-rise center of the Nigerian capital. Even at this early hour, the traffic was already grinding to a near standstill on Lagos's overloaded roads and arteries. General Mohammed, however, disdained the motorcades, with their screaming sirens and phalanxes of helmeted motorcycle outriders, that his predecessor, General Yakabu Gowon, had been partial to. They had been the source of monumental traffic jams and had caused a good deal of resentment among the already harried commuters. Besides, Mohammed enjoyed the tranquility of

the limousine, free from ringing telephones and bustling aides. It gave him time
to catch up on his reading.

He was poring over documents detailing the pervasive corruption in his oil-
rich West African nation as the traffic came to a halt. Suddenly, the windshield
exploded as a hail of 9-millimeter fire ripped through the glass and stitched the
side panels of the car, the report of the weapon drowned out by blaring car
horns and the noise made by impatient drivers locked in the traffic jam as they
thumped the sides of their vehicles. Mohammed never even had time to reach
for the submachine gun bracketed in front of him; he and his driver died
instantly.

While not technically a traffic fatality, in the traditional sense of the term,
the assassination of General Mohammed gave new meaning to what urban
expert Lewis Mumford has called "the fatal stagnation of traffic in and around
our cities."[2] According to Patrick Marnham, Mohammed died "as a result of
his government's inability to solve the traffic problem."[3] Marnham notes that it
was a simple matter to predict the general's movements since his "car was
stuck in the same place at eight each morning."[4]

The general's death underscores one of the chief security problems of our
era—namely, that at no time is a potential victim more vulnerable than when he
or she is in transit between two locations, especially when riding in an automobile. The figures speak for themselves: in 80 percent of all terrorist kidnappings,
the victim is snatched from an automobile, and the same usually holds true for
assassination attempts.

This is not a new phenomenon. Before the advent of the automative age,
assassins often struck while their victims were on horseback or riding in
carriages, unprotected by the moats and high walls that usually afforded them
shelter from attack. To cite a few examples, King Henry IV of France was struck
down by a crazed assassin who attacked his carriage as it wound through the
narrow, dirty, and congested streets of sixteenth century Paris. An attempt was
made in 1878 on the life of King Humbert of Italy, who was traveling by
carriage through Naples, by a knife-wielding unemployed cook. Remember also
that Czar Alexander II was riding in a horse-drawn sleigh when he was mortally
wounded by a bomb thrown by a Russian anarchist.

During the seventy or eighty years since the internal combustion engine
replaced the horse-drawn carriage, scores of world leaders and public figures have
perished at the hands of assassins while riding in automobiles, including Arch-
duke Francis Ferdinand, whose death precipitated World War I; the thirty-fifth
president of the United States, John F. Kennedy; former Nicaraguan dictator
Anastasio Somoza; Dominican Republic strongman Raphael Trujillo; UN medi-
ator Count Folke Bernadotte; Chief Public Prosecutor Siegfried Buback of
West Germany; Nazi Reichsprotector Reinhard Heydrich; Spanish Prime Minister
Luis Carrero Blanco; and many others. Somoza's Paraguayan exile came to an
abrupt end in 1980 when his Mercedes was hit by a bazooka shell and then

raked with submachine gun fire. Somoza was literally torn to pieces and the car turned into a heap of charred and twisted metal. In February 1981, Turkey's Deputy Security Chief Mahmut Dikler was assassinated by leftist gunmen who attacked his car at a busy Istanbul intersection, pumping it full of hundreds of rounds of automatic weapons fire.

In recent years, less-successful attempts have been made on the lives of Jordan's King Hussein, French President Charles de Gaulle, former British governor-general of Cyprus Sir John Harding, and the late shah of Iran's twin sister, Princess Ashraf, when they were traveling by automobile. De Gaulle had been the target of so many assassination attempts that after an attack on his Citroen DS 19 limousine, which had been ambushed and peppered with submachine gun fire, he simply sighed, brushed the glass off his suit, and muttered, "What, again?"

The number of politicians and businessmen abducted from their cars is staggering. Two of the most sensational incidents in recent years involved West German industrialist Hans Martin Schleyer and former Italian Premier and leader of the Christian Democrats Aldo Moro. In both cases, terrorists halted the car carrying the target, killed the bodyguards, and escaped without a trace with their victim in tow. Both Schleyer and Moro were murdered subsequently by their abductors.

Bombs have been secreted both in cars and in roadbeds as assassination devices. On 26 June 1979, for example, a bomb buried in the roadbed narrowly missed killing NATO Commander (and former Secretary of State) Alexander Haig. Haig's Mercedes 600 limousine and a chase car carrying three security men were traveling at high speed along a country road near Mons, Belgium, en route to NATO headquarters, when Haig spotted two motorcycle riders speeding away from an overpass. A split second later, a loud explosion rent the air behind him, leaving a crater in the roadbed five feet deep and twelve feet across. Haig's Mercedes was thrown into the air, but neither he nor the driver was injured. The chase car, however, was demolished, but its occupants escaped with only minor injuries. To this day it is not known definitively who the would-be assassins were, although speculation has centered on the Italian Red Brigades. In the aftermath of the attack, General Haig used a helicopter to commute between his chateau and NATO headquarters.

Prime Minister Robert Mugabe of Zimbabwe also narrowly escaped the detonation of a bomb buried in the road in 1979. However, the British Ambassador to Ireland, Christopher Ewart-Biggs, was not so fortunate. On 21 July 1976, Ewart-Biggs and his secretary were murdered by the explosion of a 200-pound cache of gelignite that had been hidden in a culvert and electronically detonated beneath his 4.2-litre Jaguar. Two others in the car were injured severely but survived. Two months later to the day, exiled Chilean cabinet minister Orlando Letelier and a young co-worker died when a radio-detonated bomb tore their car apart on Washington, D.C.'s embassy row as they motored to work.

Ironically, it is believed that the bomb had been triggered prematurely by a high-frequency radio transmission from one of the embassies facing on Sheridan Circle.

Bombs planted in cars, wired to go off when the ignition was switched on, have also claimed innumerable victims. Mohammed Boudia, leader of a Black September cell in Paris, was killed by the Israeli Mossad one morning in 1973 when, after spending the night with a girlfriend in the Latin Quarter, he climbed into his white Renault and started the engine. An explosive charge placed behind the seat went off, taking the luckless Boudia with it. The Paris police still refer to the incident as the "Boudia barbecue."

From the foregoing discussion, it should be clear that threatened individuals should take extensive security precautions during the transportation mode, not only in terms of modifications to their vehicles but also with respect to their driving patterns and techniques.

Hardened Vehicles. If, as some observers have noted, the automobile is the mistress of the modern technological man, it is also assuming, under some circumstances, the role of mother, wife, and protector. Indeed, a whole new industry has grown up in recent years to provide specially designed, custom-built, terror-proof automobiles and other vehicles to the world's threatened men and women. Such vehicles are usually extensively modified, or hardened— that is, attack resistant—versions of standard production cars and trucks. Virtually any vehicle can be terror proofed, and the selection of vehicle depends largely on one's taste, pocketbook, and the use to which it will be put. Contrary to popular belief, however, most hardened vehicles are not luxury cars and limousines because they are too conspicuous and attract too much attention. Some of the most popular models given the security treatment in the United States include the Chevrolet Caprice, the Oldsmobile 88, the Jeep Wagoneer, and several Dodge products, in addition to the ubiquitous Mercedes 450 SEL. Whatever the choice of model, the car should be painted a common, nonflashy color, preferably white or tan, to make it more difficult to follow on a crowded street. Moreover, dirty cars are always less conspicuous than clean, highly polished cars. One should also resist the temptation to mount a forest of antennae atop the vehicle since in many countries they indicate an owner of influence or wealth.

In years past, hardened vehicles were basically slow, lumbering limousines with heavy armor plating. They weighed too much to handle effectively, and the extra weight of the armor plating put a severe strain on the brakes, suspension, and drive train. Over the past two decades, however, new lightweight, space-age materials like Kelvar, a fiberglass and resin compound that was developed during the Vietnam War, have revolutionized the armored car business, providing maximum protection with only a marginal increase in weight. Nevertheless, while different levels of protection are available, it should be noted that, even using the most advanced materials, the amount of armor still involves some trade-offs in terms of performance and handling. Thus, the higher the level of protection, the less maneuverable the vehicle. One firm offers six basic levels of protection, ranging from class I, which will stop bullets from a .38 special or a .45 Colt, to class VI, which is impervious to 7.62-millimeter armor-piercing NATO ordnance. Grade VI, the heavyweight top-of-the-line armored limousine normally used by heads-of-state, is a virtual fortress on wheels. In view of its extraordinary weight and marginal roadability, such cars only have value when operated in a convoy or motorcade. The average purchaser of a hardened vehicle, however, needs only mid-level protection, resistant to most grenades, assault rifles, 9-millimeter parabellum submachine guns, and magnum force weapons.

In a well-protected vehicle, typically the door panels, engine bulkhead, roof, and trunk wall are covered with Kelvar, often in combination with aluminum oxide ceramic tiles, nylon ballistic cloth, or nylon laminates. The battery case, radiator, engine compartment, and fuel tank also are reinforced and the floor of the vehicle is made blast proof. Many manufacturers are using fuel cells developed for racing cars, often wrapped in nylon batting, to prevent perforation of the fuel tank and to reduce the possibility of a fire or explosion during hostile action.

Dense plastic or bullet-resistant glass—usually layered glass with a layer of transparent sheet polycarbonate in the middle—is a standard feature of virtually all hardened cars. Because of the weight and thickness of glass (often 35 millimeters thick) capable of stopping a high-velocity bullet, door and window frames must be reinforced and widened. Once the regular glass has been replaced with bullet-resistant glass, the side windows will not roll up and down. This puts an extra premium on outfitting the vehicle with a durable and reliable air conditioning system in tropical countries. Most hardened vehicles also use compartmentalized, or run flat, tires that will stay on the rim and permit the car to be driven at speeds in excess of 70 miles per hour even if punctured by bullets. Dual reinforced bumpers, mounted on both the front and rear of the car, permit the driver to ram other vehicles and obstructions in the road without harm to his vehicle. The trunk, doors, and bonnet should be secured by special locks and antihijack bolts to prevent them from being pried open.

Among the more novel features sported by some of the most exotic and sophisticated hardened vehicles are devices that lay down an oil slick behind the car, release a heavy smoke screen, or spit tacks on the road. A remote-control starter, which allows the car to be started from a safe distance, is useful in the event someone has wired a bomb to the ignition. In addition, a variety of companies manufacture alarms, bomb-scanning devices, and tampering-detection systems. High-intensity lights mounted on the rear bumper will make it difficult, if not impossible, for hostiles to pursue a vehicle at night at close range, and a pulsating high-intensity light atop the car will make it similarly impossible for a sniper to get a clear fix on the vehicle, even if he is using a night vision scope. Nozzles that spray tear gas, acids, chemicals, or poisons, hidden in the fender wells behind reflectors, are extremely valuable in discouraging mob attacks. Former Iranian General Taghil Latifi, who was dragged from his Mercedes and severely beaten by a Tehran mob, probably would have escaped injury if his car had boasted such a system. In order to prevent those inside the car from being overcome by the tear gas or spray from the nozzles, or to ensure against harm from a gas attack launched by hostiles, it is recommended that a special air conditioning system be installed that, at the flick of a switch, can be turned into an integrated ventilation system that recirculates the air already inside the car. A similar spray system also can be purchased that douses fires with fire-repressant chemicals. Another mob deterrent involves making the lower edge of the car razor sharp so that if hostiles try to lift the car up and tip it over, their hands will be sliced off.

Most of the accessories that have been described have chiefly a defensive function, but other gadgetry and modifications are available for those who believe that the best defense is a good offense. Gun ports enable the occupants inside the car to return hostile fire without endangering themselves, and gun racks, both hidden and exposed, can be built into the front or rear seats or installed underneath the dash. A well-outfitted automotive arsenal should include a variety of weapons, each with a different range and utility. Time after time, for sheer intimidation power and mayhem, the best weapon is an automatic, short-barrel shotgun loaded with double-O buckshot or flechettes. Despite their limited range and accuracy, submachine guns are recommended because of their rapid rate of fire and the fact that they are relatively easy to use in the cramped confines of an automobile. Assault rifles are unwieldy inside an automobile, and most pistols lack stopping power and a sufficient rate of fire to be effective. It should be noted that even a relatively unskilled individual can employ a shotgun or submachine gun with devastating effect, but it takes constant practice and good eye to be a competent pistol marksman.

Other useful devices for the aggressive driver include a hostile-fire indicator, which resembles a clock and indicates from which direction an attack is coming; night vision driving/aiming devices; ejection seats to catapult undesirable passengers out of the car; grenade launchers; and a loudspeaker/microphone system that permits the occupants of the car to communicate with those on the outside. In spite of all of the fancy gadgetry, however, according to the Italian firm of Fontauto, the largest automotive security company in that country, the single most effective deterrent of vehicle assaults is a piercing siren or air horn that both frightens and disorients the attackers.

Although it smacks of James Bond, one Miami security man has a custom-built Cadillac with two machine guns built into the front grille; when he throws the car into a complete spin, he can "take out" everything in a 360-degree arc. The Cadillac also has four shotguns loaded with double-O buckshot mounted in the rear taillight assembly. If being chased, his strategy is to turn a sharp corner and broadside the pursuit vehicle with all four shotguns simultaneously. Unless the pursuit car is hardened, the shotgun blasts will play havoc with it.

Well-constructed and -designed hardened vehicles are, as the old television commercial for one of Detroit's products used to purport, truly "something to believe in." They do not take all of the risk out of driving, but they certainly do diminish one's chances of "becoming a highway fatality." Indeed, most terrorists and kidnappers, if they discover that an individual has excellent security, usually will select another target who is more vulnerable rather than to risk an encounter in which they might come out the loser. After all, too many potential victims with inadequate security exist to go after those few who have taken appropriate precautions. This brings up an interesting point. Despite the advanced state-of-the-art with respect to automotive security, it is always amazing to note how many individuals, with both the means and the need, have resisted efforts to get them to use a hardened vehicle. Alexander Haig's Mercedes, which he was riding in at the time of the assassination attempt described earlier, was an ordinary showroom model without even rudimentary hardening.

Exiled Nicaraguan Dictator Anastasio Somoza had rejected the idea of purchasing a heavily armored automobile, valued at more than $200,000, shortly before his death, maintaining that Paraguay's strongman Alfredo Stroessner ran a tight ship and that an assassination attempt in Asunción was unlikely. Aldo Moro was equally stubborn, a fact that cost him his life. Moro ignored the suggestions of his security advisors and refused to travel in an inconspicuous armored vehicle, preferring instead a readily identifiable, unhardened blue official car.

In many respects, the attack on Moro, which resulted in the deaths of his chauffeur and five-member escort, and ultimately Moro himself, represents a casebook example of how not to protect someone. In addition to declining the protection afforded by a hardened vehicle, Moro, who was a man of meticulous habit, rejected any notion of varying his routes and travel times. On 16 March 1978, the day of his abduction, he left to attend mass, as he did every morning, at the usual time and by the regular route. As his car, followed by a police vehicle, approached an intersection at the confluence of two narrow Rome streets, the exit was blocked by another car, which was later reported stolen, with Venezuelan tags and registration. At that moment, Moro's car was struck from behind by the police vehicle, whose driver was following too closely and not paying proper attention. The three *carabiniere* in the police car died instantly when the windshield was raked with fire (nearly eighty rounds) from Skorpion Vz61 machine pistols. The terrorists used pistols in the attack on Moro's car presumably to avoid indiscriminate fire and to reduce the chances of accidentally hitting Moro, which happened anyway. Even if they had had time to react, it is doubtful that the three police officers could have put up effective resistance since they were only armed with small-caliber sixteen-shot pistols hidden beneath their coats. Moreover, none of the officers had any more than rudimentary knowledge of executive protection methods, and at best, they would have been forced to improvise in a situation that demanded reflexive action.

Both Moro's bodyguard and chauffeur, who were riding in the front seat of the official car, were also killed, and the wounded Moro was pulled from the back seat and kidnapped, only to be executed later by the terrorists. There has been speculation that, had Moro's chauffeur, an old family retainer, been trained in aggressive/evasive driving techniques, especially ramming, it might have been possible to escape the trap. According to an Italian police official, if the chauffeur had rammed the car blocking the intersection and bulldozed his way on through, Moro might still be alive today.

By contrast to Moro's slipshod security precautions, the terrorists, members of Italy's Red Brigades, had taken months to plan the operation, working it out to the last detail. More than sixty members of their network were involved, including the twelve-member contingent that actually carried out the attack, and in excess of $20,000 had been spent on firearms and preparations.

Avoiding Vehicle Attacks. During the period of Henry Kissinger's famous shuttle diplomacy in search of a Middle East peace, he decided to visit Syrian President Assad in Damascus, overruling his security advisors who felt that protecting the U.S. secretary of state would be virtually impossible given the internal tensions in Syria, not to mention numerous threats against his life by radical Palestinian groups. The chief problem was how to get Kissinger safely from the airport to the presidential palace, a distance of some eighteen miles. Syrian security forces were viewed as only marginally competent and the army as unreliable. Kissinger's security men did not want Syrian soldiers with automatic weapons flanking the road all the way into the city. If a conspiracy were hatched, it would be like running a gauntlet. However, if the military could not be trusted, who was available to repel attacks by Palestinian terrorists or Moslem fundamentalists? Even more disconcerting was intelligence suggesting that Iraq, Syria's arch enemy, might sponsor an assassination plot against Kissinger just to embarass the Syrian government.

Ultimately, a plan was worked out with which the U.S. security contingent was able to live and in which the Syrians were willing to participate. When Kissinger arrived at the airport, he immediately transferred to a hardened limousine that was part of a convoy of vehicles. The convoy then left the airport at high speed for Damascus. The road leading into the city had been closed to all traffic, and Syrian troops lined both sides, one man every thirty paces. Instead of facing the highway, however, the soldiers had been ordered to stand with their backs to it, and instead of holding their automatic rifles across their chests, every weapon rested on the ground, to be picked up only in an emergency and, even then, only at the direct command of an officer.

Kissinger's security men rode into the city leaning out of the windows of the vehicles in the convoy, their weapons cocked and ready to kill—by prior agreement with the Syrians—any soldier who attempted to pick up his rifle.

Kissinger's trip to Damascus involved some strange logistics and security arrangements, but they paid off inasmuch as the visit was made safely.

From a planning perspective, the key to good vehicle security is unpredictability. Every effort should be made, when commuting between frequently visited locations, to avoid routine patterns since virtually all terrorists or would-be kidnappers and assassins monitor their victim's habits to determine the most vulnerable moment and place to strike. The route between one's home and place of business, in particular, should be varied constantly, along with the time of arrival and departure.

Route selection merits careful consideration and should not be left to the last moment. In addition to a primary route, several backup or alternate routes should be selected. The quickest and most direct route is not always the safest route, especially if it means traveling on congested roads or through high-risk neighborhoods. Route planning should always be done in secrecy, and the fewer people who know the route in advance the better so that a breech of security, either accidental or intentional, will be less likely. A trusted aide should be informed on a secure phone or, if that is not possible, by means of a coded message, as to the intended route and estimated time of arrival at the particular destination. If the principal misses the agreed-upon arrival time or is overdue by more than a reasonable period of time, prearranged emergency procedures should be initiated.

When traveling on an expressway or four-lane highway, the car should stay on the inside lanes so as to make it more difficult for hostiles to force it to the side of the road. A constant, steady speed under the legal limit should be maintained. In dangerous regions, it is advisable to travel in convoy or accompanied by one or more escort vehicles. A so-called crash car can run interference in front and spot potential trouble situations, and if the road is suddenly blocked, it can ram the obstruction. A rear escort vehicle can prevent the principal's car from being forced to the side of the road or pinned between hostile vehicles. It can also open up a rear avenue of retreat should the situation warrant it.

Each vehicle should observe a reasonable interval from the car in front of it in order to reduce the likelihood of rear-end collisions and the possibility of the entire convoy becoming trapped or boxed in. Nevertheless, visual contact should be maintained, and all of the escort vehicles should be linked by means of a secure communications system with the principal's car. In some instances, in order to add an additional variable to any terrorist assassination or kidnapping plan, it is advisable for the principal to alternate, at random, the vehicle he rides in.

Evasive/Aggressive Driving Skills. One's vehicle security is only as good as the driver. Drivers and chauffeurs not only should be highly trained and in excellent physical condition (to ensure good reflexes and alertness), but also they should be screened carefully to ascertain whether anything in their backgrounds would render them unfit for such work or susceptible to being compromised. For example, one chauffeur in Latin America, who was burdened by gambling debts, was paid a large sum of money to leave the doors unlocked on his employer's hardened vehicle, permitting terrorists to kidnap the victim at a stop light. The chauffeur, incidentally, was shot to death by the terrorists for his complicity.

Fueled by attention in the media, schools are springing up all around the world to teach chauffeurs, bodyguards, and potential kidnap victims how to avoid being stopped on a road or highway by resorting to a series of evasive maneuvers designed to escape entrapment and to outrun pursuers. Known as evasive or aggressive driving, many of the basic maneuvers trace their origin to auto racing and the skills perfected by Southern moonshiners, Hollywood stuntmen, and Prohibition-era rum-runners.

Perhaps the most basic maneuver is the 180-degree so-called bootlegger's turn, or California bootleg as it is known in some circles. If a sudden obstruction should appear in the road, the driver—traveling at a speed of between 45 and 60 miles an hour—jerks on the emergency brake, cranks the steering wheel abruptly to the left, fishtails the car around until completing a U-turn, releases the emergency brake, and accelerates away in the opposite direction. Another basic maneuver is the J-turn, commonly called the reverse 180. It is used most often when the forward momentum of the car has stopped and there is no room to make a bootlegger's turn. The J-turn involves throwing the vehicle into reverse and backing away at high speed, then whipping the wheel to one side, forcing the car to swing around until it is facing the opposite direction, at which time it should be possible to leave the scene by the same route as one entered.

Despite all of the glamour and hyperbole associated with such maneuvers, however, they are usually more effective on a movie lot than in real life. Most vehicle attacks by terrorists occur on crowded city streets, at stoplights, or when entering or exiting from parking garages. Only rarely will an attack take place on a high-speed expressway or lonely country road where such maneuvers can be utilized. This writer knows of no incident where evasive driving maneuvers such as the bootlegger's turn or reverse 180 saved a would-be victim, although surely there must be a few cases on record.

Such skills are clearly not a panacea in terms of avoiding motor vehicle attacks. By contrast, ramming techniques are not part of the curriculum at many antiterrorist driving schools, but they represent perhaps the most important auto survival skill that can be mastered. Since many vehicle attacks involve blocking the target vehicle and forcing it to a stop on a narrow and crowded street, as in the Moro incident, dramatic maneuvers are out of the question. Under such circumstances, the best, and often only, tactic is to ram the obstruction, knocking it out of the immediate path and opening a hole large enough for escape. Since they are sometimes inadequate for the task, it is advisable, as previously noted, to replace factory bumpers with dual reinforced bumpers, although the positioning of the hit is more important than the strength of the bumpers. When ramming a car crossways in the road, for example, it should be hit near the front or rear end with just enough force to spin it out of the way rather than broadside, which could disable the ramming vehicle.

The first rule of survival in any vehicle attack is never to stop moving; when that happens escape is usually impossible. A moving vehicle cannot be trapped or boxed in. In an emergency, drive over lawns, up sidewalks, even through shops and buildings. Remember that an automobile is a formidable weapon: do not hesitate to run down assailants or to hit another car trying to force your vehicle over to the side of the road. If the particular vehicle you are driving is not a hardened model, it should be noted that a human body can do considerable damage. If struck head-on, a body is likely to be thrown onto the hood or through the windshield. In one instance on record, the driver of a car under attack struck one of the terrorists, decapitating the man and propelling his head back through the windshield. The severed head landed on the seat next to the driver and caused him to lose control of the car and crash.

If pursued by another car, it should never be allowed to draw alongside; the driver can weave from side to side, thereby forcing it to stay behind. Only if there is no other choice should those in the target vehicle attempt to fight it out with the attackers. Since the assailants normally will have better cover and weapons, there is no disgrace in fleeing from the scene of the engagement as quickly as possible. From a purely practical standpoint, the driver of the car should not be expected to return hostile fire and drive at the same time, since his driving and not his marksmanship almost always will offer the best chance of escape. Good driving technique requires both hands on the steering wheel and maximum concentration.

As noted earlier, small-caliber pistols are no match against an adversary who is armed with automatic weapons. Providing a chauffeur with a pistol, which has utility only at close range, is often to sign his death warrant and perhaps that of the passenger as well since ineffective resistance is, in most cases, worse than no resistance at all. Moreover, unless the chauffeur has been checked out on his weapon and is a competent marksman, he may be more of a threat to others in the car than to the assailants in the excitement and confusion of a terrorist attack. This goes for the passenger as well.

To summarize, although it is but one element in a total security package, good vehicle security is essential to any threatened person. Hardened automobiles represent a compromise between the family car and a tank, but because of recent technological advances, modern war wagons do not have to be lumbering and homely. No one can be completely secure, but with a well-designed and constructed hardened vehicle, prudent planning, evasive/aggressive driving skills, and an appropriate arsenal, most terrorist and criminal threats during the transportation mode can be managed and controlled successfully.

Residential Protection

Despite the fact that one usually is more vulnerable in his or her residence than at any other time except when in transit, sophisticated residential security is unknown in many parts of the world and often consists solely of security guards, attack animals, and high walls. This was illustrated by a security audit performed of the presidential palace in Bogota, Columbia. The audit showed security to be almost nonexistent. Access to the palace was gained through a nonreinforced wrought-iron gate that was open most of the time. Armed troops patrolled the grounds, but they were visible targets from outside the fence or from any number of tall office buildings and church steeples in the immediate vicinity. Unlocked manholes led from outside the complex into the restricted grounds. There was no method of checking identification at the main gate; one was simply admitted if his or her name appeared on a handwritten list at the guardhouse. Each visitor was given a security badge to be worn for the duration of the visit, but at the conclusion of the visit, several members of the audit team kept their security badges, a fact the guards at the gate failed to notice since they made no attempt to count the badges to see if the number of badges corresponded to the number of people exiting the area. The security guards, moreover, had so little familiarity with their firearms that they had to look at the name on the side of their submachine guns, in response to a query from a member of the audit team, to determine the make and caliber of their weapons.

Palace architects had attempted to install heavy bullet-resistant glass in the windows but had neglected to reinforce the window frames, hence many of the windows and frames had fallen out and shattered on the ground. There was a clear line of fire from the roof of the nearby university into the president's bedroom, and figures within the palace could be picked off easily by snipers from dozens of vantage points around it. Once the grounds were penetrated, it was an easy matter to scale the building and to enter it by means of unlocked ventilation shafts or by plastic-bubble skylights held in place solely by clamps. There was a helicopter pad high atop the palace, but not only was the helicopter so vulnerable from surrounding buildings that it could be downed, in the words of one expert, "with a crossbow," but also tricky winds and crosscurrents rendered the pad totally unsafe.

There is little excuse for the almost total absence of security just described. A residence or building of almost any size and design can be turned into a nearly impregnable fortress with only superficial changes to its outward appearance.

The modern equivalent of a medieval moat, intrusion-detection systems (microwave/seismic/laser field/seismic-magnetic) will pick up any unauthorized attempts to penetrate a secure perimeter and warn those inside by means of an alarm. Closed circuit television cameras can also be used to guard strategic access points; however, television monitors must be manned on a continuous basis and thus are only as good as the people operating them. Other external safeguards include deadbolt locks, reinforced doors, bullet-resistant windows, high-intensity outdoor or periphery lighting, and steel bars, window grilles, or shutters (that close from the inside). In order to secure a residence from rioters or bombs, fragmentation screens or netting in front of the windows usually will prevent grenades, stones, or bombs from being thrown through the windows. Sliding doors can be made secure by inserting a metal rod or broom handle in the door track. Trees or poles that an intruder might scale to get over an outer wall or to gain access to the upper floors of the house should be removed or included in the overall security system.

All automobiles should be kept in secure garages to prevent tampering as well as to avoid tipping off observers as to which family members are at home. While the presence of security guards alone does not ensure effective security, it can often serve as a valuable component in an overall security system by acting as a deterrent to would-be aggressors. If armed, guards should be trained properly in the use of their weapons and in firearm safety. Most people have an exaggerated fear of guard dogs and other attack animals, and hence, they also serve as valuable deterrents to unauthorized trespassers. One prominent individual in Latin America lets lions roam his estate at night, a fact that he publicizes to ward away terrorists. Moreover, the cry of a peacock, the bark of a dog, or the honk of a goose (all excellent guard animals) can provide security personnel with advance warning of intruders.

Guards should watch for suspicious cars or panel trucks on the street outside the house, or for loiterers and other persons with no apparent business in the neighborhood, who may be casing the house and keeping track of the movements of those inside. If the police cannot or will not remove suspicious individuals, pictures of them should be taken and the make, model, and license numbers of their vehicles should be recorded.

Everyone who works in close proximity to the potential victim and his or her family should be screened carefully—that is, an exhaustive study of his or her background and references should be conducted. One should never speak in front of the household staff about the security system that protects the house or of details relating to one's personal finances and habits. It is recommended that all household staff members be required to follow strict security procedures and that the failure to observe any of the rules should be grounds for dismissal. Among the most important precautions are the following:

> Household staff should not speak with anyone, especially strangers, about the family, house, or the security system.

No one should be admitted without proper identification. If there is any doubt about the identity of a delivery or other person at the door, the individual should be refused admittance until his or her identity is verified.

Be suspicious of new delivery personnel or utility inspectors, especially if they claim to be substituting for a sick co-worker who is known to the household.

Suspicious Mail

With the development of plastique—a compound of TNT, Hexogen, and a rubber compound that "can be molded into almost any shape and can even be rolled thin to look like writing paper that can, indeed, be written on"[5]—and the Polaroid camera that uses flat batteries, terrorists can manufacture remarkably sophisticated letter bombs that have claimed many lives in recent years and have maimed even more people. Be wary of unexpected letters or parcels inasmuch as they may contain deadly chemicals or explosives. Do not attempt to open the suspicious item, but instead notify the police immediately. Never feel the suspect mail or press on it since that may be enough to trigger a detonation. Handle it with extreme caution.

A parcel or envelop should be regarded as suspicious if:

There is no return address;

The person or firm indicated on the return address is not recognizable;

The name and address are composed of letters clipped from newspapers or magazines;

The parcel has unusual features such as the contents having been inserted from the side so that the addressee will trip the explosive charge when he opens it from the top.[6]

The following list includes hints on detecting a letter bomb:

The envelop normally will be heavier than one that contains the same thickness of paper.

Explosives often sweat, causing greasy marks or stains on a package.

Explosives often have a smell similar to marzipan or almonds.

The letter or parcel may have a dead feeling like putty or clay would give it rather than the spring and flexibility of a sheaf of papers.

The letter or parcel may feel lopsided or heavy for its size.

The presence of a hairspring or a mechanism the size of a small coin may be outlined on the envelope or parcel. This is the trip mechanism.[7]

Business Security

One's place of business should be protected by access control and identification systems to thwart unwanted intruders. All employees of the firm should undergo at least a minimal security screening to ascertain whether they have arrest or criminal records, any history of political activism, unsavory friends, and any close family members who are suspected members of the underground. Closet homosexuals, compulsive gamblers, and anyone with a serious drinking problem should be removed from sensitive posts. An admitted homosexual, however, who is open about his or her predilection, usually constitutes no more risk than anyone else since the disclosure of that person's sexual preference cannot be used as a reason for blackmail.

All company telephones should be checked periodically for telephone taps and eavesdropping devices, and key offices and conference rooms also should be swept for such devices. Do not forget the confidential secretary's telephone and work area since she more often than not makes the potential victim's travel arrangements and appointments and is privy to much of his personal life. All packages and envelopes should be scrutinized by a trained employee or screening device for bombs and explosive devices. Corporate planes should be operated with the same prudence as a personal automobile—that is, they should be kept in locked hangers when not in use and the backgrounds of the maintenance personnel and flight crew carefully screened.

Possible victims should wait until the last feasible moment to make travel reservations and should not publicize them or make them known to others. When traveling alone, it is prudent to eat in the hotel rather than to go out. If one does decide to go out to shop or eat, sparsely populated areas and rough night spots should be avoided. One should always stay in public view and, if possible, dress like the natives so as not to stand out from the population. In most parts of Latin America, attire such as a three-piece suit or pair of golf slacks and sport shirt instantly will identify the wearer as an outsider, most likely as a North American. Association with prostitutes and strangers is dangerous, but if one still desires the services of a prostitute, he should resist selecting a girl who shows too much interest in him or is too forward. She may be part of a kidnap plot. Similarly, when taking a taxi, do not order one in advance or use one that is parked too conveniently in front of the hotel. Instead, hail a cab that is cruising or select one at random at a cab stand. If the taxis at a cab stand must be taken in order, stand back and let others hire the first several cabs until satisfied that it is not a setup and then select one.

Crisis Management

Although the goal of every security program is to prevent crises from occurring, even the best security systems occasionally will fail or be overridden by superior tactics on the part of hostile forces. If past incidents hold any lesson, it is that persons unprepared for a crisis suffer most when it occurs. An ad hoc or hastily organized response to a crisis increases the risk of error, and in the matter of a kidnapping, errors can be fatal.

In the event that the first line of defense fails and a worst-case scenario develops, especially when it involves life and death stakes such as in a kidnap or hostage situation, it is critical that preestablished emergency procedures be in place to provide a comprehensive framework for an organized response to the incident. This is known as crisis management and involves "a unique management process that develops strategic responses in crisis situations through preselected and trained managers (the Crisis Management Team) using existing skills plus specialized processes to minimize loss of organizational assets."[8] The benefits emanating from an organized response to a crisis, as opposed to a makeshift response, are obvious and too numerous to list, and it should suffice to say that no government or corporation can afford to ignore such contingency planning if it is desirous of developing appropriate strategies designed to achieve a successful resolution of security-related crisis. While governments and corporations usually develop an in-house crisis management capability, vulnerable individuals often retain outside security firms, specializing in crisis management techniques, to fulfill this function in the event that the principal or a member of his family is kidnapped or threatened in some way. Any number of firms in the United States and abroad provide crisis management services on a consulting basis.

Crisis-Management Group

The crisis management group (CMG) should be composed of senior management officials and security experts with full authority to collect all of the factual data pertaining to the crisis and to mobilize the resources necessary for its successful resolution. The composition of CMGs will vary, but an individual responsible for each of the following functional categories should be named to the unit: security, communications, legal, financial/insurance, public relations, personnel/medical, and top management. If possible, all of the individuals selected for the CMG should reside in the same city (normally where the organization's headquarters are located), not be subject to extensive routine travel demands, have proven leadership abilities and sound judgment, and be required to fulfill the demands of the CMG personally and not delegate responsibilities to a staff member. Alternates or deputy members also should be chosen in the event that one of the principal members is on vacation or indisposed when the crisis arises, and a chairman should be selected to preside over the group. Outside consultants may be brought in to provide experience and support services to the CMG and to help implement the decisions that are reached.

Clear lines of authority within the CMG should be established and individual responsibilities defined. For example:

Security: Normally such matters fall under the purview of the firm's security chief. He will be expected to provide expertise in analyzing the threat, developing options, and implementing the CMG's decisions. He should also take steps to minimize the possibility of further attacks or incidents by invoking emergency security procedures at all company facilities.

Communications: This individual coordinates all communications to and from the adversary, the host government (if the event takes place outside the United States), intermediaries, and law enforcement personnel to ensure that the company speaks with only one voice and does not send conflicting signals to any of the other parties involved.

Legal: The legal officer provides counsel to the CMG regarding the legal implications of the particular incident and the options being considered to resolve the situation. This individual may be called upon to devise a strategy for circumventing the laws of nations that prohibit the payment of money in extortion and kidnapping incidents.

Financial/Insurance: The designated individual must arrange for the funds necessary to implement the decisions of the CMG, especially in the event that it is necessary to pay a ransom. The person should have expertise in or knowledge of surreptitious movement of funds across national borders. If the company carries kidnapping or some other kind of relevant insurance, he must also coordinate the CMG's actions with the insurance company.

Public Relations: This individual is the chief spokesman of the CMG and liaison with the press and television media and should answer all inquiries in a controlled and thoughtful manner in order to project a sense of strength and assurance. Should it be necessary to undertake a covert hostage retrieval mission or some other controversial action, he must devise a proper strategy and method of releasing the information to the public.

Personnel/Medical: In a kidnapping situation, the medical coordinator provides all relevant information regarding the victim(s), especially medical data, and serves as liaison to the victim's family and to the other employees of the company.

Top Management: This individual acts as the representative of top manage-

ment and the board of directors and keeps them informed of the deliberations and actions of the CMG.

Decision-Making Preparations

Once the CMG has been selected and is in place and operational responsibilities
have been affixed, then individual preparation should commence. Each member
of the team must familiarize himself with his individual responsibilities so he
will be ready to assume his duties at a moment's notice in a professional and
expeditious fashion. The CMG should be provided with a charter delineating its
authority by the governing councils of the company or institution. A pre-event
threat-analysis survey should be conducted to determine the identity and nature
of potential threats, and this should be followed by the development of a
relevant data base and contingency plans addressing each threat category.

With the adoption of specific step-by-step procedures for responding to
crises, the CMG will be ready to simulate various crises, employing standard
gaming techniques, both to gain practical experience and to coalesce as a group.
At the conclusion of each simulation, a crisis readiness survey should be prepared, identifying weaknesses in the CMG's performance and appraising the
company's or institution's overall ability to meet the challenge simulated in the
exercise. It goes without saying that every effort should be made to correct any
shortcomings noted by the survey.

Crisis Phase

As soon as news of a potential event or serious threat is received by the communications manager of the CMG, he should immediately contact the chairman
of the group, and a decision should be reached whether or not the specific
threat or event merits the convening of the CMG. If it appears to be a legitimate
emergency, the group should be notified at once, using a prearranged code or
message, and the members should assemble at a predesignated location.

Some specialists advocate incident diagramming as a means of organizing
all of the relevant information associated with the event so that the essential
facts can be assimilated in a thorough and comprehensive manner. When this
is completed, it is time to identify the range of options available to the CMG
for reacting to the event. These should be ranked according to risk, cost, and
probable success and evaluated from a technical, legal, financial, and logistical
standpoint. Once a decision has been made, the CMG must see that it is
properly implemented.

A step-by-step response to a kidnapping crisis is outlined later in this
chapter.

Kidnapping. Once among the rarest of crimes, kidnapping for ransom has, in recent years, reached epidemic proportions around the world. Thousands of people, usually business executives, diplomats, and political leaders, are kidnapped every year and held for ransom; and where in the past the motive nearly always was criminal, today an increasingly large percentage of all kidnappings are politically inspired. While political kidnappings are virtually a daily occurrence in nations like Italy, El Salvador, and Argentina, there have been few politically motivated kidnappings in the United States; the celebrated Patricia Hearst kidnapping is the only high publicized incident of its type during the past decade. Nevertheless, convictions for criminal kidnappings in the United States are up fivefold over fifteen years ago, indicating a considerable increase in this activity. Moreover, Americans living and working abroad are prime targets for foreign terrorists, and a significant number have been kidnapped, although figures are incomplete since many of the incidents are never reported to the authorities.

The spectacular growth of kidnapping as a favorite tactic of terrorists is explained perhaps by the fact that, relatively speaking, it is an extremely low-risk tactic. As a method of financing a revolutionary movement, kidnapping is not only safer but also more lucrative than robbing banks or skyjacking and holding the passengers and plane for ransom.

During the past decade and a half, tens of millions of dollars have been paid to a variety of terrorist groups in Argentina, Guatemala, Italy, West Germany, Belgium, Mexico, Uruguay, Spain, El Salvador, and a host of other countries for the safe return of abducted executives, government officials, and members of their families. Foreign corporations in Argentina have been particularly hard hit, and in one case, a U.S. corporation is reported to have paid $10 million for the return of one of its executives. The family of Argentine brothers Juan and Jorge Born, moreover, paid a record $60 million ransom to the Montoneros guerrillas for their safe release. A Guatemalan newspaper estimated that during one sixteen-month period, over $2 million in ransom was collected by kidnappers in eleven separate incidents involving Guatemalan citizens.[9] However, the newspaper noted that it was difficult to determine which incidents were carried out by political terrorists and which were the work of common criminals posing as such. Some criminals have attempted to make their kidnappings appear to be the work of political terrorists as a means of throwing law enforcement personnel off their trail. Indeed, in the wake of the Hearst kidnapping in the United States, *Atlanta Constitution* editor J. Reginald Murphy was abducted by a purported terrorist organization that identified itself as the American Revolutionary Army. It subsequently turned out that the so-called army consisted only of the kidnapper and his wife, who had actually committed the crime for the money and had no political motivations whatsoever.

General Security Precautions. It is a fact that the terrorists or kidnappers will have kept the potential victim under surveillance for some time, perhaps even for a period of months, before making a move. The attack, when it does come, can be expected to be staged and executed carefully, the product of weeks of preparation and often a good deal of money, and aimed at the most identifiable weakness in the victim's security. The terrorists, moreover, likely will have planned for all contingencies, leaving very little to chance. Unless the victim is extremely well prepared, and in many cases simply lucky, once the attack has been initiated the odds are that the kidnapping will be successful. Thus, the best insurance against a kidnap attempt is for the potential victim not to give the terrorists an opportunity to strike in the first place.

The essence of good security is common sense and the adoption of a comprehensive program designed to reduce the individual's vulnerability. Inasmuch as the kidnappers, not the victim, will determine the time, place, and strategy of the attack, a personal security program will necessarily have to be all encompassing and provide a consistent level of protection during every hour of the day in order to be effective. If security procedures are disregarded even for a moment, that may be all the opportunity alert terrorists need in order to strike. For example, a prominent businessman in Central America refused to observe security precautions or to be accompanied by his bodyguards when he visited his mistress, which he ordinarily did three days a week at approximately the same hour. Of course, it was only a matter of time before terrorists, observing his movements, concluded that that was the optimal time to abduct him—and abducted he was. To the extent possible, therefore, the potential victim should seek to make his activities as unpredictable as possible, avoiding rigid patterns and routines. The value of unpredictability can be illustrated by an incident that occurred in prerevolutionary Iran. Several antigovernment safe houses were discovered by the authorities, who found in one of the houses a list of nearly 200 potential kidnap victims who had been under observation by the terrorists. In every case where the potential victim was unpredictable, the terrorists had crossed his name off the list.

One's route between home and business, and the time that he or she commutes each day, should be varied constantly. A full itinerary of the potential victim's daily schedule should be provided to a trusted aide or personal secretary, and if he or she fails to make an appointment or to call within a prearranged time interval, emergency procedures should commence at once. Business and social schedules should never be publicized in advance. Interviews should not be given to the press without first checking the credentials of the reporter, and even then care must be exercised to provide as little information as possible about one's family, residence, and personal habits.

Good communications are essential to good security. Linking home, office, car, yacht, and/or plane to a central communications system should be considered. Most important of all, the potential victim should be alert to anything unusual or out of the ordinary during his or her daily activities. For example, one should not enter a store in which everyone is standing listlessly and no one is talking; it is probable that the store has been occupied by terrorists in preparation for the victim's arrival. An accident or stalled vehicle may be a hoax designed to slow down traffic or to block a critical thoroughfare. It is well to note that terrorists may use a diversion such as a trash fire or a comely young woman in a provocative dress to distract one's security detail or chauffeur momentarily in order to gain the advantage.

If one suspects that he or she is being followed, either on foot or in the car, walk or drive around the block an extra time to make certain.

Planning for an Emergency. Anyone who suspects that he or she is a likely terrorist target and who is not covered under a corporate or institutional crisis management umbrella should develop a personal emergency plan to be implemented in the event of a kidnapping or other emergency.[10] The plan should designate the person(s) who will negotiate with the kidnappers, emergency financial arrangements for his or her family, and how the ransom money will be obtained. Insurance policies, passport, medical records, and other vital documents should be readily available and in a place accessible to a trusted aide or member of the victim's family. The potential victim may find it desirable to give a limited power-of-attorney to a partner, attorney, aide, or member of his family, to become effective if he is kidnapped, so that important business decisions can be made in his absence.

If the individual requires daily medication, a four-week supply of any such medicine should be kept on hand for an emergency of this kind. A member of the victim's staff or family should be prepared to communicate the victim's dependence on medication to the kidnappers and to provide them with a supply of the necessary drugs if requested to do so. The potential victim should always carry a second pair of eyeglasses in case those he or she is wearing are lost or damaged in the abduction.

Along different lines, the potential victim may want to cut up a carbide-steel hacksaw blade and carry a two-inch piece secreted in his pants cuff with its cutting edge taped. The blade can be used to saw out of captivity or to cut one's bonds if tied up. A far more complex security precaution involves tiny transmitters or tracking devices that emit a powerful signal and that can be worn by the potential victim—in the heel of his shoe, for example—or hidden in his car. The transmitter is programmed to send out an alert or distress signal under certain conditions and can be used to track the victim once he has been kidnapped. Helicopters are employed to home in on the signal and to isolate it in a particular sector or quadrant of a city or rural region. Trucks or vans with sophisticated tracking and monitoring equipment are then used to pinpoint the exact location of the signal. If the victim can be located within a half hour of his abduction, the chances are extremely good that his captors will not be prepared for a rescue attempt and most likely can be overpowered with little resistance. In tests of this system in the Los Angeles region, a man wearing one of the transmitters was given a car and fifteen minutes head start and was told to drive in any direction he desired. In every instance, the tracking teams were able to locate him within a half hour of elapsed time. Campbell's Soup Company is just one of many corporations that has placed such tracking devices in its executives' cars.

In the case of a kidnapping, the following sections provide responses that could, if followed carefully, facilitate a successful resolution of the crisis and contribute to the safe and expeditious return of the victim.[11]

Confirmation of the Event.   The first priority is to confirm beyond a reasonable doubt that the event or threat is bona fide. The importance of obtaining an absolute verification of the event can be demonstrated by an incident that took place in Latin America in recent years. A foreign corporation was notified that one of its senior executives had been kidnapped, and the caller demanded a $50,000 ransom in exchange for his life. The caller said that the company had only thirty-six hours to make the drop and that if the deadline expired, the executive would be executed. The company was told that the kidnapper's demands were nonnegotiable and that no other communications would be forthcoming. A hasty check by the company revealed that no one knew the whereabouts of the executive. Predicated on that fact and the call from the kidnapper, the company authorized payment of the ransom. Two days later, however, the executive appeared and was at a loss to explain the commotion his presence created. It turned out that he had not been kidnapped at all but had slipped away for a tryst with his mistress. He had instructed one of her servants to call his office and say that he was taking off several days, but instead, the servant had engineered the hoax and absconded with the ransom.

Presence of a Representative at the Scene.   Once the incident has been verified, send a representative to the scene. The field representative, as he is called, can be either an executive of the company or a member of a reliable security firm. The presence of a man on the spot is clear evidence of corporate concern. The personal qualifications of the field representative are maturity, intelligence, good judgment, and an ability to communicate effectively. In this connection, if the event takes place in another country, a knowledge of local customs and language is desirable and, in some cases, essential. The field representative should be in good health and capable of spending days, perhaps even weeks, away from home, living under what may be difficult conditions. If the field representative is to accomplish his mission, he must subjugate and control his own feelings and emotions and, in the case of a kidnapping, concentrate solely on the release of the kidnap victim. If the negotiation period drags on, in time it may be necessary to have a backup field representative or at least staff support to alleviate physical wear and tear on the field representative.

Chain of Command. The field representative reports directly to the CMG and should not have authority to make critical decisions without consultation, except when the victim's life is in imminent danger and when it is impossible to communicate with the CMG. The responsibility of the CMG is to provide all necessary logistic support to the field representative. This should be done in an expeditious manner, and the CMG should be prepared to cut corporate red tape wherever and whenever necessary.

Communications Link. After arriving on the scene, the field representative should immediately establish a secure channel of communications to the CMG. If it is necessary to use open telephone or telex lines, which can be easily monitored and permit little privacy, it is recommended that a preestablished code or cipher be utilized to maintain the confidentiality of communications to and from the CMG. At the very least, it is wise to substitute innocuous words for key words like *ransom* and for the names of important local contacts. Similarly, the victim never should be referred to by name. Different phrases can be utilized to indicate various options and courses of action.

Duties of the Field Representative. The field representative should obtain all possible information regarding the kidnapping, including possible suspects or, if the perpetrators are known, their identities, habits, modus operandi, and so forth. This information can be of critical importance—for example, some terrorist groups have a better history of smooth ransom exchanges than others.

If it is suspected that the victim was injured in the abduction, his or her complete medical records should be available to facilitate treatment upon release. If life-sustaining drugs are required (insulin, medication for high blood pressure or a heart condition), it is prudent to stockpile a supply of the medication, and efforts should be made at once to communicate this fact to the kidnappers. If the kidnap victim wears glasses, there is a likely chance that the original pair may have been lost or damaged in the abduction and subsequent captivity, thus making it good policy to have a second pair on hand.

Establishment and Maintenance of Contact with the Kidnappers. Contact can be made in a variety of ways, but in most instances, the kidnappers will identify a specific channel of communication to be used for the duration of the negotiations, such as an ad in a newspaper or a particular individual. The field representative should have written proof of his identity and, if necessary, his authority to negotiate.

Care of the Victim's Family. If the kidnapping occurs outside of the United

States and the victim's family is still in the particular country, appropriate security measures should be taken to prevent additional attacks on family members or related harassment. In most instances, it is wise to withdraw the victim's family from the host country. Religious counseling and medical care should be made available to family members, but only at their request. The family should be kept informed of any developments as they relate to efforts to secure the victim's release.

Negotiating Plan. Based on the information collected by the field representative and from other sources, a detailed negotiating plan should be formulated by the CMG. The plan should include an assessment of the elasticity of the ransom demand(s), focusing on the minimum and maximum estimates of a negotiated ransom payment, and detailing the steps by which the ransom will be paid. An analysis of previous kidnap cases has shown that the lack of a firm negotiating plan was a significant handicap in effecting the release of kidnap victims. A sound, comprehensive negotiating plan represents a team approach and permits a wide variety of perspectives and different kinds of knowledge to be factored into the decision-making process.

Effect of Local Laws. The legal representative on the CMG is responsible for reviewing all local laws, customs, and regulations impinging upon kidnapping cases. It is well to note that certain countries have laws that may affect a corporation's continued presence and activities in the host country after a kidnapping occurs. For example, some countries forbid negotiating with terrorists or giving publicity to terrorist groups, while others prohibit the paying of ransoms. If domestic laws are broken in the process of ransoming or retrieving a kidnap victim, the company may have to bear the consequences.

William F. Niehous was the victim of Venezuelan laws prohibiting his employer, Owens-Illinois, from negotiating with kidnappers or complying with their demands. While laws of this kind ultimately may deny support and sustenance to terrorist organizations, it is often at the sacrifice of the kidnap victim, a wholly unacceptable solution to the friends, relatives, and employers of the victim. In such situations, negotiations for the release of the captive often have to be moved to a third country and cloaked in secrecy.

Kidnap Insurance. There has been a tremendous growth in kidnap and ransom insurance in recent years, and one source estimates that companies throughout the world paid more than $100 million in premiums to insurance companies in 1979.[12] First offered in 1938 by Lloyd's, which still controls the largest share of the market, in recent years firms such as the Chubb Group, Republic, INA, and American International Group also have entered the market. As a result, corporate premiums have been declining in price since 1978. Premium rates typically are figured on the basis of "the country, the quality of the security system in place, the type, size and visibility of the company, the executives to be covered, their travel patterns and the deductible amount."[13] Kidnap insurance is not limited to corporations, however. Recently, the Japanese Foreign Ministry purchased an insurance policy on each member of the Japanese foreign service stationed abroad. Even individuals who are fearful of being kidnapped may find such policies a good investment. One wealthy landowner in El Salvador, for example, paid an annual premium of $750,000 for $5 million of insurance coverage and still considered it a bargain. Nevertheless, because of mounting instability in that country, his insurance company has indicated that his policy will not be renewed.

The existence of a kidnap policy should be kept a closely guarded secret because knowledge that a substantial policy is in force may serve as an incentive to terrorists to kidnap the policyholder since they may reckon that payment of the ransom will be sure and swift. A second problem with kidnap insurance is that not all insurance companies pay automatically and some will attempt to negotiate the ransom downward, a process that may take several months or longer.

Verification of the Hostage's Safety. Before any negotiation takes place, the negotiator or field representative must demand and receive proof that the victim is still alive and in good health, and that such verification be provided by the kidnappers on a continuous basis. The receipt of personal articles belonging to the victim does not constitute satisfactory verification since it only establishes that the victim was at some time in the hands of the terrorists and provides no assurance as to his welfare or condition. Similarly, letters from the victim can be forged or postdated and therefore are also unacceptable. Direct communication by telephone from the victim to someone who knows him or her extremely well is the best method of verification, but photographs of the victim holding the front page of a major daily newspaper with the headline clearly legible also will suffice. If tape recordings of the victim are used, the victim must describe recent athletic scores or news items so that the tape can be time locked; otherwise it, too, will not constitute adequate verification. The failure to press for continuous verification of the victim's well-being may suggest to the terrorists that they can execute him and still collect the ransom.

Field Representative's Security. Terrorists are capable of any treachery. In several incidents, the field representative/negotiator was taken prisoner by the kidnappers and held for ransom along with the original victim. Thus, the field representative must take steps to ensure his own security and to prevent the hijacking or interception of the ransom once it is in his possession. Precautions may include a secure dwelling, bodyguards, a hardened automobile, and body armor. The field representative should not take unnecessary risks. Thus, meetings and exchanges should only be held in areas where both the field representative and the kidnappers feel secure.

Payment of Ransom. Terrorists normally will demand some kind of ransom in exchange for the kidnap victim. Most often the ransom will take the form of money, although sometimes it will also involve the release of prisoners, the free distribution of food to the poor, and even salary increases and bonuses for workers in a particular plant or factory. Nearly all kidnappers can be negotiated with; few actually desire the death of their hostage(s) and prefer instead to realize their ransom demands, if only in part. Even groups with fearsome reputations like the JRA, which carried out the notorious Lod massacre, are clever negotiators and in recent years have not been known to harm their hostages if they fail to receive all that they demand.

All negotiations take time and should not be rushed precipitously unless there is genuine concern for the hostage's well-being. If the ransom demand is paid too rapidly, the kidnappers may conclude that they asked too little. This occurred during an incident in Central America, and the kidnappers tripled the ransom.

Once an understanding has been reached by both sides concerning the amount of the ransom to be paid, a delivery schedule and procedures to implement the delivery must also be agreed upon. It is always preferable if the kidnap victim can be exchanged simultaneously for the ransom. The dropping of the ransom payment at a predesignated location in return for a promise that the victim will be released later involves placing trust in the good faith of the terrorists to perform their part of the bargain.

Money is both bulky and quite heavy in large amounts and requires a good deal of strength and stamina to be carried any distance. One million dollars in $50 bills, for example, weighs 45 pounds and fills a large suitcase. Usually, however, kidnappers will demand nonserialized $10 and $20 bills, which are easier to circulate without attracting attention. It takes 50,000 $20 bills, weighing 112.5 pounds, to make a ransom of $1 million.

Sophisticated kidnappers are familiar with most money identification techniques and, consequently, will often repack the money in their own suitcases or bags to guard against the possibility of a hidden transmitter built into the original containers. Moreover, should they discover that they have been double-crossed, the ransom is sure to be increased and the hostage's life may even be placed in graver danger.

Hostage Retrieval. In the event that it is impossible to comply with the terrorists' ransom demands—for example, if they adamantly refuse to release the victim unless certain political prisoners are freed from jail, which the government maintains is out of the question—then it may be necessary to mount a private sector rescue operation. To do so one must enter the twilight world of a handful of highly specialized firms with political-military-intelligence capabilities and a willingness to undertake extremely difficult tasks for a sum of money commensurate with the risk involved. Although many self-styled mercenaries may indicate a desire to attempt such missions, most will spend a good deal of the client's money and produce few results, and should they actually mount a rescue effort, they are likely to get both themselves and the kidnap victim killed. Indeed, there is no room for amateurs in this esoteric field. Several of the world's largest insurance underwriters are affiliated with firms skilled in hostage negotiation and retrieval.

Since rescue attempts may violate any number of national statutes and involve a good deal of risk for those engaged in the effort, who may be forced to combat both the terrorists and an enraged national government, such services are expensive and are beyond the reach of all but powerful multinational corporations and individuals of substantial means. For a large insurance company, however, such an expenditure may make good business sense. For example, if the client is covered by a $5-million ransom policy and he can be freed for $1 million, the insurance company will save $4 million.

Perhaps one of the most dramatic private sector rescues in recent years was a largely in-house effort mounted at the behest of Texas millionaire H. Ross Perot when two employees of his Dallas-based computer company, Electronic Data Systems (EDS), were arrested and imprisoned in Iran. The Iranian government, engulfed in turmoil in the final days before the departure of the shah, had fallen in arrears in its payments to EDS. Moreover, the more prudent U.S. firms could see the handwriting on the wall and rapidly were pulling out of Iran as the internal situation continued to deteriorate with every passing hour. This, of course, infuriated the government of Prime Minister Shahpur Bakhtiar, which was attempting to enlist support for its shaky transition regime, and it sought to hold EDS hostage by seizing two of its employees.

Perot contacted the late Arthur "Bull" Simons, a retired colonel who had led a 1970 raid deep into North Vietnam to rescue U.S. POWs. Perot explained his decision this way:

> Protecting American citizens is a role that our government should perform. Private companies, private individuals shouldn't be involved in this sort of thing. But if your government is not willing to protect American citizens, and if you have people in your company imprisoned in a country, you have an obligation to get them out of there.[14]

Simons ruled out a direct assault on Ghasr Prison, where the two men were being held, since it was heavily fortified and guarded. Instead, he and his lieutenants organized a mob attack by Iranian revolutionaries on the prison. As thousands of inmates poured out of the prison, the two Americans were able to escape unnoticed. After a rendezvous with Simons and his party, they began a two-day trek to safety in Turkey. Had they encountered trouble on the way out of Iran, a backup team—complete with planes, helicopters, and weapons— was standing by in Turkey waiting to go in to airlift them out.

In retrospect, Perot and his commandos displayed considerable ingenuity and resourcefulness in a situation where most companies would simply have thrown up their hands in despair. However, not all rescue missions meet with the same success, often for reasons wholly outside the control of those undertaking the attempt. One rescue mission that never got off the ground but that might have saved the life of a wealthy coffee planter from El Salvador, kidnapped by members of the clandestine Armed Forces for National Resistance, was sabotaged by the sordid jealousies, petty bickering, and greed displayed by members of the victim's family. Family members were reluctant to pay the ransom demanded for the return of their kidnapped patriarch since it would have severely depleted the family coffers. As an alternative, they contacted a firm, specializing in hostage retrieval, that rapidly was able to ascertain where the victim was being held and began to make preparations to free him with a team of commandos. Inexplicably, however, the family hesitated. As a consequence, the kidnap victim was murdered when the deadline set by the terrorists for payment of the ransom expired without action by the family, and his body subsequently was discovered stuffed into the trunk of an abandoned car in San Salvador. It was later speculated that the family, in a calculated action designed to produce the death of the old man, let the deadline pass so that they could divide up his estate.

Another rescue effort that never took place involved a contingency operation to spirit the deposed shah of Iran out of Panama if the government in that Central American country, in which the shah had taken refuge, had refused to permit his departure and appeared ready to extradite him back to Iran.

Preparation of a Postincident Report. At the conclusion of a terrorist incident, a postincident report should be prepared so that deficiencies may be corrected and what was learned can be shared with others. In this connection, knowledge is perhaps the most valuable defense to kidnapping and other forms of terrorism.

How to React if Kidnapped. No hard and fast rules exist for behavior in the event that one is kidnapped, but the following recommendations reflect the experiences and suggestions of a number of business executives and diplomats who survived abduction and kidnapping.[15]

If attacked, resist only if there is a good probability of repelling the terrorists and escaping; futile resistance may only result in needless death and suffering. Stay calm and do not provoke your captors, but comply with their orders and do not be alarmed if handled roughly. In view of the fact that terrorists or gunmen are likely to be nervous and agitated, do not do anything to aggravate the situation or to excite them needlessly.

Although one may be stuffed in the trunk of a car or blindfolded on the floor of the back seat, stay alert and make mental notes of all voices, movements, external sounds, odors, distances, and the passage of time between the place of abduction and the location to which one is taken.

Once in captivity, one must try to accept the predicament without undue emotion because the terrorists will respect strength. Strive always to maintain self-control and good humor, and never despair since courage, patience, and optimism are fundamental to one's survival. U.S. businessman William F. Niehous, held in captivity by leftist terrorists for three and a half years in the Venezuelan jungle before being accidentally discovered by the authorities, said that there were times he had given up hope, but he had never completely lost hope.[16] Never beg or fawn over your captors; maintain your basic integrity and do not argue or debate politics with them. Nevertheless, try to develop basic rapport with them. Most terrorists do not hate their victims, and the existence of a human bond lessens the likelihood that victims will be subjected to physical harm. In this connection, JRA terrorists, in an effort to prevent personal bonds from developing, rotate guards frequently and prohibit all but necessary communication with the prisoners. It should also be noted that the terrorists secretly may be taping all of the hostage's conversations and interrogation sessions so they can use comments taken out of context for propaganda purposes. Do not offer suggestions or instructions to one's terrorist captors because, in the event that they act upon one of the suggestions and it does not succeed, they may respond with punishment or some other form of retaliation.

Do not be alarmed by feelings of humiliation during captivity.[17] Powerlessness often breeds self-contempt. Moreover, terrorists often keep their captive only partially clad and under constant supervision even when performing necessary bodily functions. Obviously, being reduced to childlike dependency where one's captors are both the source of all necessities as well as permission to engage in the simplest tasks or amusements is both demeaning and humiliating. However, one adapts quickly to such a regimen and usually is no worse for it. In some extraordinary cases, psychiatrists have detected what they call the Stockholm syndrome in some former hostages and kidnap victims, defined as strong attachments or feelings of love directed toward one's captors that stem from seeing the terrorist as an authority figure and feelings of impotency by the captive.

In order to preserve one's health, exercise regularly, using isometric exercises if the area of confinement is too small for more vigorous forms of exercise. Although the food may be unfamiliar, of poor quality, and unpalatable, try to eat all of it. By staying in good physical condition, one's mental health is improved, and resistance to disease and permanent disability is increased. Request reading material to help pass the time; most terrorists will provide books, newspapers, and even writing materials to their captives.

If the terrorists continue to wear hoods or to shield their faces, consider it an encouraging sign that suggests that they expect ultimately to release their captive and are taking the precaution of covering their faces to minimize any possibility of future recognition. If they have marked their captive for death, there is little reason to hide their faces.

Escape. Under most circumstances, escape is not advisable and may only result in death, injury, or punishment. More than likely, the terrorists already will have considered all the avenues of escape, and if an opportunity presents itself, the victim may be overlooking some drawback or disadvantage. One's release almost always will be secured from the outside; thus, patience is advised. Over 80 percent of all companies whose executives have been kidnapped have paid ransom demands, and few kidnap victims have been harmed by their captors. Niehous, for example, was assured from the outset that no matter what happened, he never would be harmed: "From the first day of the kidnapping until the last, they [the kidnappers] said that I would never be shot, never be killed. They would always release me alive. Why, I don't know, except they said they were no assassins."[18] Experience indicates that the odds are overwhelmingly in favor of eventual release if the kidnap victim remains cool and patient.

In the event that the kidnappers ask the victim to compose letters indicating that he is still alive or appealing to his family, government, or company to spare his life by complying with the terrorist's demands, it may be possible to convey information to the authorities without the terrorists' being aware of it. A kidnapped millionaire coffee planter in Central America, for example, sent the following message: "I am well. Today I played three games of chess and won one." From all outward indications the message was innocuous. However, the victim was a chess master, and only one man in his country could beat him two games out of three: a leftist university professor. His captors did not grasp the implication inherent in the message that the professor was obviously involved in the kidnapping. Such ploys, however, are extremely dangerous and must be done with a good deal of finesse lest one's captors read between the lines and discover the hidden message in the communication.

If one is convinced that he is going to be killed and that his only chance lies in escape, it is helpful to know how to kill or stun with one's bare hands since the likelihood that the kidnappers will leave a weapon unattended is almost nonexistent. Among the most destructive blows to vital points of the human body are the following[19]:

A well-placed karate chop to the side of the neck will cause a drastic drop in blood pressure and interrupt the supply of blood to the brain, rendering the victim almost immediately unconscious.

A three-finger strike to the throat or a strong grip on the thyroid cartilage will result in extreme pain and even death (if forceful enough) since the victim chokes on his own blood.

One may attack the spinal chord with a sharp blow of the fist to the back of the victim's neck, resulting in severe trauma, unconsciousness, and often, death.

Any blow to the spine, temple, or behind the ear with one's fist or, preferably, a rod-shaped object can be fatal.

Kicks under the armpit, to the testicles, or to the solar plexus are all effective and painful blows when engaged in hand-to-hand combat.

Slamming one's cupped hands over the ears of an adversary will produce severe pain, dizziness, or unconsciousness.

In a desperate fight for your life, especially if down on your back, rip the attacker's ear lobes with your teeth, gouge his eyes, or jam your fingers into his nostrils. Any of these tactics usually will result in the adversary's releasing pressure on you momentarily and flinching back in pain. Another release is to pinch the adversary's trapezius muscles at the base of the neck with all your strength.

If armed with any heavy rod-shaped object and faced with a foe with a knife or gun (at close range), strike at the kneecaps, the inside of the wrist, or the tip of the elbow (the so-called crazy bone).

If armed with a knife in the presence of a guard or sentry, slip up behind him and, if right-handed, cup your left hand over his mouth, jerk his head upward, and push forward with the knife across the side of his neck below the angle of the jaw. A one-and-a-half-inch-deep slash will sever the jugular vein and often the carotid artery. The victim will be rendered unconscious within five seconds, and death will usually follow in another seven seconds. A knife thrust from behind into the kidney region, while pulling the victim backward with your other hand, is also a recommended killing technique.[20]

A list of the weapons that a kidnap victim can improvise from ordinary articles and household substances is also helpful in critical life-and-death situations:

A bar of soap in a sock or wrapped in a towel can be used as a blackjack.

A coffee or beer mug is an effective weapon with which to strike an adversary, and a solid hit to the top of the shoulders can break the collarbone.

Boiling water can be hurled on a guard.

A spoon can be used to gouge an adversary's eyes.

Powdered soap or laundry detergent thrown in the face of a guard will often permit you to get the drop on him.

A pen or pencil may be gripped like a knife and used to stab at the throat, eyes, ears, and the nerves behind the ears. A smoking pipe, held by the bowl like a pistol, can be used in the same manner.

A lightbulb, held by the base with a cloth or towel to protect your hand, will produce dozens of painful cuts if smashed into an adversary's face.

Most aerosol sprays can be used to blind an adversary and, if sprayed over the flame of a disposable lighter, will make a devastating flamethrower as the mist is ignited.

Folded eyeglasses can be used to strike hammerlike blows at an adversary, and the lenses, if made of glass, can be shattered and the shards of glass (gripped with a piece of cloth) can be used as a knife.[21]

Responsibility of Corporations to Protect their Employees

U.S. jurisprudence has maintained that one is not obligated to impoverish himself to save another unless some kind of special duty is in force. Historically, corporations were not regarded as having such a special duty toward their employees. Today, however, this precept is under substantial challenge. The landmark case involves Gustavo Curtis, the American manager of Industrias Gran Colombia (IGC), a subsidiary of Beatrice Foods Company, a U.S.-based multinational.

On 28 September 1976, Curtis and his chauffeur, Simon Chacon, were on their way home in heavy evening rush hour traffic in Bogota when their car was struck from behind by a green Renault. Curtis and Chacon got out to inspect the damage and saw that the two men in the Renault appeared to be drunk. Suddenly, another car pulled up with four people inside, two men and two women. Curtis and Chacon were forced into separate cars at gunpoint, and Chacon was released a short time later. He immediately alerted IGC that Curtis had been abducted, and attention focused on the leftist M-19 revolutionary movement as the probable force behind the kidnapping.

A week passed without word from the terrorists, and then, on 6 October, IGC's attorney received two letters from Curtis. The letters indicated that the terrorists wanted a $5-million ransom and included were the names of two prominent Colombian citizens that the terrorists had designated as intermediaries. The following day, Beatrice Foods retained the U.K. security firm, Control Risk Limited, to take charge of the case, and its representative, Simon Adams-Dale, arrived on the scene on 9 October. Adams-Dale, who did not speak Spanish and was not particularly familiar with Colombia, soon made contact with the terrorists, but over the next month he was unable to make any real progress in view of the fact that he was forced to divide his time between several cases, one as far away as Argentina, and because both he and the parent company, Beatrice Foods, were suspicious that Curtis might somehow be involved in his own kidnapping as a means of defrauding his company. As a result, the management of Beatrice Foods wanted a $100,000 ceiling on any ransom paid.

Although Adams-Dale subsequently changed his mind, Beatrice Foods officials continued to subscribe to the notion that the kidnapping was bogus and refused to raise the ransom limit. Adams-Dale, moreover, appeared to have no real plan to effect Curtis's release or to negotiate with the terrorists.

On 15 February 1977, the terrorists, in a surprise call to IGC's attorney, James Raisbeck, lowered without explanation their ransom demand from $5 million to $3 million. Beatrice Foods, however, continued to reject any payment of that magnitude, stating that investigators hired by the company had turned up information suggesting that Curtis's wife Vera was a party to the kidnapping. A month later, in mid-March, Adams-Dale was joined by a new negotiator from Control Risk named Arish Turle. The impasse continued between the company and the kidnappers until early May when officials of Beatrice Foods finally conceded that the kidnapping was not a hoax. What changed their view was a tape received from Curtis describing his poor state of health and the results of a lie detector test administered to Vera Curtis that absolved her from any complicity in the affair. Thus, on 18 May, the terrorists and the company finally came to terms, and Curtis was released in exchange for a ransom of $430,000. The following day, Turle, Adams-Dale, and Raisbeck were arrested by Colombian authorities for paying a ransom—a crime under Colombian law.

A year later, on 25 March 1978, Curtis and his wife filed suit in federal court in New York City, asking $185 million in damages from Beatrice Foods on the grounds that the company had not done enough to protect him or to effect his release. The case, the first to question the conduct of a company whose employee has been kidnapped by political terrorists, generated considerable controversy. Although the case was dismissed, it is only a matter of time before a plaintiff somewhere wins a similar case, and when that happens, corporations will have to reevaluate their security responsibilities to their employees, not to mention the very desirability of continuing operations in high-risk areas of the world.

The Curtis case spawned litigation on behalf of other plaintiffs. The wife of William F. Niehous, in one example, filed suit for an undisclosed sum of money against her husband's employer, Owens-Illinois, just three months prior to his release. After Niehous's return, the suit was withdrawn.

Private Security Firms

The old expression that in every cloud there is a silver lining is nowhere better illustrated than in the example of the security industry that is turning the misfortunes of others into a big business. According to one Wall Street investment banker, the sale of private security services, hardware, and training is the largest growth industry in the world. Since the founding of the nation's first private security firm in the 1850s by Allen Pinkerton, the sale of security services has grown to a \$12-billion-a-year industry.[22] Today, more than 5,000 security firms operate in the United States. They range from small, one- or two-man, operations to full-service giants like the Wackenhut Corporation, Pinkerton's Inc., and Burns International Security Services, Inc. Business has never been better for Burns International, which registered a 44 percent jump in its income since 1972, and Wackenhut, which posted a 20 percent increase in profits in 1979 over the previous year.

As with size, the quality of most security companies and the range of services they offer vary widely from firm to firm. While industrial security programs, uniformed guards, couriers, detectives, and armored-car deliveries still comprise over 60 percent of the security business, measured from the standpoint of revenues, as terrorist violence against business executives and individuals climbs throughout the world, the sector of the industry that specializes in counterterrorist and crisis management services has expanded rapidly. In addition to a plethora of firms that teach evasive/aggressive driving skills and techniques, many new companies have appeared in the last five years that concentrate on bodyguard training and executive protection techniques. For example, Cobray International, Inc., operated by right-wing gadfly and developer of the famous Ingram muzzle silencer Mitchell Livingston WerBell III, instructs students in self-defense techniques such as martial arts, small arms marksmanship, and specialized training in the use of unconventional weapons including screwdrivers, hatchets, knives, files, and even ballpoint pens. His students include everyone from policemen to business executives, from housewives to bodyguards. By contrast to the flamboyant WerBell, however, most of the more sophisticated firms in the counterterrorist business maintain a very low profile, and from outward appearances, their personnel more nearly resemble the IBM sales force than mercenaries for hire.

Conclusion

James Hougan has described the purveyors of private intelligence and security services as "spooks," and he maintains that serious dangers are associated with the growth of a massive private security industry in the United States, including the "emergence of a new sort of totalitarianism, an industrial regime of secret agents and manipulators operating within the framework of a state that has become only nominally democratic."[23] Similarly, James A. Nathan warns that the proliferation of private security firms, especially those boasting paramilitary capabilities, could result in a kind of "new feudalism" in which multinational businesses, confronted with government impotence in the face of terrorist assaults, decide to take the law into their own hands.[24] By contrast to the arguments advanced by Hougan and Nathan, the phenomenal growth and expansion of the private security industry in recent years are by no means the product of dark and conspiratorial forces but simply the private sector's natural response to the rising wave of crime and violence that is afflicting both the industrial democracies and the developing countries. Moreover, neither Hougan nor Nathan has been able to advance any alternative solutions to the problem of terrorism to alleviate the need for private security companies. Nathan's endorsement of the concept of an international prison for terrorists will hardly contribute to the security of multinational corporations or their employees and is a totally infeasible proposition. While Nathan raises the issue of whether the United States should provide training to foreign security forces engaged in counterterrorist operations, he never really takes a stand. His suggestion of an international information clearinghouse that identifies and keeps tabs on suspected terrorists is already in place, though not in name, and takes the form of official and unofficial cooperation between the world's security and intelligence services. However, if Nathan thinks that such an information clearinghouse would contribute materially to the rescue of kidnapped business executives or assist in repelling terrorist attacks, then he is sadly mistaken. In such circumstances, action responses are demanded.

In conclusion, while the private security industry must be monitored carefully to ensure that laws are not violated and to prevent the erosion of civil liberties, the real fear, in an age of rising anxiety and uncertainty, much of it the result of escalating global terrorism, should not be too much security but rather the lack of it.

Notes

1. This is the last line in chapter XIV of *The Prince* by Niccolò Machiavelli, and is subject to many varied translations. The translation used in this text appears in Bergan Evans, *Dictionary of Quotations*, (New York: Avenel Books, 1978), p. 613. In the translation by Christian E. Detmold (*The Prince*, [New York: Washington Square Press, 1963], p. 109), the passage appears as, "That defense alone is effectual, sure, and durable which depends upon yourself and your own valor."

2. Lewis Mumford, *The Highway and the City* (New York: Harcourt, Brace & World, 1963), p. 238.

3. Patrick Marnham, *Fantastic Invasion* (New York: Harcourt Brace Jovanovich, 1980), p. 165.

4. Ibid.

5. Robert Moss, "Counter Terrorism," *The Economist*, Brief Booklet no. 29, p. 10.

6. Richard Clutterbuck, *Living with Terrorism*, (London: Faber & Faber, 1975), pp. 82-83.

7. Ibid.

8. Lloyd W. Singer and Jan Reber, "A Crisis Management System," *Security Management* (September 1977), pp. 8-9.

9. Terri Shaw, "Pacification in Guatemala: Terrorism a Way of Life," *Washington Post,* 7 March 1971.

10. Some of the material in this section appears in N.C. Livingstone, *Crisis Management for Kidnap and Extortion Incidents: Family and Victim,* vol. 1 (Washington, D.C.: Joseph J. Cappucci Associates, Inc., 1979).

11. Some of the material in this section appears in N.C. Livingstone, *Crisis Management* (Washington, D.C.: Joseph J. Cappucci Associates, Inc., 1979).

12. "Corporate Security: Top Management Mandate," *Duns Review* (January 1980), p. 115.

13. Ibid.

14. H. Ross Perot, quoted by Richard Shenkman, "Rescue by the Private Sector," *National Review* (30 May 1980), p. 623.

15. Some of this material appears in Livingstone, *Crisis Management for Kidnap and Extortion Incidents.* See also U.S. Department of State, "Countering Terrorism: Security Suggestions for U.S. Business Representatives Abroad," Department of State Publication 8884 (Washington, D.C., 1977).

16. William F. Niehous, quoted in "Kidnap Victim Returns to U.S.," *Washington Post,* 2 July 1979.

17. See Brian Jenkins, "Hostage Survival," *Protection of Assets* (New York: The Merritt Company, 1974), pp. 18-81 through 18-98.

18. Niehous, "Kidnap Victim Returns."

19. See N. Mashiro, *Black Medicine: The Dark Art of Death,* vol. 1 (Boulder, Colo.: Paladin Press, 1978), for his study of the vital points of the human anatomy.

20. See William L. Cassidy, *The Complete Book of Knife Fighting* (Boulder, Colo.: Paladin Press, 1975), pp. 69-72.

21. See N. Mashiro, *Black Medicine: Weapons at Hand,* vol. 2 (Boulder, Colo.: Paladin Press, 1979).

22. Bruce Cory, "Police for Hire," *Police Magazine* (September 1979), p. 40.

23. James Hougan, *Spooks* (New York: William Morrow and Company, 1978), p. 463.

24. James A. Nathan, "The New Feudalism," *Foreign Policy* (Spring 1981), pp. 156-166.

10 A New U.S. Policy to Control and Suppress Terrorism

We can get so lost in humanitarian concerns as a nation, we could float off into oblivion.
                                                    —Nelson Rockefeller[1]

Although more than a decade has passed since the defeat of the Arab armies by Israel in 1967, the student rebellions in France and the United States, and the decision by the USSR to provide significant levels of aid and training to terrorist movements around the world as a means of surrogate warfare against the West—all of which have stimulated and fostered the growth of international terrorism—a viable policy for the control and suppression of terrorism, designed to respond to and manage terrorism-related crises, has yet to emerge in the United States.[2] According to President Reagan's former National Security Advisor Richard Allen, the United States is "way behind the power curve" with respect to understanding terrorism and being prepared to meet terrorist challenges.[3] Allen maintains, "We've been very fortunate so far that all violent forms of terrorism have not been inflicted upon our people here."[4]

The inability to achieve a national policy addressing terrorism can be attributed to three factors. First, powerful voices have always existed within the foreign policy community that maintain that terrorism is not a significant problem and, therefore, that it does not constitute a real threat to the security and well-being of the United States. Those who hold this view allege, for the most part, that the problem has been oversensationalized and that it amounts to little more than a few pinpricks against the United States when viewed in the larger context of the U.S. global strategic picture. Representative of such thinking, FBI Director William Webster has downplayed the terrorist threat publicly and even has reduced domestic terrorism from twelfth to thirteenth on the bureau's list of priorities. Second, little institutional machinery within the U.S. government has been designed to make policy in this area or to address terrorist incidents in any systematic manner. Third, the control and suppression of terrorism was regarded by several recent administrations as inimical or somehow antithetical to other, more important, policy goals. During Secretary of State Henry Kissinger's drive for detente with the USSR, information relating to Soviet and Eastern bloc support of international terrorism was consciously suppressed or simply not collected lest it seem to cast doubt on the Soviet commitment to the process of easing tensions between the superpowers. However, the climate created by the Carter administration's human rights campaign was most damaging and retarded efforts to construct a viable U.S. policy to address the issue of terrorism.

Terrorism and Human Rights

In 1976, the promise of fresh and moral leadership from beyond the banks of the Potomac was widely embraced by a U.S. public that was weary of scandal and foreign policy failures. The disillusionment that accompanied the defeat of U.S. policy goals in Southeast Asia, revelations about questionable U.S. conduct elsewhere in the world, the seemingly convergent nature of Kissinger's policy of détente with the Soviet Union, and the agony of Watergate left the public feeling that the United States was drifting, that it had lost its sense of direction and purpose, especially in the area of foreign policy.

In a nation beset by self-doubts, the human rights issue was tailor-made for newly elected President Jimmy Carter, who came to office the least prepared president in modern times with respect to foreign policy. One would have to go back to Calvin Coolidge to find a president with so little foreign policy experience and background. By adopting the human rights issue as his own, Carter was able to translate the moral precepts he held so dear, and which were an integral part of his evangelical Christianity, to the complex area of foreign policy.

Speaking at commencement exercises at Notre Dame University in May 1977, President Carter, in office for barely four months, announced that, henceforth, a commitment to human rights would be a "fundamental tenet" of U.S. foreign policy.[5] In view of the widespread denial of human rights in the contemporary world, it was difficult to find fault with the basic intent of the Carter policy. However, almost from its inception, the human rights policy raised a number of troubling and difficult questions with respect to how the policy would be applied and administered and against whom, not to mention its impact on other competing policy goals like efforts to combat international terrorism.[6]

The human rights campaign, as administered by a singularly guileless and untutored collection of Carter administration appointees at the State Department, rapidly deteriorated into one of the greatest foreign policy fiascoes in modern times. At best, it merely perplexed friends and allies of the United States; at worst, it antagonized many and contributed materially to the downfall of a few, such as the Peacock Throne in Iran and the Somoza regime in Nicaragua. By the time an exasperated electorate resoundingly rejected the Carter administration in 1980, the once-vaunted human rights policy had become the chief symbol of a failed foreign policy characterized by inconsistency, vacillation, and disarray.

One casualty of the Carter administration's moralistic binge was the failure to respond decisively to terrorist threats or to develop new initiatives to control or eliminate terrorism. Indeed, during the Carter administration, the fight against terrorism was accorded very low priority because it was felt that a strong anti-terrorist policy would be destructive to the advancement of human rights. Countries accused of human rights violations—including those combating extern-ally fostered terrorism and insurgencies—often were villified publicly and denied U.S. economic and military assistance. While right-wing governments in Latin America, the Philippines, Iran, and South Korea came under constant fire for human rights abuses, communist governments and one-party despotisms in the Third World, especially Africa, escaped censure. The administration's policy was characterized not only by inconsistencies and obvious hypocrisy—such as the decision to support Pol Pot's so-called Democratic Kampuchea in the UN, one of the few certifiable monster regimes on earth that reportedly had massacred one-quarter of its entire population—but also by an almost complete failure to distinguish between authoritarian governments, which only suppress their citizens' political rights, and totalitarian governments, which repress both the political and individual rights of their populations. The ultimate irony, as former Secretary of State Kissinger predicted, was "a posture of resignation towards totalitarian states and harassment of those who would be our friends and who have every prospect of evolving in a more humane direction."[7]

The Carter Administration's Record on Terrorism

The Carter administration tended to view terrorism not so much as a problem but instead as the symptom of larger problems—namely, poverty, injustice, and repression. Thus, the administration focused its efforts on finding remedies to what its leading foreign policy experts considered the root causes of terror-ism rather than on efforts to suppress and control terrorism itself. Carter administration officials hoped that increased U.S. foreign assistance, together with efforts to mediate or defuse long-standing sources of tension and instabil-ity, would result in a diminishment of global terrorism. Unfortunately, such alternatives to violence are complex, time consuming, and expensive and smack of utopianism rather than pragmatism.

The administration also placed new emphasis on preventative efforts designed to discourage terrorist attacks or at least to make such attacks more difficult. However, despite tightened security at embassies and diplomatic missions, a series of terrorist assaults on U.S. embassies and diplomatic personnel rocked the Carter administration and tested its mettle and resolve. In 1979, U.S. Ambassador to Afghanistan Adolph Dubs died when Afghan police—with the approval of the State Department—stormed the U.S. embassy after Dubs had been taken hostage by Moslem militants. The following year, U.S. Ambassador to Colombia Diego Asencio was taken captive, along with thirteen other ambassadors, in the embassy of the Dominican Republic in Bogota. After a sixty-day standoff, Asencio and the other hostages were finally released. Most serious of all was the crisis that followed the storming of the U.S. embassy in Tehran. For 444 days, the ensuing hostage crisis dominated the Carter administration agenda and the thoughts of the U.S. people and, in the end, was responsible, in large measure, for the repudiation of Jimmy Carter's presidency at the polls.

In view of the criticism leveled at the Carter administration for its handling of the Iranian hostage crisis, it is only appropriate that some effort be made to assess the administration's performance during this period as well as to describe the alternative steps that could have been taken to bring the matter to an earlier and perhaps more satisfactory conclusion.

First, the Carter administration can be criticized legitimately for not taking adequate precautions designed to avoid the kind of crisis that occurred once the decision had been made to admit the ailing shah to the United States for medical treatment. This could have been accomplished either by beefing up security at the U.S. embassy in Tehran or by greatly reducing the size of the diplomatic staff. The president and his senior advisors reportedly were surprised at the violent reaction of the Iranians to what they viewed as essentially a humane action. The deposed shah's arrival in the United States all but invited the crisis, and the failure to recognize this fact or to take appropriate action was inexcusable.

Second, President Carter made a fundamental error of judgment during the early stages of the crisis by publicly ruling out the use of force. This was clearly interpreted by both the Iranians and U.S. allies abroad as a sign of weakness and lack of resolve. Moreover, it meant that the administration relinquished any chance of seizing the initiative in addressing the crisis; with the exception of the disastrous rescue attempt, the United States would be forced simply to react to Iranian demands and actions. Even if certain options are considered by policymakers to be outside the range of acceptable alternatives, this information should never be communicated to the adversary. Carter's conciliatory posture and ill-advised pronouncement not only relieved the Iranians of any need to prepare for military retaliation on the part of the United States but also effectively eliminated the chief inducement for them to negotiate seriously and in good faith with Washington.

Force, however odious, must always remain the ultimate sanction in dealing with terrorists. The threat of severe retaliation is one of the best deterrents in preventing hostile or aggressive actions from occurring. As several observers have noted, few Soviet embassies have suffered the fate of the U.S. embassies in Iran, Pakistan, and Libya, not to mention the assassination of four U.S. ambassadors in recent years. Although the Soviet embassy in Tehran was overrun briefly in December 1980 by angry Afghan students and refugees protesting the Soviet occupation of their homeland, Iranian authorities quickly restored order. Two strongly worded Soviet protests to the Iranian government left little doubt that Moscow would not tolerate a recurrence of the incident. Indeed, there is nearly universal recognition around the world that the USSR will exact harsh retribution for assaults on its foreign missions and diplomatic personnel.

The Carter administration's assumption of rational behavior on the part of Iranian policymakers was hopelessly naive and played into the hands of hard-line militants in Iran whose aim was to humiliate the United States. By presuming that rationality would ultimately triumph in Iran, the United States unnecessarily delayed any resolution of the crisis, content to stand by and wait for a Thermidorean reaction to set in that would temper the revolutionary atmosphere and make it possible for the Iranian government to exert its authority over the situation. Each passing day not only distracted U.S. policymakers from addressing other pressing concerns but also increased the chance that some physical harm, accidental or otherwise, would come to the hostages.

Third, almost immediately, in the aftermath of the hostage seizure, the U.S. government, at the very least, should have conveyed to Iranian authorities the price they would have to pay if any harm came to the hostages. President Carter's statement that he would hold the Iranian government responsible for the hostages' safety was imprecise and ambiguous, especially to revolutionaries accustomed to dealing in stark language and exaggerated rhetoric, and therefore carried with it little weight. His failure to identify an implicit course of punitive action and to commit the United States to it, in the event that the hostages were harmed, directly endangered their lives.

Carter should have served notice on the Iranians, in no uncertain terms, that they could expect severe military and economic retaliation if the hostages were killed, or perhaps even if they were put on trial. U.S. restraint in the face of such a grave provocation was a dangerous precedent and an incentive to other outlaw regimes to seize U.S. hostages in order to win concessions or to seek restitution for old grievances. The United States should have indicated that, as with Germany and Japan during World War II, nothing less than the replacement, from within or without, of the revolutionary power structure in Iran and the punishment of its leaders would suffice if the United States was forced to initiate hostilities. By spelling out in precise detail the severity of the U.S. response, moderate elements in Iran might have taken the initiative and either overthrown the regime or forced a swift resolution of the crisis had they concluded that the hostages' lives were in imminent danger and that such action was the only way of avoiding a disastrous war with the United States. Moreover, the United States should have gone on record as willing to accept the partition of Iran, including Iraqi control over oil-rich Khuzestan province and a pro-Soviet rump government in the northeastern provinces bordering the USSR, as a predictable consequence of its military intervention. This would have laid to rest the notion on the part of many Iranian policymakers that the U.S. desire to maintain the territorial integrity of Iran as a buffer to the USSR would preclude any massive U.S. military intervention, no matter how extreme the provocation.

Fourth, consideration should have been given to a formal declaration of war on Iran in the wake of the hostage seizure. Congressional approval of a presidential request for a declaration of war not only would have been an unmistakable sign of U.S. political unity but also would have communicated to its wavering allies, the government of Iran, and the USSR the depth of U.S. anger over the hostage issue and, in so doing, would have constituted a clear statement of U.S. commitment to finding a rapid and acceptable solution to the crisis. A formal declaration of war would have carried with it no obligation to initiate immediate hostilities but rather would have expanded the president's latitude for action and strengthened his ability to isolate Iran economically and politically.

Fifth, the safe return of the hostages is more attributable to various events than to any policy or design of the Carter administration; in fact, it could be said that they were freed not as a result of efforts by the Carter administration but in spite of such efforts. Indeed, their ultimate release probably had more to do with the election of President Reagan than anything else, although the Iran-Iraq War and the Soviet invasion of Afghanistan were also factors.

In this connection, the one inescapable conclusion that emerges from the hostage crisis is that the adoption of a policy of conciliation when dealing with terrorists is to court disaster. Two hostages attempted to commit suicide during their captivity. Had they succeeded, or had one or more of the other hostages been accidentally killed, the lives of all of the hostages would have been placed in severe peril. Only as long as all were alive and in reasonably good health was there any room for a peaceful resolution of the crisis; once a hostage was harmed, the crisis would have taken on a life and momentum of its own, rendering conflict all but inevitable. In short, while a firm response may have involved risks to the hostages, greater risks were associated with the Carter administration's policy of inaction and delay.

As a result, the stalemate over the hostages should not have been permitted to last as long as it did. At some point, preferably during the first ninety days, an ultimatum—in the spirit of Secretary of State Hay's famous cable calling for "Perdicaris Alive or Raisuli Dead"—should have been transmitted to the Iranian government, informing the Iranians that if the hostages were not released within a specified period of time, the United States would declare war on Iran, mine the waters around Kharg Island, launch air strikes against the pumping stations controlling the flow of oil through Iranian pipelines, suspend most-favored-nation status to any country that continued to trade with Iran, and underwrite a massive covert, economic, and propaganda offensive against Iran and its leadership. After hostilities between Iran and Iraq had commenced, serious consideration could also have been given to providing political and military assistance to Baghdad. Tehran should have been informed further that any effort to retaliate by harming the hostages, attempting to close the Strait of Hormuz, attacking U.S. allies on the Arabian Peninsula, or striking at the U.S.

fleet would be met with a massive military response. The targets of such a response would have included the Iranian fleet; air bases and other military installations; all centers of economic activity, especially refineries, cotton mills, the steel mill complex at Isfahan, and the heavy machinery plant at Arāk; and finally, airports, railroads, bridges, and communications facilities. Air strikes against the religious seat of government at Qom and the capital of Tehran also could have been contemplated.

Sixth, by making the safe return of the hostages, for all intents and purposes, the sole objective of the United States, President Carter and his administration, indeed even the president's reelection campaign, became themselves hostages of the Iranians. By vowing initially to suspend all personal campaign appearances until the hostages were freed, the president adopted what amounted to a siege mentality that only strengthened the resolve of the militants to hold on to the hostages since, in addition to their enormous propaganda value, they were a means of actually influencing domestic politics in the United States. A slow paralysis descended over the White House. Other vital issues—the economy, SALT II, the Middle East—took a back seat to the president's single-minded pursuit of a solution to the hostage crisis, and this, in turn, reinforced the media's preoccupation with the issue. As a consequence, the seizure of the U.S. embassy and the hostages succeeded beyond the wildest dreams of the Iranian militants because of the unwitting cooperation of the president and U.S. policymakers.

By placing entirely too much emphasis on the fate of the fifty-three hostages, to the exclusion of other national and strategic interests, President Carter was perceived by much of the world, not to mention the Iranian militants holding the hostages, as willing to permit the United States to suffer any humiliation as long as the hostages remained unharmed. This impression encouraged the Iranians consistently to overplay their hand, confident that they possessed the one trump card—namely, the safety of the hostages—that would ensure U.S. restraint. The administration's failure to take decisive action in Iran in the face of a direct challenge to its citizens and national interests by a weak and isolated nation certainly contributed to the Soviet decision to invade Afghanistan in December 1979, inasmuch as the Soviet leadership was confident that its aggression would be met with little more than angry words and symbolic gestures by the Carter White House. After all, if the United States would not take strong action in Iran, where the lives of fifty-three U.S. hostages and its national pride were on the line, then surely it would not risk a confrontation over a remote piece of real estate where its national interests were, at best, obscure.

Seventh, the Carter administration missed numerous opportunities to influence events in Iran while there was still hope of salvaging, if not the shah's regime, then a government more compatible than the ayatollah's with U.S. interests in the region. Evidence suggests, for example, that the United States squelched efforts by the U.S.-trained and -equipped Iranian military, while it was still reasonably intact, to seize control of the country by means of a coup d'état. After the onset of the hostage crisis, perhaps the most significant missed opportunity was the failure of the United States to launch a rescue attempt or military initiative in December 1979, concomitant with the Soviet invasion of Afghanistan. Not only would the Soviets have been too preoccupied with their own intervention to mobilize effective opposition to the U.S. move, but also the Iranians clearly would have been distracted by the military action in neighboring Afghanistan, thus providing the U.S. rescue force with an extra margin of surprise.

Eighth, the United States has long been on record as opposing the payment of ransoms to terrorists. While not technically a ransom inasmuch as the assets transferred to Tehran in exchange for the hostages originally belonged to Iran, having been frozen by executive order in the aftermath of the hostage seizure, nevertheless, the Carter administration's willingness to negotiate with hostage takers set a dangerous precedent that may come back to haunt this nation in the future since, historically, one successful case of blackmail has often stimulated another. Former Secretary of State Kissinger put the matter most succinctly, "If terrorist groups get the impression that they can force a negotiation with the United States and an acquiescence in their demands, then we may save lives in one place at the risk of hundreds of lives everywhere else."[8]

This was not the first time that President Carter had ignored the no-concessions policy with respect to terrorist blackmail. Early in his presidency, he agreed to the demand of a crazed bank robber in Indianapolis who had taken a police officer hostage and wanted to speak to the president of the United States. While the police officer was ultimately released, as Steve R. Pieczenik, a former deputy assistant secretary of state, has noted, "Carter had set an unfortunate precedent by making it clear that he was more than willing to put the presidency itself on the line."[9] Oblivious to such concerns, Carter tried once again, that same month, to turn the Oval Office into the Situation Room when he indicated that he wanted to assume direct control of the negotiations in the Hanafi Muslim takeovers in downtown Washington, D.C. Fortunately, cooler heads prevailed, and Carter was dissuaded from doing so by White House aides.

Institutional Machinery for Combating Terrorism

Only in the area of revamping the institutional machinery for dealing with terrorism was the Carter administration's record at all favorable. After an extensive review of U.S. government policy and capabilities with regard to responding to the problem of terrorism, in 1977 the National Security Council issued a presidential review memorandum known as PRM-30. Although many, if not most, of the recommendations contained in the memorandum were rejected, two special units—in accordance with PRM-30's recommendation—were established to coordinate the federal response to terrorist crises. The first, known as the working group, is a broad-based unit (twenty members) that draws membership from every agency of the federal government with even a remote connection to the subject, including the Department of Agriculture. The second, and more critical unit, functions as an executive committee. In addition to an official from the Department of State who chairs the committee, this unit is made up of representatives of the Departments of Defense, Justice, Treasury, and Transportation; the CIA; the Joint Chiefs of Staff; and the National Security Council.

The two units just described perform essentially planning and coordination functions. From an operational point of view, different agencies, depending on the nature of the terrorist incident, are designated as the lead agency for the purposes of actual management of each crisis. The Department of State is the lead agency with respect to international incidents, the only exception being the FAA that has purview over skyjacking incidents both at home and abroad. The FBI and the Justice Department have lead authority in the event of domestic threats, but this authority is shared with state and local jurisdictions. Under the Carter administration, the Federal Emergency Management Agency (FEMA) was created and was delegated the task of planning for and responding to the consequences of terrorist acts.

Despite this reorganization, the federal capability to manage terrorist incidents and to develop coherent and effective policies for the control and suppression of terrorism remains fragmented and poorly coordinated. According to Kupperman and Trent:

> As of today, we are poorly prepared to deal with nationally disruptive acts of terrorism. Our capability to manage terrorist crises is limited. Our state of preparedness is not adequately developed. The international community is not integrated into preplanned modes of response. Research on terrorist behavior, target hardening, and the problem of restoration after attack is only in its infancy.[10]

Steve R. Pieczenik has called attention to the lack of experienced personnel within the federal structure for dealing with terrorist crises.[11] This is especially true at the Department of State. The Office for Combating Terrorism at State, the department's key institutional component charged with addressing the problem, has—since its inception—traditionally been a dumping ground for foreign service officers with no special expertise in the field and without sufficient stature to merit appointment to a diplomatic post. Similarly, the personnel at FEMA are more accustomed to dealing with floods and natural calamities than to addressing terrorist incidents, and as a consequence, they are ill suited for the task of responding in a meaningful way to the problem.

The Reagan Administration

Only eight days after his inauguration, President Reagan, welcoming home the hostages from Iran, announced, "Let terrorists be aware that when the rules of international behavior are violated, our policy will be one of swift and effective retribution."[12] Although the specific meaning of "swift and effective retribution" was not spelled out, there could be little question that the Reagan administration was committing itself to a far stronger posture with respect to terrorism than previous administrations.[13]

Former Secretary of State Haig has described efforts to suppress and control terrorism as a major objective of American foreign policy and has asserted that international terrorism would "take the place [in U.S. policy] of human rights . . . because it is the ultimate abuse of human rights."[14] In a televised interview, former National Security Advisor Richard Allen continued the strong tone of the administration's rhetoric, maintaining that international terrorism was a threat to the United States and to U.S. foreign policy objectives, and he assailed the USSR for its support of terrorist movements around the world.[15]

Reflecting the administration's new hard line on terrorism and its reinterpretation of human rights, in the 4 May 1981 declaration on terrorism issued by the North Atlantic council (NATO) ministerial meeting in Rome, the assembled foreign ministers and representatives of the NATO bloc "condemned all acts of terrorism regardless of their origins, causes or purposes as a flagrant violation of human dignity and rights."[16]

Thus, early in the new administration's life, the president and his principal foreign policy spokesmen put the administration squarely on record as opposing terrorism in its every incarnation and manifestation and vowed strong action against the perpetrators and supporters of international terrorism whenever the United States, its citizens, or diplomatic personnel were targets of such violence. In addition, the human rights doctrine had been redefined to place far greater emphasis on the protection of individual citizens, both in the United States and abroad, from attacks against their lives and property by nonstate actors seeking to overturn existing political systems by means of violence.

Despite the strong rhetoric of the Reagan administration, however, by the end of its first year in office, observers were dismayed to find that little in the way of substantive policy dealing with the problem of terrorism had emerged. Critics of the new emphasis on terrorism decried it as a tempest in a teapot and wondered aloud whether the administration could make a case to justify its tough stance, let alone develop a realistic policy to match its rhetoric.

In a more general sense, some real and positive steps have been taken to impress upon the USSR and its surrogates that the United States no longer will tolerate terrorist activities that threaten the United States, its Western allies, and friendly nations in the Third World. U.S. advisors and equipment have been dispatched to El Salvador to assist the local government in responding to a Cuban- and Nicaraguan-backed insurgency. Sanctions imposed during the Carter administration against friendly nations for alleged human rights abuses have been dropped. Proposals have been drafted to expand the authority of the CIA so it can collect information on terrorist groups operating in this country and to authorize the disruption of their activities. The United States has stepped up pressure on the renegade government of Muammar Qaddafi in Libya, first by expelling Libyan diplomats and later by engaging in aerial hostilities over the Gulf of Sidra. By the end of 1981, the message to the USSR was unmistakable: Any improvement in relations with the United States would be linked to, among other things, a reduction in Soviet support of international terrorism.

A New U.S. Policy

Before recommending new steps toward a solution, the broad outlines of the current official U.S. policy regarding terrorism should be reviewed. First, the United States opposes any payment of ransom for the release of kidnapped Americans or other concessions to terrorist blackmail. U.S. policymakers maintain that to do so would be to encourage further acts of terrorism and endanger still more Americans. However, while embraced in theory, such a posture is not always translated into practice. The United States has, as noted earlier, during the Carter administration, turned a blind eye to the payment of ransoms by third parties to effect the release of hostage Americans, as in the capitulation of the Colombian government to demands of terrorists holding 18 diplomats including U.S. Ambassador Diego Asencio, hostage in Bogota in 1980. The terrorists initially demanded a $50-million ransom and the release of 311 political prisoners, but ultimately they settled for a $2.5-million ransom and safe passage to Cuba. Similarly, the Carter administration pledged what in effect was the payment of a ransom for the return of U.S. hostages in Iran. The United States further maintains that the responsibility for dealing with threats to diplomatic personnel or the abduction of Americans must fall on the local, or host, government. Should the host government fail to live up to its obligations, or more seriously, should it encourage or give assistance to the hostage takers as in Iran, the policy is unclear. However, Reagan administration officials leave little doubt that the United States, choosing from a variety of economic, political, and military sanctions, would respond decisively.

The United States also encourages various levels of cooperative action by states with a common interest in opposing terrorism. This cooperation takes many forms. Nevertheless, diplomatic efforts to reach bilateral and multilateral agreements for the control and suppression of terrorism have produced only limited results to date. Despite major international agreements pertaining to issues such as air piracy and the protection of diplomatic personnel, such agreements are still only effective and enforceable at the pleasure of the signatories. Moreover, in the case of the two pending 1977 protocols to the four 1949 Geneva conventions relating to armed conflicts, such efforts actually may be counterproductive. Although more is written later about this subject, the two protocols would extend—under some circumstances—prisoner-of-war status to terrorists.

Among the other recommendations for international cooperation being studied by the U.S. government is the American Bar Association proposal for the creation of an international criminal court for terrorists. However, like similar recommendations for an international prison for terrorists or an international police force to combat terrorism, such proposals stand little, if any, chance of ever being adopted. Likewise, little in the way of substantive action to suppress terrorism can be expected from the UN. As Paul Wilkinson has observed, "The United Nations has proved to be a broken reed on the whole subject of terrorism."[17] Indeed, nothing better illustrates the ineffectiveness of the world body than its inability to come to grips with the problem of terrorism. A two-year effort to find new solutions to the problem collapsed after diplomats failed to arrive at a commonly accepted definition of terrorism.

More productive have been cooperative efforts on a limited scale, involving governments collaborating informally on an incident-by-incident basis. This cooperation has taken the form of sharing intelligence data, hardware, and techniques for combating and controlling terrorism. Counterterrorist commando teams from one country are frequently aided by advisors and equipment from other countries, both before the fact and in the actual conduct of operations. Some nations conveniently have overlooked the operations of counterterrorist strike teams within their borders and, in several instances, have assisted the hit team in carrying out its mission. In one notable case, Communist Bulgaria cooperated with West Germany in apprehending and extraditing three members of the June 2 movement, a successor group to the Baader-Meinhof gang. Two of the terrorists were snatched by a German undercover squad at a Black Sea resort and spirited out of the country and back to Germany. The third terrorist was arrested by Bulgarian authorities and turned over to the West German government. To illustrate the expanding parameters of cooperation, it should be recalled that in 1977 the government of Somalia permitted West German GSG-9 commandos to rescue a Lufthansa jetliner that had been hijacked by four terrorists and flown to Mogadishu. The German unit had received training from Israel's General Intelligence and Reconnaissance Unit 269, and two U.K. SAS commandos took part in the assault. The United States aided the German mission not only with intelligence data and by interceding with the Somali government but also unconfirmed reports indicate that U.S. personnel were on site at Mogadishu.

In view of the futility of most multilateral efforts to control and suppress terrorism, however, the United States should concentrate on a policy of self-help, consistent with Article 51 of the UN Charter that expressly reserves to states the inherent right of self-defense. In this connection, the United States should take comprehensive steps to insure that it is prepared in the event of a major terrorist crisis. Such preparation would include the development of a comprehensive counterterrorist program that would analyze threats and develop proper countermeasures, establish appropriate procedures to coordinate the government's response in the event of a terrorist crisis, and implement government emergency programs in the aftermath of a serious event.

The main elements of a comprehensive U.S. policy for dealing with terrorism are as follows:

1. Every effort must be made to restore the prestige and professionalism of U.S. intelligence agencies, which form the first line of defense to terrorism. During the mid-1970s, inquiries into alleged CIA abuses got out of control; constructive reform gave way to mindless persecution. The CIA was accused of innumerable misdeeds—most never proved—and portrayed in the press as a dangerous institution, full of assassins and miscreants, a shadow government that threatened the very security of the nation. This led to a breakdown of morale and a pervasive malaise throughout the agency. "As a result," noted James Schlesinger, "all of the old war stories [came] out,"[18] and this fed the hysteria all the more. Foreign intelligence services became reluctant to share their secrets lest they appear two weeks later in *The New York Times*. More than 2,800 intelligence officers retired, many prematurely, or were dismissed. Clandestine activities were abandoned in many instances because, as one official put it, "everyone was watching." The climate of fear and recrimination led to a paralysis of action, and the agency failed to provide timely warnings regarding the collapse of the Peacock Throne in Iran, the Cuban penetration of the Sandanista rebellion in Nicaragua, and the Soviet invasion of Afghanistan.

Under the Reagan administration, the rebuilding of the CIA has begun, although not without some initial missteps like the appointment of Max Hugel, who later resigned, as spymaster. Among the chief deficiencies that should be addressed by the new leadership at the CIA are the following. The agency's human intelligence collection effort needs to be significantly revitalized. The penetration of terrorist organizations and the compromise of leading terrorists must be made a top priority, and the agency's paramilitary capability should be rebuilt in view of the obvious limitations of Delta-type units under military control. The CIA also should be given greater responsibilities with respect to penetrating and subverting foreign terrorist elements within the United States. The requirement that U.S. intelligence agents have strong evidence that U.S. corporations and citizens abroad are agents of a foreign power, or engaged in terrorism or the sale of illegal drugs, before they can be put under surveillance should be eliminated.

Congress should review recent restrictions—for example, the attorney general's guidelines for domestic security and foreign counterintelligence investigations (the so-called Levi guidelines), the Freedom of Information Act, the Privacy Act, and the Foreign Intelligence Surveillance Act—that have impaired the ability of the CIA, the FBI, and other intelligence agencies to collect and utilize intelligence data pertaining to terrorist organizations and their domestic and international support apparatus.[19] In this connection, priority should be given to eliminating the criminal standard for intelligence collection, developing new protections for intelligence sources and methods, and restoring the ability of the government to retain and disseminate intelligence information pertaining to noncriminal activities of Americans.[20]

2. State-sponsored terrorism no longer can be tolerated. In this connection, as former CIA Director William E. Colby recently testified before a congressional committee, "The Soviets must be seen to be responsible for the obvious consequences of their actions, and not be able to hide behind the 'plausible denial' that the groups they trained and supplied, the proxies they support in Cuba, Libya and among Palestinians, are operating on their own."[21] Any improvement in relations with the USSR, therefore, must be predicated on a significant reduction of its global support of terrorist violence. Increased pressure also should be applied against Cuba to end its support of revolution in Africa and the nations of Latin America. Terrorist sanctuaries must be eliminated. Nations that train, harbor, or support terrorists should be isolated diplomatically, economically, and in terms of their communications links with the West. Such nations should be denied U.S. foreign assistance, and their applications for loans and technical assistance should be opposed by the United States at the World Bank, the International Monetary Fund (IMF), and regional development banks. A major diplomatic and propaganda offensive should be launched in the UN and other world forums against nations that support international terrorism.

3. The United States should come to the aid of friendly governments that are confronted with endemic terrorism not only by lending public support to their struggles but also by providing them with intelligence, hardware, training, economic assistance, and even U.S. military advisors. It should be stressed that while governments under siege occasionally may be guilty of human rights violations, the United States should work with those governments to assist them in reducing such violations instead of publicly condemning and villifying them as happened during the Carter years. The widespread use of torture and mass arrests usually is self-defeating and shortsighted, and most governments, if provided with more effective alternatives, readily will opt for tactics that do not undermine their base of domestic as well as international support. Some human rights violations will, nevertheless, always occur because if, as Joseph Stalin once observed, "You cannot make a revolution with silk gloves," then it is surely too much to expect that it is possible to defeat revolutions with silk gloves.

4. The Libyan regime of Colonel Muammar Qaddafi must be overthrown,

either through covert and clandestine means or, in the face of extreme provocation, by U.S. military intervention. As the quartermaster, instructor, and financier of more than forty terrorist groups ranging from the PFLP to the IRA, Libya represents an unacceptable threat to Western security. Qaddafi has threatened to attack U.S. nuclear depots in Europe and to cause an international catastrophe after U.S. jets shot down two Libyan fighters over the Gulf of Sidra in August 1981. He has also sought for some time to purchase or steal fissionable material in order to build a so-called Moslem bomb. Libya has attempted to destablize nearly a dozen nations in Africa over the past decade and has provided support to Islamic terrorists in Iran who were instrumental in the overthrow of the shah. Moslem extremists who assassinated President Anwar Sadat of Egypt also received support and encouragement from Libya. Qaddafi is suspected of launching attacks against the lives of U.S. diplomats in Europe and reportedly dispatched hit teams to kill President Reagan, Vice-President Bush, and several cabinet officers.

Ample precedent exists in U.S. history to justify its intervention in Libya. Historically, Libya was a base for pirates operating along the Mediterranean coast. Although Presidents Washington and Adams followed British practice and paid tribute to the Barbary pirates for safe passage of U.S. vessels, when the pasha of Tripoli increased the levy on the United States in 1801, President Thomas Jefferson dispatched warships to the Mediterranean. After four years of military action and the imposition of a blockade, the Barbary states capitulated and signed a peace treaty with the United States in which they agreed, among other things, to indemnify the United States for its losses.

5. With respect to indemnification, nations should present international claims against states that fail to prevent terrorist attacks launched from their territory or that aid and abet international terrorists by means of training and supplying weapons and money. Certainly Israel could present such claims against Lebanon, and even Italy (or Vatican City) could assert a claim against Bulgaria for the assistance it gave to Mehmet Ali Agca, the Pope's attempted assassin.[22]

6. Delta and the other antiterrorist strike units are self-contained multipurpose forces that are supposed to be able to carry out counterterrorist operations like rescuing hostages as well as to engage in conventional military operations including intervention in foreign conflicts, the protection of critical assets anywhere in the world, and rapid deployment to repel aggression. Unfortunately, because of their totally military nature and composition, such units suffer from obvious limitations in combating terrorists and are essentially one dimensional inasmuch as their only form of response in meeting terrorist challenges is the application of force.

At present, such units lack a clandestine and covert dimension and, therefore, the ability to engage in so-called deniable missions and black work. Consideration must be given to increasing Delta's capabilities in this area or, alternately, to rebuilding the paramilitary capability of the CIA.

7. The U.S. Senate should not ratify Protocols I and II to the 1949 Geneva Convention relating to the Treatment of Prisoners of War.[23] Initialed under the Carter administration in 1977, the protocols accord prisoner-of-war status to captured terrorists/insurgents under certain conditions. If ratified by the United States, it is conceivable that members of the Weatherman/Black Liberation Army captured in the aftermath of the October 1981 murder of a Brinks guard and two policemen could demand prisoner-of-war status, including incarceration in a special military facility instead of a criminal detention center, with all of the rights and privileges granted under the Geneva Convention and their treatment overseen by representatives of an outside nation or nations, perhaps even including countries like India, Sweden, the USSR, or Libya. This is not fantasy: Members of the Puerto Rican FALN, on trial in Chicago in February 1981, alleged that they were prisoners of war entitled to be tried by an international tribunal. Similarly, IRA prisoners in Belfast's Maze Prison went on a seven-month campaign of hunger strikes, resulting in the deaths of ten prisoners before it was abandoned in October 1981, to achieve various demands including recognition as political prisoners by the U.K. government.[24]

8. Congress should rescind the ban it imposed in 1975 on foreign aid funds being used to provide training and other support activities to foreign police units. The denial of U.S. technology and police techniques to foreign governments engaged in counterinsurgency and counterterrorism activities almost surely resulted in an increase in human rights violations since those governments often reverted to heavy-handed tactics against terrorists, such as mass arrests, torture, and the sponsorship of death squads. Modern police methods, together with an emphasis on professionalism and up-to-date technology, would have permitted those governments to react in a more restrained and surgical manner to terrorist violence and likely would have achieved the same results without the political fallout that occurred with other methods.

9. In the wake of discoveries relating to the activities of former CIA agents in Libya, Congress should move quickly to enact the International Terrorism Crime Act of 1981 into law, or some similar measure that would achieve the same purpose. Introduced by Senators Bentsen, Roth, and Cannon, this bill would make it a crime for U.S. citizens to manufacture, sell, or export military weapons, equipment, or technology or to provide training and expertise to other nations and individuals for the purpose of aiding and abetting international terrorism.

10. Recent steps have been taken with respect to shoring up U.S. embassy security and improving the protection of diplomatic personnel abroad. In this connection, the State Department has undertaken a comprehensive program to improve embassy security, emphasizing new access controls, nonlethal denial systems in U.S. embassies and consulates, and the construction of safe havens or bunkers where personnel can take refuge until rescued. An expanded two-day course on coping with violence abroad has been instituted for all State

Department, Agency for International Development, and International Communications Agency (ICA) personnel assigned overseas. The course focuses on topics such as bomb recognition, residential security, and hostage survival. New contingency planning and crisis management programs for dealing with terrorist incidents have been put into effect, and various practice exercises have been run to test the effectiveness of such procedures. Efforts are also underway to work out improved counterterrorist coordination with close allies of the United States.[25]

Consistent with President Reagan's pledge that the United States shall never again permit its diplomats to be taken captive with impunity, the comprehensive security improvement program initiated in 1981 to increase security at U.S. embassies and diplomatic missions abroad should be continued in succeeding years. The $10 million appropriated in fiscal year 1981 for this purpose should be regarded as but the first phase of a long overdue upgrading of embassy security.

11. The question of how a nation conducts its diplomacy in a world of terrorism is clearly at issue when one stops to consider that more U.S. ambassadors have died of hostile action since World War II than military personnel of the rank of general or higher. Obviously, it would defeat the purposes of diplomacy to turn embassies into armed enclaves or fortresses. One need only view the bunkerlike design and construction of the U.S. embassy in Bogota, for example, to glimpse the architecture of fear. Similarly, the new Swedish embassy in Cairo has been described as a "forbidding concrete structure with a single entrance, narrow slits for windows, and a protected inner courtyard backing on the Nile—for quick escape by boat if necessary. More than anything, it is said to resemble Hitler's bunker."[26] Contact with local natives is vital to understanding the pulse of a nation and to assess its political and economic climate properly. However, fear of violence often restricts diplomats to certain safe areas and inhibits their ability to collect vital information and to make proper contacts. Indeed, in pre-Khomeini Iran, contact with opposition groups and leaders was likely to put a diplomat's life in danger.

To help reduce the threat to U.S. government and diplomatic personnel, the United States should consider placing a bounty—perhaps as much as $250,000 cash—on the heads of terrorists, named by U.S. intelligence, whose actions have contributed to or resulted in the death of U.S. representatives. The bounty would be collectible in cash at any U.S. embassy in the world upon proper verification of the terrorist's identity. Consideration might also be given to the creation of an action team, based on the concept of the Israeli Wrath-of-God unit that systematically has hunted down the perpetrators of the Munich massacre, that would carry the war to the terrorists in their lairs, eliminating those responsible for shedding Americans' blood. If it were a near certainty among terrorists that they would meet the same fate as their victims, it can be postulated with some certainty that there would be fewer attacks on

U.S. diplomats and other U.S. government personnel. Recall that only after pirates were made universal criminals, punishable by any nation without regard to nationality or the location of the crimes, was piracy stamped out. Until modern times, private individuals were even permitted to enforce the prohibition against piracy, and the U.S. Constitution provides for the granting of letters of marque and reprisal by Congress.

12. As Senator John P. East has pointed out, currently no federal statute expressly recognizes a separate category of crimes defined as terrorism.[27] Terrorists are punished under existing statutes pertaining to crimes such as murder, arson, robbery, and kidnapping. The failure to distinguish terrorist acts from ordinary criminal acts results not only in confusion over what exactly constitutes terrorism but also often means that local law enforcement agencies and courts have the primary jurisdiction with respect to terrorist crimes. Local prosecutors and law enforcement personnel, however, often are not adequately trained or equipped to deal with terrorists. Senator East recommends that terrorism be defined as a federal crime and that appropriate penalties be established to punish terrorists. The FBI would therefore become the lead law enforcement agency with both the responsibility and authority for responding to all terrorist crimes within the United States. With respect to penalties, the death sentence should be made mandatory for those convicted of terrorist acts that result in the loss of life or the wanton maiming and disfigurement of innocent persons.

13. It is estimated that up to 2 percent of all U.S. passport applications are fraudulent. Since relatively unrestricted mobility is certainly a precondition for most acts of terrorism, the State Department should be provided with the additional personnel it needs to crack down on passport fraud. In addition, immigration and passport controls should be strengthened greatly in order to apprehend suspected terrorists upon their arrival in the United States, before they have an opportunity to commit acts of violence or engage in other illegal acts.

14. In view of the fact that police are usually the first to engage terrorists or to respond to terrorist incidents, new emphasis must be placed on upgrading police capabilities to deal with the problem. In this connection, most city police departments are just beginning to learn how to cope effectively with hostage/barricade situations and other terrorist threats. Moreover, few policemen have any real knowledge of the modus operandi of terrorist organizations they are likely to encounter.

The Special Tactics Unit of the Special Operations Division of the Washington, D.C., Police Department, or its New York and Los Angeles counterparts, could well serve as models for the rest of the nation. This unit was created to respond to terrorist and related incidents in the nation's capital. It is deployed about twenty-five or thirty times a year, although all but about a dozen of the incidents are of a traditional hostage/barricade nature and lacking a terrorist dimension. The unit is composed of three platoons, each composed, in turn, of three squads. Each platoon is a self-contained mobile response unit. D.C. police believe that small, cohesive, multifaceted units give them more flexibility than highly compartmentalized and overly specialized units in other cities. Each platoon contains hostage negotiators, rescue teams, and tactical intelligence specialists. Members of the units are typically combat veterans trained in skills such as marksmanship, hand-to-hand combat, intelligence collection, building and helicopter rappeling, first aid, and terrorist psychology. The unit maintains close links to the Secret Service, the FBI, various intelligence agencies, and to federal antiterrorist commando units like the Delta team stationed at Fort Bragg.

Great emphasis is placed on speed in reacting to a crisis; special tactics squads can be on the scene and ready to respond to any kind of incident within half an hour. "The security of the Western world," explained one police official, "may in the end depend on a man getting through a door . . . and getting through it first."[28]

15. A crash program to study and assess the vulnerability of key elements of the U.S. defense, economic, and energy infrastructure from the standpoint of the threat posed by terrorists and saboteurs should be commenced at once. Upon completion, a major effort to harden those elements that are deemed most vulnerable could begin. In addition, Congress should enact into law a provision that identifies all critical modes of activity whose survival is vital to the well-being and security of the United States—for example, record storage centers, key computer centers controlling communications and energy flows, power-generating facilities, satellite ground stations, regional air traffic control centers, and certain production facilities—and that requires an internal security design statement to be filed, and certain provisions satisfied, before construction of new facilities that fall into this category can go forward.

Conclusion

A hard-line policy dealing with terrorism, emphasizing a quick, efficient, and—if necessary—brutal response has been demonstrated to be highly effective in controlling and suppressing terrorism. Indeed, numerous Western nations have mounted successful counterattacks against terrorists in recent years, and as the *Washington Post* observed, "[S]uccesses can be contagious: they can deter would-be terrorists, and they can encourage governments to plan and take intelligent counter-action, rather than simply wring their hands."[29]

This is not to say that the resort to force will be an appropriate or ideal strategy with respect to every terrorist incident or against every terrorist movement, especially those with legitimate grievances and demands. Nevertheless, were it possible to remove or eradicate injustice, poverty, political repression, and all forms of inequality, it would be politically naive to believe that terrorism would disappear. Persons who glorify violence for its own sake and individuals and groups that embrace terrorism for a variety of purely selfish or distorted motives that may or may not have any legitimacy or basis in fact will always exist. Moreover, as long as the USSR and other nations view terrorism as a low-cost strategy for achieving geopolitical goals, and therefore provide terrorists with support and sustenance, the problem will not soon disappear and, instead, will only grow in intensity.

Notes

1. Nelson Rockefeller, quotation during executive session of the Commission on the Organization of the Government for the Conduct of Foreign Policy (Murphy Commission), U.S. Capitol, 1975.

2. According to Arnaud de Borchgrave, Western intelligence services believe that the Soviet decision to support international terrorist groups was taken at the Tri-Continental Conference in Havana in 1966 and implemented two years later.

3. "Richard Allen Analyzes International Terrorism," *Congressional Record*, 9 April 1981, p. E1748.

4. Ibid.

5. President Jimmy Carter, Presidential Address, University of Notre Dame, 22 May 1977, in *Weekly Compilation of Presidential Documents* 13 (30 May 1977):776.

6. Contrary to the belief that, while Henry Kissinger directed it, U.S. foreign policy was essentially value free and motivated solely by realpolitik considerations, during this period interest in human rights was renewed. Kissinger worked for free emigration of Soviet Jewry, the release of political prisoners in Chile, and on behalf of humanitarian concerns in Cyprus, South Korea, Bangladesh, and a host of other countries. However, unlike the Carter administration, Kissinger made no effort to grandstand on the issue of human rights, preferring instead to work quietly behind the scenes, where he felt that the greatest gains could be made. Only at Helsinki did the United States publicly espouse human rights concerns. The Ford administration only reluctantly participated in the OSCE Conference at the urging of its European allies. By insisting on comparatively strong human rights provisions in basket 3 of the Helsinki accord, the Ford administration hoped to mute domestic opposition to the real substance of the agreement, especially from ethnic and religious groups.

7. Henry Kissinger, "Continuity and Change in American Foreign Policy," *Congressional Record*, U.S. Senate, Sept 20, 1977, p. S 15218.

8. Henry Kissinger, quoted in "Beyond the Call of Duty," *Time*, 1 September 1975.

9. Steve R. Pieczenik, "Terrorist Policy: It Could Scare You To Death," *Washington Post*, 15 February 1981, © The Washington Post. Reprinted with permission.

10. Robert Kupperman and Darrell Trent, *Terrorism: Threat, Reality, Response* (Stanford, Calif.: Hoover Institution Press, 1979), p. 177.

11. Pieczenik, "Terrorist Policy."

12. President Ronald Reagan, *Editorial Research Reports*, 27 March 1981, p. 231.

13. Secretary of State Alexander Haig, at a press conference that same day, described the president's remarks as "consciously ambiguous."

14. Reagan and Haig Statements about Terror," *Editorial Research Reports*, (27 March 1981), p. 232.

15. "Richard Allen Analyzes International Terrorism," *Congressional Record*, 5 April 1981, p. E1748.

16. *Department of State Bulletin* (July 1981), p. 41.

17. Paul Wilkinson, *Terrorism and the Liberal State* (New York: New York University Press, 1979), p. 231.

18. James Schlesinger, comment to author, Washington, D.C., 1975.

19. Senator John P. East, "Congress and Terrorism," draft article for the *International Security Review* (November 1981), p. 5.

20. Ibid.

21. U.S., Congress, Senate, Committee on the Judiciary, Subcommittee on Security and Terrorism, Testimony of William E. Colby, 97th Cong., 1st sess., 24 April 1981, p. 5.

22. I am indebted to Professor Alfred P. Rubin of the Fletcher School of Law and Diplomacy for his insight on the matter of indemnification.

23. United Nations, "Respect for Human Rights in Armed Conflicts," U.N. Document A/32/144, 15 August 1977.

24. For further information regarding Protocol II, see Robert D. Chapman, "The New Terrorist Weapon: Protocol II," *Security Management*, (July 1981).

25. U.S., Congress, Senate, Committee on Foreign Relations, Testimony of Richard T. Kennedy, 97th Cong., 1st sess., 10 June 1981, pp. 32-68.

26. *Time*, March 17, 1980, p. 30.

27. Senator John P. East, "Congress and Terrorism," p. 3.

28. Interview with D.C. police official, not for attribution.

29. Editorial, "Egypt Foils a Libyan Hijacking," *Washington Post*, 25 August 1976.

Bibliography

Books

Alexander, Yonah, ed. *International Terrorism: National, Regional and Global Perspectives.* New York: Frederick A. Praeger, 1976.

Archer, Denis, ed. *Jane's Pocket Book of Pistols and Sub-Machine Guns.* New York: Collier Books, 1976.

Arendt, Hannah. *On Revolution.* New York: Viking Press, 1965.

_____. *On Violence.* New York: Harcourt, Brace & World, 1975.

Aristotle. *Politics.* New York: Modern Library, 1943.

Arms and Armour Press, in Association with the International Institute for Strategic Studies. *The Military Balance 1978-79.* Dorking: Bartholomew Press, 1979.

Art, Robert J., and Kenneth N. Waltz, eds. *The Use of Force.* Boston: Little, Brown & Company, 1971.

Asprey, Robert B. *War in the Shadows,* vols. 1 and 2. Garden City, N.Y.: Doubleday, 1975.

Batalov, E. *The Philosophy of Revolution.* Moscow: Progress Publishers, 1975.

Begin, Menachem. *The Revolt.* London: W.H. Allen, 1951.

Bell, J. Bowyer. *Transnational Terror.* Washington, D.C.: American Enterprise Institute for Public Policy Research, 1975.

_____. *On Revolt.* Cambridge: Harvard University Press, 1976.

_____. *Terror out of Zion.* New York: St. Martin's Press, 1977.

_____. *A Time of Terror.* New York: Basic Books, 1978.

Brinton, Crane. *The Anatomy of Revolution.* New York: Vintage Books, 1965.

Brodie, Bernard, and Fawn M. Brodie. *From Crossbow to H-Bomb.* Bloomington: Indiana University Press, 1973.

Brzezinski, Zbigniew. *Between Two Ages.* New York: Viking Press, 1970.

Burchett, Wilfred, and Derek Roebuck. *The Whores of War.* Harmondsworth, U.K.: Penguin Books Ltd., 1977.

Burke, Edmund. *Reflections on the Revolution in France.* Garden City, N.Y.: Doubleday, 1961.

Burnham, S., ed. *The Threat to Licensed Nuclear Facilities.* Washington, D.C.: Mitre Corp. 1975.

Burton, Anthony. *Urban Terrorism: Theory, Practice and Response.* New York: Free Press, 1975.

Calder, Nigel. *Nuclear Nightmares.* New York: Viking Press, 1979.

Camus, Albert. *Notebooks, 1935-1942.* New York: Harcourt Brace Jovanovich, 1978.

_____. *Notebooks, 1942-1951.* New York: Harcourt Brace Jovanovich, 1978.

Carroll, Lewis. *The Annotated Alice.* New York: Bramhall House, 1960.

Cassidy, William L. *The Complete Book of Knife Fighting.* Boulder, Colo.: Paladin Press, 1975.

———. *Political Kidnapping.* Boulder, Colo.: Sycamore Island Books, 1978.

Chapman, Robert D. *The Crimson Web of Terror.* Boulder, Colo.: Paladin Press, 1980.

Clark, Richard C. *Technological Terrorism.* Old Greenwich: Devin-Adair Company, 1980.

Cline, Ray S. *Secrets, Spies and Scholars.* New York: Acropolis Books, Ltd., 1976.

Clutterbuck, Richard. *Protest and the Urban Guerrilla.* London: Cassell & Co., 1973.

———. *Living with Terrorism.* London: Faber & Faber, 1975.

Clyne, Peter. *An Anatomy of Skyjacking.* London: Abelard-Schuman, 1973.

Crozier, Brian. *A Theory of Conflict.* New York: Charles Scribner's Sons, 1974.

Cunningham, William C., and Philip J. Gross. *Prevention of Terrorism: Security Guidelines for Business and Other Organizations.* McLean, Va.: Hallcrest Press, June 1978.

Dallin, Alexander, and George W. Breslauer. *Political Terror in Communist Systems.* Stanford, Calif.: Stanford University Press, 1970.

Debray, Regis. *Revolution in the Revolution?* New York: Grove Press, 1967.

Demaris, Ovid. *Brothers in Blood.* New York: Charles Scribner's Sons, 1977.

Dobson, Christopher. *Black September: It's Short, Violent History.* New York: Macmillan, 1974.

———. *The Terrorists.* New York: Facts on File, 1979.

Dobson, Christopher, and Ronald Payne. *The Carlos Complex: A Study in Terror.* New York: G.P. Putnam's Sons, 1977.

Eckstein, Harry, ed. *Internal War.* London: Collier-Macmillan Limited, 1964.

Ellis, John. *Guerrilla Warfare.* New York: St. Martin's Press, 1976.

Fanon, Frantz. *The Wretched of the Earth.* New York: Grove Press, 1968.

Frankford Arsenal. *Improvised Munitions Black Book.* Cornville, Ar.: Desert Publications, 1977.

Friedmann, Wolfgang, Oliver J. Lissitzyn, and Richard C. Pugh. *International Law.* St. Paul, Minn.: West Publishing Co., 1969.

Frommer, Harvey. *The Martial Arts.* New York: Atheneum, 1978.

Giap, Vo Nguyen. *People's War, People's Army.* New York: Frederick A. Praeger, 1967.

Godson, Roy, ed. *Intelligence Requirements for the 1980's: Elements of Intelligence.* Washington, D.C.: National Strategy Information Center, 1979.

Graham, Hugh Davis, and Ted Robert Gurr. *Violence in America,* Report submitted to the National Commission on the Causes and Prevention of Violence. New York: Bantam Books, 1969.

Gray, J. Glenn. *The Warriors.* New York: Harper & Row, 1967.

Grivas, George. *The Memoirs of General Grivas*, edited by Charles Foley. New York: Frederick A. Praeger, 1964.

_____. *General Grivas on Guerrilla Warfare*. New York: Frederick A. Praeger, 1965.

Gross, Feliks. *Violence in Politics*. The Hague: Mouton, 1972.

Guevara, Che. *Guerrilla Warfare*. New York: Monthly Review Press, 1961.

_____. *The Complete Bolivian Diaries of Che Guevara*, edited by Daniel James. New York: Stein and Day, 1968.

Guhin, Michael A. *Nuclear Paradox: Security Risks of the Peaceful Atom*. Washington, D.C.: American Enterprise Institute, 1976.

Hacker, Frederick J. *Crusaders, Criminals, Crazies*. New York: W.W. Norton & Company, 1976.

Hobbes, Thomas. *Leviathan*. New York: Collier Books, 1966.

Hoffmann, Stanley. *The State of War*. New York: Frederick A. Praeger, 1965.

Hougan, Jim. *Spooks*. New York: William Morrow and Company, 1978.

Hubbard, David. *The Skyjacker: His Flights of Fantasy*. New York: Macmillan, 1977.

Hyams, Edward. *Terrorists and Terrorism*. London: J.M. Dent and Sons, 1975.

Jackson, Geoffrey. *People's Prison*. London: Faber & Faber, 1973.

_____. *Surviving the Long Night: An Autobiographical Account of a Political Kidnapping*. New York: Vanguard Press, 1974.

Jenkins, Brian. *International Terrorism: A New Mode of Conflict*. Los Angeles: Crescent Publications, 1975.

Kafka, Franz. *The Trial*. New York: Vintage Books, 1969.

Knutson, Jeanne M., ed. *Handbook of Political Psychology*. San Francisco: Jossey-Bass, 1973.

Koestler, Arthur. *Darkness at Noon*. New York: Time Incorporated, 1962.

Kupperman, Robert, and Darrell Trent. *Terrorism: Threat, Reality, Response*. Stanford, Calif.: Hoover Institution Press, 1979.

Laqueur, Walter. *Guerrilla: A Historical and Critical Study*. Boston: Little, Brown & Company, 1976.

_____. *Terrorism*. Boston: Little, Brown & Company, 1977.

_____. *The Terrorism Reader*. New York: New American Library, 1978.

Leachman, Robert B., and Phillip Althoff, eds. *Preventing Nuclear Theft: Guidelines for Industry and Government*. New York: Praeger, 1972.

Lenin, V.I. *State and Revolution*. New York: International Publishers, 1943.

Livingston, Marius H., ed. *International Terrorism in the Contemporary World*. Westport, Conn.: Greenwood Press, 1978.

Lotz, Wolfgang. *A Handbook for Spies*. New York: Harper & Row, 1980.

Mallin, Jay. *Terror and the Urban Guerrilla*. Coral Gables, Fl.: University of Miami Press, 1971.

Malraux, Andre. *Man's Fate (La Condition Humaine)*. New York: Modern Library, 1961.

Mao Tse-tung. *On Guerrilla Warfare.* New York: Frederick A. Praeger, 1961.

Marighella, Carlos. *For the Liberation of Brazil,* translated by John Butt and Rosemary Sheed. London: Penguin Books, 1970.

Marnham, Patrick. *Fantastic Invasion.* New York: Harcourt Brace Jovanovich, 1980.

Mashiro, N. *Black Medicine,* vols. 1 and 2. Boulder, Colo.: Paladin Press, 1978 and 1979.

Mazlich, Bruce. *The Revolutionary Aesthetic.* New York: Basic Books, 1976.

McLuhan, Marshall, and Quentin Fiore. *The Medium Is the Message.* New York: Bantam Books, 1967.

McPhee, John. *The Curve of Binding Energy.* New York: Farrar, Straus and Giroux, 1974.

Minnery, John. *How to Kill,* vols. 1, 2, 3, and 4. Boulder, Colo.: Paladin Press, 1973, 1977, 1979, and 1979, respectively.

Miron, Murray S., and Arnold P. Goldstein. *Hostage.* New York: Pergamon Press, no date.

Morf, Gustave. *Terror in Quebec: Case Studies of the F.L.Q.* Toronto: Clarke, Irwin Publishers, 1970.

Morgenthau, Hans J. *Politics among Nations.* New York: Alfred A. Knopf, 1971.

Moss, Robert. *Counter Terrorism.* London: *The Economist,* Brief Booklet no. 29, no date.

Mumford, Lewis. *The Highway and the City.* New York: Harcourt, Brace & World, 1963.

Nasution, Abdul Haris. *Fundamentals of Guerrilla Warfare.* New York: Frederick A. Praeger, 1965.

National Advisory Committee on Criminal Justice Standards and Goals. *Disorders and Terrorism.* Washington, D.C.: Law Enforcement Assistance Administration, 1976.

Niebuhr, Reinhold. *The Children of Light and the Children of Darkness.* New York: Charles Scribner's Sons, 1960.

Nieburg, H.L. *Political Violence.* New York: St. Martin's Press, 1969.

Nuclear Energy Policy Study Group. *Nuclear Power Issues and Choices.* Cambridge, Mass.: Ballinger, 1977.

O'Ballance, Edgar. *Language of Violence.* San Rafael, Calif.: Presidio Press, 1979.

Organski, A.F.K. *World Politics.* New York: Alfred A. Knopf, 1968.

Orwell, George. "Politics and the English Language." In *The Orwell Reader.* New York: Harcourt, Brace & World, 1956.

O'Sullivan, P. Michael. *Patriot Graves.* Chicago: Follett Publishing Company, 1972.

Paine, Lauran. *The Terrorists.* London: Robert Hale and Co., 1975.

Parker, Donn B. *Crime by Computer.* New York: Charles Scribner's Sons, 1976.

Parry, Albert. *Terrorism: From Robespierre to Arafat.* New York: Vanguard Press, 1976.

Pfaltzgraff, Robert L., Geoffrey Kemp, and Uri Ra'anan, eds. *The Other Arms Race.* Lexington, Mass.: D.C. Heath and Company (no date).

Phillips, David. *Skyjack.* London: Harrap, 1973.

Plischke, Elmer. *Microstates in World Affairs.* Washington, D.C.: American Enterprise Institute for Public Policy Research, 1977.

Porsecanski, Arturo C. *Uruguay's Tupamaros.* New York: Praeger Publishers (no date).

Possony, Stefan T., and L. Francis Bouchey. *International Terrorism: The Communist Connection.* Washington, D.C.: American Council for World Freedom, 1978.

Powers, Thomas. *The Man Who Kept the Secrets: Richard Helms and CIA.* New York: Alfred A. Knopf, 1979.

Pranger, Robert J., and Roger P. Labrie, eds. *Nuclear Strategy and National Security Points of View.* Washington, D.C.: American Enterprise Institute, 1977.

Pruitt, Dean G., and Richard C. Snyder. *Theory and Research on the Causes of War.* Englewood Cliffs, N.J.: Prentice-Hall, 1969.

Ratliff, William E. *Castroism and Communism in Latin America, 1959-1976.* Washington, D.C.: American Enterprise Institute for Public Policy Research, 1976.

Revel, Jean-François. *Without Marx or Jesus.* Garden City, N.Y.: Doubleday, 1970.

Rose, Richard. *Northern Ireland: Time of Choice.* Washington, D.C.: American Enterprise Institute for Public Policy Research, 1976.

Rosenfeld, Alvin. *The Plot to Destroy Israel.* New York: G.P. Putnam's Sons, 1977.

Russell, Bertrand. *History of Western Philosophy.* London: George Allen & Unwin, 1967.

Sax, N. Irving. *Dangerous Properties of Industrial Materials.* New York: Van Nostrand Reinhold, 1978.

Saxon, Kurt. *The Poor Man's James Bond.* Eureka, Calif.: Atlan Formularies, 1972.

Schieler, Leroy, and Denis Pauze. *Hazardous Materials.* New York: Van Nostrand Reinhold, 1978.

Schreiber, Jan. *The Ultimate Weapon: Terrorists and World Order.* New York: William Morrow and Company, 1978.

Schultz, Richard H., Jr., and Stephen Sloan. *Responding to the Terrorist Threat.* New York: Pergamon Press, 1980.

Silone, Ignazio. *Bread and Wine.* New York: Signet, 1973.

Skolnikoff, Eugene B. *Science, Technology, and American Foreign Policy.* Cambridge, Mass.: MIT Press, 1967.

Smith, Colin. *Carlos: Portrait of a Terrorist.* New York: Holt, Rinehart & Winston, 1976.

SIPRI. *Weapons of Mass Destruction and the Environment.* New York: Crane, Russak & Co., 1977.

_____. *World Aramaments and Disarmament: SIPRI Yearbook 1977.* Cambridge, Mass. MIT Press, 1977.

Sterling, Claire. *The Terror Network.* New York: Holt, Rinehart & Winston, 1981.

Stevenson, William. *A Man Called Intrepid.* New York: Harcourt Brace Jovanovich, 1976.

_____. *90 Minutes at Entebbe.* New York: Bantam Books, 1976.

Stoessinger, John G. *The Might of Nations.* New York: Random House, 1965.

Swift, Jonathan. *Gulliver's Travels.* New York: New American Library, 1960.

Taber, Robert. *The War of the Flea.* New York: Citadel Press, 1970.

The Merritt Company. *Protection of Assets.* Los Angeles, 1974.

Tinker, Jerry M. *Strategies of Revolutionary Warfare.* New Delhi: S. Chand and Co., 1969.

Trotsky, L. *The Defense of Terrorism.* London: George Allen & Unwin, 1935.

van der Linde, Peter, and Naomi A. Hintze. *Time Bomb.* New York: Doubleday, 1978.

von Glahn, Gerhard. *Law among Nations,* 2d ed. London: MacMillan, 1970.

Walter, E.V. *Terror and Resistance: A Study of Political Violence.* London: Oxford University Press, 1969.

Watson, Francis M. *Political Terrorism: The Threat and the Response.* New York: Robert B. Luce Co., 1976.

Weiss, Peter. *The Persecution and Assassination of Jean-Paul Marat: As Performed by the Inmates of the Asylum of Charenton under the Direction of the Marquis de Sade.* New York: Atheneum, 1978.

Wilkinson, Paul. *Political Terrorism.* New York: John Wiley & Sons, 1974.

Willrich, Mason, and Theodore B. Taylor. *Nuclear Theft: Risks and Safeguards.* Cambridge, Mass.: Ballinger Publishing Company, 1974.

Journals, Newspapers, and Periodicals

Abrahamson, Dean E. "Nuclear Theft and Nuclear Parks." *Environment,* July/August 1974.

Allen, Henry. "CBS' Black Humor Sunday." *Washington Post,* 20 January 1979.

Alpern, David M. "More Outrages." *Newsweek,* 26 December 1977.

Anderson, Jack.. "Terrorist 'Fish' in a Sea of Tourists." *Washington Post,* 16 May 1974.

Anderson, Jack, with Jack Mitchell. "The Diary of a Hostage." *Parade.* 13 April 1980.

Anderson, Jack, and Les Whitten. "Terrorists' Use of A-Arms Feared." *Washington Post*, 29 August 1975.

Apple, R.W. "A Loose Alliance of Terrorists Does Seem to Exist." *The New York Times,* 23 October 1977.

Babcock, Charles R. "Alleged Financier of Guerrilla Group is Indicted in N.Y." *Washington Post,* 13 April 1978.

_____. "Ethnic Nationalists Fight Their Wars on American Soil." *Washington Post*, 20 April 1980.

Barnir, Dov. "Were Israelis Terrorists, Too?" *New Outlook,* February 1975.

Beall, Marshall D. "Hostage Negotiations." *Military Police Law Enforcement Journal*, Fall 1976.

Bell, Robert G. "The U.S. Response to Terrorism against International Civil Aviation." *Orbis,* Winter 1976.

Benjamin, Milton R. "Growth of Plutonium Supply Forecast." *Washington Post,* 25 February 1980.

Biggs-Davison, John. "The Strategic Implications for the West of the International Links of the IRA in Ireland." *Foreign Affairs Research Institute* 17 (1976).

Blumenthal, Fred. "Bad News for Terror Bombers." *Parade,* 25 July 1976.

Bradshaw, Jon. "A Dream of Terror." *Esquire,* 18 July 1978.

Branigin, William. "Official of PLO Critically Hurt in Murder Attempt." *Washington Post*, 26 July 1979.

Burgess, Anthony. "The Freedom We Have Lost." *Time*, 8 May 1978.

Burn, Gordon. "Kill, Carlos, Kill—Run, Carlos, Run." *Oui*, July 1976.

"Businessmen and Terrorism." *Newsweek*, 14 November 1976.

Calvert, Peter. "The Diminishing Returns of Political Violence." *New Middle East*, May 1975.

Cherio, P. "Security Requirements and Standards for Nuclear Power Plants." *Security Management*, January 1975.

Clairborne, William. "Cyprus Sentences Two Palestinian Terrorists to Die." *Washington Post,* 5 April 1978.

_____. "Begin Seeks Death for Extreme Acts of Terror in Israel." *Washington Post*, 25 April 1979.

Clark, Dennis. "Which Way the IRA?" *Commonweal,* 5 January 1973.

Coates, Joseph F. "Urban Violence—The Pattern of Disorder." *Annals of the American Academy of Political and Social Science*, January 1973.

Colebrook, Joan. "Israel—With Terrorists." *Commentary,* July 1974.

Collins, Whit. "Counter-Terrorist Technology for Everyday Use." *Security World*, October 1978.

"Collision Course over the PLO." *Newsweek,* 3 September 1979.

Cook, Don. "A Terrorist's Many 'Connections'." *Washington Post*, 7 September 1975.

"Corporate Security: Top Management Mandate." *Dun's Review*, January 1980.

Cory, Bruce. "Police for Hire." *Police Magazine,* September 1979.

Council for Ter-American Security. "Guatemalan Private Sector Targets of Terrorists." West Watch Advisory, 13 June 1980.

Crile, George, III. "Our Heritage—The Exile Cuban Terrorists." *Washington Post*, 7 November 1976.

Crittenden, Ann. "Surge in Nuclear Exports Spurs Drive for Controls." *The New York Times*, 17 August 1975.

Crozier, Brian. "The Direct Support." In *International Terrorism: The Soviet Connection.* Jerusalem: Jonathan Institute, 1979.

Daniels, Stuart. "The Weathermen." *Government and Opposition* 9 (Autumn 1974).

"A Daring Rescue at Princes Gate." *Time*, 19 May 1980.

Davidson, William, and Louise FitzSimons. "The Violence of the Dispossessed." *Washington Post*, 28 May 1972.

De Janos, Sigmund, and Stephen Lieff. "Technoaggression—An Alternative Mode of Warfare." *Conflict* 1 (1980).

Dotto, Lydia. "The New Computer Criminals." *Atlas World Press Review*, August 1979.

Drake, Elisabeth, and Robert C. Reid. "The Importation of Liquefied Natural Gas." *Scientific American*, April 1977.

Drummond, William J., and Augustine Zycher. "Arafat's Press Agents." *Harper's*, March 1976.

Dugard, John. "International Terrorism: Problems of Definition." *International Affairs*, January 1974.

Dunkin, Tom. "Terrorists Beware! WerBell's Cobray School." *Soldier of Fortune,* January 1980.

Ebon, Martin. "Apocalyptic Terrorists." *The Humanist*, November/December 1978.

"Egyptian Blunder at Larnaca." *Daily Telegraph*, 22 February 1978.

Elliot, Major John D. "International Terrorism: Threat to U.S. Security?" *Armed Forces Journal International*, September 1976.

"The Fallout from Entebbe." *Newsweek*, 19 July 1976.

Feld, Bernard T. "The Menace of a Fission Power Economy." *Bulletin of the Atomic Scientists*, April 1974.

Firngarn, Rodney D. "Terrorism—Tool of the Gun Grabbers!" *Guns and Ammo*, January 1979.

Fitchett, Joseph. "Paris Aid to Saudis Cited in Ending Mosque Siege." *Washington Post*, 28 January 1980.

_____. "Arafat Denies Demanding Destruction of Israel." *Washington Post*, 2 August 1980.

Flood, Michael. "Nuclear Sabotage." *Washington Post*, 9 January 1977.

Follath, Erich. "Israel's Elite Intelligence Corps." *World Press Review*, May 1980.

"The Friendly People Whose Job Is to Make Your Shopping Safer." *Ulster Commentary*, February 1975.

Fromkin, David. "The Strategy of Terrorism." *Foreign Affairs*, July 1975.

Frye, Alton. "How to Ban the Bomb: Sell it." *The New York Times Magazine*, 11 January 1976.

Gallagher, Lt. Col. Harold D. "Combat Support in Wars of National Liberation." *Naval War College Review*, September/October 1972.

Gavzer, Bernard. "The Search for a Way to Combat Terrorists." *Parade*, 20 May 1979.

Getler, Michael. "Hunt for Terrorists Focuses on 'Swiss Problem'." *Washington Post*, 12 April 1978.

Geyer, Georgie Anne. "Faceless Terror." *Washington Post*, 23 July 1979.

Gilbert, Sari. "Learning to Live with Terrorism in Italy." *Washington Post*, 29 July 1979.

Gott, Richard. "Whatever Happened to the Tupamaros?" *The Guardian*, 25 May 1974.

Greenway, H.D.S. "Uranium-Caper Story Spurs Concern over Israeli Reactor." *Washington Post*, 30 April 1977.

Gross, Leo. "International Terrorism and International Criminal Jurisdiction." *American Journal of International Law*, July 1973.

Hadley, Arthur T. "America's Vulnerability to Terrorism." *Washington Post*, 4 December 1977.

Hamid, Rashid. "What Is the PLO?" *Journal of Palestine Studies* 4 (Summer 1975).

Hanna, Vincent. "Internment: What Are the Facts?" *The Listener*, 19 and 26 December 1974.

Hannay, William. "International Terrorism: The Need for a Fresh Perspective." *International Lawyer*, April 1974.

Harrison, Paul. "The Dark Age of Ulster." *Human Behavior*, October 1975.

Hassel, Conrad V. "Terror: The Crime of the Privileged; An Examination and Prognosis." *Terrorism* 1 (1977).

Homan, Richard L. "Israeli Forces Occupy South Lebanon." *Washington Post*, 16 March 1978.

Horowitz, Irving Louis. "Political Terrorism and State Power," *Journal of Political and Military Sociology*, Spring 1973.

Howard, Walter W. "Terrorists: How They Operate a Worldwide Network." *Parade*, 18 January 1976.

Howe, Russell Warren. "Zion: Born in Blood." *Washington Post*, Book Review, 26 June 1976.

Hutchinson, Martha Crenshaw. "The Concept of Revolutionary Terrorism." *Journal of Conflict Resolution*, September 1972.

"The IRA Reborn." *Newsweek*, 27 February 1978.

"Israel 'Severs the Arm'." *Time,* 27 March 1978.

Jacobson, Philip. "Terrorists at Large." *Washington Post*, 6 November 1977.

Janke, Peter. "Terrorism in Argentina." *Journal of the Royal United Services Institute for Defense Studies* 119 (September 1974).

Jenkins, Brian M. "International Terrorism: A New Kind of Warfare." *Rand Paper Series*, June 1974.

_____. "Terrorism and Kidnapping." Rand Paper Series, June 1974.

_____. "International Terrorism: A Balance Sheet." *Survival*, July/August 1975.

_____. "Upgrading the Fight against Terrorism." *Washington Post*, 27 March 1977.

Johnson, Haynes. "Terrorism: The Crime of Our Time." *Washington Post*, 10 March 1977.

Johnson, Kenneth F. "Guatemala: From Terrorism to Terror." *Conflict Studies*, no. 23 (May 1972).

Jungk, Robert. "The Menace of 'the Atom State'." *Atlas World Press Review*, July 1978.

Kahn, E.J., Jr. "How Do We Explain Them?" *New Yorker*, 12 June 1978.

Karber, Phillip A. "Newspaper Coverage of Domestic Bombings: Reporting Patterns of American Violence." *Targets and Tactics*, January 1973.

_____. "Urban Terrorism: Baseline Data and Conceptual Framework." *Social Science*, January 1973.

_____. "The Psychological Dimensions of Bombing Motivations." *Targets and Tactics* 1 (June 1973).

Kraft, Joseph. "History in His Veins." *Washington Post*, 4 December 1977.

Kramer, Larry. "Anti-Kidnapping Business Thriving." *Washington Post*, 1 April 1979.

Krosney, Herbert. "The PLO's Moscow Connection." *New York*, 24 September 1979.

Kupperman, Robert H. "Treating the Symptoms of Terrorism: Some Principles of Good Hygiene." *Terrorism* 1 (1977).

Lamborn, Robert. "Is Executive Protection Psycho-Therapy?" *Security Management*, January 1978.

Lapp, Ralph E. "The Ultimate Blackmail," *The New York Times Magazine*, 4 February 1973.

Laqueur, Walter. "The Futility of Terrorism." *Harper's*, March 1976.

_____. "The Continuing Failure of Terrorism." *Harper's,* November 1976.

Lardner, George, Jr. "Terrorism Study Head Calls it 'Very Minor Part' of Crime." *Washington Post*, 13 March 1977.

"Leningrad Trial of Would-Be Hijackers." *Current Digest of Soviet Press*. Translated and condensed from *Pravda* and *Isvestia*, 1 January 1971.

Livingstone, N.C. "Weapons for the Few." *Conflict* 1(1979).

_____. "Low-Level Violence and Future Targets." *Conflict* 2 (1980).

_____. "Terrorism: The International Connection." *Army*, December 1980.

_____. "Is Terrorism Effective?" *International Security Review* 6 (Fall 1981).

_____. "States in Opposition: The War against Terrorism." *Conflict* 3 (1981).

_____. "Fighting Terrorism: The Private Sector." *Conflict* 3 (1981).

Livingstone, N.C., with James P. Kelly. "Could the President Survive a Real-Life James Bond Movie?" *The Washingtonian*, September 1981.

Lord, Christina. "Italy." *European Community*, May/June 1978.

Lovins, Amory B., and L. Hunter Lovins, and Leonard Ross. "Nuclear Power and Nuclear Bombs." *Foreign Affairs,* Summer 1980.

Lyons, Richard D. "CIA Secrets: Poison Pellets, Marshmallows." *The New York Times*, 16 June 1980.

MacPherson, Myra. "The Hostage-Takers: An Epidemic of People Gone Mad." *Washington Post*, 20 February 1977.

Mallin, Jay. "The Military vs. Urban Guerrillas." *Marine Corps Gazette*, June 1973.

Mallison, W.T., Jr., and S.V. Mallison. "The Concept of Public Purpose Terror in International Law: Doctrines and Sanctions to Reduce the Destruction of Human and Material Values." *Howard Law Journal* 18 (1973).

Mansfield, Stephanie. "Armored Car Business Booms." *Washington Post*, 2 July 1979.

Mardis, Jaime. "In Italy, Car Trouble for Kidnappers." *Washington Post*, 19 June 1979.

May, William F. "Terrorism as Strategy and Ecstasy." *Social Research*, Summer 1974.

McCombs, Phil. "Nations Turn to Force to Combat Terror." *Washington Post,* 15 March 1978.

McCormack, Richard T. "The Twilight War." *Army*, January 1979.

McDonald, Ronald H. "The Rise of Military Politics in Uruguay," *Inter-American Economic Affairs* 28 (Spring 1975).

McKittrick, David. "The Irish Connection." *World Press Review,* November 1979.

Means, J. "Political Kidnappings and Terrorism." *North American Review*, Winter 1970.

Meighan, Don G. "How Safe Is Safe Enough?" *The New York Times Magazine*, 20 June 1976.

Mitchell, Henry. "A Tale of Terror, Peace and Our Times." *Washington Post*, 5 August 1976.

Moraes, Dom. "Indian Revolutionaries with a Chinese Accent." *The New York Times Magazine*, 8 November 1970.

Moss, Robert, "International Terrorism and Western Societies." *International Journal*, Summer 1973.

"Most Barbarous Assassins." *Time,* 22 May 1978.

Mullen, Robert K. "Mass Destruction and Terrorism." *Journal of International Affairs*, Spring/Summer 1978.

"Murder and Massacre on Cyprus." *Time*, 6 March 1978.

"The New War on Terrorism." *Newsweek*, 31 October 1977.

Nieburg, H.L. "The Threat of Violence and Social Change." *American Political Science Review*, December 1962.

Norman, Geoffrey. "Black Berets to the Rescue." *Esquire*, 11 April 1978.

Nossiter, Bernard D. "Democracy's Future Called Grim Because of Past Failings." *Washington Post*, 9 October 1977.

O'Brien, Pat. "NRA Snags Passage of Anti-Terrorism Bill." *Airline Executive*, December 1978.

O'Neill, Major Bard E. "Israel and the Fedayeen: Persistence or Transformation." *Strategic Review*, Spring 1976.

Orme, Stanley, and Sean Walsh. "Violence in Northern Ireland." *Washington Post*, 31 January 1976.

O'Toole, Thomas. "Weapons-Grade Uranium Offer Probed by FBI." *Washington Post*, 19 March 1978.

――――. "Uranium Theft, Extortion Plot Laid to Worker at GE Plant." *Washington Post*, 2 February 1979.

Paust, Jordan J. "Terrorism and the International Law of War." *Military Law Review* 64 (Spring 1974).

Phillips, James G. "Energy Reports/Safeguards, Recycling Broadens Nuclear Power Debate." *National Journal Reports*, 22 March 1975.

――――. "Energy Report/Controversy Surrounds Proposed Nuclear Export Policies." *National Journal Reports*, 10 May 1975.

Pierre, Andrew J. "The Politics of International Terrorism." *Orbis*, Winter 1976.

Pierson, Lt. Col. Earl F. "The United States Role in Counterinsurgency." *Naval War College Review*, January/February 1973.

"Policing Plutonium: The Civil Liberties Fallout." *Harvard Civil Rights-Civil Liberties Law Review* 10 (1975).

Raimundo, Jeffrey. "LNG: Where, When and Why?" *Sierra*, June 1978.

Randal, Jonathan C. "Obstacles Keep New Blood from PLO Leadership." *Washington Post*, 3 March 1980.

Reid, Robert C. "The Importation of Liquefied Natural Gas." *Scientific American*, April 1977.

"Religious Wars: A Bloody Zeal." *Time*, 12 July 1976.

Rescorla, Richard. "Emergency Planning and the Security Manager." *International Security Review*, January 1979.

Restak, Richard. "The Origins of Violence." *Saturday Review*, 12 May 1979.

Ribicoff, Sen. Abraham. "Diplomacy Is NOT Enough." *Airline Pilot*, September 1978.

Rollow, Jonathan, and Yoichi Teraishi. " 'Nice' Terrorists Shake Japanese." *Washington Post*, 13 July 1975.

Rose, Gregory F. "The Terrorists Are Coming." *Politics Today*, July/August 1978.

Rosenblum, Mort. "Terror in Argentina." *New York Review*, 28 October 1976.

Rosenfeld, Steven S. "How Should the Media Handle Deeds of Terrorism?" *Washington Post*, 21 November 1975.

Rothstein, Raphael, and Zeev Schiff. "Why the Fedayeen Kill the Innocent." *Chicago Tribune*, 11 June 1972.

Rozakis, Christos L. "Terrorism and the Internationally Protected Persons in the Light of the ILC's Draft Articles." *International and Comparative Law Quarterly* 23 (January 1974).

Russell, Charles A., and Bowman H. Miller. "Profile of a Terrorist." *Terrorism* 1 (1977).

Saab, Jocelyn. "The Suicide Squads of Ahmad Jibril." *Washington Post*, 2 March 1975.

Scheinman, Lawrence. "Safeguarding Nuclear Materials." *Bulletin of the Atomic Scientists*, April 1974.

Schnall, David J. "Native Anti-Zionism: Ideologies of Radical Dissent in Israel." *Middle East Journal*, Spring 1977.

Schoenberg, Harris O. "Terror Legitimized." *Midstream*, March 1979.

Schuler, G. Henry M. "Beyond Billy: The Importance of Investigating Libya's Treacheries." *Washington Post*, 27 July 1980.

Scoville, Herbert, Jr. "The Technology of Surveillance." *Society*, March/April 1969.

Segre, D.V. and J.H. Adler. "The Ecology of Terrorism." *Encounter*, February 1973.

Shales, Tom and Ken Ringle. "Weighing the Media's Coverage at the Close of the Crisis." *Washington Post*, 12 March 1977.

Shaw, Terri. "Pacification in Guatemala: Terrorism a Way of Life." *Washington Post*, 7 March 1971.

Shenkman, Richard. "Rescue by the Private Sector." *National Review*, May 1980.

Silverman, Jerry M., and Peter M. Jackson. "Terror in Insurgency Warfare." *Military Review*, October 1970.

Simpson, Howard R. "Terror." *U.S. Naval Institute Proceedings*, 96, April 1970.

Singer, Lloyd W. and Jan Reber. "A Crisis Management System." *Security Management*, September 1977.

Singer, Michael and David Weir. "Nuclear Nightmare." *New West*, 3 December 1979.

Smart, I.M.H. "The Power of Terror." *International Journal* 30 (Spring 1975).

Sowell, Thomas. "The Terrorist as Celebrity." *Washington Star*, 9 August 1978.

Sterling, Claire. "The Terrorist Network." *The Atlantic*, 1978.

Stevenson, John R. "International Law and the Export of Terrorism." *Department of State Newsletter*, December 1972.

"Terrorism." *Skeptic*, January/February 1976.

"The Strange Affair at Larnaca Airport." *The Economist*, 5 February 1978.

Strobl, Walter M. "Extortion: The Remote Method of Bank Robbery." *Security World*, August 1978.

_____. "Round-the-Clock Executive Protection." *Security World*, January 1979.

Sulzberger, C.L. "The New Realm of Terror." *Arkansas Gazette*, 27 December 1977.

Taylor, Maxwell D. "Analogies (II): Was Desert 1 Another Bay of Pigs?" *Washington Post*, 12 May 1980.

Taylor, Theodore. "Nuclear Theft and Terrorism." *Sixteenth Strategy for Peace Conference Report*, The Stanley Foundation, 1975.

"Terrorism: The Global War." *Latin American Times*, May 1980.

"Terrorists Force Lessons in 'Psychology of Siege'." *American Medical News*, 20 June 1977.

"Terrorists Kill 3, Take 70 Hostages at OPEC Meeting." *Arkansas Gazette*, 22 December 1975.

"Terror Proofing." *Autocar*, June 1979.

"The Terrorists Declare War." *Time*, 27 March 1978.

Thompson, W. Scott. "Political Violence and the 'Correlation of Forces'." *Orbis*, Winter 1976.

"The U.S.: A Haven for Terrorists?" *Politics Today*, November/December 1979.

"Top Targets of Terrorists: U.S. Businessmen." *U.S. News & World Report*, 26 November 1979.

Waltzer, Michael. "The New Terrorists." *New Republic*, 30 August 1975.

Weinberg, Alvin M. "Social Institutions and Nuclear Energy." *Science* 177 (7 July 1972).

Weisel, Jonas. "Schools Putting Anti-Terrorists in the Driver's Seat." *Washington Post*, 18 December 1977.

"Welcome Sign to Hijackers." *International Herald Tribune*, Editorial, 16-17 June 1979.

"West Germany: The Hit Women." *Newsweek*, 15 August 1977.

Wilhelm, John L. "Psychic Spying." *Washington Post*, 7 August 1977.

Wilkinson, Paul. "Three Questions on Terrorism." *Government and Opposition* 8 (1973).

Will, George F. "'Mad Logic' and Ulster Violence." *The Washington Post*, 8 February 1976.

_____. "The Soul of Terrorism." *Newsweek*, 31 October 1977.

"Will 'Hot Pursuit' Stop Terrorism?" *U.S. News & World Report*, 19 July 1976.

Williams, H.E. "Handling Vehicle Attacks." *Security World*, October 1978.

Willrich, Mason, and Theodore B. Taylor. "Nuclear Theft." *Survival* 16 (1974).

Winegarten, Renee. "Literary Terrorism." *Commentary*, March 1974.

Wolf, John B. "Controlling Political Terrorism in a Free Society." *Orbis*, Winter 1976.

Woolsey, R. James. "Sometimes Long Shots Pay Off." *Washington Post*, 28 April 1980.

Young, Gavin. "Despair Keeps Movement Alive for Palestinians." *Washington Post*, 17 May 1973.

Young, Patrick. "A 'Criminal Personality'?" *Washington Post*, 20 November 1977.

Publications, Monographs, Studies, and Reports of the Government and Other Organizations

American Society of International Law. "Proposal for a Research Project on Legal Aspects of International Terrorism." Submitted to the Department of State in response to solicitation no. RFP-ST-75-28, 24 March 1975.

Becker, Louise Giovane; Marjorie Ann Browne; Suzanne Cavanagh; and Frederick M. Kaiser. "Terrorism: Information as a Tool for Control." Washington, D.C.: Congressional Research Service, Library of Congress, 1978.

Bennett, Carl A.; William M. Murphy; and Theodore S. Sherr. "Societal Risk Approach to Safeguards Design and Evaluation." Washington, D.C.: U.S. Energy Research and Development Administration, June 1975.

Bouthoul, Gaston. "International Terrorism in its Historical Depth and Present Dimension." 55633, SM/SKP (French) (Washington, D.C.: U.S. Department of State, 25 February 1976).

Central Intelligence Agency. "Personnel Protection Guide." Washington, D.C., June 1975.

_____. *International Terrorism in 1978*. Washington, D.C.: National Foreign Assessment Center of the CIA, 1979.

Civil Defense Preparedness Agency. *Vulnerability of Total Petroleum Systems.* Washington, D.C., May 1973.

Comptroller General of the United States. "Assessment of U.S. and International Controls over the Peaceful Uses of Nuclear Energy." Washington, D.C.: 14 September 1976.

Dixon, Barbara. "Assassinations and Assassination Attempts on American Public Officials, 1835-1972." Washington, D.C.: Congressional Research Service, Library of Congress, 6 October 1972.

Donnelly, Warren H., and Donna S. Kramer. *Congress and the Control of Hazards of Marine Transportation of Liquefied Natural Gas.* Washington, D.C.: Congressional Research Service, Library of Congress, 1977.

Drake, William R., and Thomas E. Kelly. "Community Crime Prevention and the Local Official." Washington, D.C.: Law Enforcement Assistance Administration and the National League of Cities, U.S. Conference of Mayors, 1975.

Dukert, Joseph M. "High-Level Radioactive Waste: Safe Storage and Ultimate Disposal." Washington, D.C.: U.S. Energy Research and Development Administration, 1975.

Fairchild Stratos Division. "Offshore LNG Receiving Terminal Project," vol. 2. Report, 31 July 1977.

Federal Aviation Administration. *Semiannual Report to Congress on the Effectiveness of the Civil Aviation Security Program, for the Period of January 1-June 30, 1979.* Washington, D.C.: U.S. Department of Transportation, 1979.

Fuel Cycle Task Force. "Nuclear Fuel Cycle." Washington, D.C.: U.S. Energy Research and Development Administration, 1975.

Hoffacker, Lewis. "The U.S. Government Response to Terrorism: A Global Approach." *Department of State Bulletin*, 18 March 1974.

Horner, Charles. " 'The Usual Suspects': The State, and the Status of Terrorism." Mimeographed. Paper prepared for the Conference on Totalitarianism and Terrorism, 24 April 1980.

Iran Task Force. "Iran: Consequences of the Abortive Attempt to Rescue the American Hostages." Washington, D.C.: Congressional Research Service, Library of Congress, 2 May 1980.

Jenkins, Brian M. "Format for Case Studies and Post-Mortems of Bargaining Events." A working note prepared for the Defense Advanced Research Projects Agency, October 1973.

Johnson, Thomas O. "Nuclear Energy: Key Issues." Babcock & Wilcox energy brief, July 1975.

Joint Chiefs of Staff. "Memorandum for the Secretary of Defense, Subject: Report on Rescue Mission." JCSM-122-80, Washington, D.C., 6 May 1980.

Joseph J. Cappucci Associates, Inc. "The Development of Security for Executives through Countering Terroristic Activities in Their Region." Washington, D.C., no date.

_____. "Residential Security Guide." Washington, D.C., no date.

Kupperman, Robert H. "Facing Tomorrow's Terrorist Incident Today." Washington, D.C.: Law Enforcement Assistance Administration, October 1977.

League of Nations. *Proceedings of the International Conference on the Repression of Terrorism.* League of Nations Doc. C.94.M.47. 1938.V. Geneva, 1 June 1938.

Livingstone, N.C. *Crisis Management for Kidnap and Extortion Incidents: Family and Victim,* vol. 1. Washington, D.C.: Joseph J. Cappucci Associates, Inc., 1979.

_____. *Crisis Management.* Washington, D.C.: Joseph J. Cappucci Associates, Inc., 1979.

Medical Research Council. *The Toxicity of Plutonium.* London: Her Majesty's Stationery Office, 1975.

Merin, Kenneth. "Aircraft Hijackers: Extradition and the Political Offense Exception." Washington, D.C.: Congressional Research Service, Library of Congress, 19 November 1976.

Molnar, Andrew R., with Jerry M. Tinker and John D. LeNoir. "Human Factors Considerations of Undergrounds in Insurgencies." Research project prepared for the Special Operations Office of the American University, operating under contract with the Department of the Army, 1965.

National Commission on the Causes and Prevention of Violence. *To Establish Justice, to Insure Domestic Tranquility.* Washington, D.C.: U.S. Government Printing Office, 1969.

Nixon, Richard M. "Action to Combat Terrorism." Memorandum by the President to the Secretary of State, 25 September 1972. *Weekly Compilation of Presidential Documents,* 25 September 1972.

Organization of American States. *Documents Prepared by the Inter-American Juridical Committee on Acts of Terrorism and, Particularly Kidnapping, Extortion, and Assaults against Persons.* General Secretariat, OAS/Official Records/ser.P/English, AG/doc.68. Washington, D.C., 13 January 1971.

Rosenbaum, David M.; and John N. Googin; Robert M. Jefferson; Daniel Kleitman; and William C. Sullivan. "Special Safeguards Study. Mimeographed. Washington, D.C.: U.S. Atomic Energy Commission, 1974.

Rothberg, Paul F. "Liquefied Natural Gas: Hazards, Safety Requirements, and Policy Issues." Washington, D.C.: Congressional Research Service, Library of Congress, December 1977.

Stephens, Maynard M. "Vulnerability of Total Petroleum Systems." Report prepared for the Defense Civil Preparedness Agency, DAHC 20-70-C-0316. Washington, D.C.: U.S. Government Printing Office, 1976.

Telecommunication Publishing Inc. "Protecting Your Privacy: A Comprehensive Report on Eavesdropping Techniques and Devices and Their Corresponding Countermeasures." No date.

United Nations. General Assembly. *Report of the Ad Hoc Committee on International Terrorism.* Suppl. 28, A/9028, 1973.

_____. *Observations of States Submitted in Accordance with General Assembly Resolution 3034 (XXVII),* A/AC.160/1/Add.5, 31 July 1973.

U.S. Army. *Special Forces Demolition Techniques.* Extract from Army Field Manual FM 31-20, December 1965. Boulder, Colo.: Paladin Press, no date.

U.S. Atomic Energy Commission. "Conceptual Design Criteria for Safeguarding Nuclear Material in Facilities." Report prepared for the Division of Nuclear Materials Security. Upton, N.Y.: Technical Support Organization, Brookhaven National Laboratory, 1974.

———. "Reactor Safety Study: An Assessment of Accident Risks in U.S. Commercial Nuclear Power Plants," Summary Report, draft. Washington, D.C., August 1975.

U.S. Congress. Commission on the Operation of the Senate. *Major U.S. Foreign and Defense Policy Issues.* Prepared by the Congressional Research Service of the Library of Congress. Washington, D.C.: U.S. Government Printing Office, 1977.

U.S. Congress. General Accounting Office. *Automated Systems Security— Federal Agencies Should Strengthen Safeguards over Personal and Other Sensitive Data.* Washington, D.C.: U.S. Government Printing Office, 1979.

U.S. Congress. House. Committee on Foreign Affairs. Subcommittee on Europe. *Northern Ireland: Hearings.* 92nd Cong., 2d sess., February and March 1972.

U.S. Congress. House. Committee on Internal Security. *America's Maoists— The Revolutionary Union: The Venceremos Organization: Report.* 92nd Cong., 2d sess., 1973.

U.S. Congress. House. Committee on Internal Security. *Terrorism: Staff Study.* 93rd Cong., 2d sess., 1974.

U.S. Congress. House. Committee on Internal Security. *Terrorism, Parts 1 and 2: Hearings.* 93rd Cong., 2d sess., 1974.

U.S. Congress. House. Committee on Internal Security. *Terrorism, Part 3: Hearings.* 93rd Cong., 2d sess., June, July, August 1974.

U.S. Congress. House. Committee on Foreign Affairs. Subcommittee on the Near East and South Asia. *International Terrorism: Hearings.* 93rd Cong., 2d sess., June 1974.

U.S. Congress. House. Committee on Foreign Affairs. Subcommittee on International Organizations and Movements. *Problems of Protecting Civilians under International Law in the Middle East Conflict: Hearings.* 93rd Cong., 2d sess., 4 April 1974.

U.S. Congress. House. Committee on Small Business. Subcommittee on Energy and Environment. *Problems in the Accounting for and Safeguarding of Special Nuclear Materials: Hearings.* 94th Cong., 2d sess., 26 April, 7 May, and 20 May 1976.

U.S. Congress. House. Committee on International Relations. Special Subcommittee on Investigations. *The Palestinian Issue in Middle East Peace Efforts: Hearings.* 94th Cong., 1st sess., 1976.

U.S. Congress. House. Committee on the Judiciary. Subcommittee on Civil and Constitutional Rights. *Federal Capabilities in Crisis Management and Terrorism: Staff Report.* 95th Cong., 2d sess., 1978.

U.S. Congress. House. Committee on the Judiciary. Subcommittee on Civil and Constitutional Rights. *Federal Capabilities in Crisis Management and Terrorism: Hearings.* 95th Cong., 2d sess., 16 August, 15 and 28 September, and 4 October 1978.

U.S. Congress. House. Committee on Public Works and Transportation. Subcommittee on Aviation. *Aircraft Piracy, International Terrorism: Hearings.* 96th Cong., 1st sess., 28 February, 1 March 1979.

U.S. Congress. Joint Committee on Atomic Energy. *Nuclear Reactor Safety: Hearings.* Vols. 1 and 2. 93rd Cong., 2d sess., 1974.

U.S. Congress. Joint Committee on Atomic Energy. *Staff Analysis of Responses Received on April 11, 1975 Letter Soliciting Views on Various Energy Issues.* Staff Analysis, Subcommittee on the Liquid Metal Fast Breeder Reactor (LMFBR) Program. Mimeographed, 94th Cong., 1st sess.

U.S. Congress. Joint Committee on Atomic Energy. *Development, Use, and Control of Nuclear Energy for the Common Defense and Security and for Peaceful Purposes.* Annual Report to the U.S. Congress pursuant to Section 202(b) of the Atomic Energy Act as amended. 94th Cong., 1st sess., 1975.

U.S. Congress. Joint Committee on Atomic Energy. Subcommittee to Review the Liquid Metal Fast Breeder Reactor Program. *Review of National Breeder Reactor Program: Report.* 94th Cong., 2nd sess., 1976.

U.S. Congress. Senate. Committee on Government Operations. Subcommittee on Investigations. *Riots, Civil and Criminal Disorders: Hearings.* 97th Cong., 2nd sess., 31 July, 4, 5, and 6 August 1970.

U.S. Congress. Senate. Select Committee to Study Governmental Operations with respect to Intelligence Activities. *Alleged Assassination Plots Involving Foreign Leaders.* Interim report, 94th Cong., 1st sess., 1975.

U.S. Congress. Senate. Committee on the Judiciary. Subcommittee to Investigate the Administration of the Internal Security Act and Other Internal Security Laws. *Terroristic Activity: Hearings.* 94th Cong., 1st sess., 14 May 1975.

U.S. Congress. Senate. Committee on the Judiciary. Subcommittee to Investigate the Administration of the Internal Security Act and Other Internal Security Laws. *The Trans-Alaska Pipeline: Problems Posed by the Threat of Sabotage and Their Impact on Internal Security: Report.* 94th Cong., 2nd sess., 1976.

U.S. Congress. Senate. Committee on the Judiciary. Subcommittee on Criminal Laws and Procedures. *Control of Explosives: Report.* 95th Cong., 1st sess., 1977.

U.S. Congress. Senate. Committee on Governmental Affairs. *Reorganization Plan No. 3 of 1978, Establishing a New Independent Agency, the Federal Emergency Management Agency: Report.* 95th Cong., 2d sess., 1978.

U.S. Congress. Senate. Committee on Governmental Affairs. *An Act to Combat Terrorism, Hearings on S. 2236.* 95th Cong., 2d sess., 1978.

U.S. Congress. Senate. "Debate on S2236." *Congressional Record.* 25 October 1977.

U.S. Congress. Senate. "Debate on the Omnibus Antiterrorism Act of 1979. 5 February 1979.

U.S. Congress. Office of Technology Assessment. *Transportation of Liquefied Natural Gas.* Washington, D.C.: U.S. Government Printing Office, 1977.

U.S. Congress. Office of Technology Assessment. *Nuclear Proliferation and Safeguards.* Washington, D.C.: U.S. Government Printing Office, 1977.

U.S. Congress. Office of Technology Assessment. *Taggants in Explosives.* Washington, D.C.: U.S. Government Printing Office, 1980.

U.S. Department of Defense. "Security Criteria and Standards for Protecting Nuclear Weapons." Directive 5210.41. Washington, D.C., 30 July 1974.

U.S. Department of State. "Protection of Dignitaries." Communication to the Senate Foreign Relations Committee. Washington, D.C., 3 July 1975.

U.S. Department of State. *Countering Terrorism: Security Suggestions for U.S. Business Representatives Abroad.* Publication 8884. Washington, D.C.: U.S. Government Printing Office, January 1977.

U.S. Department of the Treasury. *Explosives Incidents, 1978 Annual Report.* Washington, D.C.: Bureau of Alcohol, Tobacco and Firearms, 1979.

U.S. Department of the Treasury. "Firearms and Explosives: Target of 1980 Priorities." *Newsletter.* Washington, D.C.: Bureau of Alcohol, Tobacco and Firearms, 4 January 1980.

U.S. Energy Research and Development Administration. *ERDA Headquarters Plan and Procedures for Response to Major Emergencies: Emergency Action and Coordination Team (EACT).* Interim Revision. 23 May 1975.

U.S. Energy Research and Development Administration. Division of International Security Affairs. "LDC Nuclear Power Prospects, 1975-1990: Commercial, Economic and Security Implications." Washington, D.C., 1975.

U.S. Environmental Protection Agency. *Proceedings of Public Hearings: Plutonium and the Other Transuranium Elements*, vol. 1. Washington, D.C., 10-11 December 1974.

Westinghouse Electric Corporation. Advanced Reactors Division. "Our Only Reasonable Alternative: The Case for the Liquid Metal Fast Breeder Reactor." 1975.

White House. "Briefing by the Secretary of Defense, Harold Brown." Internal transcript, 25 April 1980.

Unpublished Materials

Carter, Jimmy. Text of letter to the Speaker of the U.S. House of Representatives and the President Pro Tempore of the Senate. 26 April 1980.

Chisholm, Major Henry J. "The Function of Terror and Violence in Revolution." Master's thesis, Georgetown University, Washington, D.C., 1948.

Crozier, Brian. "Terrorism: The Problem in Perspective." Mimeographed. February/March 1976.

Franck, Thomas M., and Bert B. Lockwood, Jr. "Terrorism: What Is it? What Is it Not? Should it Be Suppressed, Regulated, Condoned or Encouraged? Some Preliminary Thoughts towards an International Convention on Terrorism." Mimeographed.

Gurr, Ted Robert. "Some Characteristics of Contemporary Political Terrorism." Mimeographed. March 1976.

Hoffacker, Ambassador Lewis. "The U.S. Government Response to Terrorism: A Global Approach." Remarks made before the Mayor's Advisory Committee on International Relations and Trade and the Foreign Relations Association, New Orleans, Louisiana, 28 February 1974.

Horowitz, Irving L. "Political Terrorism and Personal Deviance." Summary of remarks at a conference sponsored by the Bureau of Intelligence and Research and the Planning and Coordination Staff, U.S. Department of State, 15 February 1973.

Jenkins, Brian M. "International Terrorism: Trends and Potentialities." Mimeographed paper. March 1976.

Johnson, Chalmers. "Perspectives on Terrorism." Mimeographed. 1976.

Leachman, R.B. "Preventive Criminology Applied to Fissionable Materials." Research paper sponsored by a grant from the Research Applied to National Needs Office of the National Science Foundation, (no date).

Marighella, Carlos. "Minimanual of the Urban Guerrilla." Mimeographed.

Milbank, David L. "International and Transnational Terrorism: Diagnosis and Prognosis." Mimeographed. Draft working paper prepared for the Conference on International Terrorism. Washington, D.C.: Department of State, 25-26 March 1976.

Miller, William H. "Facts on Sabotage and Diversion of Nuclear Material at Nuclear Power Plants." Mimeographed. Information paper.

Schelling, Thomas C. "Nuclear Energy and National Security." Paper prepared for the Committee for Economic Development (CED), 10 December 1975.

Weather Underground. "Prairie Fire." Mimeographed.

Index

About the Author

Neil C. Livingstone is vice-president of Gray and Company, the largest public-affairs/public-relations firm in Washington, D.C., concentrating on foreign policy and national security matters. Mr. Livingstone is also president of the Institute for Subnational Conflict and director for Terrorism and Low-Level Warfare at the American Security Council.

Until 1979, he was an equity owner, vice-president, and member of the Board of Directors of Air Panama International, Panama's national airline. He also served as vice-president for administration and operations of Joseph J. Cappucci Associates, Inc., an international security and crisis-management firm.

Prior to entering the private sector, Mr. Livingstone worked on Capitol Hill, first as an assistant to Senator Stuart Symington and later as special assistant for foreign-policy matters to Senator James B. Pearson, a member of the Senate Foreign Relations Committee. He completed his Ph.D. dissertation in 1981 at the Fletcher School of Law and Diplomacy.